PRINCIPLES
OF
MARKETING

PRINCIPLES OF MARKETING

fourth edition

JAY DIAMOND, Professor
Nassau Community College

GERALD PINTEL, Professor Emeritus
Nassau Community College

 Prentice Hall, Englewood Cliffs, New Jersey 07632

Library of Congress Cataloging-in-Publication Data

DIAMOND, JAY.
 Principles of marketing / Jay Diamond, Gerald Pintel. — 4th ed.
  p. cm.
 ISBN 0-13-714668-X
 1. Marketing. I. Pintel, Gerald. II. Title.
HF5415.D4847 1991
658.8—dc20

90–6856
CIP

Editorial/production supervision
 and interior design: **Janet M. DiBlasi**
Cover design: **Patricia Kelly**
Manufacturing buyer: **Mary Ann Gloriande**

© 1991 by Prentice-Hall, Inc.
A Division of Simon & Schuster
Englewood Cliffs, New Jersey 07632

Printed in the United States of America
10 9 8 7 6 5 4 3

ISBN 0-13-714668-X

Prentice-Hall International (UK) Limited, *London*
Prentice-Hall of Australia Pty. Limited, *Sydney*
Prentice-Hall Canada Inc., *Toronto*
Prentice-Hall Hispanoamericana, S.A., *Mexico*
Prentice-Hall of India Private Limited, *New Delhi*
Prentice-Hall of Japan, Inc., *Tokyo*
Simon & Schuster Asia Pte. Ltd., *Singapore*
Editora Prentice-Hall do Brasil, Ltda., *Rio de Janeiro*

CONTENTS _____

v

Part 3   The Marketing Mix: Development of the Product

7   THE PRODUCT   147

Part IV   The Marketing Mix: Getting the Product to Market

11   CHANNELS OF DISTRIBUTION   267

PREFACE

The fourth edition of *Principles of Marketing* represents an extensive revision of the earlier editions. The intention of the text remains the same: to introduce students to the various marketing fundamentals and to provide the theoretical knowledge necessary for entry into the field.

The five-part format is carried over from the third edition and includes a new chapter, Direct Marketing, added to Part Four, The Marketing Mix: Getting the Product to the Market. Direct marketing and telemarketing have become the mainstays for many marketing companies in the sale of their products and services. This new chapter carefully examines this approach and explores the role it plays for both large and small companies in the distribution of their goods.

In addition to the vignettes about specific organizations or concepts that introduce each chapter, a new feature, a Marketing Profile, is found throughout the text. Stories about companies and products such as Mattel's Barbie doll, RJR Nabisco's Premier smokeless cigarette, Bristol-Myers, *Lear's* magazine, Nordstrom's department stores, and The Goodyear Tire & Rubber Company underscore specific marketing concepts and their relationships to marketing principles. Each profile is accompanied by artwork that has been supplied by the companies being examined.

Since the world of marketing is constantly changing, with many products failing and new ones being introduced in their places, a wealth of information on these successes and failures is explored. The return of the raisin to consumer popularity, Barbie doll's continued domination in the doll market, the Merkur's failure versus the Acura's success, and Pizza Hut's use of the computer to speed up home delivery are featured along with others. This edition also includes a significant amount of new illustrative materials as well as charts and graphs that have been brought up to date.

All the features of the third edition, including learning objectives at the beginning of each chapter, important points at each chapter's conclusion, review questions, and case problems are retained in this edition.

A study guide that serves as an aid for review purposes features a host of questions, case problems, and projects. An instructor's manual provides all the answers to the questions and case problems in both the text and study guide and sample examination questions for each chapter.

The authors wish to thank Jack Mandel for his contribution to the case problem for the chapter on direct marketing, Ellen Diamond for work with the illustrative materials, and Mary Cole for the typing of the manuscript.

We also wish to acknowledge the following people and their companies for the materials they have contributed for this edition of *Principles of Marketing*: Larry Haeg, Pillsbury; Joanne Lawrence, Beecham Group p.l.c.; Kathleen C. McCown, Bristol-Myers Company; Anne Gardinier, Beatrice/Hunt Wesson; Joy Perilli, AT&T; Michael Spencer, Acura; Candace Irving, Mattel Toys; Eva Rossman, PepsiCo, Inc.; Jack Conmy and Jane Donovan, Dupont Company; Christine Jacobs, Foote, Cone & Belding; Sean Sullivan, Macy's; Francoise Max, L'Oreal/Cosmair, Inc.; James Pypelink, Bloomingdale's; Linda Peavy, Harley-Davidson, Inc.; Wendy Good, Adolph Coors Company; James Podany, Sears, Roebuck and Co.; R. D. Mitchell, BMW of North America; William A. Hammer, Sara Lee Corporation; L. A. Weis, Ford Motor Company; Christine Hon, Borden, Inc.; Janet Dougherty, Chrysler Corporation; Kerry McNulty, Domino's Pizza; Jeanette Fleisher, Harry Levine Associates; and Patricia M. Lent, The Procter & Gamble Company.

PRINCIPLES OF MARKETING

1

THE NATURE OF MARKETING

Learning Objectives

Upon completion of the chapter, you will be able to:

1. Define and give examples of the four utilities of marketing.
2. Write a brief paragraph on six functions of marketing.
3. Discuss the importance of marketing, including the effect of marketing on costs, people employed, the standard of living, and importance to the individual firm.
4. Describe the evolution of marketing from its infancy in America to the present day.
5. List and discuss the elements of the marketing mix.
6. Explain why the study of marketing may benefit the student's career.

"RAISIN" PROFITS

Those shriveled, funny-looking, little critters, better known as raisins, have been on grocer's shelves as long as most of us can remember. They have been the mainstays of the baker's ingredient shelves and as snacks in children's lunch boxes. Awareness had been generally centered upon the product's nutritional value, and sales were, if not spectacular, steady.

The California Raisin Advisory Board, which was formed in 1949 to promote the sale and consumption of raisins, employed the services of Foote, Cone & Belding to increase raisin awareness and ultimately to improve sales. The agency immediately developed a research project to determine who the users were and which groups failed to make the product part of their meals. Two important points were uncovered in the study. First, the children who were the dominant raisin eaters abandoned the product in their teenage years as soon as they felt some independence. The raisin was replaced with potato chips, candy, pretzels, and other more socially acceptable snacks. Second, the mother who spent her time baking was now a member of the work force and no longer had the time or energy left for making cakes and breads in her kitchen. Thus, the void was found in a very large market segment, the 25- to 50-year-old population.

Courtesy: Foote, Cone & Belding.

Foote, Cone & Belding was determined to reach this group and make them raisin eaters once again. It was decided that raisins needed a personality that would catch people's attention. After many failed attempts, Claymation, the use of animated clay figures that sing and dance, transformed the product's awareness. All over people were looking forward to the little clay raisins' television appearances. Along with the parade of clay raisins, complete with sunglasses and dancing feet, came a tune that captured the attention of the consumer. "I Heard It Through the Grapevine" became as familiar as the lyrics to many popular tunes. The two most popular formats have been the "Raisin Ray" arrangement, which features a Ray Charles raisin, and the "Lunch Box" segment, which depicts construction workers in hard hats.

The multimillion-dollar television campaign has transformed the business of raisins into a giant industry. The magic of the imaginative clay dancing figures has captured the hearts of the consuming public and is still "raisin" profits for the industrial participants.

INTRODUCTION

In a primitive society marketing is limited and simple because most primitive people are nearly self-sufficient and goods and services rarely need to be exchanged. Where exchanges are required, surplus goods are usually taken to a neighbor or neighboring village and bartered (traded) for the neighbor's surplus. As the society evolves toward a more technical economic level, specialization occurs. Certain individuals may become toolmakers, others farmers, and still others healers. The exchange of goods and services then becomes a necessity, since the toolmaker's only means of securing food and clothing is by marketing the tools in exchange for the surpluses being offered by the farmer, the hunter, and other specialists.

The more the society progresses, the more workers become specialized. The toolmaker no longer hunts or farms and marketing gains steadily in importance. At this point the exchange of goods and services becomes indispensable. Producers must offer their products at the market to obtain the means of acquiring the goods and services that they need for continued production.

THE MARKET

The term *market* is used in many ways and, consequently, cannot be simply defined. When the term *market* is used to express the exchange of goods, the American Marketing Association suggests the following definition:

> The aggregate of forces or conditions within which buyers and sellers make decisions that result in the transfer of goods and services.

When the term *market* is used to represent a demand for a product, the American Marketing Association suggests this definition:

> The aggregate demand of the potential buyers of a commodity or service.

Frequently, the word *market* is used to define a specific geographical area. In that case, the following definition is appropriate:

> The place or area in which buyers and sellers function.

The word *market* may also be used as a verb, that is, to define an activity. To market is

> To perform business activities that direct the flow of goods and services from the producer to the consumer or user.

Obviously, since the term *market* may be used correctly in many ways, no single definition can be entirely suitable. A reasonable working definition that combines the main features of three just listed is as follows:

> A market is an area in which the aggregate of forces or conditions result in decisions that satisfy demand by the transfer of goods and services.

MARKETING

Since the market is an absolute requirement in all but the most primitive, self-sufficient societies, the problem of getting goods to the market, or more properly, from the producer to the user, becomes basic. Because great distances and competing products may be involved, it becomes highly complicated and essential for the successful operation of a business. The American Marketing Association's committee on definitions describes marketing in this way:

> The performance of business activities that direct the flow of goods and services from the producer to the consumer or user (customer).

Another definition of marketing is as follows: "Marketing is the total system of interacting business activities designed to plan, price, promote, and distribute satisfying goods and services to present and potential customers."

It would seem from the definition that marketing covers all business activities. This is not the case. The key to the decision of whether or not marketing is involved in a particular business activity is the use of the word *direct* in the definition. Thus, tasks that significantly change the product, such as manufacturing, mining, and agriculture, are not included in the term *marketing*, although they are directed by marketers. Activities such as market research, product planning, and product design are the responsibility of the marketing division. The marketing manager is not concerned with the manufacturing process, but he or she is responsible for the type of goods that are produced and for the timing of their production. Similarly, although not involved with accounting, the marketing function must direct pricing and credit policies. The marketing division, therefore, is involved in almost every activity of the firm. It is directly responsible for such activities as selling, advertising, transportation, and promotion, and indirectly for production and accounting.

Historical Aspects

Prior to the Industrial Revolution, marketing was of relatively little importance to American business. The early farming communities were comparatively self-sufficient. The people raised their own crops, made their own clothes, and required very little of the outside world. With the passing of time, individuals began to concentrate on the production of goods most appropriate for their abilities. Farmers, rather than planting all the foodstuffs required by their families, concentrated their energies on the particular crop for which they and their land were best suited. This created the two things that are the basis of marketing: a surplus of the product produced and a demand for the necessities no longer produced.

In early colonial times in the United States, population was clustered around the great ports of the Eastern Seaboard. The colonists produced raw materials for the European economy and were themselves a market for European finished products. As the population moved westward, there was a beginning of domestic manufacturing, which resulted in a decrease of the dependence of the colonists upon foreign markets. The Revolutionary War and the War of 1812 added impetus to this development by reducing European trade and placing domestic production in a preferred competitive position. At this point marketing was still a relatively minor business function because surpluses were minimal and easily distributed since the demand generally exceeded the supply.

The Industrial Revolution resulted in a growth of urban areas at the expense of the rural population. This accelerated marketing growth by increasing the effect of the two factors most important to the distribution of goods: the demand of the urban centers for the necessities of their people and raw materials for production, and the surplus production of their factories. The extension of the railroad network after the Civil War provided a means for transporting goods into and out of the urban centers and facilitated the movement of manufacturing centers away from the Eastern Seaboard. As of the late 1800s, the supply (surplus) began to catch up with the demand. Until this time, marketing was little more than transportation. Now competition began to take on importance. This led to styling and packaging changes, to the beginning of advertising, and even to the use of drummers (salespersons).

It was not until the close of World War I and the emergence of mass production as a factor in American industry that the importance of marketing was established. Until then, the demand for goods had exceeded the supply and expensive marketing systems were not required. With mass production, the supply of goods became almost unlimited, whereas the demand for goods, though growing, lagged behind. This occurred for the first time in American history in the 1920s. The result was a buyer's market (more goods available than purchasing power) rather than a seller's market (more purchasing power available than goods). Such conditions led to fierce competition among producers to increase their share of the market.

One way of increasing sales is to give customers what they want, when they want it, where they want it, and at a price they are willing to pay. This is another way of saying that the answer to overproduction is improved marketing.

The Utilities of Marketing

To operate successfully, a business must create four basic utilities: form, place, time, and ownership. The value of goods is determined by the creation of one or more of these utilities.

Form is created by extracting goods from nature and changing them to satisfy human needs. It refers to manufacturing and production. Although marketing is not concerned with the manufacturing process, it directs production into the areas that will satisfy consumer demand. In other words, the milling of wheat into flour and the baking of bread are not the concern of marketers, but the types of bread to be made and the quantities of each category to be produced must be directed by the marketing division. The marketing manager must see to it that the form goods take is keyed to customer demand.

Place is created by moving goods from the facility at which they are produced, through intermediary places such as the wholesaler's, to the location at which customers will buy them. Place is very much the utility of the marketing division. It requires selection of various transportation systems, as well as channels of distribution, which are routes (through the hands of various wholesalers and other middlemen) by which goods flow from the producer to the consumer.

Time is created by storing goods until they are required by the customer. It entails the use of warehousing and storage facilities that are usually selected and supervised by the marketing division.

Ownership is created by getting the goods into the hands of customers (wholesale or retail).

The utilities just listed are so interrelated that it is impossible to evaluate their individual importance. They are equal in importance, and all must be performed efficiently if a business is to operate successfully. If bread is to be supplied to a customer, it is as important to ship the wheat to the miller and baker, keep the wheat until customers want it, and have it where they need it, as it is for the wheat to be grown and milled into flour.

The Functions of Marketing

There are eight specialized activities or functions involved in marketing.

Buying.   This requires the recognition of the needs of an enterprise; the selection of the best source of supply; and the negotiation of price, shipping dates, and other matters.

Selling.   This is a function that requires the understanding of customer demand, the discovery of buyers, and negotiation.

Transportation.   Place utility involves the function of transportation. It involves the physical movement of goods from the producer to the user.

Storage.   Time utility frequently requires the use of storage. It involves the holding and preserving of goods until they are required by the users.

Grading (Dividing or Bulk Breaking).   Agricultural and extractive (lumber, mining, and so on) industries require definite standards of quality and the sorting of goods into standardized grades. Only in this way can buyers be certain of what they are buying. Grading is frequently carried out by middlemen as well as producers. (In Figure 1–1 you will see workers grading tomatoes.)

Financing.   This function is concerned with the management of the money and credit required from the producer to the ultimate consumer. (The financial transactions arising from production are *not* considered part of the financing function of *marketing*.)

Risk Taking.   The marketing of goods and services involves a considerable amount of risk taking. Minimizing such risks is an important function of marketing.

Market Information.   Increasingly, managerial decision making has become more dependent on comprehensive market information. As the growth of an institution increases the distance between the decision makers and the market, information becomes more important. This is the prime reason for the importance of the computer, essentially an information producer, to industry at all levels.

The Importance of Marketing

The importance of marketing to an industrial economy can be pointed out in many ways. Among these are the cost, the number of people employed, the effect on the standard of living, and the importance to the individual firm.

FIGURE 1–1
Workers grading tomatoes. (*Courtesy:* Beatrice Company.)

Cost. In our complex, dispersed, highly competitive society, marketing costs are extremely high. A recent estimate stated that it cost as much to market goods as to produce them. There is little doubt that marketing costs have increased relative to production costs. The relationship of marketing costs to total costs varies considerably from industry to industry. For example, agricultural products that require little or no processing between producer and consumer frequently have marketing costs in excess of 70 percent of the retail price. Automobiles and heavy farming equipment, on the other hand, are marketed at a cost of about 35 percent, whereas ladies' apparel requires about 60 percent of the retail price for distribution from the manufacturer to the consumer.

People Employed.   Although it is difficult to estimate the number of people employed in marketing jobs, most experts agree that between one-fourth and one-third of the total working population is engaged in marketing activities. Included in these figures are all persons employed in retailing, wholesaling, transportation, warehousing, and communications industries, as well as those involved in the marketing functions of manufacture, finance, service, agriculture, and other business activities that are not classified primarily as marketing. Another interesting employment statistic is that during the last one hundred or so years there has been a threefold advance in total employment, whereas retailing and wholesaling jobs have increased twelve times. There is reason to believe that the proportion of marketing jobs to total employment will continue to increase.

Effect on the Standard of Living.   Ours has been described as an economy of affluence. This means that we produce and consume far in excess of our basic needs. We are not forced to consume all that is produced, but not to do so would result in serious economic disorder. It is the function of marketing to convince us to consume the mass of products turned out. Where marketing is able to successfully build a high demand, new jobs are created and both the individual and national standard of living are increased. This does not mean that the economic health of the United States is dependent upon marketing alone, but rather that inefficient distribution can lead to economic problems. Companies that can enlarge their profits through effective marketing are able to raise the standard of living of their owners and their employees and to hire new employees.

Importance to the Individual Firm.   As our technological capabilities grow, our production facilities are able to turn out ever-larger surpluses of goods. The gap between necessities and output constantly widens. To dispose of the surplus at a profitable level becomes more difficult and complicated. Product lines are expanding, and competition, both from similar products and substitutes, is growing keener. As a result, effective marketing is becoming steadily more important to the individual firm. The National Association of Manufacturers put it this way:

> In this exciting age of change, marketing is the beating heart of many operations. It must be considered a principle reason for corporate existence. The modern concept of marketing recognizes its role as a direct contributor to profits as well as sales volume.
>
> No longer can a company just figure out how many widgets it can produce and then go ahead and turn them out. To endure in this highly competitive, change-infested market, a company must first determine what it can sell, how much it can sell, and what approaches must be used to entice the wary customer. The president cannot plan; the production manager cannot manage; the purchasing agent cannot purchase; the chief financial officer cannot budget; and the en-

gineer and designer cannot design until the basic market determinations have been made.

Marketing must be understood to be a dynamic operation requiring the efforts and skills of a *team* of specialists.

The Development of Marketing Management

As American industry poured an ever-increasing surplus of goods into a highly competitive market, the function of marketing gained in importance. This has resulted in improved organization and management within the marketing division and has accorded greater importance to the position of the marketing manager in the overall operation of the company. The development of marketing from its rudimentary, relatively unimportant stage to its present far-reaching level of importance has been traced by the executive vice-president of the Pillsbury Company through four evolutionary stages that demonstrate the growth in significance of marketing management.

Production Stage.   When Pillsbury began milling fine flour in 1869, it found itself in a seller's market. That is, the demand for its product far exceeded its production capabilities. Since sales and distribution offered no problems, the company's management was primarily concerned with the improvement, expansion, and efficiency of production. The company employed salespeople, but they were not very important.

Sales Stage.   By 1930 the steadily increasing production of flour by Pillsbury and its competitors had changed the seller's market to a buyer's market. At that time there was a greater supply of flour on the market than was needed to satisfy customer demand. Competition became very keen and selling rivaled production in importance. The organization of a company at this stage of development is shown in Figure 1–2. Examination of the figure discloses that the functions of marketing are split up among many divisions. However, the importance of the sales area has been established, as indicated by the fact that the sales manager is equal to the other division managers. Note that the marketing executive is called sales manager and is responsible for none of the marketing functions beyond that of sales.

Market-planning Stage.   By the 1950s Pillsbury began to put out products other than flour. The company sought to improve its position in a highly competitive flour market by making convenience baking products, such as a variety of cake, biscuit, and roll mixes. Since the success of such products required a comprehensive understanding of the market, the marketing function increased in importance. Figure 1–3 depicts the organization of a company at the market-planning stage of development.

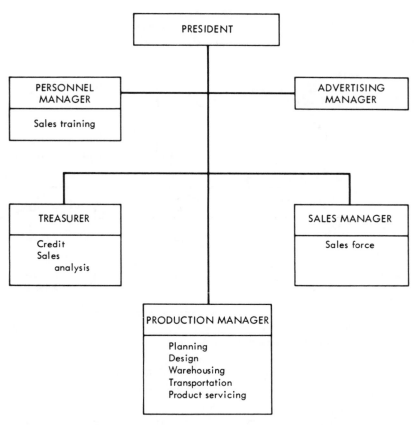

FIGURE 1–2   Organization chart of a sales-oriented firm, showing the responsibility for marketing functions.

Figure 1–4 indicates an improvement in the relative importance of the marketing function in a company at the market-planning stage of development. Since the department manager's responsibility is no longer limited to selling, the title has been changed from sales manager to marketing manager. Recognition has been given to the fact that efficient performance of the marketing function requires that many of the marketing activities, such as advertising, marketing research, sales analysis, and the training of sales personnel, have been transferred to the responsibility of the marketing division. At the market-planning stage the marketing manager's importance to the firm has increased to the point where the marketing manager is now equal to the production manager.

Market-control Stage.   The market-control stage at Pillsbury has the total company effort guided by marketing concepts. This entails a recognition of the fact that corporate success may be measured by the manner in which the company

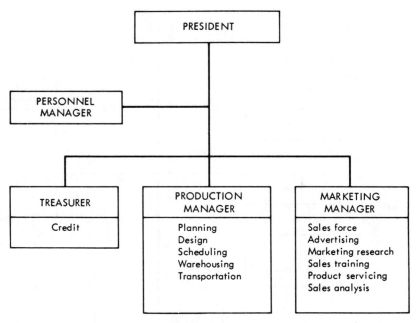

FIGURE 1–3 Organization chart of a marketing-oriented firm, showing the responsibility for marketing functions.

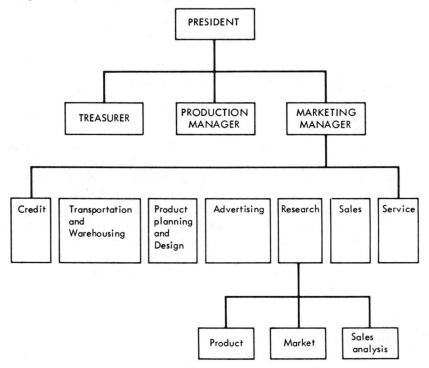

FIGURE 1–4 Organization chart of a firm with a fully integrated marketing division.

satisfies its consumer market. Since customer satisfaction is clearly a marketing function, the marketing division becomes, of necessity, the most significant of the company's functions and is responsible for the control and direction of all the company's efforts, including such nonmarketing areas as production and finance. Figure 1–4 indicates the organization of a marketing-oriented company with a fully integrated marketing division in which the marketing manager is directly responsible for all the marketing functions.

The Marketing Mix.   It is apparent from the previous discussion that the evolution of marketing has resulted in directing all the company's efforts toward giving customer satisfaction at a price that will bring in maximum profits. Under this system it is the marketer's responsibility to estimate the size and demand of the market and to direct the company's efforts toward the profitable satisfaction of such demand. This represents a complete turnabout from the relatively competition-free situation a century ago in which the emphasis was on production, with marketing filling a simple, unimportant role.

To fulfill this responsibility, the marketing manager must first estimate the target market. This is done by selecting a particular segment of the market (college students, housewives, and so on) and then fitting the marketing plans of the company to the satisfaction of this particular group. It is important for the marketing student to understand that the reason for the marketing division's growth to encompass almost all of a company's efforts is that, in today's market, the satisfaction of consumer demand requires a totally integrated company effort.

Considering the wide variety of ways in which goods can be designed and sold (color, style, quality, various advertising media and distribution methods, and so on), market planning is an extremely complicated problem.

A careful study of the marketing problem indicates that it consists of four areas that must be blended together to achieve marketing success. These are known as the marketing mix and consist of

1. Product.
2. Place.
3. Promotion.
4. Price.

Good market planning requires that the marketing mix be under continuous study and that the individual factors be constantly altered to adjust to a changing market. This may include changed product design, promotional and selling methods, distribution channels, or price adjustments. This regular review is as important to successful as to unsuccessful products. Perhaps the greatest error in American marketing history was Ford's refusal to alter the enormously successful Model-T automobile to meet the changed demand that was forced by General Motors' streamlining.

Each element of the marketing mix will have one or more chapters devoted to it later in the text. However, a brief overview at this point will be helpful.

Product.   Generally speaking, the companies that are growing most quickly are those that are spending the most money for product research and development. A short time ago the average life of a food product was about ten years. Presently marketers are delighted to have a product with a life of more than three years. The success of a company's product line depends upon decisions in the following areas: selecting the right product, knowing when to add new products to the line, dropping products from the line at the right time, and branding and packaging. (Note that in marketing, branding and packaging are considered part of the product.)

Place.   In marketing, the term *place* is used to indicate the method used to get the goods to the target market. The choices are very great. Questions that must be answered in solving the problem of place include the following:

1. What sort of wholesale and retail institutions should be used?
2. Should the goods be marketed through multiple outlets or, in the case of consumer goods, through a few exclusive stores?
3. Where should the outlets be located?
4. Would a consumer product do best in discount, low-priced stores, or in high-prestige, well-serviced stores?
5. How should the goods be shipped and warehoused to ensure their availability when the customer wants them?

Promotion.   Promotion involves communicating with the target market about the product, place, and price of the goods. There are many ways in which this information can be directed to the consumer, and the marketing division must select the media that are best suited to the particular marketing mix. Sales promotion, advertising, and personal selling are the elements that must be considered in the determination of a promotion policy.

Price.   In addition to product, place, and promotion, the marketer must also select the proper price at which the goods must be sold. Some of the factors involved in this decision are competitors' actions, existing practices on markdowns and discounts, target profits, and legal restrictions.

All four elements of the marketing mix are so closely interrelated that it is impossible to consider one more important than the others. The success of an institution's marketing program depends upon the effectiveness of each and every element of the marketing mix. The continued success of the program depends upon the ease and rapidity with which the institution adjusts its marketing mix to the constantly changing consumer market.

A MARKETING PROFILE

Barbie Doll

In an industry where new toys come on the market year after year, quickly replacing last year's entry, Mattel Toys has captured a vast segment of the market with a product that continues to grow in popularity.

In 1959, a new, exciting doll was developed and introduced at the Toy Fair, March 1959. Barbie, the 11½-inch fashion doll, would defy the professional buyers and become an international institution. Through innovative advertising on television, the Barbie Teen Age Model became a resounding hit.

Just as fashion designers respond to the times with changes in their collections, so have the designers of the Barbie costumes and hair creations. Hundreds of people keep Barbie current. In 1964 as the "Carnaby Street" look saw hemlines rise and hair lengths grow longer, so did the Barbie look. In the 1970s Mattel changed Barbie's appearance to "prairie," "granny" and disco styles. At the end of the decade, the doll's face was resculpted to incorporate the trends of the day.

In 1968 Christie, Barbie's first black friend, was added to the line and Hispanic Barbie was born in 1980. The doll is now available domestically in almost any ethnic guise in the "Dolls of the World" collection. Along with Barbie has been a select supporting cast beginning with boyfriend Ken in 1961, girlfriend Midge in 1963, and little sister Skipper in 1964.

In 1989 Barbie celebrated her thirtieth anniversary. The figures that accompany the product are astounding:

- A Barbie doll is sold every two seconds.
- Over 250 million Barbie fashions have been produced since 1959.
- Over 20 million fashions are sold every year.
- More than 75 million yards of fabric have gone into making Barbie fashions.
- Barbie doll has had more than 1.2 million pairs of shoes.
- Complementing her fashions, Barbie doll has "owned" more than 35,000 handbags and carry-alls.
- Over 6,000 different fashion designs have been created especially for Barbie.
- At least 100 new outfits are currently designed for Barbie annually.
- The bridal gown has been the No. 1 selling fashion every year since the beginning. Over 5 million gowns have been sold.
- Over 50 million additional fashions for Ken, Skipper, and other friends have been made.
- Barbie is being featured in the 1990 Ice Capades.

The product has been effectively marketed since its inception with timely introductions of companion models. The Barbie family tree shows how productive one "family" can be.

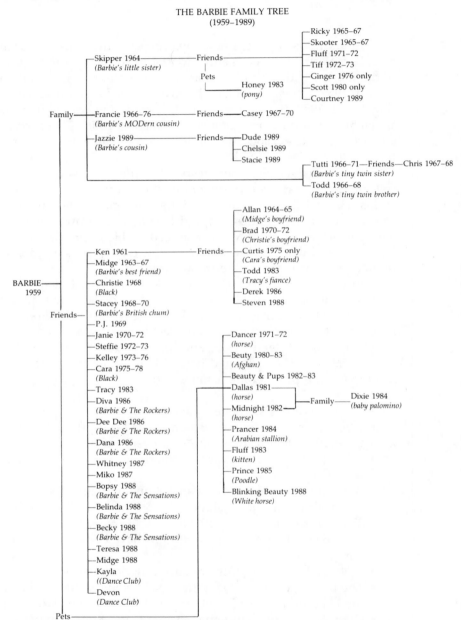

THE BARBIE FAMILY TREE
(1959–1989)

Skipper 1964 — Friends
(Barbie's little sister)
Pets — Honey 1983 *(pony)*

Ricky 1965–67
Skooter 1965–67
Fluff 1971–72
Tiff 1972–73
Ginger 1976 only
Scott 1980 only
Courtney 1989

Family — Francie 1966–76 — Friends — Casey 1967–70
(Barbie's MODern cousin)

Jazzie 1989 — Friends — Dude 1989
(Barbie's cousin) — Chelsie 1989 — Stacie 1989

Tutti 1966–71 — Friends — Chris 1967–68
(Barbie's tiny twin sister)
Todd 1966–68
(Barbie's tiny twin brother)

BARBIE — 1959

Ken 1961 — Friends
Midge 1963–67
(Barbie's best friend)
Christie 1968 *(Black)*
Stacey 1968–70 *(Barbie's British chum)*
P.J. 1969
Janie 1970–72
Steffie 1972–73
Kelley 1973–76
Cara 1975–78 *(Black)*
Tracy 1983
Diva 1986 *(Barbie & The Rockers)*
Dee Dee 1986 *(Barbie & The Rockers)*
Dana 1986 *(Barbie & The Rockers)*
Whitney 1987
Miko 1987
Bopsy 1988 *(Barbie & The Sensations)*
Belinda 1988 *(Barbie & The Sensations)*
Becky 1988 *(Barbie & The Sensations)*
Teresa 1988
Midge 1988
Kayla *((Dance Club)*
Devon *(Dance Club)*

Friends —
Allan 1964–65 *(Midge's boyfriend)*
Brad 1970–72 *(Christie's boyfriend)*
Curtis 1975 only *(Cara's boyfriend)*
Todd 1983 *(Tracy's fiance)*
Derek 1986
Steven 1988

Dancer 1971–72 *(horse)*
Beuty 1980–83 *(Afghan)*
Beauty & Pups 1982–83
Dallas 1981 *(horse)*
Midnight 1982 *(horse)* — Family — Dixie 1984 *(baby palomino)*
Prancer 1984 *(Arabian stallion)*
Fluff 1983 *(kitten)*
Prince 1985 *(Poodle)*
Blinking Beauty 1988 *(White horse)*

Pets —

Figures 1–5 and 1–6 feature highlights of the Barbie collection that has spanned its thirty-year history.

FIGURE 1–5   Barbie through the years. (*Courtesy:* Mattel Toys.)

The Computer and Marketing

Among the various areas of American businesses that turned to electronic data processing, marketing was one of the slowest. There are several reasons for this:

1. The company that originally acquired a computer for clerical reasons generally found itself with a small data-processing installation that was unable to handle the increased capacity required by the solution of marketing prob-

FIGURE 1–6   Barbie and her friends, 1989. (*Courtesy:* Mattel Toys.)

lems. Any increase in the size of a data-processing system is generally extremely expensive.

2. Trained programmers and other specialists required to develop the procedures needed to solve marketing problems were in short supply.

3. Top-level management was more likely to give higher priorities to the problems of the financial and accounting departments than to the more intricate problems posed by marketers.

4. Marketing problems are complicated. For the computer to operate effectively, the information entered must be absolutely complete and accurate. Such information is not always available in a form that can be used by a computer. Getting this information into usable shape may be expensive and time consuming.

Despite these formidable obstacles, the use of the computer in marketing is increasing rapidly. Polls taken of computer-using firms indicate a constantly growing use of the computer for marketing decision making. Some of the reasons for this trend are

1. Technological advances in the electronic data-processing field, which have led to better usage of computers in terms of getting information into and out of the system with a minimum of effort and training.

2. It was found that the high cost was worthwhile, since vital decision-making information is made quickly available by computerized installations. For example, a large ladies' apparel chain rented a computer for inventory control. One day the buyer of ladies' sweaters decided she would like to know which sizes were most popular. This is a simple computer problem and the information was readily available. Then she wanted to know about the popularity of various colors, and was given the answer. Then she wondered if bright colors were better in small sizes than in large sizes. This goes on and on, until the buyer is so well equipped with information that she can perform with far greater efficiency. At this point it is foolish to compare the cost of the computer with the salaries of the clerks it replaced, since the information the device supplies is far more important than the job for which it was originally installed. This, incidentally, is also an example of why computers that were purchased to work six hours a day are now working twenty-four hours a day.

3. The insistence of top-level management that the constantly growing investment in electronic data processing produce a greater return in more business areas.

4. The desire to match the considerable competitive advantage of the firms that use electronic devices for the solution of marketing problems.

5. The emergence of the managerial scientist on the business scene.

Figure 1–7 illustrates NCR's Tower 1632 computer.

FIGURE 1–7
NCR Tower 1632 computer.
(*Courtesy:* NCR.)

Pizza Hut has been one of the most successful fast-food restaurants in the United States. The company has also entered the home delivery market, which is the fastest-growing segment of the restaurant business today. One problem encountered with home delivery of hot foods is their delivery while still hot. Pizza Hut has resolved its problem by utilizing a computerized system. In major markets, customers call a single number that connects them with a computerized customer service center that is linked to all Pizza Hut delivery units. The order is automatically transmitted to the facility nearest the caller's home for immediate preparation and delivery. Figure 1–8 illustrates Pizza Hut's computerized delivery system.

To sum up, efficient marketing depends upon information. Much of the necessary knowledge has always been available in the records, but analyzing such mountainous records and producing timely, accurate informational summaries have not been possible until now.

Pizza Hut's delivery system:

Delivery Countdown–an innovative approach to a high-potential market. The order is called in... confirmed... routed to the nearest delivery unit. The hot Pizza Hut pizza is placed in a special pouch for transport... and arrives at the customer's door within 30 minutes.

FIGURE 1–8
Pizza Hut's computerized delivery system.
(*Courtesy:* PepsiCo, Inc.)

Careers in Marketing

The trend in America over the last thirty years has been for marketing to become the most important single factor in a business enterprise. Unquestionably, this trend will continue. Some time ago, the American Marketing Association went so far as to say, "Every company president elected from 1965 on will be a marketing expert." This might seem to be an overstatement, but it is probably close to the truth, especially when we consider the role played by David Garth, a marketing specialist, in helping to elect Jimmy Carter to the presidency.

Newcomers to many jobs receive higher starting salaries than do marketing graduates, but marketers generally catch up and pass them over a number of years. One author, comparing the earnings of graduates in business and industry in the fields of engineering, accounting, marketing, and general business, found the marketing graduates' earnings to be equal to the others after five years and to exceed the others after ten years.

Educational requirements have become increasingly stringent in business and industry. It is presently very difficult to find a job in a training position for a middle-management position without a minimum of an associate's degree. Holders of bachelor's degrees and masters of business administration have a decided advantage in the competition for top-level management positions.

The recent growth of management to a total business function has vastly broadened the variety of jobs available in marketing. Specifically, the most significant marketing positions are as follows:

Advertising and Sales Promotion.   In this vast area, which continues to show enormous growth particularly in television advertising, job applicants have many choices. Account executives, the persons in the middle between the company and the advertising agency, are the experts who totally understand the marketing needs of the companies they represent. While their responsibilities are not creatively oriented as are those of the copywriters and illustrators, they must be able to focus on work produced by these people and explain its significance to a successful advertising campaign. The salary range for such people is from $30,000 to $75,000.

Media buyers are responsible for selecting the most appropriate media for their customers. They must be totally familiar with all of the media and be prepared to fit the clients' needs, within a specific budget allocation, to the medium or media which promises the best return. In this aspect of advertising, the salary range is from $25,000 to $50,000.

With the competition facing marketers today, the role of the sales promotion director has taken on new importance. Whether it is in the form of continuity promotions where encyclopedias, dinnerware, and so on are offered in supermarkets; tie-ins of filters given free with the purchase of an automatic coffee maker; or personal appearances by authors in the promotion of their novels in bookstores, sales promotion is a growing field. The people involved must be creative in the sense that they must be able to develop promotions which motivate consumers to buy. Executives in this exciting field earn from $30,000 to $100,000.

Product Managers.   The most important individuals involved in the planning and control of a company's products are the product managers and brand managers. They are totally concerned with the product from its inception. Their involvement includes development of the product, test marketing, advertising and promotion, sales analysis, distribution decision making, pricing, packaging, and so forth. Those with extensive background in formal marketing education coupled with practical experience in many of the areas mentioned are best suited for careers in product and brand management. Earnings generally range from $30,000 to $75,000.

Marketing Research.   For those people who are statistics oriented and have a comprehensive understanding of the social and psychological motivations of consumers, research is a perfect area. The daily routine includes such tasks as questionnaire designs, sample selection, tabulation and analysis of data, report writing and presentation, and making recommendations to marketers. In this area, it is possible to be employed by marketing institutions which have their own research departments as is the case with the giants in the field such as General Foods, Sears, General Motors, and so on, or to work for marketing research organizations such as A. C. Nielsen who sell their services to clients. This analytical field pays from $30,000 to $50,000 for research analysts and $40,000 to $100,000 for marketing research directors.

Sales.   The area of marketing which generally offers the initial step into the field for the college graduate is sales. Without the salesperson few companies would be able to market their products successfully. Whether the company is industrially oriented or focuses upon consumer goods, few sales could be closed without significant professional selling. A career in sales offers the individual a wide range of products and services as well as opportunity for advancement to sales or marketing management. The salary, often based on commission for incentive, usually ranges from $20,000 to $75,000, but it is not inconceivable for the gifted salesperson to earn upwards of $100,000.

Retailing.   While retailing has often been given a bad rap for offering notoriously low salaries, this has been corrected to some degree in recent years. Although starting salaries are still often below those of other entry-level marketing jobs, the gap is not as wide as it once was.

Retailing provides a wealth of opportunities for those who are willing to work long hours and during evenings and weekends when other people are away from their jobs. College graduates enter executive training programs which provide on-the-job training as well as classroom instruction in such areas as merchandising, control, store operations, management, and advertising and sales promotion. Each company offers its own "ladder" with ultimate choices to be made by the store and the employee. Typical positions in retailing include department manager, buyer, merchandise manager, service manager, employment director, visual merchandiser, advertising manager, and sales associate. With the present-day expansion of the chains and department stores, the opportunities are considerable. Macy's is expanding to the South: J. C. Penney is restructuring its merchandising format to become more fashion oriented; Sears is concentrating on more name brands with a slight deemphasis of private brands, the Limited empire is expanding all of its divisions, including The Limited, Limited Express, Victoria's Secret, Lerner Shops and Henri Bendel. Much attention is being focused upon off-price retailing as well. With the steady increase in the population, the population explosion to the South and West, and store expansion to meet these needs, retailing is a place for a rewarding career. Salaries range from $15,000 to $75,000, with top executives earning significantly more.

Transportation.   A little-known field by most students involves the transporting of goods from the producer to the consumer. With the recent growth of air express, the field has taken on new dimensions. Concerns of the people in transportation focus upon delivery routes, time of transport, safety of products, and cost of shipment. Salaries range from $20,000 to $40,000.

Wholesaling.   This area of marketing includes positions in purchasing, warehousing, and selling. Any marketing student knows that the function of most wholesalers is to assemble goods from many manufacturers, warehouse them, and sell them to their customers who are usually retailers. People who choose wholesaling should be service oriented. That is, they should have the ability to motivate others to purchase merchandise from them that is available from other wholesale resources. Salespeople usually earn from $22,000 to $50,000 in wholesaling.

Public Relations.   More and more profit and nonprofit organizations are organizing public relations staffs. The object of the public relations person is to build the company's image. Handling complaints, dealing with the public's problems concerning the company, and interfacing with the media are just a few of the tasks performed by these individuals. Essential for such a position is the ability to communicate effectively both orally and in writing. While a knowledge of marketing is certainly an advantage, the individual's formal education should have centered on communication or the liberal arts.

International Marketing.   Consumers as well as marketers instantly are made aware of the internationalization of businesses through continuous reports in newspapers and magazines and on television. One need only to examine merchandise offerings to find that American firms are actively engaged in a multitude of foreign ventures in automobiles, video recorders, cameras, clothing, food, appliances, and so on. College graduates who have a command of another language and who are willing to travel and reside in foreign countries will be perfectly suited to explore the many possibilities offered in a career in international marketing. While the salaries tend to be comparable to those in America, they are sometimes higher as an incentive to attract the best people. Many of those in international marketing who must relocate abroad find that their money buys even more in some places than it would at home.

Customer Services.   Many companies are establishing customer service programs which enable both the company's customers and the consumers to have direct contact. The customer service representative is best described as a combination troubleshooter and goodwill ambassador whose aim it is to foster good relations and project a positive image. Handling complaints, dealing with problems, evaluating suggestions, and communicating with the proper company department for customers are just some of the duties and responsibilities of such a job. The salary range is from $20,000 to $30,000.

Resident Buying Offices.   Retailers are generally located away from their wholesale markets but, nevertheless, need to be within earshot to know about market conditions. Since time and money make regular visits to the market impossible except for major purchases, retailers employ the service of market representatives professionally known as resident buyers. For a fee, the resident buying offices enable retailers to feel the pulse of the market without leaving their stores. With approximately three hundred of these businesses flourishing, this field provides graduates (an associate's degree is accepted at this level) with the opportunity to learn all about manufacturers' offerings and retail management. This industry offers people positions primarily as assistant buyers, buyers, and merchandise managers. While the starting salary is low ($15,000 is typical), the worker will gain invaluable market experience for future positions.

There are careers in many other areas of marketing in addition to those discussed. Industrial marketing runs the gamut of jobs from product design to sales; purchasing agents buy everything from raw materials to supplies that are used to run a business; credit managers deal with money matters at both the manufacturers' and retailers' levels; and systems analysts are involved in the quantitative problems encountered in business, to name a few more.

The outlook for marketing occupations appears to be positive based upon projections made by the United States Department of Labor's Bureau of Labor Statistics. The listing in Table 1–1 indicates the number of new jobs expected

TABLE 1–1.   Outlook for marketing careers

Marketing Occupations	Present–1995	
	New Jobs	*% Increase*
Retail and Wholesale Buyers	76,000	30
Purchasing Agents	52,000	27
Designers	73,000	41
Insurance Sales Agents	90,000	25
Manufacturers' Sales Workers	64,000	15
Retail-Trade Sales Personnel	898,000	27
Wholesale-Trade Sales Workers	327,000	30
Industrial Trucking	70,000	18
Travel Agents	26,000	43

Source: United States Department of Labor, Bureau of Labor Statistics.

between the present and 1995 and the percentage gain in those numbers. While the list is by no means complete in terms of all marketing jobs, the overall outlook shows a definite upswing in marketing careers. The careful examination of government publications, newspapers, trade journals and other materials are excellent sources of career opportunities which may provide not only an analysis of the various job titles but projections in terms of market needs.

Important Points in the Chapter

1. As a society progresses economically, specialization of work occurs, resulting in surpluses. Marketing becomes indispensable, since these surpluses must be exchanged for the necessities that are the surpluses of other workers.

2. There are many ways in which the word *market* is used. One of these is: a market is an area in which the aggregate of forces or conditions result in decisions that satisfy demand by the transfer of goods and services.

3. *Marketing* may be defined as the performance of business activities that direct the flow of goods and services from the producer to the consumer or user.

4. The marketing division is directly responsible for such activities as selling, advertising, transportation, and promotion and is indirectly involved in production and accounting.

5. The two basic elements of a marketing system are the surplus of a good or service in one sector of the economy (the producing sector) and a demand for such good or service in another sector of the economy (the consuming sector).

6. The Industrial Revolution increased the importance of marketing because a surplus of manufactured goods was produced at urban centers, whereas the urban population required food and other farm products that were produced outside the cities.

7. When the demand for goods exceeds the supply, the emphasis of a nation's business is on production. After World War I, mass production resulted in a situation in which the supply of goods exceeded the demand. Marketing then came into its own, since it is responsible for the distribution of excess goods.

8. A business enterprise must perform four functions: form (production), place (transportation to the customer), time (getting goods to the consumer when demanded), and ownership (transfer of title). The marketing division is fully responsible for place, time, and ownership and must direct form.

9. Some reasons why marketing is important to our economy are the effect on price, the effect on number of people employed, the effect on the standard of living, and the importance to the individual firm.

10. The evolution of business from the production stage, the sales stage, and the market-planning stage to the market-control stage has coincided with the increased importance of the role of the marketing manager.

11. The four areas that must be blended together to achieve marketing success are called the marketing mix. The marketing mix consists of product, place, promotion, and price.

12. With the enormous marketing investments made by industry, the career outlook is especially favorable in such areas as advertising, marketing research, sales, retailing, international marketing, and customer services.

Review Questions

1. Explain the relationship between specialization and marketing.

2. Indicate four ways in which the term *market* is used. Give examples of each.

3. Give the American Marketing Association's definition of *marketing*.

4. Which business activities are the full responsibility of the marketing division? Which business activities are directed rather than fully controlled by marketing?

5. The two basic elements of marketing importance are surplus and demand. Discuss these in terms of the growth in importance of marketing in the post–World War I period.

6. How do marketers use the word *time?* Explain their responsibility in the area of time.

7. What is meant by *passing title?* What is the marketer's responsibility in this area?

8. Discuss the effect of marketing on our standard of living.

9. How important is marketing in our society with regard to the number of people employed in marketing? What are the future trends in regard to marketing employment?

10. Explain the market-planning stage of marketing development at Pillsbury. Relate it to the production stage and the sales stage at that company.

11. Discuss the market-control stage of marketing development at Pillsbury. How has the relative importance of the marketing division changed during the evolution from the production, sales, market-planning, and market-control stages?

12. What are the four elements of the marketing mix?

13. Explain the importance of promotion to marketing. Indicate methods of promotion.

14. Which is the most important element of the marketing mix?

15. Why is the marketing mix of a successful product kept under careful study?

16. Discuss the compensation of marketers at the first level of employment and at later levels.

17. Indicate the outlook for marketing careers in the future. Give details.

Case problems

Case Problem 1

Techtronics, Inc., is a medium-sized electronics manufacturer whose total production is an electronic component shipped directly to the NASA space agency. The firm was extremely successful throughout the 1970s, but in 1987 it became apparent that federal budget cutbacks would present serious problems in the future.

In view of this ominous threat, the company, during the late 1970s and mid-1980s, designed consumer products in the hope of offsetting lost government business. Although these consumer products were well designed and competitive, they did poorly on the market and the company was forced to abandon them.

The company's top management consists of five extremely bright, capable engineers. They are fine research people and their production-planning capabilities are excellent. This, teamed with up-to-date equipment, ensures a high level of product research and production.

At present, the research department has developed a device that can be attached easily to a TV antenna that will increase its range and bring in extra channels. Competitively, the product is inexpensive, of excellent quality, and suited to yield a high profit.

Questions

1. What do you think should be done to make the firm more marketing oriented?
2. What organizational changes would you recommend to put the firm in a better position to sell on the consumer market?

Case Problem 2

Tropicania is an emerging African nation that achieved its independence ten years ago. At great personal sacrifice and with the help of foreign aid, the country has since its formation built many schools and hospitals and supplied a minimal standard of living to its citizens. Although this has been a great stride forward, the country's standard of living is still very low.

The government, having raised the conditions to minimal standards, is now ready for an economic step forward. The goal is an improved standard of living for its citizens. Foreign aid is available for use in any way the government wishes.

The economy of Tropicania is chiefly agricultural. Typically, the farms are family owned, and the crops grown are those necessary to family survival. When possible, individual farmers grow a little cotton, which they are able to sell for currency with which they buy simple manufactured products and tools. The soil and climate are excellent for the growth of a long-staple variety of cotton that is avidly sought after by wealthier nations for the manufacture of high-quality clothing.

The problem faced by the government is to decide the form that foreign aid should take in raising the country's living standards. For example, the aid could be in the form of manufactured products used by the people, machine tools for manufacturing a variety of high-demand products, and so on.

Assignment

1. Develop a program that would have the most beneficial long-run effect on Tropicania's economy.

2

MARKETING RESEARCH

Learning Objectives

Upon completion of the chapter, you will be able to:

1. Enumerate four areas of marketing research and give examples of each.
2. Define and explain the importance of the scientific method of marketing research.
3. Discuss the importance to the researcher of problem identification and definition.
4. Differentiate between primary and secondary data and give examples of each.
5. List and describe four methods of gathering marketing research information.
6. Explain the importance of sampling.

WILL THE CROWDS CHEER
WHEN IT REACHES LOS ANGELES?

The out-of-town tryout is certainly not new to the theater industry. No matter how brilliant the script, how creative the sets, and how masterful the performers, the show always opens first out of town. Whether it is Philadelphia, Boston, or Washington, D.C., the most generally accepted tryout towns, or it's a tour across the nation, the final product is polished and repolished before its major introduction to the Broadway critics.

Marketing of products follows a format that is similar. Whether it is Procter & Gamble, General Foods, or any of the other giants in the field, the company wants to get the kinks out of a product before major distribution takes place. One of the vital areas of research is test marketing of products. Before enormous sums of money are committed by the producer (sometimes the expenditures run into the millions), test marketing is done to evaluate the public's reaction to the product, its package, and its advertising and promotional campaigns.

One of the most valuable aspects of research is test marketing. The problem is to find a market that is typical of the eventual market the company seeks. The objective is to reproduce the typical American city. The market must have the right demographics and all the other requisites that make it a miniversion of the potentially vast market the company is heading for.

There are many test markets which are considered to be most appropriate for the producers of American-made goods. The list is by no means stable. While one city might be favorable one year, next year could find it falling from favor among the market researchers. Peoria, Illinois, for example, once high on the test market ladder, was dropped because of a high unemployment rate, as was the Tampa–St. Petersburg area of Florida, because of a high percentage of senior citizens.

As evidenced by their test marketing actions, many marketers view Syracuse, New York, as one of the most, if not *the* most important testing cities. Since 1980 more than 100 products have been test marketed in Syracuse. Brown Cow Yogurt, Extra Mild Kielbasa, Hopfenferle Beer, and Polar B'ars are just some of the products whose companies have had the citizens of Syracuse try them before distribution to the big time. Dancer Fitzgerald Sample, the advertising agency, rates Syracuse as one of the top eight test markets.

A by-product of Syracuse being a test market is its rise to one of industry's centers for research. At this time, with the prospects for the area to continue to be a mini-America, more than fifteen marketing research companies have set up shop in the region.

It should be understood, however, that all the research undertaken by even the most sophisticated marketers does not guarantee success. Many marketing researchers still tread carefully even after the test market scores a *yes* for the product. They recall disasters such as the Procter & Gamble fiasco when Rely tampons had to be recalled after the toxic shock syndrome scare.

|| Statistically, about 50 percent of the products that reach the test market stage are eliminated, and of those that are finally introduced nationally, about 30 percent fail.

|| Will the crowds cheer in Los Angeles? Only sometimes!

INTRODUCTION

Decision making and problem solving are probably the most important aspects of marketing management. Should a new soft beverage be packaged in a reusable or disposable container? Will the addition of a new compact car to an automobile manufacturer's line find a new market to increase overall company sales, or will it cut into sales of the company's other, established models? In the late 1950s Corning Glass Works was faced with many problems concerning its prospective new product, Corning Ware. One major problem was the effect on Corning's already successful line of Pyrex. One decision that had to be reached was whether or not to associate the new product with the Pyrex name, thereby possibly jeopardizing Pyrex's position, or to market Corning Ware separately. It is quite obvious that in order to make such decisions intelligently, a good deal of information is needed by marketers. Marketing research, broadly defined, involves investigation of marketing problems and formulation of the necessary recommendations to solve these problems. *Market research* and *marketing research*, although often used interchangeably, are actually different and should not be substituted for each other. *Marketing research* refers to the investigation of *all* marketing problems, whereas *market research* deals exclusively with problems associated with markets.

Marketing research had its formal beginning in the early 1900s. Throughout the years, businesses, having realized the value of the dollars spent for research in terms of improving their marketing positions, continue to increase their expenditures for marketing research. Companies spend millions of dollars each year to have those questions answered that will improve the chance of success of their companies and products. Table 2–1 features the top 20 U.S. Research Organizations. Although, from every indication, marketers will continue to increase their research expenditures, it should be understood that even with extensive marketing research programs some products and companies have failed in the past and others will do so in the future. One need only to look at the Ford Motor Company's marketing of the Merkur XR4Ti for an example. The Merkur and a number of other well-known marketing mistakes will be examined in Chapter 8.

TABLE 2–1. Top 20 U.S. research
organizations in 1988[1]

Rank 1988	Organization	1988 total
1	A. C. Nielsen	$880.0
2	IMS International	365.0
3	Arbitron/SAMI/Burke	320.0
4	Information Resources	129.2
5	Research International	103.4
6	MRB Group	78.2
7	WESTAT	64.3
8	M/A/R/C Inc.	51.1
9	NFO Research	40.9
10	Maritz Marketing Research	39.9
11	Market Facts	37.8
12	Elrick & Lavidge	31.4
13	NPD Group	29.8
14	Yankelovich Clancy Shulman	24.5
15	Chilton Research Services	23.7
16	Walker Research	21.7
17	Louis Harris & Associates	19.4
18	Starch INRA Hooper	19.0
19	Intersearch Corp.	19.0
20	Pharmaceutical Data Services	18.3

[1]Dollars are in millions.

Source: June 5, 1989, *Advertising Age*

CLASSIFICATION OF MARKETING RESEARCH ACTIVITIES

Research is not confined to a specific aspect of marketing but is part of every marketing function. Only a few very large businesses, with upward of $100 million in sales volume, have formally organized research departments equipped to deal with all the areas that require examination. Smaller companies, although able to research some specific areas, call upon private marketing research companies if extensive investigation is necessary. Generally, the following classifications represent all the activities of research.

1. Research on products and services
    a. Customer acceptance of proposed new products
    b. Comparative studies of competitive products
    c. Evaluating competitive product developments
    d. Determining present users of present products
    e. Evaluating proposed new products or services
    f. Market tests or test market activities

     g. Determining sources of customer dissatisfaction

     h. Seeking new uses of present products

     i. Product line simplification

     j. Packaging studies

2. Research on markets

     a. Competitive position of company products

     b. Analysis of market size

     c. Estimating demand for new products

     d. Sales forecasting

     e. Determining characteristics of markets

     f. Analysis of territorial potentials

     g. Studying trends in market size

     h. General business forecasting

     i. Studying relative market profitability

     j. Studying economic factors

     k. Studying shifts in market composition

     l. Changes in consumer-type importance

3. Research on sales methods and policies

     a. Establishing or revising sales territories

     b. Measuring variation in territorial yield

     c. Evaluating present sales methods

     d. Competitive pricing studies

     e. Analysis of salespersons' activities

     f. Price studies

     g. Appraising proposed sales methods

     h. Measuring salespersons' effectiveness

     i. Distribution cost studies

     j. Setting sales quotas

     k. Development of salespersons' standards

     l. Sales compensation

     m. Effectiveness of promotional devices

4. Research on advertising

     a. Advertising effectiveness

     b. Competitive advertising and selling prices

     c. Motivational or qualitative studies

     d. Selecting media

Although marketing institutions differ in their research emphasis, it is generally agreed that research on markets receives the greatest amount of attention from marketers. Without the determination of significant market information, it is unlikely that marketing managers can proceed to any other marketing activities.

MARKETING RESEARCH EXAMPLES

To make the foregoing list more meaningful to marketing students, a specific example of a marketing research problem will be discussed under each major classification.

Research on Products and Services

A well-known manufacturer of cookware was contemplating the addition of an electric coffee maker to its line of products. The company's design team developed many different styles, from which one was to be selected for production. Management narrowed the field down to two models. It then assigned to the marketing research department the task of determining which would be more successful. The research staff felt that the best qualified person to make the ultimate decision should be the primary user of the product, the homemaker. Briefly, the approach employed in solving the problem was as follows. A test market (a city, town, or other area with a population considered typical of the manufacturer's entire market) was selected and a number of homemakers were chosen to use both coffee makers in their homes for a specified period. At the end of the period, each homemaker completed a questionnaire that provided meaningful information with which a final choice could be made by the company. After tabulating these data (and measuring many other factors), the company decided upon the model it would market.

Research on Markets

A real estate developer tentatively decided upon a site on which to build a shopping center. From the real estate agent's point of view, the location was easily accessible by public and private transportation, and the amount of land was sufficient for a substantial number of stores plus ample parking. The last problem was to analyze the size of the potential customer market. A marketing research firm was employed to assess the market. After careful analysis, the research firm suggested that the plan to develop the site be dropped because survey results indicated that because of the short distance to similar nearby shopping centers, the size of the potential market was not sufficient to warrant the venture.

A MARKETING PROFILE

Bristol-Myers Company

The host of products that the Bristol-Myers Company manufactures for distribution to customers in the United States and abroad cuts across many categories. Consumer products such as Clairol Ultress and Windex, health care formulas like Jobst used for swelling control after specific surgical procedures, pharmaceuticals such as Bu Spar, a unique antianxiety agent, Final Net, one of the world's leading nonaerosol hairsprays, and Mum Roll-On and Stick deodorants are just some that make up the Bristol-Myers family.

Aggressive companies always look to strengthen their positions through the addition of new products and penetration of new markets. Bristol-Myers, one of the more ambitious participants in marketing research, has recently completed an in-depth study that strongly indicated the potential of a market that is often ignored or underestimated.

In its report, "America Comes of Age," the company recognized the importance of this ever-increasing market and its importance to profits. By conducting scores of personal interviews, it found a market that is alive and well and coming of age in a most vital manner. The misconceptions of the gray market, or senior citizens group, is that they are seeking new pleasures in life instead of wiling away the hours in rocking chairs. Such individual responses as "I'm just learning how to swim," from a 72-year-old, "I'm never going to be old," from a 71-year-old member of the Over-the-Hill Hockey League, made up of men from ages 59 to 89, "I felt older in my late 30's and early 40's than I do now" from a 74-year-old woman, and "I can teach reading because I read for 60 years. I can hear them when they make mistakes," from a legally blind, 84-year-old reading teacher.

The company's research found that although people over 50 make up only one quarter of the population, they control half of the nation's discretionary spending, which amounts to $130 billion a year. With this newly recognized vitality, the life expectancy ever increasing, and the earnings potential from this market, research has shown the way for Bristol-Myers to capture its fair share of these consumers' purchases.

The photograph accompanying this profile, from the company's annual report, 1988, shows the vim and vigor of this once neglected market segment.

FIGURE 2–1
Senior Citizens on vacation in New York. (Laimute E. Druskis)

Research on Sales Methods and Policies

It has been the policy of a high-priced men's coat and suit manufacturer to sell its merchandise to retail outlets on an exclusive basis. That is, only major department stores, one in each city, could carry the line. For the past few years, management was confronted with declining sales, even though each store was the finest in its respective city and the stores' sales were steadily increasing. This was a problem for a marketing research company. The study conducted by the research consultants showed that although department store sales were on the rise, men's high-priced clothing was being purchased, more commonly, from small specialty stores. It was recommended that in the future, company policy should change from exclusive to selective distribution (a chosen few in each city) and that emphasis should shift from the department store to the specialty store.

Research on Advertising

A mail-order wholesaler had always received a large percentage of orders through advertising. The media she had continuously and successfully used were trade papers and direct mail. She had never really determined which medium was more successful in achieving results. In an attempt to measure media effectiveness, a new statement form (mailed to customers monthly) was prepared by the wholesaler. In addition to the amount due the wholesaler, a listing was incorporated that asked the customer where he or she had learned about the various products. After a few months, tabulation of the data showed that trade paper advertising accounted for an insignificant proportion of sales. Trade paper advertising was suspended and the savings eventually led to an increased profit.

THE SCIENTIFIC METHOD

The term *scientific* is loosely used in marketing. Often so-called research studies are merely the educated opinions of marketers. If a method of research is to be considered scientific, there must be a systematic procedure for the solving of problems. The scientific method is adequately defined as follows:

> We can distinguish that which actually is scientific by two criteria: that it is *systematic* and *impartial.* Nothing deserves to be called scientific unless it is carried out in a systematic fashion, which requires accurate problem definition and measurements, orderly data gathering, organized arrangement of knowledge within the total framework of knowledge, and systematic methods in all other respects. Impartiality is of course the ability to place the meaning on evidence without the distortion of preconceived notions of its nature or foregone conclusions.

THE RESEARCH PROCEDURE

Although the problems to be solved might employ different techniques, the procedure used by marketing researchers generally breaks down as follows.

Identification of the Problem

A number of factors might contribute to the eventual investigation of a problem. It might be the decrease in sales of a line's particular product or perhaps a decline of an entire line of goods. Although management could be aware of the decline in sales, the actual cause of the problem might not be apparent. Similarly, a wholesaler might be concerned with the effectiveness of promotional campaigns and wonder whether or not they substantially contribute to sales. Whichever area troubles management, it must be clearly identified before research can begin.

Definition of the Problem

In the discussion of their business problems, executives usually resort to generalities. Marketing researchers, however, are trained to solve specific problems. What the problem is must be clearly determined. For example, mentioning that the entire line of a manufacturer is declining in sales is too general a statement. It should be specified how much it has declined and where the decline has taken place.

Making the Study

Sometimes the costs to solve a problem are extravagant. The practicality of searching for a solution must be decided in terms of dollars and relative worth.

Secondary Data.   Once research has been decided upon, secondary sources are usually studied for pertinent data. The data from these sources have already been compiled and are called secondary data. Their information may play an important role in the solution and sometimes may be all that is needed, so that original research can be omitted. Some of the common sources of secondary data are

1. *Company records.* Records of sales orders, sales according to territories, product returns, periodic reports of sales personnel, and advertising expenditures in some instances will provide sufficient information to solve the problem.

2. *Libraries.* An unlimited number of business periodicals is available to researchers in public libraries: for example, *Advertising Age, Chain Store Age, The Journal of Marketing,* and *Business Week.* To facilitate finding the appropriate business literature, a *Business Periodical Index* is available. These publications are significant in that they often provide survey results that might be similar or pertinent to the study being made. They may contain adequate data to render a new and original research project unnecessary.

3. *Trade associations.* These organizations are groups of businesses with similar interests. Most industries have trade associations. One of the largest is the National Retail Merchants' Association, with almost every important retail store a member. Trade association activities include regular meetings to discuss problems in the trade, training seminars, and sometimes the publication of journals.

4. *Government agencies.* An abundance of material is available from all levels of government. At the federal level, the monthly catalog of the Government Printing Office is a publication constantly used by researchers. It provides an extensive listing of everything published by the government. The Department of Commerce, of which the Bureau of the Census is a part, provides a census of business, one of population, and one of agriculture. These may be extremely valuable to marketing research projects. Other federal sources of data are the many regulatory agencies, for example, the Federal Communications Commission, the Federal Trade Commission, the Bureau of Labor and Statistics, and the Food and Drug Administration. At the state and municipal levels, the consumer affairs departments provide information concerning consumer protection. With the consumer movement now so prominent, these departments are being tapped more frequently for information.

5. *Private agencies.* Many established service organizations provide data that otherwise might only be obtainable through original research. Compilers of such vital data are A. C. Nielsen Co., noted for broadcast audience measurement and other consumer data, and Dun & Bradstreet, a leader in credit information. These companies supply pertinent research data.

6. *Advertising media.* The various communications media, such as newspapers, magazines, radio, and television, make studies that are of interest to researchers. Studies of population, readership, and income are examples of the statistics made available by the media.

7. *Colleges and universities.* Throughout the country, many institutions of higher learning organize research facilities which explore marketing and other business problems. Some colleges, through their courses in marketing research, involve students in research projects that are often high-quality undertakings which serve the needs of the business community. Whichever college approach is used, marketers often make use of college-based research studies.

Primary Data.   Although careful examination of secondary data often provides valuable information, an original study is often still needed. If so, primary data (that is, compiled firsthand) must be collected. The methods by which the information is gathered are numerous. Final determination of the technique or combination of techniques to be employed is generally dictated by the particular problem. The facts that must be gathered firsthand by a company can be obtained from a number of different sources of primary data:

1. *Company salespersons.* The sales force is the link between the company and the customer. Management often seeks the advice of salespersons on matters of market information. Sometimes the sales staff acts in a formal manner and interviews customers to gather information that could be vital to future company decision making. Since sales personnel usually have estab-

lished sound rapport with those to whom they sell, the information they procure is often used by research teams.

2. *Potential customers.* Prospects, or potential customers, are fine primary sources. They often provide insights into reasons they did not purchase products in the past or what management might do to make their offerings more desirable. In studying this group it is important to make certain that all persons to be surveyed meet the general criteria established to be classified as potential customers. If caution is not exercised in selecting this group, the data gathered might be inappropriate and less credible for decision making.

3. *Regular customers.* This group is a fine source. Since they have been involved with the company, they can provide meaningful insight into many areas of marketing. Problems concerning product design and quality, services, terms, and so forth are just some of the areas with which customers have had firsthand experience.

Methods Used to Gather Information

Observation Method.   Probably the simplest method used to collect raw data is the observation or counting technique. The individual assigned to the task merely counts and records what he or she sees without talking to those being studied. Traffic counts and fashion or style counts are often used by marketing research teams.

Traffic counts are used at various times. In the supermarket chain, top management, in trying to evaluate the location for a new unit, is interested in how much traffic passes the proposed site. It is unlikely that general traffic information is sufficient to satisfy the needs of the researcher. Classifications such as pedestrian traffic, automobile traffic, and traffic generated by buses and trains might be devised to see how important each one is. Similarly, recorders might be assigned to tabulate from which direction the traffic originates. Forms are constructed to make the task of recording simple. Usually, just a checkmark placed next to predetermined categories is all that is necessary to record the information. The traffic observation might be used by a retailer to help determine store entrance locations.

Fashion counts are used by both manufacturers and retailers as aids in determining which styles are being purchased and worn by consumers. A shirt manufacturer, in determining which colors and styles to produce, might make a fashion count. A retail buyer, in trying to determine additional purchases for the present season, might also use this method of research. These counts, which are merely recorded observations of people, are also helpful in recognizing trends. A survey of this type, checking a practical kind of merchandise and taken at periodic intervals in places where a company's clientele assembles, might reveal factors that would be of interest in future purchasing. For example, a shoe store catering to the jet set might want to determine whether both shoes and boots

```
┌─────────────────────────────────────────────────────────────────────┐
│                          FASHION COUNT                                │
│                                                                       │
│                Item Counted:   LADIES' FOOTWEAR                        │
│                                                                       │
│                   LOCATION: _____                   │
│                                                                       │
│   CLASSIFICATION          BOOT STYLE              SHOE STYLE           │
│                                                                       │
│   SHOE                    ANKLE                   SANDAL               │
│   BOOT                    MID-CALF                OPEN-TOE PUMP        │
│   OTHER _____            ABOVE THE KNEE          CLOSED-TOE PUMP      │
│                           HIP                     T-STRAP              │
│                           OTHER _____            HIGH HEEL           │
│                                                   MEDIUM HEEL         │
│                                                   FLAT HEEL           │
│                                                   OTHER _____        │
│                                                                       │
│                              COLORS                                   │
│                                                                       │
│   TINTS                   SHADES                  NEUTRALS             │
│                                                                       │
│   PINK                    BLUE                    BLACK                │
│   BLUE                    GREEN                    WHITE               │
│   YELLOW                  GOLD (MUSTARD)          SILVER               │
│   GREEN                   ORANGE                   GOLD (METALLIC)      │
│   MELON                   RED                                          │
│   TAN                     PURPLE                                       │
│   AQUA                    BROWN                                        │
│   OTHER _____            OTHER _____                                 │
│                                                                       │
│          PLACE CHECK MARKS NEXT TO THE APPROPRIATE ITEMS              │
└─────────────────────────────────────────────────────────────────────┘
```

FIGURE 2–2   Fashion count checklist used by manufacturers and retailers to determine which styles are being purchased and worn by consumers.

should be replenished in inventory and in which amount. By selecting various places where the jet set come together the firm can rapidly learn what their clientele is wearing. The opening night of the opera or the first horse show of the season are events sure to attract scores of jet setters. Through the use of a simple form, as pictured in Figure 2–2, all the pertinent information can be easily recorded. The exact number of people to observe to make the survey meaningful is determined by statistical formulas. After the data have been recorded and tabulated, it is relatively simple to rank, in order of importance, what was studied. For example, if half the women observed wore boots, it would indicate that half the inventory should consist of boots to satisfy customer needs.

To determine trends several counts could be taken to see whether there is a decline or an increase. For example, 50 percent of the women wore boots at one observation; however, two weeks later another count might indicate 53 percent.

This increase in percentage should be reflected in the proportion of shoes and boots in stock.

Questionnaire Method.   Although observation is used by marketers, it is by no means as widely employed as the questionnaire. Whereas the counting technique is relatively simple, the questionnaire is more complex and therefore more costly and time consuming. One major difference is that observation can actually take place without consumer awareness, whereas a questionnaire requires cooperation from those being studied.

Marketing managers can select the method by which they will collect data from three types of questionnaires: telephone, mail, and interview. The choice is based upon several factors:

1. Size and location of the area to be surveyed
2. Availability of personnel to assign to the project
3. Availability of funds
4. Amount of time allocated to gathering of the data

A study of both the advantages and disadvantages of each type will show which method is the most appropriate for a particular project.

Telephone advantages

1. People cannot be reached faster in any other way.
2. Telephone calls are relatively inexpensive.
3. Questioning can be carried out from a central point, without sending people into the field (Figure 2–3).
4. Information is obtained very quickly.

FIGURE 2–3
Telephone survey personnel. (*Courtesy:* McNeil Consumer Products Company.)

Telephone disadvantages

1. People without telephones cannot be reached. Businesses catering to the lower socioeconomic groups may not be able to contact their customers using this method.
2. People are frequently reluctant to answer callers they cannot see.
3. People living outside the local calling zone might not be called because of the high cost involved.
4. Calls might be annoying to customers.

Mail advantages

1. Postage is relatively inexpensive even though postal rates have increased.
2. Wide distribution (for trading areas of nationally distributed products) does not affect the cost for any person being questioned. Telephone costs would be different because of toll calls.
3. Time allotted for studying and answering questions is longer.
4. Interviewer cannot have an influence, as might happen in an interview.
5. Field staff is eliminated.

Mail disadvantages

1. Rate of return is very small. A 5–10 percent response is considered to be average. In the case of consumer panels or focus groups (to be discussed later in the chapter), a 25–40 percent return is average.
2. Cost per return is very high, since the cost of the unanswered questionnaires must be considered part of the overall cost of the survey.
3. Questions might not be completely understood without an interviewer.
4. The time it takes to receive the answer is longer than it is for interview or telephone.
5. Persons responding might not be truly representative of the sample.

To overcome the disadvantages of the time lag and the small number of returns, business managers sometimes offer premiums to those from whom information is being sought as a motivational device. The results are usually better when inducements are offered.

The personal interview may take place at an individual's home, on the job, at subway entrances, in front of a retailer's store entrance, or in other places where people come together. This is the only method employing face-to-face involvement. The questions may be of either the short-answer variety or open-ended, with the respondent giving a complete reaction to the question.

Interview advantages

1. Trained interviewers have great success in the percentage of people who will grant interviews.
2. Questions that are not completely clear can be explained.
3. Additional probing can be carried on by using the open-ended question. This is not possible via the mail.
4. Observations may also be recorded.

Interview disadvantages

1. Responding to an interviewer may cause interviewees to color their responses because of embarrassment, for example, the response to such questions as age and income.
2. Employment of experienced interviewers is costly.
3. Interviewers' bias might be reflected in responses.
4. Interviews in the home might come at an inopportune time.

Preparation of the Questionnaire Form.   Although the researcher might select the most appropriate questionnaire technique to obtain information, the number and caliber of answers is directly dependent on the questionnaire design. It is necessary to make certain that a high-quality form has been produced. Sufficient time should be allocated to structuring the document to be used, or the survey could bring disastrous results or none at all. Among the factors to be considered are

1. The occupations of those being questioned.
2. The educational level of those being questioned.
3. Prejudices of those to be interviewed.

In constructing the form to be used, the following requirements are vital:

1. Questions must be easily understood. The language must be compatible with the intelligence of those to be interviewed. This is particularly true in the case of the mail questionnaire, where no interviewer will be available to clarify questions.
2. Generalities must be avoided by eliminating words such as *usually, frequently, generally,* and *occasionally,* which tend to prohibit a clear-cut response. For example, an answer to the question, "Do you frequently shop at Value-Rite?" will not disclose how often the customer shops at Value-Rite and the percentage of purchases that are made there. This information may be important to the study.
3. Questions should be arranged in sequential order, so that each preceding question makes for a smooth transition to the next.

4. Questions should be concise and to the point.

5. The questionnaire should not be too long. This might discourage a response. For example, a one-page form is most satisfactory for use by retailers.

6. The design must be organized in such a manner that recording is simple. Caution must be taken to provide enough space for responses, particularly if open-ended questions are used.

7. The questionnaire should be organized in such a manner that tabulation of the results is simplified.

8. Factual questions should be limited to obtaining data that can be clearly remembered by the respondents.

9. Leading questions should be eliminated.

10. Questions that are too intimate or that raise personal prejudices should be omitted.

11. The questionnaire should as much as possible be limited to obtaining facts or opinions.

12. Questions containing more than one element should be eliminated.

13. Questions should always provide for conditional answers.

There are three major types of questions used. They are open questions which give the respondent freedom to answer in any manner chosen, multiple choice which permit one or more answers from predetermined responses, and dichotomous questions which offer a choice between two answers. Examples of these types of questions are found in the sample forms in Figures 2–4, 2–5, and 2–6.

Experimental Method.   This method of gathering information employs either the observation method or the direct approach or both. In some instances marketers would like to see the results of a controlled experiment, which this method permits. Experimentation might be risky on a large scale, but management often experiments on a small scale. For example, a company might want to change the disposable container now used to package its soft beverage to a reusable container, in order to deal with the country's ecology problem. The tremendous amount of disposable containers presents many problems that contribute to the destruction of the environment. Before calling for this major packaging change, which might seriously hamper sales, the company would select a test market in which it could sample the new package while the balance of its soft drink distribution is normal. Theory has it that the results of these experiments will hold true in the overall distribution of the company's product.

This method is an excellent research procedure in that it actually simulates the company's complete marketing activities. The disadvantages involved are the high costs of experimentation and the length of time necessary to carry out the project.

8007
C005-A2
483

PIZZA SAUCE PRODUCT TEST
_____FIRST CALLBACK_____

Home Testing Institute
P.O. Box 9200
Port Washington, NY 11050

Time Started:_____

1-6
7-8   Time Ended:_____

9-1   Interviewer's Name:_____

Date:_____

CALLBACK SCHEDULE		I.I.	ATTEMPT			RESULT											
Date	Time			Date	Time	Comp.	NA/ BSY	Disc. + Not In Srv.	RNA For Dur.	CB	Didn't Receive	Didn't Use	Inc.	Ref.	TQ	NSP Wrong #	Other - Explanation RNA
			1		A.M. P.M.												
			2		A.M. P.M.												
			3		A.M. P.M.												
			4		A.M. P.M.												
			5		A.M. P.M.												

Hello, this is _____ calling for Janet Hall of Home Testing Institute. May I please speak with the female head of your household? (IF NOT AVAILABLE, MAKE CALLBACK ARRANGEMENT) (REINTRODUCE YOURSELF IF NECESSARY) I'd like to ask you a few questions about the pizza sauce we recently sent you to use.

1a. Did you receive the two cans of pizza sauce we sent you to use?

Yes ( ) 1 ──▶(SKIP TO Q.2a)

No ( ) 2 ──▶(MAKE CALLBACK ARRANGEMENT IF WITHIN INTERVIEWING SCHEDULE AS FOLLOWS, OTHERWISE TERMINATE)

b. You should receive the pizza sauce within the next few days. Please use the 1st product as soon as possible after receiving them. We will be calling you back to get your opinions in a couple of days.

2a. Did you use one can of the pizza sauce? (IF USED BOTH, TERMINATE)

Yes ( ) 1 ──▶(SKIP TO Q.3)

No ( ) 2 ──▶(IF WITHIN INTERVIEWING SCHEDULE ASK Q.2b, OTHERWISE TERMINATE)

b. Could you please do so within the next day or so?

Yes ( ) 1 ──▶(ARRANGE FOR CALLBACK)

No ( ) 2 ──▶(TERMINATE)

3. What was the code number of the can you used?

#_____ 13-15

(IF RESPONDENT CANNOT TELL NUMBERS OF CAN SHE USED, ASK FOR NUMBERS ON REMAINING UNUSED CAN AND RECORD BELOW)

Unused Can#_____ 16-18

4. Assuming the product you used 1st was available in a store where you regularly shop, how likely would you be to buy this product in the future, would you say you...(READ CHOICES AND CHECK ONE)

Definitely would buy it.... ( ) 5
Probably would buy it...... ( ) 4
Might or might not buy it.. ( ) 3
Probably would not buy it.. ( ) 2
Definitely would not buy it ( ) 1

5. Taking all things into consideration, how would you rate the 1st pizza sauce? That is, would you say you...(READ CHOICES AND CHECK ONE)

Liked it extremely.......... ( ) 7
Like it somewhat............ ( ) 6
Liked it slightly........... ( ) 5
Neither liked nor disliked it ( ) 4
Disliked it slightly........ ( ) 3
Disliked it somewhat........ ( ) 2
Disliked it extremely....... ( ) 1

FIGURE 2–4 Telephone survey (excerpted). (*Courtesy:* Home Testing Institute, Inc., one of the NPD Group of Marketing & Research Companies.)

U2003-1
484
VCR
A

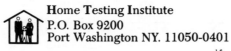

Home Testing Institute
P.O. Box 9200
Port Washington NY. 11050-0401

1-6
7-8
9-1
10-5

VIDEOCASSETTE RECORDER QUESTIONNAIRE

PLEASE READ THIS DEFINITION BEFORE CONTINUING

A **Videocassette Recorder** (VCR) is an electronic machine that allows you to videotape both the picture and sound of programs, movies, sporting events, etc. off your television. These videotape recordings can then be **played back** at some future time as you desire. A VCR can also be used to play "pre-recorded" videocassettes (of new/classic movies and other types of programs) which can be bought or rented.

1. Does your household own a videocassette recorder (VCR)?

    11
    Yes.... □1 ───────►(Go to Question 6)
    No .... □2 ───────►(Continue)

2. Please check all of the reasons why you do not currently own a videocassette recorder. (**Check all that apply**)

    12
    Do not know what a videocassette recorder is .... □1
    Do not watch TV enough .... □2
    Would watch TV too much....................... □3
    Cannot afford one .... □4

    Not worth the cost............................ □5
    Waiting for price to come down .... □6
    Do not like to watch movies enough............... □7
    Pre-recorded videocassettes of movies cost too much □8

    Blank videocassettes for recording cost too much .... □9
    Currently own a videodisc player .... □0
    Don't have a TV set............................ □x
    Waiting for new advanced VCR to be available ...... □y

    Other (Write in):
    _____ 13

3. In the **next 12 months**, does your household plan to purchase a videocassette recorder? (**Check one box**)

    14
    Definitely will purchase..... □1
    Probably will purchase...... □2 ───►(Continue)
    May or may not purchase.... □3
    Probably will not purchase □4 ───►(Go to Question 5)
    Definitely will not purchase □5

4. If you **probably or definitely** will purchase a videocassette recorder in the next 12 months, how likely are you to purchase or rent movies on pre-recorded videocassettes? (**Check one box**)

    15
    Definitely will purchase or rent ..... □1
    Probably will purchase or rent ...... □2
    May or may not purchase or rent .... □3
    Probably will not purchase or rent ... □4
    Definitely will not purchase or rent   □5

5. In the **last 12 months** has your household **rented** a videocassette recorder?

    16
    Yes.... □1 ───────►Total number of days rented _____
    No .... □2   17-19

    Now go to Question 31   80-2

FIGURE 2–5 Mail questionnaire (excerpted). (*Courtesy:* Home Testing Institute, Inc., one of the NPD Group of Marketing & Research Companies.)

1. When was the last time you took a vacation:

	5 Days or More (Check One)	Less Than 5 Days (Check One)
Within the last 6 months	1	1
6-12 months ago	2	2
1-2 years ago	3	3
2-3 years ago	4	4
3+ years ago	5	5

2. How often do you usually take a vacation in which you travel away from home? (Check One)
   Two times a year or more....... 11-1
   Once a year....... 2
   Once every two years....... 3
   Once every two to five years... 4
   Less than once every five years 5

3. Do you plan to take a vacation in 1984? Yes 12-1 No 2 Don't know 3

3a. If "Yes", have you decided where you will go on vacation in 1984? Yes 13-1 No 2

4. Do you plan to take a vacation in 1985? Yes 14-1 No 2 Don't know 3

4a. If "Yes", have you decided where you will go on vacation in 1985? Yes 15-1 No 2

5. When taking a vacation, what method of transportation do you normally choose? (Check All That Apply)
   Air.. 16-1   Personal car 3   Bus............. 5
   Train 2   Car rental.. 4   Other_____

6. When taking a vacation, what type of accomodations do you normally choose? (Check All That Apply)
   Hotel 17-1   Campsite...... 3   Other
   Motel 2   Friends/family 4   _____

7. Do you prefer to make:
   All of your arrangements through a travel agent. 18-1
   Part of your arrangements through a travel agent 2
   None of your arrangements through a travel agent 3
   80-2

1. Write in the age and sex of each household member AGE 16 AND OLDER.

	Household Members 16 and Older			
	#1	#2	#3	#4
Age:	___ yrs 9-10	___ yrs 24-25	___ yrs 39-40	___ yrs 54-55
Sex: Male..	11-1	26-1	41-1	56-1
Female	2	2	2	2

PLEASE ASK FOR EACH PERSON:
2. How many times have you attended a movie in the PAST 3 MONTHS? (If none, write in 0)...............

3. AIRLINE USAGE
   Number of times flown in the PAST 12 MONTHS........
   For business purposes....
   For non-business purposes

4. Number of times rented a car in PAST 12 MONTHS:.....

5. Number of occasions stayed away from home ON BUSINESS in PAST 12 MONTHS:...........
   For a convention/seminar....
   For other business purposes
   12-23   27-38   42-53   57-68
   80-3

H4HT046-1

H4HT047-1   184   <002595 9>231051 59   99   51

FIGURE 2–6   Personal interview. (*Courtesy:* Home Testing Institute, Inc., one of the NPD Group of Marketing & Research Companies.)

Perhaps not a disadvantage, but rather a major difficulty with the experimental method, is the control of relevant variables. When employing this research technique, it is necessary to select markets that are identical in all significant aspects. For example, in the case of the change to reusable containers mentioned above, it might be impossible to find two distinct groups that possess all the significant identical factors. If only one out of all the factors is different, this might have an effect on acceptance of the proposed container. When the variables are uncontrollable, the results might not be truly comparable.

Consumer Focus Group Method.   As marketing research costs escalate, many companies have begun using the research tool that is known as the *consumer panel* or *consumer focus group*. For a cost ranging generally from $15 to $25, participants will spend a few hours voicing their opinions on products which manufacturers are considering adding to their company's product line. Where typical comprehensive surveys can approach tens of thousands of dollars, a focus group, for an amount as little as $1,200 to $2,000, can provide the information necessary to introduce, alter, or halt production of a product.

The success achieved by many offerings has been attributed to this type of research. General Mills acknowledges that a significant amount of information

FIGURE 2–7
Research panel. (*Courtesy:* McNeil Consumer Products Company.)

was gained through a focus group's recommendations and perceptions on their Hamburger Helper product. General Mills, in fact, reports that at least one focus group meets every day somewhere in the United States. In the undertaking of a recent major market segmentation study, Levi Strauss & Company first organized focus groups to kick off its research project. The basic concept of Pepsi Light came as a result of such groups who complained about the bitter aftertaste of the diet sodas. The Kissing Barbie version of Mattel's Barbie doll came from a consumer group comprised of little girls who thought Barbie should kiss Ken!

In the organization of the focus group, which generally numbers eight to ten people, care is exercised to make certain that members of the group are compatible. Disagreement is appropriate, but arguing is detrimental to the group's proper functioning. Generally, men and women are not mixed because, as reported by one organizer of such panels, women are sometimes inhibited by men. Similarly, age groups are not mixed.

Of paramount importance to the success of this type of research is the ability of the moderator to carefully guide the group. Often, moderators have a background in industrial psychology and employ these communicative skills, which motivate the participants to play a meaningful role. A criticism of the groups has been that poorly trained moderators are sometimes used with the results proving to be less meaningful. Fig 2–7 illustrates a large focus group or research panel.

It should be understood that the focus group is but one method to gather information and is generally used in conjunction with other information-gathering techniques for decision making.

Sampling.   After preparing the necessary forms to be used, a determination must be made regarding the number of people to be included for the survey to be meaningful. It is neither necessary nor practical to involve every conceivable individual in a group. For example, a manufacturer with a potential market of six million persons need only investigate a part of this population. The segment of the population selected is known as a sample. The sample is most effective when its members are truly representative of a group to be studied. The size and selection of the sample is based upon many considerations and should be carefully decided on with the help of a statistician.

There are numerous sampling techniques employed by researchers. Whichever technique is judged by the research team to be most appropriate, it must be representative of the total group. Without this, we cannot be certain that the results achieved will be sufficiently accurate for ultimate use in the research.

Included in the types of samples employed are the following.

Random sampling. In this technique, each unit in a predetermined group has an equal chance to be selected. For example, if the study wanted to determine customer preference in supermarkets in Des Moines, Iowa, a complete list of all the shoppers in Des Moines would be needed and a small percentage sampled.

Nonrandom sampling. This is the same as random sampling except that the sample is restricted to the particular group to be sampled. Thus in Des Moines, Iowa, supermarkets, if we restricted the sample to women with large families, we would be using nonrandom sampling.

Area sampling. It is frequently impractical to study a complete area as in the foregoing example. In this case, Des Moines might be divided into separate streets, which could then be selected at random. After this is completed, it could be decided to interview each household on the selected streets.

Collection of Data

The actual collection of data depends on the technique to be used. A choice must be made among available methods—mail questionnaire, interviewing, telephone questioning, observations, and customer focus groups. Whichever technique or combination of techniques is employed, the investigators involved must be thoroughly trained. Companies employing the services of a professional research organization need not be concerned, but those using their own employees or college students (often used) to collect data must make certain that there is a thorough understanding of the investigative methods. Role playing is a successful method of training laypersons to conduct personal interviews. For example, one individual assumes the interviewer's identity and the other the interviewee's. In this way an individual trained in the art of questioning can observe, criticize, and make recommendations to improve questioning techniques. In the area of observations, investigators must be familiar with what they are observing and recording. Pepsi-Cola collects data though taste testing as pictured in Figure 2–8.

FIGURE 2–8
Consumer taste testing.
(*Courtesy:* Pepsi-Cola USA.)

Processing and Analysis of Data

After the investigators submit the raw data collected, the data must be processed. Processing involves arranging data in proper form for analysis. All data sheets must first be inspected and corrected or modified to guarantee that the information is stated appropriately for tabulation. The data must then be classified into categories. This step is simplified if care was exercised in the preparation of the questionnaire. Without being classified into homogeneous groupings, the data cannot be analyzed. The next step, particularly if data-processing machines are to be used for the purpose of tabulation, is coding. This involves a code being devised for assignment to each type of reply. For example, code 6 might mean blue and code 12 might stand for red. These codes can then be fed into the computer for quick processing. Coding can be eliminated if the questionnaire was precoded, with each item having a number assigned to it on the original form. Actual tabulation can be done by machine, as mentioned, or by hand. Small samples that can be tabulated by hand are often employed by small retailers. More common in marketing research is the machine tabulation, which mechanically and more quickly and efficiently performs the steps involved in manual tabulation.

After the data have been compiled and summarized, analysis takes place. The amount and kind of analysis depend upon the research project. Some studies, such as the fashion count, might only be used to determine which colors are most popular and in what percentages. Other studies might require more sophisticated statistical analysis and interpretation. This phase of the research project is most important, since future decisions will be based upon it. Knowledgeable research analysts are best used to evaluate all possible courses of action and make final recommendations. If a company is conducting its own study, it is

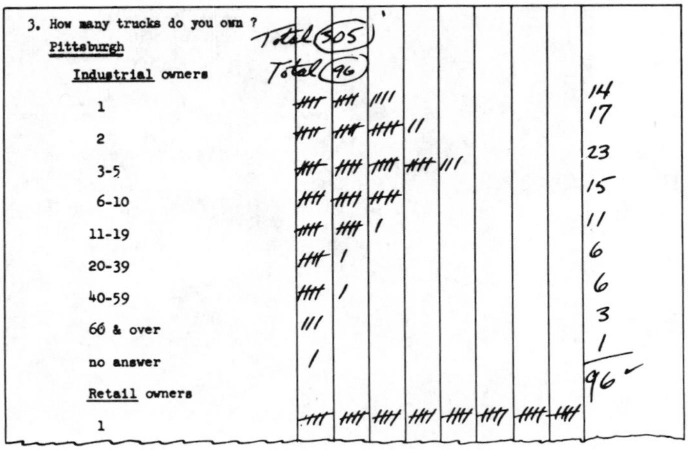

3. How many trucks do you own ?	Total (505)
Pittsburgh	
Industrial owners	Total (96)
1	14
2	17
3-5	23
6-10	15
11-19	11
20-39	6
40-59	6
60 & over	3
no answer	1
	96
Retail owners	
1	

FIGURE 2–9
Form for hand tabulation.

advisable that everyone in management connected with the project review the recommendations of the chief researcher before implementing the suggestions.

Preparation of the Research Report

A written report should be prepared outlining the findings of the investigation. It should include the data, analysis, and recommendations, bound in permanent form. Also included should be any pertinent graphic displays, such as bar charts, line graphs, and pictograms. This can serve for future reference and related studies.

Most complete research reports follow the areas covered in this chapter. They are

1. Definition of the problem.
2. Methodology used in this study.
3. Analysis.
4. Recommendations.
5. Appendices, to include data from both secondary and primary sources.

COST OF MARKETING RESEARCH

It is not uncommon for a research project to cost in excess of $250,000. Generally, the larger expenditures are allocated to the study of new products. Although the formal investigations carried out by research consultant firms tend to be more dependable than studies made exclusively by a company's own staff, businesses that are unable to afford outside assistance can still adequately make use of marketing research. The gas station, in determining whether customers prefer trading stamps or lower prices, need only ask its customers. This is marketing research.

New product research expenditures continue to increase. Business managers are willing to pay these costs in exchange for information that might alter the design of their proposed product and therefore make it more successful. Often, after a study has been completed, manufacturers scrap their plans for a new product entirely. It is more sensible to spend $250,000 in research than to lose several million dollars in the production of something that will not appeal to the consuming market.

THE FUTURE OF MARKETING RESEARCH

With the success businesses have enjoyed through marketing research involvement, it is certain that there will be significant increases in research budgets. Companies that have heretofore limited their investigations to those made by their own personnel, will employ the services of research organizations.

Of particular significance to the future of research is the computer and its limitless applications. No doubt the computer will make the greatest contribution to the continued growth and success firms have enjoyed through marketing research.

Important Points in the Chapter _____

1. Marketing research relates to the investigation of marketing problems and the recommendations needed to solve the problems.

2. Marketing research is generally categorized into research on products and services, market research, sales methods and policies research, and advertising research.

3. The scientific method involves the systematic and impartial procedure for the solving of problems.

4. Generally, the research procedure followed by investigating teams is as follows:

   a. Identification of the problem.
   b. Definition of the problem.
   c. Investigation of secondary sources of information.
   d. Securing primary information.
   e. Sample selection.
   f. Collection of data.

g. Processing and analysis of data.

h. Preparation of the report.

5. The amounts spent on marketing research are expected to continue to increase, since the results of research continue to make companies operate more effectively.

6. The computer, through its speed and accuracy, promises to make greater contributions to marketing research management.

Review Questions

1. Define *marketing research.*

2. Can the terms *marketing research* and *market research* be used interchangeably? Defend your answer.

3. What arrangements do large companies generally make for their research? Are the arrangements the same as those for small companies? Discuss.

4. Into how many categories is marketing research usually divided? List and briefly describe each category.

5. Which area of marketing research usually receives the greatest amount of attention? Why?

6. Briefly define *scientific method.*

7. What is the first step in the research process?

8. Differentiate between secondary and primary data.

9. How important are trade organizations to the research team?

10. Of which single governmental source can researchers avail themselves for the most complete listing of government publications?

11. Are the advertising media helpful to marketing researchers? How?

12. Describe the observation method employed in gathering information.

13. In what principal way does the questionnaire method differ from the observation method?

14. Compare the telephone and mail questionnaires. Which is less costly to operate? Which brings the quickest response?

15. Discuss some of the major disadvantages of the personal interview.

16. Briefly describe the areas to be considered in the preparation of a questionnaire.

17. Which research method often combines observation with the direct approach? Why do marketers often use this method?

18. Define the term *sample*. Why do marketers use a sample?

19. How are data tabulated? Why are the data coded?

20. The amounts spent on marketing research continue to increase. Why are marketers willing to spend such huge sums for research?

21. Describe the importance of consumer focus groups to marketers.

Case Problems

Case Problem 1

David's Emporium is a large department store with six branches, all of which are located in the New York City area. For the past twenty years the organization has steadily increased its advertising expenditure and its sales.

The advertising dollar has been spent on newspapers, television, radio, direct mail, and magazines. The effort has been effective on an overall basis, but management has not really determined whether or not all the media employed have been producing results in direct proportion to the investment. For example, is radio, with an annual expenditure of 5 percent of the advertising budget, bringing in only half as much as television, for which 10 percent is being spent?

In an effort to ascertain the true worth of the present allocation of the advertising money, a marketing research consultant has been retained to help the company.

Questions

1. Should David's continue their present system, which has proved to be successful? Why?
2. Pretend you are the research consultant. What procedure would you employ in order to make sound recommendations to David's Emporium?

Case Problem 2

International Foods, Inc., has manufactured, processed, and distributed foreign and gourmet-type foods for the past five years. Initially, the firm successfully produced and sold Italian and French delicacies to supermarkets and gourmet food shops. Each year the firm added to its existing line food from one more nation. The last four years have seen the inclusion of popular Swedish, Japanese, British, and Chinese foods. All were sold to the satisfaction of the company.

Three months ago, the company added a full line of products from Greece. With the enormous increase in travel to Greece, management felt that introduction of Greek foods would be a natural. Techniques of packaging, promotion, distribution, and so on, that had been employed for distribution of the other products were used again. Immediate success was expected, but the results were dismal. Preliminary investigation showed that initially the Greek products were well received; however, repeat business was very low. International Foods, Inc., must decide how to rectify this undesirable situation.

Questions

1. Should the Greek foods be withdrawn immediately? Why?
2. What might be the problem?
3. What kind of research would you suggest if you were the director of research? Specify which techniques you would employ to discover the cause of the problem.

Part 2 The Target Market

3

CONSUMER MOTIVATIONS, HABITS, AND THE BEHAVIORAL SCIENCES

Learning Objectives

Upon completion of the chapter, you will be able to:

1. Explain the relationship between the behavioral sciences and marketing.
2. Differentiate between rational and emotional motives, giving examples of each.
3. Write a brief paper on the self-concept theory.
4. Discuss Maslow's hierarchy of needs and its importance to marketing.
5. Explain the learning process as it relates to consumers.
6. Describe the consumer as a problem solver.
7. Discuss the importance of consumer attitudes to marketing and give examples.
8. Discuss the importance of consumer habits to marketing and give examples.
9. Explain marketing utilization of motivation and habits in terms of the marketing mix.

IS IT PRESTIGE OR PERFORMANCE THAT AMERICANS WANT?

For many years Americans who achieved financial success made their way to the nearest Cadillac dealer to purchase the car of their dreams. The most successful sought the biggest models filled with the most luxurious options. The Cadillac not only fulfilled their dreams with the fine performance they sought, but their egos were equally heightened by the prestige the automobile bestowed upon them.

Recent years have witnessed the erosion of the Cadillac as the "American dream car." Talk of "too big" or "poor performance" was heard as the major reasons for the loyal followers to break rank and move on to new pastures. Were these the actual reasons or merely excuses to achieve greater prestige with a different toy? Was it that Cadillacs were now appearing in many more driveways and being driven by the middle Americans who traded up from the Oldsmobile and Buick?

The defectors spoke about unsatisfactory performance, high gas consumption, and "too big" as the reasons they abandoned their once-valued Cadillac. Few spoke of status and prestige as reasons why they now opted for the foreign car.

Many Americans did, in fact, flock to the imports for rational motives such as price, fuel economy, and efficiency. They chose the Toyotas and Datsuns (now Nissan) as their cars since they were proven performance winners. Large numbers were considered to be rational buyers who sought something better than the cars they used to buy from General Motors, Chrysler, and Ford. A large segment of the market, 1.3 million buyers, however, were not to be satisfied with these modestly priced vehicles, despite the fine performance they delivered. This buying group opted for the Mercedes, BMW, and Jaguar at double and triple what they once doled out for Cadillacs. For prices that have soared to the $70,000 range, they could now again use words like "efficiency," "performance," and "comfort" to describe their automobiles. How many readily use the word "prestige"?

INTRODUCTION

The principal object of an economic system and of the marketing institutions that make up that system is the satisfaction of consumer demand. From a marketer's viewpoint, in a capitalistic society, the successful satisfaction of consumer demand requires that the distribution of products result in a profit. A market is made up of many institutions competing for the opportunity of satisfying consumer demand at a profit. It is obvious that an important factor of marketing success is the knowledge of consumer demand. This market knowledge can be broken down into two broad areas: the habits and motivations of the consumer and the size of the population and purchasing power that is available.

In this chapter, discussion will focus upon the motivations and habits of

The flagship of the line, the BMW 750iL. (*Courtesy:* BMW of North America.)

consumers and the importance of the behavioral sciences in relation to them. Chapter 4 will center on the population and the demographics and psychographics involved in segmenting markets.

THE BEHAVIORAL SCIENCES

It is generally agreed that the study of consumer motivation dates back as far as the study of marketing itself. In recent years, more sophisticated research techniques, coupled with the enormous growth in competition, have vastly increased the importance, need, and use of better consumer information. The attraction of the behavioral scientists to marketing has now led to an even greater importance of the role that consumer motivation plays in the marketing of a product.

As we reach more deeply into the way people behave, we go beyond the areas of traditional marketing training—we turn to the behavioral scientists for answers. In recent years, marketing has evolved to the point where it is now a necessity to involve psychologists and sociologists in the solution of marketing problems.

CONSUMER MOTIVATIONS

Granted that the hard demographic factors of the market (size of the population and available purchasing power) can be determined, the marketer is faced with the need to predict which of many competing products the consumer will buy. That is, if a person has $400 that he or she wants to spend for a color television set, how can we determine which of the many competing products he or she will select? To answer this question, one must know a great deal about the psychological makeup of consumers.

An example of the importance of understanding consumer psychology can be illustrated in the marketing of powdered and, later, liquid dietary products. A number of years ago the Mead Johnson Company marketed a product called Metrecal. In Mead Johnson's view, obesity was a health problem and its marketing mix was geared to that effect. The product was first offered to physicians and later to the public under the theme that Metrecal improved health and longevity. The product was successful and dominated the market. The Pet Company introduced Sego, a competitive dietary liquid. Pet's understanding of the market was that the consumer was more interested in physical beauty than health, and their marketing mix was targeted to personal vanity and good looks. Sego overtook Metrecal and led the market with over 40 percent of total sales. Obviously, they had a better understanding of consumer psychology. Today, however the market is being lead by such product lines as Slim Fast and Nutri System.

Buying Motives

Traditionally, consumer purchasers are said to make their buying decisions on either a rational or an emotional basis. Although marketers today go well beyond this simplified breakdown in their analysis of consumer motivations, an understanding of the following material is still essential.

Rational Motives.   Rational motives are those that result from a carefully studied group of factors in which the long-run use of the article is weighed against the cost of the purchase. The information that is usually considered before such purchases are made includes

1. The cost of the purchase.
2. The cost of operation.
3. The frequency of breakdown and the dependability and cost of repair.
4. The use life of the article.
5. The effectiveness of the article with regard to the purpose for which it was bought.

Use of the term *rational* to describe purchasers who consider the foregoing list before they make purchases does not mean that a person using such a list buys intelligently. Frequently, people purchase items they do not need or cannot afford after a careful study of the available choices.

Producers should understand the rational buying motivations of consumers because the marketing of goods aimed at such consumers must follow the rational approach with reasonable consistency. That is, advertising, sales promotion, and product development must be geared to appeal to the rational buyer. Of course, this portion of the market is not available to all producers. Fashion merchandise, for example, will have very little appeal for rational shoppers, since such goods are not designed for long-range durability or use. It would be foolish for the manufacturer of something currently fashionable, which has the probability of one season's acceptance, to construct a garment that will give ten years of serviceable wear. The customer, realizing that a skirt has a relatively short fashion life, would be unwilling to pay an additional premium for durability beyond its period of popularity.

Emotional Motives.   Any listing of the emotional factors that may go into a buying decision is difficult, since the definitions tend to run together and the list would be enormous and highly technical. However, the following are some of the more common nonrational reasons upon which purchasing decisions are based.

Perception—appeal to the senses.   The five senses—touch, taste, sight, smell, and hearing—are important factors in the selling of many varieties of goods. Most people are willing to make purchases to satisfy these senses. For example, a cashmere sweater offers no better protection against cold than does one made of sheep's wool, but it feels better to the touch. Food odors attract people to certain products, and the sight appeal of fashion merchandise is critical in selling. The avoidance of displeasure might also be listed in this category. Typical of such goods are deodorants, air conditioners, and a host of nonprescription drugs.

Perception plays an important role in marketing, since it is concerned with attracting the customer's attention, the necessary first step to a completed sale. In our waking hours we are surrounded by a great number of happenings from which we select a few and leave the rest. The marketer attempts to make his product one of the noticed events. There are several ways in which this can be done:

1. Buyers are likely to perceive an event if they anticipate it. A long-distance driver who expects to stop for the night in two hours is likely to select a Holiday Inn if he sees signs: Holiday Inn 100 miles, Holiday Inn 50 miles, and so on, as he rides.
2. People are more likely to eat at McDonald's if they see a McDonald's TV commercial before dinner rather than after dinner.
3. An unusual change is more likely to be noticed. An ad in color in an otherwise black-and-white newspaper, or a drastic price reduction, are eye-catching.

Personal satisfaction.   A person's self-pride, rather than the attitude of others, may be used as a selling tool. Such characteristics as personal and home cleanliness and neatness can be appealed to by products such as soaps, cosmetics,

FIGURE 3–1   1989 BMW 635CSi. (*Courtesy:* BMW of North America.)

and waxes. It is frequently difficult for advertisers to choose the most important of several motives—for example, should a dishwashing detergent promote youthful hands or clean dishes?

As has been indicated, an understanding of the motives of buyers, both rational (aroused by appeals to reason) and emotional (aroused by appeals to appetites), is necessary to successful marketing. Generally, the promotion of a product takes into account both of these motivations in prospective customers. BMW (Figure 3–1), for example, emphasizes both quality (rational) and status (emotional) in its advertisements.

In addition to the areas of emotional motives just described, others, such as safety and protection, sociability and courtship, and prestige, status, and esteem, are also important. They are presented a little later in the chapter as part of Maslow's *hierarchy of needs*.

The Self-concept Theory.   The objection to the theory of rational versus emotional buying is that although it explains buying motives, it does not supply an underlying theoretical basis for why people buy or do not buy.

As it relates to marketing, the self-concept theory offers four definitions of self:

Real self.   The way a person thinks of himself or herself. This is the sum of one's impression of one's own personality, character, talents, and interests. The real self is extremely important, because a person's view of his or her real self is an indication of the person's capacity for happiness. The importance of the real self to marketing is that it explains why a wealthy man whose self-concept is that he is a wise and frugal buyer will drive a Volkswagen, and why advertisements of such cars may appeal in media aimed at high-income-level consumers.

Ideal self.   The way a person would like to be. This is the goal toward which one is constantly striving. Its relation to marketing lies in the fact that it explains the actions of a poor person buying silk underwear. This rash expenditure may be to satisfy an ideal self who likes fine things but dislikes obvious displays of wealth.

Other self.   One's idea of how others see him or her. This may have no relation to reality, but it is important in marketing.

Ideal other.   The way one would like others to think of him or her. The interaction between other self and ideal other explains why a young executive might give up bowling, which she loves, for golf, toward which she is only lukewarm. This action is an attempt to reach from other self to ideal other. This striving also explains the popularity of literary book clubs among people who are not at all literary.

Maslow's Hierarchy of Needs.   Abraham Maslow has theorized an order in which needs will be fulfilled by an individual, which is generally accepted by marketers and behavioral scientists. In marketing, it explains the differences in importance of the various needs and the reasons for their change. Maslow's hierarchy of needs, *in order of their importance,* are as follows:

Physiological

1. *Food, water, shelter.* These are the basic needs of survival and must be satisfied before any other needs are even considered.
2. *Safety.* After the basics of survival are achieved, there is a human need for protection. This emotional drive for self-preservation and the protection of family and friends often leads to such purchases as vitamin pills, insurance, and safety devices. Producers of such goods and services usually appeal to the fears of the consumer and indicate the manner in which their product will diminish such fears.

Social

3. *Belongingness and love.* Next in order of importance in the satisfaction of human needs is the need to be accepted by one's family and close friends.

FIGURE 3–2   The BMW 325i convertible delivers esteem and status. (*Courtesy:* BMW of North America.)

This may require joining organizations and setting up a family. The drive to mate and have children (to marry, in our society) is very strong. Many people, particularly young women, are willing to make purchases that will enhance their prospects of courtship. Clothing and cosmetics appeal to this emotion. Also in this category are homemaking products for young married couples, such as furniture and appliances and merchandise for children.

4. *Esteem and status.* This is a need for recognition and status outside the family and group of close friends. Some products become symbols of status and success. These items give an aura of prestige, leadership, and high social position to their users, and although they may be only a little more functional than competing products, they are able to command higher prices because of their identification with success. Expensive homes, automobiles, art objects, and haute couture clothing fall into this category. Figure 3–2 features the BMW 325i convertible, an automobile that promotes delivery of esteem and status to the owner.

Self

5. *Self-actualization.* This is the highest and final need in Maslow's hierarchy. It is the need to develop one's full potential by knowledge and understanding.

In the affluent western civilizations, the higher-order needs are more important than those in the lower categories of the hierarchy since the lower-order needs are often automatically provided. Consequently, marketers aim their products at the satisfaction of these needs by studying the basic processes that lead up to a purchase.

Consumers as Problem Solvers.   Another approach to understanding consumer buying involves viewing the buyer's actions as a means of problem solving. Problem solving can be broken down into the following steps:

1. *Awareness of the problem.* First there must be an awareness of the problem. For example, a student's girlfriend tells him that he needs a new pair of jeans.
2. *Accumulation of information.* The second step involves gathering information that will help in the solution. Visiting stores carrying jeans, trying on various styles and shades, observing and discussing the product with friends are common types of information gathering.
3. *Evaluation.* From the gathered information, comparisons are made. Price, style, and durability are weighed.
4. *Decision and purchase.* These follow as a result of the evaluation.

The problem-solving approach enables marketing managers to tackle new product decisions by asking these questions:

1. What consumer problems will the new product solve?
2. Is the problem serious enough to initiate a purchase?
3. Does the new product offer a substantially better solution than the product now in use?
4. Is the improvement in solving the problem offered by the new product worth the cost to develop it?
5. Will the new product run into competition? Is there anything on the market similar to the new product? If not, will we be able to handle the competition it might encourage?

The Learning Process.   In essence, problem solving is a learning process from which the marketer can earn success or failure. Behavioral scientists break learning down into individual steps. The first is *drive,* a stimulus or need that results in action by the learner. The learner's *response* is an effort to satisfy the drive by means of an action on his or her part. The manner in which the learner responds depends upon *clues* received. These are hints and bits of information from which a response can be fashioned. Having made the response, the learner evaluates it. If it was pleasing, it is considered to have been *reinforced,* so that faced with the same drive and clues in the future the person is likely to make the same response. If the response was unrewarding, given the same problem in the future the person is likely to try a different response.

Consider a long-distance truck driver who is becoming hungry (*drive*). He passes many signs that offer convenient food to drivers (*clues*). His decision is that he will stop at Stuckey's (*response*). If the meal suited him (*reinforcement*), he is likely to try that restaurant again under similar circumstances. If he is dissatisfied with the meal, he is unlikely to use that chain again in the near future.

Attitudes.   An attitude is a person's feeling toward a particular object. It is the result of experiences or knowledge of other people's experiences that have developed over a long period of time. The object in question can be any part of the marketing mix. Attitudes can be favorable or unfavorable, and knowledge of consumer attitude is vital to the marketer. A favorable attitude is, of course, beneficial to the marketer. In the event of an unfavorable attitude, the marketer is faced with two choices: either the product must be adjusted to fit the favorable attitude of the consumer, or, with much more difficulty, the consumer's attitude must be changed.

As an illustration of adjusting a product to fit the preconceived attitude that the consumer uses to judge the product, take the case of Miles Laboratories' Bactine. Bactine is an antibacterial product for minor cuts and bruises that contained the same antiseptic qualities of existing products without the sting. Miles thought it had a winner until the product reached the market and Miles found that sales did not reach expectations. Market research revealed that consumers associated antiseptic sting with healing and felt that a painless product did not have the strength to be effective. Miles' response was to add some sting. It altered the product to counter a negative consumer attitude.

Consumer attitudes are built up over a long period of time and, as a result, are very difficult to change. However, it is possible. Honda was successful in this. When it first came into the American market, it found that the majority of consumers had a negative attitude toward motorcycles and motorcycle riders. Americans associated motorcyclists with hoodlums and ruffians. To combat this, Honda launched a massive advertising campaign using the theme, "You meet the nicest people on a Honda." The advertisements featured people from all walks of life, of all ages, using motorcycles for all purposes. As a result of the advertising (in part, at least), there has been some change in attitude on the part of the American consumer.

CONSUMER HABITS

In addition to understanding the buying motives of consumers, it is necessary to know their habits. If goods are to be successfully marketed, knowledge of when, where, and how goods are purchased is required. To satisfy a consumer's demand for a new overcoat, the supplier must know when he will probably buy it (time of year), where he will probably buy it (department store or specialty store), and how he will probably buy it (one at a time?).

All the phases of the marketing mix must be geared to this information. Habits are more specific in nature than are motives. An individual may be motivated to buy a family home, but the time and place are still indefinite. In contrast, the family shopper is in the habit of food shopping, say, every Friday afternoon.

When—The Time Habit

Many businesses are seasonal, for example, toys (for Christmas). As a result, the marketing program of a toy manufacturer would be different from that of an organization that sells its product throughout the year. For example, such areas as promotion, special packaging for holiday items, special seasonal pricing, and warehousing must all be timed to the customer's habitual timing pattern. In addition, such basic decisions as whether a manufacturer of Christmas tree ornaments should hire a year-round sales force or depend upon sales agents are based on the time habit.

The time habit controls market planning for shorter time intervals as well. Food purchasing usually takes place at the end of the week when the paycheck arrives. In poor areas, it may occur when the welfare checks are mailed out. Each individual marketer must know and adjust to the timing pattern of his or her customers. For a manufacturer to bring out a line of bathing suits in August would be a serious error.

Where—The Location Habit

Consumers generally have a preestablished notion of where products can be bought. For example, razor blades can be purchased in a drugstore, a department store, or a supermarket. Once the source of supply has been established, it is not likely to be changed, for two reasons. First, a source of supply that has provided previous satisfaction is unlikely to be changed, and second, there is a fear that an unknown source may result in dissatisfaction. It must be understood that this is not a static situation. Discount stores overcame the preconception of buying exclusively from department stores. Sellers must bear in mind that repeat business is not based on product satisfaction alone. Friendly, courteous service is also necessary. This is particularly true where the product offered can be bought at a variety of locations.

To the marketer, the location habit must be broken down into two areas: where the buying decision is made and where the actual purchase takes place. The purchase of a chocolate bar is usually done impulsively and without prior planning. With this in mind, chocolate bar manufacturers must adjust their market strategy to provide wide distribution and high visibility in terms of packaging and point-of-sale displays. A study of grocery buying habits showed that only 30 percent of the purchases were planned at home; 70 percent were unplanned purchases that were decided upon when the products were noticed on the shelves. Obviously, this must be taken into account in marketing grocery items. On the other hand, automobiles, appliances, furniture, and other big-ticket items are generally not bought impulsively. In these cases, the buying decision is usually not made in the store but is the result of prior planning. Proper market strategy for this type of problem requires reaching into the customer's home to influence the buying decision. Television, newspapers, magazines, and direct-mail advertising are generally used to promote these products.

How—The Quantity Habit

Since consumer satisfaction is a vital element in marketing success, knowledge of the quantities the consumer desires plays an important role in determining market strategy. Whether the consumer's reasons are convenience or economy, the quantities offered must be in accordance with the buyer's demands. Urban and suburban buyers who shop infrequently will buy their cigarettes by the carton; people living in poor neighborhoods may buy eggs in less-than-dozen lots. Whatever the reason, the marketer must know and provide for his customer's tastes.

At the present time, the use of dozen and half-dozen packaging is common on the American scene. It will be interesting to note the effect the metric system, toward which we may someday change, will have on these quantities. Countries using the metric system package in multiples of ten.

Current Trends in Buying Habits

Although individual habits, once established, are difficult to change, the group habits of the consuming public are in a constant state of flux. Following is a partial list of some of the observable trends in consumer buying habits.

Shopping Hours. Stores, at one time, saw the bulk of sales transacted during the day and on Saturday, with one or two nights set aside for late shopping. Recently, a radical change has taken place. Many retailers remain open every night of the week and conduct business on Sunday. Those who have gone to Sunday opening generally report that business is as good then as on Saturday (until now the best day in most stores), with average Sunday sales increasing. This increase in Sunday sales is generally attributed both to the fact that more men are becoming involved in the family purchases, and to the increase in the number of working wives.

Quantities. Modern shoppers are buying in larger quantities. For one thing, they have more money. The shopper who could at one time afford only one shirt is now often able to buy three at a time. Quantity buying is a convenience, since it reduces the required number of shopping trips. Frequently, there are also savings for purchasers who buy in large quantity. Many producers package their goods to take advantage of this trend.

Self-service and Electronic Video Kiosks.   Although initiated in the super-market, self-service retailing has spread to many other areas. It appears that certain types of goods are more easily sold without a salesclerk than with one. Self-service adds greatly to customer convenience by permitting purchasers to fill their needs without having to wait for the attention of a clerk. Since self-service reduces selling costs, it is encouraged by retailers and will undoubtedly continue to grow in importance. As noted in Chapter 13, companies such as Levi Strauss, Florsheim, and Sears have installed video kiosks which take customer orders for merchandise faster than the time required by salespersons.

Change in Purchasers.   Until recently, women accounted for the major portion of all purchasing. At present, possibly because of the shortened workweek and the increase in the number of working wives, men frequently take part in buying decisions. They accompany their wives more and more on shopping trips. As a result, advertising for such household goods as foodstuffs and detergents, which was previously aimed exclusively at the homemaker, is now shifting to attract the male buyer as well.

Convenience of Use.   The rapid dominance of such products as instant coffee, wash-and-wear fabrics, and cake mixes indicates that American shoppers are anxious to buy merchandise that will increase their leisure time. It took only a few years for wash-and-wear materials requiring little or no ironing to dominate the clothing industry.

Location of Buying.   Since World War II, there have been some very significant changes in the places where people buy. As the customers of downtown department stores moved to the suburbs, the institutions followed by means of branch stores. As a result, suburban shoppers are spared the inconvenience of commuting to downtown centers for their purchases. This has led to an enormous growth in suburban shopping at the expense of the downtown shopping districts.

The type of store in which shopping is done has changed as well, as is evidenced by the emergence of the discount stores and off-price retail outlets. Another example relates to the fact that many items previously sold only in drugstores are now sold in supermarkets. To offset this condition, most drugstores now carry a wide variety of nondrug items.

One of the most successful merchandising ideas to take the country by storm is the flea market. Once popular only as an occasional event, the flea market has emerged as a place for buyers and sellers to transact business on a regular basis. Some of these markets are so successful that vendors find they must wait for months to be assigned a regular selling space. The spaces are either indoors or outdoors, depending on the climate, and are usually occupied by some other form of business most of the time. For example, in the East racetracks are being used twice a week as flea markets when racing is not in season. Roosevelt Raceway and Aqueduct, two of New York's better known racetracks, regularly house permanent flea markets. Similarly, drive-in movies have become popular market sites by day. The popularity of these markets can best be measured by the crowds of people who frequent them and the abundance of merchandise carried back to automobiles. Prices are always lower than at conventional stores, because overhead is considerably less.

The flea market concept is being carried over into more permanent and exciting surroundings. One such place is the Quincy Market on the Boston waterfront. Throngs of people flock there to make purchases.

Whether it is the carnival-type atmosphere, the variety of goods, or the better than typical prices, the flea market has caught on and has given the consumer another location for purchasing.

Off-the-beaten-path locations have grown into major retail centers for discount merchandise. In places like Freeport, Maine, and North Conway, New Hampshire, manufacturers' outlets are realizing huge profits by selling their goods at greatly reduced prices. The concept is made possible because these out-of-the-way locations do not conflict with the traditional locations.

Credit.   The use of credit purchasing is another customer convenience that has grown in recent years and will probably continue to expand, Credit buying affords purchasers the opportunity to have the use of desired goods before they have saved up the money for it. To another class of purchaser, credit buying permits purchases to be paid by check once a month, so that they do not require the frequent use of cash.

MARKET UTILIZATION OF CONSUMER MOTIVATIONS AND HABITS

The goal of a profit-seeking marketing institution is customer satisfaction. This can only be achieved by tailoring the product, its price, and its promotion to the clearly understood motivations and habits of the consumer.

The Product

The product must serve the function for which the customer was motivated to buy it. A style product, which a customer buys to be up to date, must actually be in the latest fashion and need not have the durability of a product designed for practical use. The addition of durability to a style product, or style to a functional product, would entail unnecessary costs without increasing the appeal of the merchandise.

This is not as simple as it sounds, since many products straddle the fence (a fashionable refrigerator) and other goods are treated differently by different manufacturers (foreign cars that never change style versus style-conscious domestic production). The point is that manufacturers must clearly define the motivation of the customer to whom they will appeal and design their products accordingly. Thus, Volkswagen, appealing to a rational market, will design a durable, less expensive product with little emphasis on design. General Motors, on the other hand, hoping to attract buyers that are emotionally motivated, will produce a car that emphasizes style, comfort, and prestige. When you see a Volkswagen and a Cadillac in the same garage, it clearly shows that a person may buy for both emotional and rational reasons.

The Price

The price of an article can have a considerable effect on the appeal to customer motives and habits. Customers who buy exclusive goods for reasons of image or prestige do so with the understanding that, in part, the goods owe their high status to the fact that the high price limits salability to people in the top socioeconomic level. The Cadillac is probably America's most prestigious automobile. Its ownership is the mark of success and high social position. There could be no quicker way of losing this image than a drop in price, which would make the car available to a much broader class of purchasers.

Price is an important means of appealing to both rational and emotional motives. Often, high prices indicate quality to a buyer, whereas low prices, particularly odd ones ($2.99), are an indication of a bargain.

Promotion

The promotion of goods is the most obvious area to benefit from an understanding of customer habits and motivations. The producer of toothpaste whose target is the teenage market must emphasize the cosmetic effect rather than the decay-inhibiting qualities, which would appeal to parents. Similarly, a car that is to be sold as a success symbol should not be promoted as a low-priced, economical automobile.

A product must be designed to meet the motivational needs of a specific target. It must be priced consistently with its goal, and the sales promotion and advertising must be aimed specifically at the motives of the individuals that make up the target market.

Time and Place

Having the goods available at the right time and at the right place is a question of understanding a customer's habits rather than his or her motivations. If customers habitually shop for clothing just before Easter, production and distribution must be planned so that the goods will be available for them at that time. If customers are accustomed to buying a product at a department store, the channel of distribution that is set up must ensure that it be there. A major challenge for marketers is to alter customers' habits and motivations to suit the advantages of particular businesses.

Important Points in the Chapter _____

1. Producers seek to improve their competitive position by studying the motivations, habits, and purchasing power of the market.

2. Rational purchasers make purchasing decisions by weighing the long-run use of the article against the cost of the purchase. Emotional purchasers are motivated by appeal to the senses and fulfillment of the need for courtship, protection, prestige, status, and personal satisfaction.

3. The self-concept theory explains buying behavior in terms of real self, ideal self, other self, and ideal other.

4. Maslow's hierarchy of needs theorizes that a person fulfills his or her basic physical needs first, then social and higher-level needs, satisfying each level before advancing to the next.

5. Another theory of consumer behavior treats consumers as problem solvers who first become aware of a problem, then accumulate and evaluate information, and finally make a buying decision.

6. The learning process consists of a drive (need) to which a person responds based upon clues (information) received.

7. Attitudes are preconceived positive and negative feelings toward an object. They are difficult to change.

8. To be successful in the market, producers must understand when, where, and how goods will be bought. This requires constant study, since the habits of the consuming public are always in a state of flux.

Review Questions _____

1. Why is the nature of the market of importance to marketers?

2. Differentiate between rational and emotional motivation. Give an example of each.

3. Is it important that a producer understand the motives of a rational purchaser? Why? Give an example.

4. Does perception play an important role in marketing? Defend your answer.

5. Discuss briefly the four major aspects of the self-concept theory.

6. Maslow's hierarchy of needs is thought to be significant by many marketers. Indicate, in order of importance, Maslow's hierarchy, and briefly explain need.

7. What are the major steps in problem solving as it relates to consumers?

8. In the learning process, what two other words can be best used to describe drive and clues?

9. Define *attitude*.

10. Is it true that rational buyers always buy intelligently?

11. Explain the difference between habits and motivations.

12. What do you think will be the future store hours of a department store?

13. Discuss the effect of the increase in male shopping. Why are men shopping more?

14. Sales of convenience goods have multiplied. Define, explain, and give examples.

15. Explain the importance of consumer motivation to the field of sales promotion.

Case Problem

Technico Products, a large manufacturer of electronic products, is engaged in a search for new consumer products. Until now, the company has been successful in manufacturing for the Defense Department, either as a prime contractor or as a subcontractor. In the past few years reductions in the Defense Department's budgets have resulted in the sudden cancellation of several important contracts. Realizing that more cancellations might occur in the future, Technico's management has been searching for a consumer product to take over the slack.

The company's research and development division has come up with a simplified automatic garage-door opener. The device has proven satisfactory in all the tests to which it was put and it will undoubtedly be marketable, since its cost estimates indicate that it can be offered at a competitive price.

Traditionally, automatic garage-door openers are sold at retail on an installation basis. Technico's model is so simple that it can easily be sold as a do-it-yourself item, at a considerable saving to the customer.

Questions

1. Discuss the motivational aspects of the type of consumer Technico should aim at.

2. Having decided on the motivations of the target market, discuss their effect on the product's development, price, promotion, and channels of distribution.

4

THE CONSUMER: MARKET SEGMENTATION AND PSYCHOGRAPHICS

Learning Objectives

Upon completion of the chapter, you will be able to:

1. Define a target market and explain its importance.
2. Define market segmentation and explain its importance.
3. List six examples of demographic market segmentation and indicate the future trend and importance of each.
4. Discuss Engels's laws of consumer spending and explain their validity today.
5. Define and explain the advantages of psychographics.

THE ONCE FORGOTTEN CITIZEN

Often in the past marketers shied away from older citizens because of their limited incomes, the small size of the group and its lack of importance in comparison to other age groups, and the fact that many worked until they were too ill for any pleasures. Today, the average senior is an individual who lives longer, retires earlier, and is often better off financially than his counterpart of past decades. Also, recent study tells us that the 65-and-over segment of the population is becoming the largest single age group and is expected to maintain that position for many years.

Bearing this in mind, many businesses have begun catering to the once overlooked segment of the population. One must only examine current advertisements and promotional pieces to discover the interest that is focused on these people. Whether it is the restaurants which offer discounts for seniors; the banks, many of whom provide free checking to those over 65; movie theaters which advertise "special admission for seniors"; or the colleges and universities which, in an effort to improve their numbers, offer specially designed courses for "mature" students, the marketers are responding to the fact that there is a vast opportunity out there that hasn't been fully tapped. With the enormous increases in the cost of living which face our younger age groups, the elderly are beginning to find they are needed and are being courted by many marketers.

The travel industry has recognized the potential of the over 65 market perhaps better than many other industries. Scanning the travel sections of the major newpapers, one regularly sees travel ads that are directed toward senior citizens. Many of the advertisements even announce in their headlines that this is the group to whom the ad has been directed. Cunard line's *Queen Elizabeth II* annually embarks upon a three-month-long around-the-world cruise at a cost that spirals to over $100,000 per passenger. It has been said that the average age of participants is about 70. It is not only the line's costliest trip of the year but the one that books earliest. Who else but senior citizens have the time necessary for such a purchases?

With the great strides in medicine that have increased life expectancy, and the earlier financial planning that often provides the means for things other than necessities, the segment of the market that many felt wasn't worthwhile is beginning to look more attractive to marketers.

INTRODUCTION

The ultimate success or failure of a product depends upon customer acceptance. Consequently, each element of the marketing mix—the product, the price, the promotional activities, and the means of getting the goods to the consumer— must be designed with the goal of consumer acceptance in mind. It becomes obvious, then, that a profound knowledge of the consumer is an absolute necessity. In Chapter 3, we discussed the behavioral aspects of consumers. In this chapter, our attention will be focused on market size in terms of sex, age, location, and so on.

Photograph by Ellen Diamond.

THE TARGET MARKET

Early in marketing history, business institutions were product oriented. They strove for a salable product and offered it to the total market. Competition led to scientific marketing principles. In a situation in which there is only one producer of ladies' dresses, that manufacturer can supply the whole market. As more competitors come into the field selling becomes more difficult, and each manufacturer begins to specialize in satisfying a different facet of consumer demand. Thus, we find a growing diversity among suppliers. One firm may limit its product to evening wear, another to sportswear, and so on. As competition builds, specialization becomes more acute. Among manufacturers of evening wear, we find a variety of price ranges. As competition grows within each price range, further segmentation occurs, and style, size, or workmanship becomes the specialty of the various competing producers.

The point is that successful business managers must set their sights carefully on a particular target market. Having made this selection, all marketing decisions must be based upon the effect of those decisions on the selected target market.

MARKET SEGMENTATION

By definition, market segmentation is the process of taking the total market for a product and breaking it down into submarkets or segments. The population of each segment should be similar in many important characteristics. Segmentation can go on indefinitely, with each submarket bringing us closer to our target. For example, if we were marketing small, tractor-type lawn mowers, for use by suburbanites, we would start with the total population, segment it for suburban homeowners, further segment for owners of one acre or more (the equipment is not designed for small lawns), further segment for annual earnings (the mower is expensive), further segment for sex (men are the usual buyers), and so on. With each segmentation, our target becomes clearer, but never perfect. When should we stop? This is an arbitrary decision usually based upon information that is readily available and the research budget.

A MARKETING PROFILE

Lear's *Magazine*

With more than forty-six million women in the United States over the age of 40 and the promise of that segment of the market to reach sixty-four million by the year 2000, the "Magazine for the Woman Who Wasn't Born Yesterday" was conceived.

Lear's magazine (Figure 4–1) is targeted at informed, affluent women who have reached this age and have become "an important fact of American life" according to its editor-in-chief and founder, Frances Lear. Lear's took a stab at that vastly expanding market without relying on the typical recipes, diets, household hints, and advice columns to attract men.

In addition to typical advertising that is fashion and beauty oriented, the magazine, after one year in operation, reported automotive as its second largest category, with business from General Motors, Ford, Chrysler, BMW, and Volvo. Financial advertising also plays an important role for the publication, with such world leaders as U.S. Trust, J. P. Morgan, Morgan Stanley, American Express Gold, and the Boston Company as regular advertisers.

Circulation has increased from 200,000 to 350,000 in less than one year of publication, a rate base increase of 75 percent. Readers are drawn from the 25 markets "where the action dominates and where the advertisers are."

Market segmentation permits us to narrow and refine our target. With this information we are able to improve our decision making in such areas as promotion, product durability, and styling.

LEAR'S

THE MAGAZINE FOR THE WOMAN WHO WASN'T BORN YESTERDAY

Gretchen Siebel, Marketing Executive. One of 12,500,000 traditional women over 40 with HHI above $40,000.

FIGURE 4–1   *Lear's* magazine, the periodical targeted for the over-40 woman. (*Courtesy:* Harry Levine Associates, Inc.)

Demographics

Demographics is the study of the various characteristics of the population. It is the starting point of market analysis and segmentation. Much of the demographic information used in marketing is available from the United States Bureau of the Census, Bureau of Labor Statistics, and Department of Commerce.

Next we discuss some of the major demographic segments that are of interest to marketing.

The Size of the Market—Population.   After deciding upon a target market, the next step in setting a marketing plan is the determination of the size, location, and composition of the prospective market. This is necessary because estimates of sales are a vital factor in the budgeting, production, and distribution of the product.

The size of the population is one of several factors used to help determine the extent of the market. Others are personal incomes and costs. Since most products are intended to have a relatively long life, the statistics of the size of the market are generally studied over a long period of time so that trends may be determined. Table 4–1 shows the population of the United States from 1900 to 1988.

The market for many products is dependent upon the number of people in the country. Consequently, population growth is important. It should be noted that forecasts of the rate of national population growth have been scaled downward in recent years. In fact, some experts feel that we are now in a zero-growth state. Consider the importance of this to manufacturers who are planning expansion.

Population Shifts.   A study of the U.S. population during the period covered by Table 4–2 shows that percentagewise there has been a considerable shift in favor of the Mountain, Pacific, and South Atlantic areas, but that major population centers are still to be found in the Middle Atlantic and East-North Central areas. Consequently, a producer whose target market is a densely populated area should concentrate his distribution in those areas. Products that depend upon population expansion will do well to aim at the Mountain and Pacific areas.

Another significant population shift indicated in Table 4–2 is the growth of the Sun Belt. This is an area of relatively mild weather running across the country. Reasons for the growth of these areas include the increased number of elderly, retired people who elect to move to areas of less severe winters, and the growing number of young, working-age people who prefer to spend their lives in a pleasant climate.

Farm to urban.   Producers of merchandise designed for farm consumers have long been aware of a steady decrease in farm population. Comparative statistics

TABLE 4-1. Population of the United States, 1900–1988[1]

Year	Resident population	Year	Total Population	Percent change	Resident population	Civilian population
1900	76,094	1950	152,271	1.7	151,868	150,790
1905	83,822	1951	154,878	1.7	153,982	151,599
1910	92,407	1952	157,553	1.7	156,393	153,892
1915	100,546	1953	160,184	1.7	158,956	156,595
1920	106,461	1954	163,026	1.8	161,884	159,695
1925	115,829	1955	165,931	1.8	165,069	162,967
1930	123,077	1956	168,903	1.8	168,088	166,055
1935	127,250	1957	171,984	1.8	171,187	169,110
1940	132,457	1958	174,882	1.7	174,149	172,226
1941	133,669	1959	177,830	1.7	177,135	175,277
1942	134,617	1960	180,671	1.6	179,979	178,140
1943	135,107	1961	183,691	1.7	182,992	181,143
1944	133,915	1962	186,538	1.5	185,771	183,677
1945	133,434	1963	189,242	1.4	188,483	186,493
1946	140,686	1964	191,889	1.4	191,141	189,141
1947	144,083	1965	194,303	1.3	193,526	191,605
1948	146,730	1966	196,560	1.2	195,576	193,420
1949	149,304	1967	198,712	1.1	197,457	195,264
		1968	200,706	1.0	199,399	197,113
		1969	202,677	1.0	201,385	199,145

Year	Total Population	Percent change	Resident population	Civilian population
1970	205,052	1.2	203,984	201,895
1971	207,661	1.3	206,827	204,866
1972	209,896	1.1	209,284	207,511
1973	211,909	1.0	211,357	209,600
1974	213,854	.9	213,342	211,636
1975	215,973	1.0	215,465	213,788
1976	218,035	1.0	217,563	215,894
1977	220,239	1.0	219,760	218,106
1978	222,585	1.1	222,095	220,467
1979	225,055	1.1	224,567	222,969
1980	227,757	1.2	227,255	225,651
1981	230,138	1.0	229,637	227,989
1982	232,520	1.0	231,996	230,327
1983	234,799	1.0	234,284	232,589
1984	237,001	1.0	236,477	234,762
1985	239,279	1.0	238,736	237,031
1986	241,613	1.0	241,096	239,374
1987	243,945	1.0	243,400	241,661
1988	246,113	1.0	245,602	243,910

[1]In thousands, except percent. Estimates as of July 1. Prior to 1940, excludes Alaska and Hawaii. Total population includes Armed Forces abroad; civilian population excludes Armed Forces. For basis of estimates, see text, section 1. See also *Historical Statistics, Colonial Times to 1970*, series A 6–8.

Source: U.S. Department of Commerce, *Statistical Abstract of the United States, 1989* (Washington, D.C.: U.S. Government Printing Office, 1989).

Table 4-2. Population of the United States by regions, 1950–1987 preliminary[1]

Region, Division, and State or Other Area	Population (1,000)										
	1950	1960	1970	1980	1981	1982	1983	1984	1985	1986	1987, prel.
United States	**151,326**	**179,323**	**203,302**	**226,546**	**229,637**	**231,996**	**234,284**	**236,477**	**238,736**	**241,096**	**243,400**
Region											
Northeast	39,478	44,678	49,061	49,135	49,262	49,324	49,526	49,713	49,858	50,056	50,278
Midwest	44,461	51,619	56,589	58,866	59,006	58,957	58,930	59,091	59,193	59,292	59,538
South	47,197	54,973	62,812	75,372	77,057	78,483	79,732	80,786	81,891	83,003	83,884
West	20,190	28,053	34,838	43,172	44,313	45,232	46,095	46,887	47,794	48,745	49,700
Northeast	**9,314**	**10,509**	**11,848**	**12,348**	**12,418**	**12,435**	**12,493**	**12,577**	**12,663**	**12,742**	**12,844**
ME	914	969	994	1,125	1,135	1,139	1,147	1,157	1,165	1,172	1,187
NH	533	607	738	921	937	948	959	978	998	1,027	1,057
VT	378	390	445	511	516	520	526	530	535	541	548
MA	4,691	5,149	5,689	5,737	5,754	5,746	5,764	5,795	5,823	5,834	5,855
RI	792	859	950	947	952	953	955	960	967	975	986
CT	2,007	2,535	3,032	3,108	3,124	3,128	3,143	3,157	3,175	3,193	3,211
Middle Atlantic	**30,164**	**34,168**	**37,213**	**36,787**	**36,844**	**36,889**	**37,034**	**37,136**	**37,195**	**37,313**	**37,433**
NY	14,830	16,782	18,241	17,558	17,559	17,575	17,670	17,727	17,762	17,795	17,825
NJ	4,835	6,067	7,171	7,365	7,407	7,430	7,468	7,518	7,568	7,625	7,672
PA	10,498	11,319	11,801	11,864	11,879	11,883	11,895	11,892	11,864	11,894	11,936
East North Central	**30,399**	**36,225**	**40,262**	**41,682**	**41,711**	**41,607**	**41,511**	**41,581**	**41,642**	**41,722**	**41,904**
OH	7,947	9,706	10,657	10,798	10,801	10,777	10,741	10,742	10,745	10,748	10,784
IN	3,934	4,662	5,195	5,490	5,489	5,484	5,475	5,492	5,500	5,503	5,531
IL	8,712	10,081	11,110	11,427	11,474	11,481	11,493	11,525	11,538	11,551	11,582
MI	6,372	7,823	8,882	9,262	9,210	9,118	9,054	9,060	9,085	9,139	9,200
WI	3,435	3,952	4,418	4,706	4,736	4,747	4,748	4,763	4,775	4,783	4,807
West North Central	**14,061**	**15,394**	**16,327**	**17,183**	**17,295**	**17,350**	**17,419**	**17,509**	**17,551**	**17,569**	**17,634**
MN	2,982	3,414	3,806	4,076	4,112	4,133	4,145	4,163	4,190	4,213	4,246
IA	2,621	2,758	2,825	2,914	2,918	2,908	2,905	2,904	2,880	2,850	2,834
MO	3,955	4,320	4,678	4,917	4,939	4,943	4,965	5,004	5,034	5,064	5,103
ND	620	632	618	653	661	672	681	687	685	679	672
SD	653	681	666	691	692	695	699	705	708	708	709
NE	1,326	1,411	1,485	1,570	1,583	1,590	1,596	1,605	1,604	1,598	1,594
KS	1,905	2,179	2,249	2,364	2,389	2,410	2,428	2,441	2,449	2,459	2,476

(continued)

Table 4–2. (*Continued*)

Region, Division, and State or Other Area	Population (1,000)										
	1950	1960	1970	1980	1981	1982	1983	1984	1985	1986	1987, prel.
South Atlantic	**21,182**	**25,972**	**30,678**	**36,959**	**37,797**	**38,318**	**38,878**	**39,534**	**40,214**	**40,938**	**41,684**
DE	318	446	548	594	597	600	606	614	622	633	644
MD	2,343	3,101	3,924	4,217	4,256	4,272	4,299	4,347	4,391	4,461	4,535
DC	802	764	757	638	633	627	624	624	623	625	622
VA	3,319	3,967	4,651	5,347	5,442	5,488	5,558	5,635	5,701	5,795	5,904
WV	2,006	1,860	1,744	1,950	1,961	1,962	1,963	1,952	1,936	1,917	1,897
NC	4,062	4,556	5,084	5,882	5,958	6,019	6,080	6,169	6,260	6,331	6,413
SC	2,117	2,383	2,591	3,122	3,186	3,220	3,253	3,296	3,334	3,381	3,425
GA	3,445	3,943	4,588	5,463	5,570	5,654	5,735	5,843	5,973	6,100	6,222
FL	2,771	4,952	6,791	9,746	10,194	10,475	10,578	11,053	11,373	11,694	12,023
East South Central	**11,477**	**12,050**	**12,808**	**14,666**	**14,786**	**14,873**	**14,951**	**15,040**	**15,128**	**15,200**	**15,290**
KY	2,945	3,038	3,221	3,661	3,675	3,695	3,715	3,723	3,728	3,726	3,727
TN	3,292	3,567	3,926	4,591	4,639	4,666	4,690	4,728	4,766	4,800	4,855
AL	3,062	3,267	3,444	3,894	3,928	3,944	3,963	3,991	4,020	4,050	4,083
MS	2,179	2,178	2,217	2,521	2,544	2,567	2,583	2,599	2,613	2,624	2,625
West South Central	**14,538**	**16,951**	**19,326**	**23,747**	**24,474**	**25,292**	**25,902**	**26,212**	**26,549**	**26,864**	**26,910**
AR	1,910	1,786	1,923	2,286	2,300	2,308	2,326	2,346	2,359	2,371	2,388
LA	2,684	3,257	3,645	4,206	4,300	4,383	4,441	4,462	4,485	4,499	4,461
OK	2,233	2,328	2,559	3,025	3,105	3,223	3,317	3,321	3,316	3,306	3,272
TX	7,711	9,580	11,199	14,229	14,768	15,378	15,818	16,083	16,389	16,689	16,789
Moutain	**5,075**	**6,855**	**8,289**	**11,373**	**11,742**	**12,054**	**12,319**	**12,537**	**12,768**	**12,982**	**13,167**
MT	591	675	694	787	796	805	816	823	825	817	809
ID	589	667	713	944	964	978	988	999	1,004	1,002	998
WY	291	330	332	470	494	510	516	513	510	507	490
CO	1,325	1,754	2,210	2,890	2,984	3,072	3,148	3,189	3,233	3,266	3,296
NM	681	951	1,017	1,303	1,335	1,369	1,402	1,427	1,450	1,479	1,500
AZ	750	1,302	1,775	2,718	2,808	2,884	2,958	3,047	3,161	3,279	3,386
UT	689	891	1,059	1,461	1,516	1,559	1,595	1,623	1,644	1,664	1,680
NV	160	285	489	800	845	877	895	916	940	967	1,007
Pacific	**15,115**	**21,198**	**26,549**	**31,800**	**32,570**	**33,179**	**33,777**	**34,350**	**35,027**	**35,763**	**36,533**
WA	2,379	2,853	3,413	4,132	4,237	4,279	4,304	4,349	4,406	4,463	4,538
OR	1,521	1,769	2,092	2,633	2,671	2,671	2,663	2,679	2,689	2,702	2,724
CA	10,586	15,717	19,971	23,668	24,267	24,786	25,309	25,780	26,358	27,001	27,663
AK	129	226	303	402	416	446	483	505	522	532	525
HI	500	633	770	965	980	998	1,019	1,036	1,051	1,065	1,083

[1]1950–1980, as of Apr.1; beginning 1981, as of July 1. Insofar as possible, population shown for all years is that of present area of State. See *Historical Statistics, Colonial Times to 1970*, series A 172, for population by regions.

Source: U.S. Department of Commerce, *Statistical Abstract of the United States, 1989* (W. hington, D.C. U.S. Government Printing Office, 1989)

TABLE 4–3.   Farm population in the United
States, 1950–1987

Year	Total (1,000)
1950	23,000
1960	16,000
1970	10,000
1980	6,000
1981	5,800
1982	5,600
1983	5,700
1984	5,700
1985	5,300
1986	5,200
1987	4,900

Source: U.S. Department of Commerce, *Statistical Abstract of the United States, 1989* (Washington, D.C.: U.S. Government Printing Office, 1989).

since 1920 indicate a decided trend away from the farm. This, in part, is the result of technological improvements in farm machinery that make possible increased agricultural production with fewer workers. It is likely that an increase in large corporate farms, completely mechanized, will result in a continuation of this trend. Table 4–3 illustrates the movement of population away from the farm.

Research in present-day farm population indicates that there is also a decreasing difference between farm and nonfarm consumers. Present-day farmers are well-educated, style-conscious buyers. This is of considerable interest to marketers, since the demands of rural customers are now pretty much the same as those of their urban cousins.

Urban to suburban.   The growing shift of the more affluent city dwellers to suburban communities has required a considerable adjustment on the part of business. The first step taken was to locate retail branches within easy reach of suburban customers. The next phase was the movement of light industry and administrative offices to suburban locations. On the industrial market this has led to a reshuffling of sales territories and transportation methods. The suburbs, rather than being simply places for city workers to sleep, are fast becoming places for suburban workers to live, shop, and spend their leisure time.

Working Women.   A significant change in the makeup of the labor force in the last forty years has caught the eye of marketing executives. As shown in Table 4–4, the percentage of working women has risen considerably in all age categories while the male categories haven't shown significant changes. To adjust to these changes, adjustments must be made in shopping hours (less weekday, daytime

TABLE 4-4. Labor force participation rates by marital status, sex, and age, 1960-1988[1]

Year and Marital Status	Male Participation Rate						Female Participation Rate					
	16-19 years	20-24 years	25-34 years	35-44 years	45-64 years	65 and over	16-19 years	20-24 years	25-34 years	35-44 years	45-64 years	65 and over
Married[1]												
1960	296.0	97.5	98.6	98.4	93.0	37.1	225.3	30.0	27.7	36.2	34.2	5.9
1970	95.5	95.0	98.2	98.1	91.6	30.2	36.0	47.4	39.3	47.2	44.1	7.9
1975	92.3	95.1	97.3	97.0	87.0	23.7	46.0	57.3	48.3	51.9	43.9	7.2
1980	97.3	96.8	97.5	97.0	84.8	20.4	47.7	60.5	59.3	62.5	46.9	7.2
1983	92.7	95.7	97.3	97.2	82.1	19.1	46.6	63.0	62.5	65.4	47.6	7.5
1984	96.5	96.2	97.2	97.2	81.8	17.4	43.4	63.3	64.0	66.4	49.0	7.3
1985	90.9	95.7	97.4	96.7	81.6	17.5	49.2	64.9	65.6	68.1	50.6	6.7
1986	91.8	95.8	97.3	96.3	81.8	17.3	52.9	63.1	66.4	69.0	50.4	7.0
1987	90.4	95.7	97.2	96.2	82.4	17.4	42.8	67.4	67.5	71.7	51.3	6.9
1988	95.3	95.7	97.0	96.7	82.4	17.5	46.8	65.9	68.6	72.7	52.7	7.4
Single												
1960	234.4	76.6	85.3	85.3	74.4	24.3	225.3	73.4	79.9	79.7	75.1	21.6
1970	49.0	69.0	86.2	82.3	66.6	21.0	39.5	71.1	80.7	73.3	67.8	17.6
1975	53.2	76.5	87.4	86.5	68.7	20.5	45.5	69.5	80.4	77.8	68.4	16.2
1980	56.8	79.6	87.3	79.9	65.2	20.0	49.0	72.2	84.2	78.5	62.8	12.0
1983	49.9	77.6	88.4	81.8	69.6	23.9	46.0	72.6	83.6	81.1	65.1	12.6
1984	50.8	78.5	87.4	83.2	65.6	16.7	46.4	72.1	83.5	83.0	67.0	11.8
1985	52.4	77.9	87.5	80.8	67.3	16.0	49.6	74.0	82.5	80.6	73.2	8.0
1986	50.8	80.7	88.3	84.5	61.4	17.8	50.1	75.0	81.1	79.6	69.3	8.0
1987	50.2	80.0	88.0	83.7	64.3	16.3	49.6	74.5	82.9	81.8	58.8	9.1
1988	49.7	80.1	88.4	82.4	65.9	20.7	48.7	74.8	81.8	81.5	65.2	10.9
Other[3]												
1960	(B)	88.6	82.3	84.1	78.1	18.2	237.3	54.6	55.5	67.4	58.3	11.0
1970	(B)	73.2	74.5	80.6	75.9	16.5	46.5	59.7	65.1	67.9	60.7	9.9
1975	(B)	84.7	92.4	89.3	69.4	18.0	41.9	68.1	67.5	69.4	60.4	8.1
1980	(B)	92.9	93.8	91.1	69.9	13.0	51.0	68.5	77.1	76.4	59.5	8.6
1983	(B)	89.7	91.9	90.7	73.9	13.1	45.3	68.4	77.1	77.7	59.5	7.5
1984	(B)	91.6	90.7	92.8	71.8	12.6	53.6	71.3	76.5	79.6	61.0	7.7
1985	(B)	96.9	92.9	92.1	72.8	12.7	50.9	66.5	78.9	80.6	60.7	7.9
1986	(B)	93.9	93.1	89.1	71.7	13.0	50.6	71.0	78.4	82.6	61.7	7.4
1987	(B)	90.6	92.9	91.1	73.1	11.1	(B)	67.2	77.1	83.0	61.9	7.6
1988	(B)	93.2	91.8	88.8	71.2	11.6	64.5	67.7	76.3	81.5	62.6	8.2

[1] As of March. See table 623 for definition of participation rate. Data for males include members of the Armed Forces living offpost or with their families on post. Based on Current Population Survey; see text, section 1 and Appendix III.   B For 1960, percentage not shown where base is less than 100,000; beginning 1970, 75,000.   [1] Spouse present.   [2] 14 to 19 years old.   [3] Widowed, divorced, and married (spouse absent).

Source: U.S. Department of Commerce, Statistical Abstract of the United States, 1989 (Washington, D.C.: U.S. Government Printing Office, 1989).

shopping), in the location of the purchase (in the neighborhood or place of business), and so on.

Table 4–4 indicates the changes in the size of the labor force from 1960 to 1988.

Age.   It is very useful for business to know the trend in the age distribution of the population. For example, the great increase in births during the 1940s resulted in a boom for the toy industry in the 1950s.

Table 4–5 indicates the probable trends in age segmentation until the year 1987. It is expected that the largest increase will be in the young middle-age group. Based on this information, much present-day sales promotion is aimed at this market. On the other hand, the percentage of the population in the teenager and older middle-age groups is expected to decline. Further breakdowns of the age of the population are available from Bureau of the Census reports. Such a population analysis of age by sex might be useful to marketers of razor blades, menswear, and sporting equipment, in the planning of future expansion.

The effect of the change in age mix of the population on marketing strategy can be illustrated by the following examples: Gerber, long a leading processor of baby foods, has gone into the life insurance business, and Johnson & Johnson has an advertising campaign to convince adults to use their baby oil and shampoo.

At the present time forty-eight million Americans, or 21 percent of the population is over age 55. Their spending power is twice that of the under-25 group. These people buy more luxury cars, take more and better vacations, and purchase the major share of such luxury items as expensive clothes, jewels, and furs. They are a major market segment, and business has begun catering to them with considerable success. Levi Strauss, for example, introduced roomy Action-wear slacks designed for middle-aged men, and sold fifty million pair in the last ten years. Similarly, travel agencies are offering special tours for older groups, restaurants like Mcdonald's and others offer special discounts and early-bird specials, food companies offer high-fiber, low-sodium cereals, and special retire-

TABLE 4–5.   Population age distribution to 1987

Age	Trend
Children (under 13)	Up 11%
Teenagers (13–19)	Down 17%
Young adults (20–34)	Up 13%
Young middle aged (35–49)	Up 31%
Older middle aged (50–64)	Down 1%
Elderly (65 and over)	Up 19%

Source: U.S. Department of Commerce, *Statistical Abstract of the United States, 1989* (Washington, D.C.: U.S. Government Printing Office, 1989).

ment housing developments are commonplace. Some errors have been made. H. J. Heinz offered Senior Foods, which was really baby food, and didn't make the grade. Similarly, advertising for Procter & Gamble's Attend (disposable incontinence pads) was rejected by *Modern Maturity* magazine because they felt it was disconcerting for their audience and sales started declining.

Advertising for the over-55 segment is complicated. Most older people do not think of themselves as old and are turned off by promotion earmarking products as being exclusively for the elderly. In addition, advertisers feel that products for the elderly can best be sold by the young and beautiful. Some people question this. They claim, for example, that older women would be more likely to buy clothes, cosmetics, and other personal items, if they were modeled by older models that the prospective buyer could identify with.

Sex.   Obviously, the size of the total market for women's hosiery depends upon the number of women in the population. Similarly, the sale of men's hats is predicated upon the number of men in the population. It is wrong, however, to assume that there is an equal number of men and women in the population. In fact, the numbers in each sex vary by age. Until the age of 24, men predominate. Beyond that age, women slowly become more numerous in the population. By the age of 75, women are more numerous.

Another important factor is the sex of the person making the purchase. Men's work socks, for example, are worn exclusively by men but are generally bought by women. The selection of the proper media for advertising such goods poses an interesting marketing problem.

Family Status.   Segmentation by sex and age alone rarely provides adequate information on consumer buying behavior. Further classification by family status is frequently broken down into the following nine classifications, each having its own purchasing patterns, habits, and special requirements. The life-cycle concept is the result of a study made by Wells and Guber as reported in the *Journal of Marketing Research*.

1. *Young single persons living away from their parents.* These are people with relatively few financial burdens. Deeply involved in the mating game, they become fashion opinion leaders. They are recreation-minded and involved in physical sports activities. Such people are likely purchasers of basic furniture and kitchen equipment, including appliances, with which to set up housekeeping. They offer a market for new automobiles, vacations, cosmetics, and equipment for attracting the opposite sex. The Harley Davidson Motorcycle exemplifies a product for the young single, as pictured in Figure 4–2.

2. *Newly married young couples, no children.* These young marrieds, frequently with two wage earners and limited financial responsibilities, are much better off financially than they will be when the children begin to arrive.

FIGURE 4–2   The Harley-Davidson motorcycle is a product purchased by the young single. (*Courtesy:* Harley-Davidson, Inc.)

They spend freely and are the principal buyers of durable goods, which they need to set up housekeeping. They purchase cars, refrigerators, stoves, and sensible and durable furniture. Vacations play an important part in their lives.

3. *Full nest I: Youngest child under age 16.* This group is poor in cash and other liquid assets. They are by far the most important purchasers of homes. They are generally unhappy about their financial position, particularly with the small amount of money they have saved. They show an interest in new products and are particularly susceptible to advertising. They purchase washers, dryers, TV sets, baby food, chest rubs, cough medicine, vitamins, dolls, wagons, sleds, and skates.

4. *Full nest II: Youngest child over age 16.* At this stage, financial position is usually improved, often because the wife has returned to work. This group is less influenced by advertising. They buy larger-sized packages and show an interest in multiple-unit deals. They buy many foods, cleaning materials, bicycles, music lessons, and musical instruments such as pianos.

5. *Full nest III: Older married couples with dependent children.* This group's financial position has continued to improve. More wives have returned to work. Some of the children have found jobs. Such people are not easily influenced by advertising. They are important purchasers of durable goods. They buy new, more tasteful furniture and luxury appliances. They spend on autos, travel, boats, dental services, and magazine subscriptions.

6. *Empty nest I: Older married couples, no children living with them, head of family still working.* Their financial position has reached the point at which they are satisfied. There is money in the bank, which is used for travel, self-education, and recreation. They make gifts and contributions. They prefer tested products to new ones. Homeownership is at its peak. They spend freely on vacations, luxuries, and home improvements.

7. *Empty nest II: Older married couples, no children living at home, head of household retired.* These people, although they suffer a drastic cut in income, keep their homes. They worry about their financial security, and a large portion of their income goes to medical care and products that will aid health, sleep, and digestion.

8. *Solitary survivor in labor force.* While their income remains good, they often sell their homes, since the need and effort required makes a house an inconvenience. Like the retired group, a good deal of their income goes for medical care and other health services.

9. *Solitary survivor, retired.* These people are faced with drastically reduced incomes. They have special needs for attention, affection, and security. As is the case with other retired persons, medical care and health needs make up an important part of their purchases.

Obviously, the segmentation can be broadened. Never-married, young, and middle-aged persons are examples. The extent and details of the segmentation depend upon the target market.

During the last decade, two new classifications have been growing at an enormous pace: the "yuppies" and "dinks" (double income, no kids). They spend significant sums on vacations, clothing, and a new breed of transportation, namely, such luxury cars as Chrysler's TC by Maserati of Italy featured in Figure 4–3 and the Jeep Cherokee Sport in Figure 4–4.

Number of Households.   The number of households is of considerable importance in certain areas of marketing. Demand for housing units, appliances, furniture, automobiles, and many similar items is closely related to these statistics. Table 4–6 indicates the number of projected households at intervals from 1989 to 2000. In addition, by indicating the number of persons in each household, Table 4–7 illustrates the changes in the number of people living in the average household in 1980 and 1987.

Considering the relatively short period of time between 1960 and 1982, the

FIGURE 4–3   Chrysler's TC by Maserati. (*Courtesy:* Chrysler Corporation.)

FIGURE 4–4   Jeep Cherokee Sport. (*Courtesy:* Chrysler Corporation.)

TABLE 4–6.   Households by type, projections for 1989–2000[1]

| Year and Series | Total | Family | | | | Nonfamily | | |
		Total	Married couple	Male householder[1]	Female householder[2]	Total	Male householder	Female householder
1989								
Series A	93,622	65,403	51,521	2,616	11,266	28,219	12,403	15,816
Series B	92,847	66,034	52,554	2,508	10,972	26,814	11,583	15,231
Series C	92,126	66,653	53,562	2,410	10,681	25,473	10,802	14,671
1990								
Series A	95,243	65,964	51,704	2,723	11,538	29,279	13,008	16,270
Series B	94,227	66,758	53,012	2,581	11,165	27,469	11,946	15,523
Series C	93,297	67,535	54,282	2,455	10,798	25,762	10,949	14,814
1995								
Series A	102,785	68,219	52,178	3,276	12,765	34,565	16,102	18,463
Series B	100,308	69,787	54,863	2,940	11,984	30,520	13,666	16,854
Series C	98,180	71,294	57,410	2,667	11,217	26,887	11,490	15,396
2000								
Series A	110,217	70,024	52,263	3,845	13,916	40,193	19,471	20,722
Series B	105,933	72,277	56,294	3,282	12,701	33,656	15,452	18,204
Series C	102,440	74,449	60,080	2,855	11,515	27,991	11,985	16,006

[1]In thousands. As of July. Series A reflects the assumption that the recent moderation in marriage and divorce trends will continue but that historical changes spanning the last 25 years must be taken into consideration. Series A assumes a continuation of past trends in householder proportions but changes in recent years are given more weight. Series B reflects assumptions intermediate between series A and C, namely changes in marriage and divorce will slow considerably, but will not cease during the next 15 years. Series C reflects the assumption that the rapid change in marriage and divorce may have come to an end, and householder proportions will remain constant for the next 15 years.   [2]With no spouse present.

Source: U.S. Department of Commerce, *Statistical Abstract of the United States, 1989* (Washington, D.C.: U.S. Government Printing Office, 1989).

increase in the number of households and the decreasing number of persons sharing each household present marketers with one of the most significant demographic changes of our times. Progressive marketing must adjust to this new information. For example, should A&P start selling eggs in cartons of six instead of a dozen?

Nationalities.   People of different ethnic backgrounds have different buying patterns. Moreover, despite "melting pot" theories, these patterns persist through at least several generations. Differences by country of origin are apparent in purchases of food, clothing, and home furnishings. The growth in recent years in television programming to include black and Spanish-speaking actors is an attempt to capitalize on this segment of the market.

There has always been a steady flow of South American and Central American immigrants into the United States. In recent years, political and economic problems have greatly increased the flow of Hispanics. Census counts indicate that the present Hispanic-American population is about seventeen million, with

TABLE 4–7. Households, 1980 and 1987, and persons in households by 1987

Type of Household and Presence of Children	Households						Persons in Household, 1987		Persons per household, 1987
	Number (1,000)		Change, 1980–1987		Percent distribution				
	1980	1987	Number (1,000)	Percent	1980	1987	Number (1,000)	Percent distribution	
Total households	80,776	89,479	8,703	10.8	100.0	100.0	238,261	100.0	2.66
Family households	59,550	64,491	4,941	8.3	73.7	72.1	207,772	87.2	3.22
With own children under 18	31,022	31,898	876	2.8	38.4	35.6	124,642	52.3	3.91
Without own children under 18	28,528	32,593	4,065	14.2	35.3	36.4	83,130	34.9	2.55
Married couple family	49,112	51,537	2,425	4.9	60.8	57.6	168,302	70.6	3.27
With own children under 18	24,961	24,645	−316	−1.3	30.9	27.5	102,134	42.8	4.14
Without own children under 18	24,151	26,892	2,741	11.3	29.9	30.1	66,168	27.8	2.46
Male householder, no spouse present	1,733	2,510	777	44.8	2.1	2.8	7,232	3.0	2.88
With own children under 18	616	955	339	55.0	.8	1.1	2,767	1.2	2.90
Without own children under 18	1,117	1,554	437	39.1	1.4	1.7	4,465	1.9	2.87
Female householder, no spouse present	8,705	10,445	1,740	20.0	10.8	11.7	32,238	13.5	3.09
With own children under 18	5,445	6,297	852	15.6	6.7	7.0	19,741	8.3	3.13
Without own children under 18	3,261	4,147	886	27.2	4.0	4.6	12,497	5.2	3.01
Nonfamily households	21,226	24,998	3,762	17.7	26.3	27.9	30,489	12.8	1.22
Living alone	18,296	21,128	2,832	15.5	22.7	23.6	21,128	8.9	1.00
Male householder	8,807	10,652	1,845	20.9	10.9	11.9	14,303	6.0	1.34
Living alone	6,966	8,246	1,280	18.4	8.6	9.2	8,246	3.5	1.00
Female householder	12,419	14,336	1,917	15.4	15.4	16.0	16,186	6.8	1.13
Living alone	11,330	12,881	1,551	13.7	14.0	14.4	12,881	5.4	1.00

Source: U.S. Department of Commerce, Statistical Abstract of the United States, 1989 (Washington, D.C.: U.S. Government Printing Office, 1989).

another five to eight million uncounted. By the year 2000, it is estimated that the Hispanic population will grow from its present 6.5 percent of the population to about 10 percent, while the black population will remain constant at 12 percent and the caucasians will show a slight decrease. Naturally, marketers have shown great interest in this huge segment of our population. McDonald's, Anheuser-Busch, Timex, and Pizza Hut are actively promoting their products to the Hispanic market. Coca-Cola budgeted more than $10 million in the late 1980s advertising budget to reach the Hispanic market.

There are problems. The Mexicans in California and Texas are culturally different from the Puerto Ricans and Cubans in New York and Florida. While Spanish is the universal language among Hispanics, different words have different shades of meaning among the various groups. For example, the word *bizcocho* means biscuits to some Latin Americans and cake to others.

Education. Until recently, educational attainment was rarely considered as a special segment of the market. The correlation between high educational level and annual earnings was so great that it was usually considered unnecessary to consider education separately. Recently, this has changed. Today's driver or police officer, with relatively little education, often earns as much as a well-educated college professor. Consequently, it is not correct to classify these two types within the same category. Although their annual earnings may be similar, their buying patterns are not.

Income. A market requires more than just people. People must have money to spend. An analysis of income, its distribution, and the way it is spent is essential in determining the trends in purchasing power that a marketer must know to understand the market.

Income is the result of producing and selling goods in the marketplace. The gross national product (the total market value of goods and services produced in a year) has been growing in the United States at an annual average of 3 percent. At this rate the GNP doubles every twenty years, and indications are that it will continue to do so until the year 2000 at least. Although this information is of overall interest, individual producers need more specific information. For example, the manufacturer of a high-cost prestige product would be interested to know the percentage of the population that could afford such merchandise. Table 4–8 shows the median family income.

An important trend can be determined by analyzing Table 4–8. The median income per family has increased steadily and significantly during the years pictured. This represents an increase in family income of nearly 300 percent.

Table 4–8 indicates that an enormous increase in spending power has been available to the marketplace during the years mentioned. Obviously, the next question is: How much of a family's total income has to be spent for necessities and how much is available for other goods? Basic spending refers to money disbursed for necessities. Discretionary expenditures are those that are available

TABLE 4–8. Money income of households—median household income in current and constant (1987) dollars, by race and Hispanic origin of householder, 1970–1987

Year	Median Income in Current Dollars (dol.)				Median Income in Constant (1987) Dollars (dol.)				Annual Percent Change of Median Income of All Households	
	All households[1]	White	Black	Hispanic[2]	All households[1]	White	Black	Hispanic[2]	Current dollars	Constant dollars
1970	8,734	9,097	5,537	NA	25,563	26,626	16,206	NA	[3]6.9	[3]1.7
1971	9,028	9,443	5,578	NA	25,335	26,499	15,654	NA	3.4	−.9
1972	9,697	10,173	5,938	7,677	26,344	27,637	16,132	20,856	7.4	4.0
1973	10,512	11,017	6,485	8,144	26,884	28,175	16,586	20,828	8.4	2.0
1974	11,197	11,710	6,964	8,906	25,806	26,987	16,050	20,526	6.5	−4.0
1975	11,800	12,340	7,408	8,865	24,917	26,058	15,643	18,720	5.4	3.4
1976	12,686	13,289	7,902	9,569	25,328	26,531	15,776	19,104	7.5	1.6
1977	13,572	14,272	8,422	10,647	25,454	26,767	15,795	19,968	7.0	.5
1978	15,064	15,660	9,411	11,803	26,242	27,281	16,395	20,562	11.0	3.1
1979	16,461	17,259	10,133	13,042	25,775	27,024	15,866	20,421	9.3	−1.8
1980	17,710	18,684	10,764	13,651	24,426	25,770	14,846	18,828	7.6	−5.2
1981	19,074	20,153	11,309	15,300	23,835	25,184	14,132	19,119	7.7	−2.4
1982	20,171	21,117	11,968	15,178	23,750	24,865	14,092	17,871	5.8	−.4
1983	21,018	22,035	12,473	15,794	23,976	25,136	14,229	18,017	4.2	1.0
1984	22,415	23,647	13,471	16,992	24,526	25,874	14,740	18,592	6.6	2.3
1985	23,618	24,908	14,819	17,465	24,952	26,315	15,656	18,451	5.4	1.7
1986	24,897	26,175	15,080	18,352	25,807	27,131	15,631	19,023	5.4	3.4
1987	25,986	27,427	15,475	19,305	25,986	27,427	15,475	19,305	4.4	.7

NA Not available. [1]Includes other races not shown separately. [2]Hispanic persons may be of any race. [3]Change from 1967.

Source: U.S. Department of Commerce, Statistical Abstract of the United States, 1989 (Washington, D.C.: U.S. Government Printing Office, 1989).

to a family after the basic needs have been satisfied. Until a certain income level is reached, a family has no control over its expenditures; income is needed to buy food, shelter, clothing, and other necessities. As the family's level of income rises and these basic needs are met, the family may spend the excess earnings at its discretion. One of the important marketing results of the shift in family earnings from the lowest to the highest levels is an increase in the purchasing power for discretionary spending. The rapid growth of the leisure industries is evidence of an increase in discretionary funds available in the market.

Database Demographics.   For years major industries have used census data to make future planning decisions. Unfortunately, the census did not always provide exactly what was needed in the form that it was needed. This has led to the rise of a number of companies such as Urban Decision Systems and Claritas Corp. They call their product *database.* They provide their customers with demographic information that is tailored to the customer's needs and is presented in the required format. Their customers include General Motors, J.C. Penney, the Chase Manhattan Bank, and the Republican National Committee. They start by buying the census on computer tape from the U.S. Census Bureau. This information is then streamlined, other demographic information is added where necessary, and the output provides information to the customer according to specifications. This results in more specific information on the target customer than raw census data can provide. The Ford Motor Company, for example, uses database information to project the need for dealerships in 140 urban markets. Database information is not limited to population demographics. Geographic Data Technology keeps a computerized data bank on nearly every street in the United States. Keebler, the cookie company, uses it to route its truck drivers.

FACTORS AFFECTING CONSUMER SPENDING

Further sophistication in understanding the way people spend requires a breakdown of family earnings into various categories of spending.

Engels's Laws

Ernst Engels was a German statistician who studied the budgets of wage earners in the middle 1800s. From the spending patterns of these working-class families, he published, in 1857, a group of generalizations concerning the manner in which families spend their income. These statements, called Engels's laws, are remarkably accurate even today. The following are Engels's four statements describing family spending patterns:

1. The percentage of income spent on food decreases as family income increases.
2. The percentage of income spent for household expenditures such as rent stays about the same as family income increases.
3. The percentage of income spent for clothing remains about the same as family income increases.
4. The percentage of income spent on other items (recreation, education, medical care, savings, and so on) increases as family income increases.

Although Engels's laws are still sufficiently accurate to be used as generalizations by marketers, present-day information requires that certain modifications be made.

Food.   Unquestionably, as incomes increase, people eat better. However, although they actually spend more for food, this expense diminishes in proportion to total earnings. But the decrease in food spending is less dramatic than Engels expected. Movement of the population from rural to urban and suburban areas, smaller family units, prepackaging, freezing, precooking, and eating out are no doubt responsible for higher food expenses.

Housing.   The percentage of income spent on housing is another area in which Engels is still correct. That is, although the amount spent for housing goes up as the family's income increases, the proportional share of total income allocated to housing diminishes.

Clothing.   According to Engels, the percentage of income spent for clothing remains about the same as total family income increases. This is close, but not quite accurate in our present-day economy. In fact, as the total income goes up, the proportion spent for clothing gets slightly higher as well. This may be due in part to expenditures for special-use clothing (sneakers, ski pants), which were unheard of in Engels's day. Apparently, the increased leisure time today, particularly for the more affluent, results in proportionately more expense for clothing.

Other Items.   Expenditures for such other items as education and savings increase with increased earnings, as Engels suggested. Since he could not have predicted hospitalization, Medicare, and group insurance programs, he can be excused for not realizing that expenditures for health and insurance decrease proportionately as incomes rise.

It is important for marketers to know that the trend toward higher incomes of the American families will increase the amount of discretionary spending money available in the marketplace. This will lead to an expansion of the sales of such luxury products as expensive food, clothing, travel, and amusements.

PSYCHOGRAPHICS

Introduction

As growing numbers of behavioral scientists became involved in marketing, they brought skills and training that were new to the field. For many years marketing managers had found that the traditional psychographic categories such as age, sex, and population, left much to be desired, since they gave no insights into the psychological and sociological characteristics of their target market. That is, all persons between forty and fifty years of age, earning $35,000 to $50,000 per year, do not have the same buying patterns. This was right down the behaviorists' alley. They are, after all, specialists in personality and life-style. Psychographics is nothing more than a sophisticated type of market segmentation that attempts to categorize traditional market segmentation into narrower, more useful categories.

A good example of psychographic success is the case of Source Perrier of France. They are bottlers of spring water whose sales on the American market have reached 175 million bottles per year. Their market segment is the twenty-five million Americans with incomes of $30,000 or more. They further narrow their segment by analyzing the consumer psychographic profiles within that group. Perrier describes their customers as "aspirant people who strive to improve their quality of life." Broad economic segmentation such as annual earnings, is not enough. Perrier appeals to those affluent people who also buy expensive cars and high-fashion merchandise.

To capitalize on their penetration of the U.S. market, Perrier has become the exclusive importer of Lindt chocolate from Switzerland and a fruit preserve called Bonne Maman of France. The campaign includes repackaging, sampling, and a high-powered, carefully directed advertising campaign. Lindt's sales have grown from $1 million to $15 million since 1982 and Bonne Maman from $1.5 million to $5 million in one year.

The field of psychographics is new, and no universal definition has been agreed upon. A good working definition for our purposes is that *psychographics* is the study of personality, life-style, and consumption patterns.

The advantages of psychographic segmentation are as follows:

1. It helps to narrow the target market. With psychographic segmentation, the marketing manager need not select the total population of workers between 40 and 50 years of age who are earning between $35,000 and $50,000. Instead, he or she can select from this population those who are outdoor types, those who are traditional thinkers, or those who display any other characteristic that fits the product.

2. Increased knowledge of the target market can improve both the promotional message and the media by which it is carried. For example, the mes-

sage can be pitched directly at the outdoor types and carried by media likely to attract their attention.

3. As more is known about a product's consumer, new products or refinements of existing products can be better keyed to buying patterns. This should result in improved product success.

4. Again, as more is known of the target market, the product can be placed in areas most likely to be used by consumers whose personality characteristics and living habits are as well known to the marketer as their age, sex, and economic standing.

Typical Research

Perhaps the best way to explain psychographic segmentation is to go through the findings of a particular research effort. The following was the result reported from a study made by the Newspaper Advertising Bureau, based on a psychographic questionnaire to which four thousand people responded. The purpose of the research was to categorize males and females into psychographic groups and to define the consumption patterns of each group. Following is the psychographic segmentation of the males.

Group I—"the quiet family man"—8 percent. A self-sufficient man who wants to be left alone and is basically shy. He tries to be as little involved with community life as possible. His life revolves around the family, simple work, and television viewing. He has a marked fantasy life. As a shopper, he is less drawn to consumer goods and pleasures than are other men.

Group II—"the traditionalist"—16 percent. A man who feels secure, has self-esteem, follows conventional rules. He is proper and respectable, regards himself as altruistic and interested in the welfare of others. As a shopper, he is conservative—he likes popular brands and well-known manufacturers. Figure 4–5 features a product that this psychographic group would buy.

Group III—"the discontented man"—12 percent. A man who is likely to be dissatisfied with his work. He feels bypassed by life, dreams of better jobs, more money, and more security. He tends to be distrustful and socially aloof; as a buyer, he is quite price conscious.

Group IV—"the ethical highbrow"—14 percent. A very concerned man, sensitive to people's needs; basically puritanical; content with family life, friends, and work; interested in culture, religion, and social reform. As a consumer he is interested in quality, which may at times justify greater expenditures.

Group V—"the pleasure-oriented man"—9 percent. A man who tends to emphasize his masculinity and reject whatever appears to be soft and femi-

FIGURE 4–5   The Acura Legend sedan LS, a product for the "traditionalist." (*Courtesy:* Acura Automobile Division.)

nine. He views himself as a leader, is self-centered, dislikes his work or job, and seeks immediate gratification for his needs. He is an impulsive buyer, likely to buy products with a masculine image.

Group VI—"the achiever"—11 percent. A hard-working man, dedicated to success and all that it implies: social prestige, power, and money. He is in favor of diversity, is adventurous about leisure-time pursuits, is stylish— likes good food, music, and the like. As a consumer, he is status conscious, a thoughtful and discriminating buyer.

Group VII—"the he-man"—19 percent. A gregarious man who likes action and seeks an exciting and dramatic life. He thinks of himself as capable and dominant; tends to be more of a bachelor than a family man, even after marriage. The products he buys and brands preferred are likely to have "self-expressive value," especially a "man-of-action" dimension. Figure 4–6 features products earmarked for this group.

Group VIII—"the sophisticated man"—10 percent. A man who is likely to be an intellectual. He is concerned about social issues, and admires people with artistic and intellectual achievements. Socially cosmopolitan, with broad interests, he wants to be dominant and a leader. As a consumer, he is attracted to the unique and fashionable.

FIGURE 4–6   The Harley-Davidson motorcycles and leathers are examples of products sought by the "he-man." (*Courtesy:* Harley-Davidson, Inc.)

The concept of market segmentation, particularly psychographics, is relatively new, and upon its arrival on the scene in the 1950s, its logic immediately caught the imagination of marketing specialists. At the present time, market segmentation is a widely used tool of scientific marketing. This is despite the fact that research in the area has not always shown a positive result. Some relatively negative research findings follow.

Social Class. Considerable segmentation research has been done in the area of social class. To be sure, differences do appear according to social class. For example, types of retailers preferred, spending patterns, and product differences seem to vary by social class. Similarly, preferences in television viewing are different. However, the differences are so narrow, and the overlap so great, that it becomes difficult to predict product preference based on social class.

Personality. In the area of personality, product preferences by various types of personalities are apparent but are too small to be of great importance. Thus, although there are personality differences between owners of convertibles and other automobiles, the differences are too slight to enable prediction. The same is true for smokers versus nonsmokers, and male heads of household as opposed to female.

Demographics. A study attempting to determine the relationship between toilet-tissue purchasing and fifteen demographic variables came up with no positive findings. Similar studies involving coffee, tea, and beer showed similar results.

Despite these negative or, at best, inconclusive results, market segmentation remains a vital and basic area of marketing research. Perhaps the lack of scientific confirmation is due to faulty research. For example, in the area of personality, the researcher usually uses a questionnaire to classify his subject according to personality type. Most psychologists question the reliability of this type of questionnaire.

The foregoing discussion of market segmentation should not be considered a criticism of the whole concept. No one would question, for example, the fact that babies eat baby food, that the number of households is a valid predictor of future furniture sales, or that men buy razor blades. The point is that marketing people must consider the type of market segmentation before making important decisions based upon the findings.

Important Points in the Chapter

1. Success in today's market requires in-depth knowledge of potential customers. With this understanding, the marketing mix can be keyed to ensure customer acceptance.

2. Most products are not aimed at the total market. Instead, a specific segment of the total market is selected, these prospects intensely studied, and marketing efforts are aimed at the chosen targets.

3. The study of population patterns, economic strata, and similar demo-

graphic information is required both to select the target and to design the production and marketing efforts.

4. As in the case with all consumer information, demographic information is constantly changing, and the study of these areas must be ongoing.

5. Family spending patterns were first described by Engels in 1857. With slight modifications, his findings are still valid. They describe the effect of an increase in income on expenditures for food, clothing, and so on.

6. Psychographics attempt to improve the marketer's understanding of his customers by adding information on life-styles, customer self-perception, and other psychological and sociological data. This is a relatively new area and, as yet, not completely accepted.

Review Questions

1. Define *target market* and discuss its importance in relation to business success.

2. What is market segmentation? Give examples.

3. Discuss probable future population trends in the United States.

4. Indicate two population shifts and explain their importance to marketing.

5. There is a trend toward an increased number of women in the labor force. Discuss this in relation to market planning.

6. Our age patterns are changing. In what way? How will marketing be affected?

7. Explain family status in terms of four types of households. Explain the unusual buying patterns of each.

8. We are witnessing two new classifications of household groupings. Discuss them.

9. Discuss trends in the number of households. Describe the producers that would be involved in changes in the number of households.

10. Since America is a melting pot, explain the importance of demographic information on national origin.

11. Explain recent changes in the importance of demographic information on education.

12. Indicate two important trends in income levels.

13. Define *discretionary income*. Explain its importance.

14. What is the effect of an increase in income on the percentage of income spent on housing? Why?

15. What is the effect of an increase in income on the percentage of income spent for food? Why?

16. Define and explain the uses of psychographics.

17. What advantages does psychographics offer?

18. Give some examples of the failure of psychographics to attain its promise.

19. Discuss reasons for the occasional failure of psychographic research.

20. Do you think psychographics has a future? Why?

Case Problem

The Apex Construction Company is the builder of a highly successful condominium in Dallas, Texas. (A condominium is an apartment house in which the individuals own their own apartments and share in the ownership and maintenance of such common facilities as the corridors, gardens, roofs, and heating equipment.) The building was designed to accommodate retired persons. In addition to building and selling the units, Apex operates the building on a long-term contract for the apartment owners. The operation is geared to the needs of well-to-do elderly persons. It provides for optional linen service, maid service, protection, and other services that are demanded by the residents. This, plus the apartment design (small, convenient to maintain, and terraced), has resulted in the rapid, profitable sale of the units and a long-term lucrative operating contract.

The success of the Dallas operation has provided Apex's management with the financial means and know-how to expand. They are searching for a new site and have decided to locate in a warm-weather area that is attractive to retired couples. At present there are two locations of interest to them. One is in St. Petersburg, Florida, the other in the vicinity of New Orleans, Louisiana.

Questions

1. In comparing the two locations, indicate the information concerning population and income you would require.

2. Explain the reason for your selection.

5

THE INDUSTRIAL MARKET

Upon completion of the chapter, you will be able to:

1. Define and provide examples of derived demand, inelastic demand, and fluctuating demand.
2. Discuss industrial buyers in terms of their skills and the nonproduct demands that they make on their suppliers.
3. Describe the habits of the industrial buyer, including direct buying, size of orders, frequency of purchase, and negotiating time.
4. Define and discuss reciprocity.
5. Give the advantages and disadvantages of leasing, including possible problems that may arise as a result of the use of this procedure.

CAN I PLAY GAMES WITH IT?

Probably not a day goes by when, as consumers, we are not bombarded either on television or in the print media with the latest in computer technology. Whether it's MacIntosh, IBM, or any of the others in the enormously expanding field, the message to the consumer is one that combines rational as well as emotional buying motives. Computer manufacturers are currently spending millions of dollars on promotional campaigns designed to make *their* product most appealing. "Over 200 programs for entertainment" is presently making the rounds of IBM's personal computer advertisements. Was the computer initially intended to be marketed as a fun tool or as a business tool? The latter, most assuredly!

When a company is going to try to motivate the industrial market, it doesn't utilize the same approach as it does for the consumer market. Neither the appeal to the senses such as taste nor to personal satisfaction such as prestige and status is considered in the marketing plan. "Can I play games with it?" is not the question which needs answering. The high-powered purchasing agents in the industrial market are rationally motivated. That is, their concerns are those which will bring a profit to their company, facilitate their operations, and so forth.

IBM, for example, is the producer of consumer-oriented computers as well as giant computer installations with capabilities to generate the requirements of the country's largest companies. They recognize that while the basic premise behind both types of computers is similar, the users' requirements differ radically.

With any computer company working within the industrial market, the closing of a sale may take many months. The purchasers are professionals who must be convinced by the industrial salesperson that a particular computer will be able to solve the business's problems. How much storage is there? How many terminals can be tied in? How quickly can breakdowns be repaired? Are there buy-back arrangements? How many canned programs are available? These are typical questions that must be answered.

In the industrial market, personal satisfaction of the purchaser is not the consideration for buying. "Can I play games with it?" is unlikely to enter into the negotiation of the purchase.

INTRODUCTION

In Chapter 6, goods are divided into two main categories: consumer goods and industrial goods. The classification is based upon the purpose for which the goods are intended. Those goods destined to be used in the production of other goods, or the operation of a business, are labeled industrial goods. In this chapter, the marketing of such goods will be discussed.

Considering that annual sales in the industrial market amount to hundreds

Courtesy: Rockville Camera and Video.

of billions of dollars and that the market's growth has been large and constant, it is strange to find that the marketing of industrial goods has been somewhat neglected. There are many reasons. For example, the engineering functions of the producers of industrial goods are usually considered more important than the marketing functions. This results in an overshadowing of the marketing functions, with many marketing decisions being made or at least being shared by nonmarketing experts. Another possible reason for the neglect of industrial marketing is that those who research, write, and teach marketing are not trained in the highly technical problems of the industrial marketing field and tend to steer clear of it. Considering the importance of this vast market, it is obvious that much study must be devoted to bringing the industrial market up to the level of the importance of consumer marketing.

EXTENT OF THE INDUSTRIAL MARKET

The industrial market is very broad. It includes a wide assortment of goods that must be distributed to many different types of users for varied purposes. Full understanding of the industrial market requires knowledge of its characteristics and of the buying habits and motivations of the individual industries that form it.

The enormous size and significance of the industrial market can be deduced from the fact that all the following industry groups are involved:

1. Extractive industries—lumbering, mining, and fishing
2. Agriculture
3. Construction contractors
4. Manufacturers
5. Commercial buyers—wholesale, retail, and service trades
6. Institutions—schools, colleges, and hotels
7. Government—federal, state, and local
8. Transportation, communication, and public utilities

CHARACTERISTICS OF THE INDUSTRIAL MARKET

The industrial market is characterized by certain features that are uniquely different from those involved in the distribution of consumer goods. Several of these are discussed next.

Derived Demand

Since industrial goods are used to produce consumer goods, the demand for industrial goods is derived from (that is, dependent on) the demand for the consumer goods they are destined to produce. Thus, the demand for such industrial goods as steel is dependent on the sale of such consumer goods as automobiles and refrigerators. Similarly, the demand for tanned leather is derived from the consumer demand for leather goods, such as baseball gloves and shoes.

The demand for industrial goods such as installations—the long-lived, expensive, major machinery and equipment of an industrial user, is also derived from consumer demand, but of a long-run nature. Only when consumer demand is expected to increase dramatically in the future does industry make huge expenditures for capital improvements, such as new factories or major producing equipment. Public utilities, for example, must estimate *future* population shifts so that the necessary pipelines, cables, and other equipment will be available when required.

The marketing implications of the derived demand for industrial goods are important, particularly in the area of promotion. Because the demand for industrial goods is ultimately in the hands of the consumer, many producers of goods for the industrial market do not promote their goods to their customers. Instead, they pitch their message to their customer's customers, the consumers. Thus, we find du Pont de Nemours, with no direct consumer sales involved, advertising the characteristics of dacron in the consumer media.

Inelastic Demand

The demand for a product is inelastic when an increase or decrease in the price does not significantly affect the demand for the goods. When a price increase lowers the demand for the commodity, or a price decrease results in an expanded demand, the demand may be referred to as elastic. That is, the demand varies as the price fluctuates.

The demand for industrial goods is derived from the consumer demand for the finished product. Consequently, the demand for the component parts of the consumer goods is based upon consumer demand, not upon the price charged to the producer for the industrial goods. The demand, therefore, for the industrial goods is said to be inelastic. It does not vary with price changes. When the demand for a firm's product is high, it will not let a price increase reduce its purchases. Similarly, if the consumer demand for its product is low, it will not buy more industrial goods, no matter how much the price declines.

Industrial goods are inelastic in many cases because the cost of the individual product is not significant in the total cost of the item. A change in the cost of zippers to a dress manufacturer will have no effect on the amount of zippers bought and very little effect on the profitability of the garment that is manufactured.

Although the total demand for industrial goods should be considered inelastic, the individual firm marketing such goods may be faced with a very elastic demand situation. The dress manufacturer mentioned above has a specific, inelastic demand for the number of zippers equal to the orders for dresses sold. However, another supplier of zippers may be utilized when the price for zippers changes. Price competition is not very common among suppliers of industrial goods, since any lowering of prices is usually quickly met by the competition to the disadvantage of all. Only through monopolistic conditions or outstanding reputation can producers of industrial goods consistently get higher prices than their competitors for a seemingly similar product. IBM's electronic typewriters and Weyerhauser's plywood are examples.

Fluctuating Demand

There is a wide fluctuation in the demand for many types of industrial goods. This is particularly true of the demand for basic installations and accessory equipment, for which the demand varies with general business conditions. During times of business prosperity, producers are generally optimistic about future sales possibilities and invest heavily in expanded production facilities and improved manufacturing equipment. This results in heavy orders of installations and accessory equipment. During periods of business slowdown, manufacturers find their facilities more than adequate to meet the demand of reduced sales, and orders for installations and accessory equipment dwindle. Not only does equipment that is used at less than capacity outlive its expected usefulness, but the general air of pessimism results in the continued use of equipment that should be replaced. This overuse has the effect of building up the demand for new basic equipment when the business cycle turns upward. The result is a widely fluctuating demand for major capital expenditures.

Fluctuation in demand has broad implications for marketers of heavy business goods. For one thing, sales forces cannot be increased or decreased with the rapidity required by the business cycle. Producers, then, have the choice of using middlemen or carrying an excessive sales department during periods of low sales activity. Another problem marketers must face, during conditions of fluctuating demand, is price instability. Producers, faced with periods of declining business activity, cut their selling prices substantially in an effort to keep their production lines in operation. Management of an individual firm must decide whether or not to follow suit in the face of such keen price competition. Promotion is another problem. In times of falling sales, should the promotion budget be increased or decreased?

Expert Buyers

Industrial buyers are generally much more knowledgeable regarding the products they purchase than consumers are. In fact, most large companies maintain purchasing departments that are staffed by well-informed, competent people who are responsible for purchasing. These people may be called upon to justify their choices; they are keenly aware of the importance of their decisions. Only by matching the needs of their firm with the quality, price, and service being offered by their suppliers can they be certain of fulfilling their jobs effectively.

The satisfaction of these well-trained buyers requires particularly knowledgeable sales personnel, who must have the following characteristics:

1. The ability to present the product intelligently.
2. The capability of furnishing prices and delivery dates on request. This is more difficult than it seems, since many industrial goods are sold on a designed-to-order basis.
3. The knowledge necessary to provide up-to-date information on new research, improvements in methods, and uses in the field.
4. The willingness to give prompt attention to errors in shipment, credits, and other areas of disagreement.

Since orders for industrial goods are generally large and lucrative, suppliers of such goods can afford to hire and train highly skilled personnel for selling jobs. This is necessary because the qualifications for sales jobs in the industrial market are stringent.

Few Buyers

Another peculiarity of the industrial market is the relatively small number of buyers involved. Consider, for example, the small number of producers of automobiles, locomotives, or major household appliances. In the area of basic installations, this is even more pronounced. If Consolidated Edison Company requires a new generator to expand its electrical generating capacity, it can only turn to a handful of producers who are capable of manufacturing such equipment.

An example of the number of buyers available to producers of accessory equipment and fabricated parts is found in the fact that General Electric Company produces electric motors for more than 200,000 customers, but over 90 percent of its electric motor business is done with its 5,000 major customers.

As for operating supplies, it has been estimated that 20 percent of the total market can be reached by calling on slightly more than five hundred of the largest users.

This results in violent competition, encouraged in part by industrial buyers who want to have multiple sources of supply and often seek out new suppliers. Moreover, the many small producers for the industrial market are usually equipped to produce a variety of parts, in accordance with customer specifications.

Geographic Concentration

Not only are industrial buyers few in number, they are also highly concentrated geographically. By far the most important manufacturing areas in the United States are clustered in the Northeast and Great Lakes regions. Although there is an increase in the manufacturing importance of the South and Far West, the Northeast's manufacturing concentration has not diminished in size.

Some types of industrial users have their locations dictated by the source of raw materials: for example, the lumber industry in the Northwest and copper mining in Arizona, Montana, and Utah. Other locations are selected as a compromise, so that they offer easy access to both raw materials and large markets. For this reason, there is a high concentration of the steel and automobile industries in the Great Lakes region. When highly trained scientific personnel is a prime business requirement, firms locate at such centers of specialized talent as Long Island, Boston, and the major California cities.

It would seem then that business locations are not arbitrarily selected, but dictated by a variety of sound business reasons. It is unlikely, therefore, that industrial concentrations will be altered without a change in the economic geography of the country, such as a major population shift or new sources of raw materials.

To the industrial suppliers these concentrations are a blessing, since they reduce distribution expenses. By locating near their geographically clustered market, both transportation costs and the expense of maintaining a sales force can be minimized. In turn, the suppliers of the industrial suppliers of the major manufacturers locate in these highly concentrated areas as well. All of this, of course, adds to the density of the manufacturing area.

Quality and Standardization

As the rate of technological advance increases, the importance of high-quality, standardized raw material becomes emphasized. As producers become more scientifically oriented, automatic machinery and highly trained personnel become relatively more important than raw materials. Thus, a highly sophisticated piece of equipment that has been designed to handle a specific type of material in a specific manner is too important in terms of time and money to be forced to remain idle because of poor-quality material, or goods that do not meet specifications. In much the same way, any halt in the production line results in loss of productivity of high-priced labor. Production delays are inevitable, but they should never be caused by low-quality materials or goods that do not conform to specified standards.

In some industries suppliers are able to guarantee quality and standardization with a high degree of certainty. This is not always the case with raw materials. Agricultural products offer a good example. The sugar quantity of grapes is important to wineries. Unfortunately, this cannot be accurately predicted in advance, varying as it does from season to season, farm to farm, and even vine to vine. As a result, wine makers, like many other users of raw materials, must be prepared to make adjustments from the expected quality standard.

On the whole, industrial suppliers, even of raw materials have been able to set realistic standards of quality and conform to them. In industries relying on raw materials, however, quality standards are a source of frequent irritation between the industrial producer and the suppliers.

Reliability of Supply

Just as quality and standardization are important to the industrial market, so is an uninterrupted supply of goods. Anyone who has anxiously awaited the completion of a building for his or her home or office, and who has seen production come to a complete halt because of a minor unavailable part, understands the problem. Among those industrial producers to whom equipment and labor are expensive and important, the firm supplying the necessary industrial goods is chosen as much for its ability to deliver the goods on time as for any other characteristic.

Often, the failure of the source of supply is not the fault of the supplier. Droughts, floods, freezing temperatures, and even strikes may frequently be put into the no-fault category. However, industrial users are frequently willing to pay a premium to large, well-financed suppliers rather than accept similar goods at a reduced price from a weaker competitor. The reasons for this are that enormous losses may be incurred from a forced shutdown because of a failure of the raw-material supply. A minor delay of a few hours causes labor and overhead losses. A cessation that causes a complete production shutdown may lead to cancellation of orders, perhaps permanent loss of customers, and possible loss of a skilled labor force. The dependability of supply is the chief reason for industrial purchasers to refuse to limit their purchases to a single supplier and to be always on the lookout for new sources. Many large users expand vertically (own their raw-material sources) to offset the possibility of shutdowns because of lack of supplies.

INDUSTRIAL BUYING HABITS

To understand effectively the marketing of industrial goods, one must study the habits of industrial buyers. As is the case with all phases of the industrial market, industrial buying habits are different from those of the consumer and relatively unknown to nonmarketers. Although the number of industrial purchasers is considerably smaller than the number of consumer purchasers, they constitute an important segment of marketing because their purchases are enormous compared with the consumer market.

Direct Buying

Most consumer goods are not purchased directly from the producer. Instead, they are bought through middlemen, such as wholesalers and retailers, who purchase in large quantities from producers and sell in smaller quantities to their customers. Although middlemen are important on the industrial scene, they are far less significant than on the consumer market. Both the buyer and the seller of industrial goods benefit from this fact. From the seller's point of view, the concentration of industrial users makes for a small geographic area, easily covered by the seller's salespeople, and the size of the individual industrial order is large enough to warrant a sales force, even to a producer with a limited product line. By cutting out the middleman, producers are able to use the middleman's profits to increase their own profits and to reduce their selling price.

However, manufacturers must be certain that they can perform as efficiently as the middleman. Direct buying benefits industrial customers by ensuring a close contact with their suppliers, on whom they depend for technical information and service.

Industrial buyers are involved in three types of buying situations. These are new task buying, modified rebuying, and straight rebuying.

New task buying is the most complicated. Since the merchandise has never been bought before, a great deal of both internal and external information is needed, specifications must be set, alternatives must be studied, and many people must be involved in the decision.

Modified rebuying occurs when merchandise that has been bought before is reordered with some changes. It is less complicated than new task buying and more involved than straight rebuying. Modified rebuying usually requires some nonpurchasing department involvement.

Straight rebuying is the least complicated. It is handled solely by the purchasing department in a routine fashion.

Large Orders

Basically the reason for the fact that suppliers of industrial goods are able to sell directly to their customers is that, unlike the consumer-customer who might spend $200 on a buying trip, the industrial purchaser may in one order contract for a full year's supply of goods at a cost of thousands of dollars. Consequently, a salesperson making relatively few stops a day can earn a considerable amount of commission. Because of the size of the individual orders, industrial suppliers cannot afford to lose a sale. Consequently, most suppliers pay well to get capable salespeople, are careful to price competitively, and attempt to be extremely exact in their quality control and delivery dates. To do otherwise would jeopardize a profitable customer who would be difficult to replace in the small industrial market.

Infrequent Purchases

Since orders are usually large, they are also infrequently made. This is particularly true in the case of major installations and accessory equipment designed to last for many years. Although less dramatic, purchases of industrial supplies are also not made very often, because the orders, when given, are large.

The infrequency of purchasing poses the problem to many industrial suppliers, particularly those selling major installations and accessory equipment, of not knowing when the customer is in the "buying mood." This may be somewhat offset by advertising in trade periodicals and maintaining contact through occasional visits.

Multiple Influence on Purchases

Despite the fact that industrial goods are frequently bought by a purchasing department consisting of specialists, it is unusual for one person, acting alone, to make the purchasing decision. Although the purchase order will certainly be handled by the purchasing agent, he or she must depend on the people who actually use the equipment or material for advice as to specifications. Commonly, the decision on what to buy is the responsibility of a group of executives who may include production, marketing, and cost-accounting representatives, as well as the purchasing agent.

As far as the marketing of industrial goods is concerned, the salesperson who limits his or her appeal to the purchasing agent alone is likely to miss out. People selling industrial goods must get their product message across to every person who is involved in the purchasing decision. To do this, they must fully understand the customer's manufacturing processes and problems, so that they may alter their pitch to fit every interested person.

Extended Negotiations

Since the size of the typical industrial order is very large and the number of people involved in the purchasing decision is considerable, it follows that the period of negotiation preceding a sale, particularly of major installations, is extended. Another reason for the length of negotiations is that many industrial purchases are made according to exact specifications that require many meetings before a perfect understanding between buyer and seller can be reached. Major installations are frequently purchased through competitive bidding. Where contracts are awarded through competitive bidding, negotiations are lengthened to provide time for the bidders to study the problem and prepare their bids.

Reciprocity

Many industrial firms maintain a policy of reciprocity in their purchasing procedures. That is, where possible, they buy only from firms who buy from them. Reciprocity has long been the rule in such basic industries as oil, steel, rubber, chemicals, and machinery. In today's industrial market, reciprocity has become very widespread. Some firms carefully analyze all of their purchases in an attempt to find potential customers who can be pressured into buying their products under the threat of purchase cancellations. Recent times have seen an increase in the use of reciprocity. This is no doubt due to a tightening of the nation's economic conditions, causing producers to search for ways to offset sagging sales volumes. Moreover, the increase in foreign imports is forcing domestic manufacturers to compete more strongly. Finally, many producers are diversifying their product lines by adding broad lines of new products. Reciprocity both increases the probability that their suppliers can use some of their broad line of product offerings and helps get a new product off the ground.

Generally, purchasing agents oppose reciprocity. They prefer to buy the goods that are best suited to their needs rather than to have to purchase from the suppliers to whom the company sells. However, the pressure placed upon them by the sales department is so great that reciprocity is forced on them. This last argument is somewhat less important than it used to be because in today's market most products are of such a highly standardized quality that an item made by one supplier, who refuses a reciprocal agreement, can be easily produced by another who will accept such an agreement. In the long run, reciprocity probably leads to paying higher prices, since the buyer is not shopping for goods in a competitive market.

The small company suffers most from reciprocity. Unable to fight off the demands of its giant customers, it may lose control of its own destiny. Morale losses may result in both the selling force of the small company and the buying department of its customer.

Catalogs

Producers of operating supplies, fabricated parts, repair parts, and many other standardized, low-cost products rely heavily on catalogs to sell their merchandise. There are two types of catalog selling: common catalogs in which the offerings of many companies are listed and individualized catalogs that are issued by the producer.

An individual catalog can consist of a few pages of products that have been carefully selected from the line or of an expensive book running to hundreds of pages. The Graham Field Surgical Company, a wholesaler and producer of medical supplies, distributes ten thousand catalogs of three hundred pages each to its customers. The company pays about $20 for each of the catalogs and delivers them free of charge. The cost is increased by the subsequent mailings of supplementary sheets that are required by constant changes in the line. Finally, a brand-new catalog is issued every three years to incorporate the product changes and bring the publication up to date. The high catalog cost is necessary, since practically all sales are made by catalog. Salespeople make infrequent visits to customers for the purpose of pushing new items and reminding customers of the firm's existence.

Common catalogs, sometimes referred to as trade directories, are produced by publishing companies. Space in common catalogs is sold to individual suppliers in much the same fashion as advertising space is sold. The information presented in common catalogs is generally limited to the requirements of a particular industry. Examples of such catalogs are the Chemical Engineering and Chemical Materials catalogs of Van Nostrand Reinhold publishing company.

To point up the importance of catalog use in industrial selling, a study of the purchases of about 1,400 products disclosed that 470 of them were made directly by catalog and another 360 resulted from leads found in catalogs.

Multiple Sources of Supply

To manufacturers, a constant source of supply is a critical element of success. They cannot risk limiting their resources to a single supplier who may fail them at a time of peak activity because of strikes, breakdowns, shortages of raw materials, or any other reason. Because of this, industrial buyers habitually seek multiple sources, and people selling them must not expect to be exclusive.

Computerized Buying

In many organizations, a significant amount of routine buying is done automatically by a computer. The computer is programmed, as part of its inventory control function, to compare the goods on hand for each inventory item against a desired inventory level. When the goods on hand fall below the indicated level, the computer automatically prints an order. In such cases, the industrial salesperson must try to get the firm's line into the computer program. This is far more important than the making of an individual sale.

LEASING

There is nothing new in the idea of leasing equipment rather than buying it. Traditionally, shoe manufacturing machinery (United Shoe Machinery Company), computer equipment (IBM), packaging equipment (American Can Company), heavy-construction equipment, and textile equipment have been distributed in this manner. Similarly, locomotives and freight cars have for years been purchased by insurance companies and leased to the railroads. Until recently, however, leasing has been limited to heavy equipment requiring an extensive capital outlay. During the past twenty years the idea of leasing has been extended to less expensive equipment, such as automobiles and trucks. Several major companies have recently come into being whose function it is to buy equipment from manufacturers and lease it to users. Examples of these include the U.S. Leasing Corporation and the National Equipment Leasing Corporation. In addition, such credit companies as the Commercial Credit Corporation and many commercial banks are getting into the act. Current trends seem to indicate a continued expansion of leasing arrangements.

Leasing Advantages—Lessor

Following are some of the reasons for which equipment producers encourage leasing:

1. Leasing requires a much smaller capital outlay and thus increases the number of potential customers. Many firms that could not afford to purchase equipment outright are quite capable of living up to the terms of a lease.
2. The total income from a piece of equipment distributed under a leasing arrangement is greater than that received from an outright sale.
3. The continual producer-customer contact results in a close relationship that may affect the purchase of future equipment, operating supplies for the equipment, and service contracts.

4. Leasing, which generally includes service contracts, ensures producers that their equipment will be used to its best advantage. This promotes the possibility of future sales to the customer and goodwill beyond the customer. Many pieces of equipment that are sold outright perform poorly because of inefficient servicing by outsiders. This is frequently damaging to the goodwill of the manufacturer.

5. In the rare instances in which a patent may give the manufacturer a monopoly, leasing brings in far greater profits than could possibly be obtained in an outright sale. Pitney Bowes postage meters are an example of such a situation.

6. Leasing offers an excellent method of distributing a new, untried product. A prospective customer, unwilling to risk the cost of an outright purchase, might be willing to enter a leasing agreement that may be canceled after a few months if the equipment proves unsatisfactory.

Leasing Advantages—Lessee

Following are the advantages of leasing to the lessee:

1. The smaller financial investment required by a leasing arrangement permits the use of capital for other purposes.

2. There are income tax savings involved with rentals, since the rent payments (a deductible expense) are usually higher than the depreciation deduction that would be taken on the same equipment if it were owned outright.

3. There is no hesitation in trading in obsolete equipment when it is rented. Fully owned equipment, particularly when business is slow, is not so quickly replaced.

4. It is to the owner's advantage, since he or she owns the equipment, to keep it in perfect condition. This guarantees effective servicing.

5. By leasing, a firm can test new equipment with a substantially reduced risk.

6. Equipment can be rented only when needed, or paid for only when used.

Leasing Problems

Although many firms reap substantial benefits from leasing rather than purchasing, there are problems involved as well. First, from the point of view of the lessor, leasing requires an enormous amount of capital, since all the machines being used by customers belong to him or her. Second, the risks of obsolescence, instead of being spread out among many users, fall on the shoulders of the producer of the equipment. These problems result in higher machinery costs, which are ultimately passed on to the consumer as higher prices.

PROMOTING INDUSTRIAL GOODS

The promotion of industrial goods differs from that of consumer goods in that there are far fewer, but better informed potential customers. Industrial buyers are very interested in quality, price, and the dependability of supply. The advertising aimed at them is usually rational as opposed to emotional. That is, they are more interested in performance than in pretty patterns.

Since the market is small, mass selling is ruled out in favor of direct mail. When media are used, they are generally trade journals, where technically oriented copy is displayed. Unlike consumer advertising, industrial promotion is not carried on in expectation of a sale, but rather of a lead to be followed up by a salesperson.

Prominently featured in many industrial promotions are the research and development capabilities of suppliers, their excellent service facilities, and the technical help furnished to customers.

Trade Shows

Many industries hold trade shows periodically. Once or more a year (frequently in a different city each year) trade shows are held to offer manufacturers the opportunities to show their lines and to make contacts with wholesalers and retailers. Trade shows also give producers the opportunity to learn of new developments in the industry, introduce new sales personnel, fill personnel needs, and demonstrate new equipment.

In recent years trade shows have been located in resort cities, where they have become a social as well as a business event. It is likely that trade shows are as important for cementing personal relationships between buyers and sellers as they are for making actual sales.

Important Points in the Chapter _____

1. The demand for industrial goods is dependent on the demand for the consumer products for which they will be used. Consequently, price has little effect on the demand for industrial goods. This is only true of total demand for a particular industrial product. The price charged by an individual producer for his or her product will affect its demand. The demand for industrial goods fluctuates widely with general business conditions.

2. Industrial goods are purchased by expert buyers in a geographically concentrated area. Industrial buyers are much fewer in number than consumer buyers and insist upon quality, standardization, and reliability of supply.

3. Industrial goods are usually bought in infrequent, large lots, directly from the producer. Because of the complexity of the orders, many people are involved in the buying decision and negotiations tend to be extensive.

4. Reciprocity—pressuring suppliers to buy the purchaser's product, is increasing as industrial competition becomes more severe.

5. Producers of operating supplies, fabricated parts, repair parts, and other standardized low-cost products use catalogs to sell their products. The use of catalogs minimizes the need for sales personnel.

6. There is a growing trend toward the lease of equipment instead of outright purchase. This increases the potential market of equipment producers and reduces the cash outlay of the equipment user.

7. The most important factor in the distribution of industrial goods is personal selling. In addition to the characteristics required by any salesperson, the industrial salesperson must be technically trained in the product area as well as in the problems of this particular group of customers. Frequently, engineering and scientific skills are required.

8. The promotion of industrial goods is generally limited to rational appeals for leads through direct mail or trade journals. Trade shows offer industrial producers an opportunity to show their lines, stay up-to-date, and socialize with their customers.

Review Questions

1. Discuss the industrial market in terms of types of goods handled, types of customers, and size.

2. What is derived demand? Differentiate between the derived demand for office supplies and for major installations.

3. Explain the effect of consumer demand on the industrial market in relation to the promotion of industrial goods.

4. A manufacturer of small electric motors for the industrial market must take into account the inelasticity of the demand for the product. How does this affect the total industry? The individual producer?

5. Discuss the fluctuating demand for industrial products. What effect does it have on the marketing of major installations?

6. What characteristics are required for a salesperson of industrial products?

7. How can a producer selling his or her products on the industrial market afford to employ high-priced sales personnel for his limited line of products?

8. Explain the reasons for the geographic concentration of the industrial market. How does this affect the distribution of industrial goods?

9. Why are industrial producers willing to pay a premium for high-quality, standardized products?

10. Discuss the standardization problems facing users of raw material. How may these problems be offset?

11. Some producers for the industrial market are able to get higher prices for their products than their competitors, despite a similarity of quality. Discuss.

12. Habitually, industrial buyers purchase directly from their suppliers. Why? What are the advantages to the buyer? The seller?

13. Explain the effect of buying in large orders on the marketing of industrial goods. How does this affect the frequency of purchases?

14. What is meant by multiple influence on industrial purchases? What problems does this create in the selling of industrial goods?

15. Define *reciprocity*. What are its advantages and disadvantages to a large firm? A small firm?

16. How are catalogs used on the industrial market? Describe a common catalog and an individualized catalog.

17. Explain the leasing of industrial goods. Give examples. What are the advantages and disadvantages of leasing to the producer of the equipment?

18. Discuss the advantages and disadvantages of leasing to the firm renting the equipment.

19. How are industrial goods promoted?

20. What is a trade show? What are its purposes?

Case Problems

Case Problem 1

The Fit-Rite Shoe Manufacturing Corporation has been a manufacturer of high-style, popularly-priced ladies' shoes for the past eight years. During that time, thanks to the superb style selection of the owners, the company has been extremely successful.

Each year's profits after taxes have been reinvested in the business. As a result, Fit-Rite's sales and profits have soared. At the present time the company is an industry leader with a well-earned reputation for style and value.

The extremely rapid growth of the company has required enormous demands on the company's working capital. All profits had to be immediately reinvested in expanded inventories and manufacturing facilities. At times the shortage of cash has been chronic and Fit-Rite has been forced to mortgage its assets and borrow heavily from banks.

At the moment the company's salespeople are bringing in sales far in excess of its production capacity. Undoubtedly, further expansion is warranted, but the capital required for such growth is simply not available.

The board of directors of Fit-Rite has been studying a proposal by the American Shoe Machine Manufacturing Corporation to lease the equipment required for the proposed expansion.

Questions

1. What information would be needed to make the leasing decision?
2. What are the advantages and disadvantages of leasing?
3. Should Fit-Rite expand by leasing?

Case Problem 2

The Do-All Supply Company is a producer of plastic containers for the industrial market. Its operation consists of buying plastic in powdered form, adding dyes and certain chemicals, and molding containers to the specifications of its industrial customers. It is located in an industrial area and all its customers are within a 200-mile radius of the plant.

Do-All is a family-owned company with executives comprised of a father and two daughters. The business is small but very lucrative. Sales are handled by the father, with very little effort, since all customers have been with the firm for many years and a close social relationship exists between the firm and its clients. Orders are usually large, long-term commitments which, thanks to Do-All's reputation for quality, fair prices, service, and dependability, require little negotiation.

Recently Do-All's largest customer (25 percent of gross sales) was bought out by a large chemical company. The new management has informed Do-All that if its present contracts are renewed, it should buy its raw materials from the new owners. Although the prices charged by the new chemical company are slightly higher than the amount Do-All is presently paying, the profits would still be considerable. In addition, the new company has indicated that if Do-All cooperates, it might also be given business from other units controlled by the new owners.

Questions

1. Discuss the advantages and disadvantages of the new setup.
2. What would you advise?

6

CLASSIFICATION OF GOODS: CONSUMER AND INDUSTRIAL

Learning Objectives

Upon completion of the chapter, you will be able to:

1. Explain the importance to marketers of the classification of goods.

2. Define convenience goods and describe the usual market strategy for such goods.

3. Define shopping goods and describe the usual market strategy for such goods.

4. Define specialty goods and describe the usual market strategy for such goods.

5. Define impulse goods and describe the usual market strategy for such goods.

6. Define emergency goods and describe the usual market strategy for such goods.

7. List six categories of industrial goods, provide examples of each, and discuss the market strategy for each type.

BEST FOOT FORWARD

High prices, high markup, and limited distribution are some of the characteristics of shopping goods. Convenience goods, on the other hand, are very widely distributed, and because of the competition carry a small markup. Getting customers to accept shopping goods as convenience goods would be a marketer's dream come true. Achieving the high volume of convenience goods while maintaining the high profit margin of shopping goods is the best of both worlds.

L'eggs did it! L'eggs took its high-quality, high-priced pantyhose and with the help of a clever promotion campaign and brilliant packaging, was able to place them in drugstores and supermarkets with outstanding success. Prior to L'eggs' success, high-priced pantyhose were sold only in specialty stores and department stores.

Is the marketing of L'eggs really a miracle, or is the standard definition of convenience goods too limited? The test is customer acceptance! Since this was very positive for L'eggs, quality pantyhose had previously been misclassified. Perhaps the definition of convenience goods should be that anything customers will accept as convenience goods should be classified as convenience goods. This opens a whole new area of marketing thinking. Surely there are other so-called shopping goods that have previously been placed in outlets that offer limited sales, that could be moved into the mass sales market. L'eggs did it by disregarding traditional classification approaches, and other products can probably be similarly reclassified. L'eggs had certain advantages. Its product is small and it was able to design a point-of-purchase display that required very little space. Supermarkets, whose space is at a premium, were willing to give L'eggs a chance. There must be other approaches that will work for other products.

Modern marketing demands new ideas. No matter how successful the product is and how effective the rest of the marketing mix, there is always a better way.

INTRODUCTION

As we have previously discussed, the marketing manager's responsibility can be summed up as the selection of the proper marketing mix and the constant adjustment of that mix to changing market patterns. Since different products require different marketing mixes, marketing strategy must begin with the proper classification of the product. That is, although dresses and hosiery are both women's clothing, they require a different marketing mix to be successfully distributed. As is frequently the case with general classification systems, many products are difficult to place into specific groups. They either fit into more than one of the arbitrarily established categories, or into none of them. However, if the items fit—and generally they do—marketers have the advantage of keying their strategy to the preferred marketing mix for their types of goods.

Hosiery products creatively packaged and sold as a convenience good. (*Courtesy:* Sara Lee Corporation.)

CONSUMER GOODS AND INDUSTRIAL GOODS

Products are classified as either consumer goods or industrial goods. Consumer goods and services are produced for the personal use of the ultimate consumer. Industrial goods and services are produced for industrial purposes; they will be used to produce other goods and services or to facilitate the operation of a business. Many products, such as lighting fixtures, stationery, typewriters, and electrical services, can be classified as both industrial and consumer goods. The proper classification should not be based on the type of goods but on the type of purchaser (consumer or industrial), since the marketing strategy must be entirely different for each type.

CONSUMER GOODS

Many classifications are possible, but the most common method of differentiating among goods is to sort them according to the habits and motivations of the buyers, the starting point of any good marketing strategy.

There are five categories of goods based on consumer buying habits. Each category requires a separate marketing strategy. When marketers relate their product to one of these classifications, they can make use of proved selling methods for that type of goods. The categories are

1. Convenience goods.
2. Shopping goods.
3. Specialty goods.
4. Impulse goods.
5. Emergency goods.

We shall define these classifications and discuss the marketing strategy that is best suited to each of them.

Convenience Goods

Convenience goods are bought with a minimum of shopping effort. Typical examples are cigarettes, candy, chewing gum, newspapers, magazines, and most grocery products. Some of the characteristics of convenience goods are

1. They are nondurable—they are quickly used up and frequently purchased.
2. They are often bought by brands.
3. They are inexpensive.
4. They are bought according to habit, and the buying decision is made quickly and easily. In buying cigarettes and gasoline, for example, the consumer knows his or her preference and habitually buys the same brand at the same store without price and quality comparison among competing brands.

Market Strategy.   The market strategy for convenience goods is characterized by an emphasis on *convenience*, affecting the marketing mix in the following ways:

Place.   Since shopping convenience is of utmost importance, place is a vital factor. Customers will not go out of their way to purchase convenience goods.

Frequently, the purchase is not even planned. Consequently, to be successfully marketed, convenience goods must be placed in as many outlets as possible. Customers will not search for these goods and they must be placed in front of them wherever possible. For this reason, there is constant competition among supermarket suppliers for the more noticeable eye-level shelves. Convenience goods require minimum shopping effort and maximum exposure. Their distribution requires a large sales force, and many producers turn to middlemen to perform the place function. This is economically sound because the middlemen can place the lines of many manufacturers at once, thereby reducing the placing cost for each line.

Price.   Although brand identification is important in the marketing of convenience goods, most consumers believe that competing goods are similar in quality. As a result, most convenience goods are very competitively priced, and an increase in the price of one producer's merchandise might encourage the customer to switch to another brand. Thus, an increase of a few cents a gallon of gasoline often results in a change of brands. On the other hand, many customers are willing to pay a premium price for an increase in shopping convenience. Home delivery of newspapers, milk, and bakery products are examples of this.

Promotion.   Convenience goods require mass selling to be successful; therefore, they need large promotional budgets. The industrial giants who produce most of these goods are among the largest advertisers in the nation. Their promotion is aimed at brand identification.

It is common practice among distributors of convenience goods to invest heavily in in-store and point-of-purchase displays. Liquor dealers go so far as to trim the windows of stores at no charge to ensure the preferential display of their products.

Shopping Goods

Shopping goods are purchased only after making comparisons as to the suitability, price, quality, and style of the item. Before purchasing such goods, the shopper usually visits several stores. Typical shopping goods are furniture, automobiles, coats, and appliances. Some of the characteristics of shopping goods are

1. They are relatively durable and long-lasting.
2. They are generally high-priced items.
3. They do not stress brand identification.
4. They require much shopping time and a difficult buying decision.

There are two types of shopping goods, homogeneous goods and heterogeneous goods.

Homogeneous Goods.   These are the goods that the consumer considers to be of equal suitability, quality, and styling. Comparison with competing merchandise is limited to price. Some examples of homogeneous goods are refrigerators and television sets.

Heterogeneous Goods.   These are the goods that the consumer compares for suitability, quality, and styling, with price relatively unimportant, but not totally ignored. Some examples of heterogeneous goods are furniture and famous-brand clothing.

Shoppers frequently do not know all the characteristics of the goods they buy—as they do when buying convenience goods—and part of the shopping effort is spent learning about the product. An automobile purchaser, for example, learns about the features of a particular model from the salesperson. This extra time spent in shopping is relatively unimportant because the purchase of shopping goods is generally planned and there is no rush to get the product.

Market Strategy.   As in all market planning, the strategy used in distributing shopping goods is based on the target customer's habits and motivations.

Place.   For shopping goods the customer is willing to visit more than one store. As a result, shopping goods do not require a maximum number of outlets. Producers place their merchandise in relatively few stores, generally near others, and in similar types of shops so that it is convenient for customers to make comparisons. In addition, retailers carrying shopping goods do not want competition from the same manufacturer's goods at a nearby store, so frequently they are granted territorial exclusivity. A woman interested in a coat will go to a location that has several stores at which she can make comparisons. Any store located by itself is not likely to be visited. As far as place is concerned, both heterogeneous and homogeneous goods are given the same treatment. Because the number of retail outlets is comparatively small, many producers of shopping goods maintain their own sales staffs and do not use middlemen for the distribution of their products.

Price.   Regarding price, there is a sharp differentiation between homogeneous and heterogeneous shopping goods. Shoppers for homogeneous goods are chiefly interested in price, and any variation in selling price generally has an immediate and drastic effect on sales volume and profits. Consequently, homogeneous goods are highly competitive in price and yield relatively small profits.

Price is a secondary factor in the sale of heterogeneous shopping goods. Furniture, clothing, and jewelry are bought for reasons of style and quality, resulting in higher markups and better profitability. Heterogeneous shopping goods have in general a highly individual styling. This makes comparisons difficult. Selections depend more on suitability and taste than on price differences.

Promotion.   The advertising of both homogeneous and heterogeneous shopping goods is usually the responsibility of the retailer, although many producers encourage the promotion of their products by means of advertising allowances or outright cash grants.

Large manufacturers of nationally distributed products indulge in institutional advertising. This is a means of drawing the public's attention to the brand name. Unlike retail advertising, which is usually promotion- or product-oriented, institutional advertising is concerned with a company's overall image in style and quality rather than with the features of specific items in its line.

Although the retail advertising of homogeneous shopping goods attempts to point out the important features of the product, the main advertising thrust is in the area of price. Advertisers of heterogeneous shopping goods, on the other hand, are more interested in informing the public of the quality and styling of their merchandise.

Specialty Goods

Specialty goods are those products for which consumers are willing to make a special purchasing effort. Substitutions will not be made because of a brand name or a characteristic that the customer insists upon. Typical are gourmet foods, stereo components, stamps for collectors, or prestige-brand men's suits. Shoppers for these goods are willing to travel to far-out locations at which they can buy them. They do not make comparisons before purchasing and are relatively disinterested in price. Specialty goods are generally found in low as well as high price ranges and are mostly sold either in a high-image retail store or under a thoroughly accepted brand name (Corning Ware, Hickey-Freeman men's suits, and Rolls-Royce automobiles).

Market Strategy.   Every producer would like his product to be classified under the specialty-goods label. Such merchandise is the most sought after and yields the highest profits. Once this level is attained, the marketing mix chosen must be carefully planned.

Place.   Characteristic of specialty goods is the customer's insistence on the particular product. With regard to place, this insistence brings about a willingness to travel a considerable distance to make the purchase. As a result, specialty goods are generally restricted to single outlets in each geographical area. Since the outlets are few in number, distribution brings minor problems and is inexpensive. Middlemen are rarely found in the distributive channels of specialty goods. This permits a very close, cooperative relationship between the manufacturer and the retailer, which works to the benefit of both parties.

Price.   Here again, the customer's insistence on the product sets the stage for the market strategy. Producers of specialty goods are able to capitalize on the

FIGURE 6–1   A Häagen-Dazs product. (*Courtesy:* Pillsbury Company.)

customer's degree of motivation for the product by charging a relatively high price for it. This should not be understood to mean that producers of specialty goods set extravagant prices. Remember, every producer tries to get his product into the specialty goods category. Unusually high prices form one of the surest ways to lose that advantage. However, the markup on specialty goods is usually higher than normal.

Promotion.   Much of the advertising of specialty goods is done by retailers, frequently with producer cooperation. Such mass media as newspapers and billboards are used. The advertisements generally serve to remind the public where a product can be bought; they do not contain any specific information. The buying public is capricious. Once a product has achieved the specialty goods status, a high advertising budget is required to keep it there.

More and more specialty foods are being brought to the marketplace to satisfy the needs of the consumer. One product that fits this description is Häagen-Dazs ice cream. While most ice creams used to fall into the convenience category, the introduction of Häagen-Dazs set this product apart from most other entries. Its use of a European sounding name (it's actually the Pillsbury Co which is based in Teaneck, N.J.), has helped make this a specialty product. While many "pricey" ice creams have tried to copy Häagen-Dazs, it still is the leader in sales in specialty ice cream. Figure 6–1 features a Häagen-Dazs product.

Impulse Goods

Many authors consider impulse goods to be a specific type of convenience goods. By definition, impulse goods are those bought without planning. A woman goes to a supermarket with a shopping list. If she buys a box of strawberries that was not on her list, that purchase is impulsive. Impulse goods are relatively low-priced products, such as drugs, toys, food, inexpensive clothing, and cosmetics.

Market Strategy.   The market strategy for impulse goods is the same as that for convenience goods in general.

Place.   Impulse goods do not compete with other similar products. Instead, they are in competition with other goods that could take a part of the consumer's dollar. A child with a quarter to spend can buy either candy or ice cream. His selection frequently depends upon the product that is most prominently displayed. Impulse goods must be widely placed in heavy traffic areas. They should be displayed on the most obvious shelves. The checkout counter in most supermarkets is a prime location for these items.

Price.   As is the case with most other convenience goods, impulse goods are highly competitive and sensitive to price differences. One reason is that substitutions are easily made. The shopper who sees a candy bar will not buy it if it is overpriced, since a cheaper one is available a few steps away.

Promotion.   Impulse goods require massive advertising in the largest media. Such advertising is the responsibility of the producer, who must impress not only the consumer but also retailers, to ensure their willingness to give the product prime display space.

Since the location in the store is vital to the success of impulse products, manufacturers devote high budgets to point-of-purchase and in-store displays.

Emergency Goods

Emergency goods must be purchased immediately to fill an urgent need. They may be convenience goods—for example, a mother discovers that she is out of milk after the stores are closed—or shopping goods—for example, a sudden need for an umbrella.

Market Strategy.   Most of the goods sold under emergency conditions are convenience goods. Market strategy for emergency goods is chiefly concerned with getting them to the places where the customer expects them.

Place.   A customer, needing goods in an emergency, has an idea of where they can be found. A woman with unexpected Sunday company knows where to find an open store. The producer whose goods are carried by that store will make the sale.

Many retailers stock emergency goods in anticipation of their customers needs. The neighborhood gas station sells very few snow tires—until it snows. Small downtown stores suddenly come up with umbrellas and rubbers in a rainstorm.

Price.   In return for the convenience of getting the goods in an emergency, the customer is willing to pay a higher than normal price. The neighborhood grocer can only compete with the supermarket giants by taking the role of an emergency store and remaining open seven days a week and far into the night. In return for this service, customers are willing to pay a premium for their foodstuffs.

Promotion.   A manufacturer promoting his convenience goods is promoting his emergency goods at the same time, since they constitute the identical merchandise sold under a different condition.

For the most part, emergency goods are sold in neighborhood stores, and the necessary promotion requires nothing more than informing the neighborhood customers of the store's location and working hours. This may be done by handbills, limited direct mailings, local newspaper advertising, or signs in the window.

Difficulty in Classification

Most marketing managers find it very difficult to classify their goods according to the categories just discussed. A motel is a good example of this. A tired salesperson might take the first motel she comes to (a convenience good). Another motorist may keep driving until he finds the best value (a shopping good). Yet another driver may reserve a room in advance in the particular spot she considers best (a specialty good). It is not at all unusual to find the same product classified in different ways, both by different shoppers and by the same shopper at different times. This does not mean that a marketing strategy based on product classification is worthless. An alert marketer can classify a product in two or more categories and employ a separate marketing strategy and distribution channels for each category, with the most important category getting the major effort.

Since the marketing mix (market strategy) is based upon product classification, the system described earlier for classifying goods is important. However, there is an unquestionable need for more research in this area.

A MARKETING PROFILE

The Goodyear Tire & Rubber Company

When Frank A. Seiberling founded the Goodyear Tire & Rubber Company in 1898, little did he know that it would develop into the world's first billion-dollar rubber company. He was the 38-year-old son of an entrepreneur who developed successful businesses in Akron, Ohio. The depression of the 1890s brought downfall to all the family businesses and a chance meeting, in Chicago, with H. C. Nelbs, an Ohio businessman. Seiberling purchased a small plant from Nelbs for $13,500, and through borrowing from friends and relatives, Seiberling was able to begin his operation. The Goodyear Tire & Rubber Company was born. Eighteen years later, the company had become the world's largest tire company, with sales of $100 million.

Today, Goodyear is the industry's giant. Its tire and rubber product sales exceed $9 billion, and it employs 135,000 workers in 101 manufacturing facilities in 28 countries. Despite its being the nation's leading radial tire producer, and an important factor in the U.S. aerospace program, it continues to carefully employ every marketing tool to maintain its position.

Goodyear is the industry's largest advertiser, its 1988 advertising budget exceeding $95 million. Its world-famous blimps are seen by millions in the skies and on television. Its U.S. blimps regularly roam the country on carefully arranged public relations schedules participating in charitable events, public service programs, municipality anniversary celebrations, ecological studies, and other national events. Every major sporting event such as the World Series features a Goodyear blimp.

Whether it's the tires on our automobiles, the rubber surfaces of the people movers in airports, the moving ramps in major stores, the tires on the autoracers' cars, breakwaters of scrap tires to protect the shorelines, or commercial tires for trucks and farm vehicles, Goodyear sets the pace for the industry.

INDUSTRIAL GOODS

In many cases the same goods may be classified as industrial or consumer goods, but it is important that they be classified and distributed separately, since the market strategies required in the distribution of the two types are completely different.

FIGURE 6–2   Commercial tires for farm equipment. (*Courtesy:* Goodyear Tire & Rubber Company.)

Most of the discussion of consumer goods was familiar to the reader. The products' names were commonplace, the places in which such products were to be found were widely known, and the examples of the promotion of the goods were always in the public eye. The industrial market, on the other hand, involves massive annual sales, employs millions of people, is widely dispersed throughout the country, but is relatively unknown to the consuming public. Industrial goods rarely make the newspapers, are not promoted in the consumer media, and are not labeled with familiar brand names.

CLASSIFICATION OF INDUSTRIAL GOODS

Industrial goods may be divided into the following categories:

1. Raw materials
2. Fabricating materials and parts
3. Installations
4. Accessory equipment
5. Supplies
6. Services

FIGURE 6–3   Tire production in Danville, Virginia. (*Courtesy:* Goodyear Tire & Rubber Company.)

Raw Materials

Raw materials are industrial goods that will be used in the production of other goods. Such goods may be sold in their natural state or processed to the extent necessary to ensure safety or economy of shipping or handling. Iron ore from which some of the unusable elements have been removed (to save shipping costs) is an example of the minor processing that is done on raw materials. Raw materials are generally divided into two categories:

1. Products found in their natural state, such as ores, oil, and lumber
2. Livestock and agricultural products, such as grains, fruits, vegetables, tobacco, and cotton

Figure 6–4 features a new material, Dupont's liquid crystal polymer, that has been manufactured into a developmental connector for electronic appliances.

Marketing Strategy.   The two categories of raw materials pose completely different marketing problems.

FIGURE 6–4   DuPont's liquid crystal polymer, a raw material used in electronic applications. (*Courtesy:* DuPont Company.)

Natural state.   Raw materials in their natural state are characterized by limited supplies, small numbers of large producers, and importance of transportation costs to high-bulk products with a low cost per unit. Since extractive industries must be located where the product is found, the cost of transportation is often a major part of the overall cost of the product.

These characteristics require that physical handling be minimized and that the channels of distribution be short, with rarely more than one middleman involved. Brand identification is relatively unimportant to industrial users, who are more concerned with low prices and certainty of supply. Advertising and sales promotion are minimal and sales are frequently made by a contract for a total year's needs.

Vertical integration (the ownership of the raw-material source by the manufacturer) is common with natural-state raw materials. For example, U.S. Steel owns its own iron mines and the Weyerhauser Lumber Company its own forests. Similarly, many petroleum, copper, and aluminum companies own their own raw material sources.

Agricultural products.   These are sold on the industrial market to such businesses as restaurants, canners, and packers. Although they fit the definition of raw materials, they require another marketing strategy. Agricultural products are perishable seasonal goods that are grown some distance from the market. They must be graded and standardized. Agricultural products are generally produced by many small farmers. All of this means that the goods need a great deal of handling, which can only be done through long channels of distribution. Many middlemen are necessary to deliver the goods from the farmer to the industrial user. Their functions include gathering lots from small producers, standardization and grading, storing, refrigerating, transporting, and selling. Typical of most industrial products, very little attention is paid to the promotion or branding of agricultural goods that are destined for industry.

Fabricating Materials and Parts

Many manufacturers, particularly when technical, highly complicated products are involved, purchase rather than construct some of the component parts of their product. These parts become a part of the product, either in the same state in which they are received or after further refinement. Generally, such fabricating materials and parts are custom-made according to the specifications of the buyer.

The automobile industry is a prime example of the industrial market for fabricating materials and supplies. The major producers are essentially assembly plants that put together such parts as bodies, tires, carburetors, batteries, and so on, that have been purchased (frequently from affiliated companies) rather than internally produced.

The individual fabricated part that is included in the product may lose its identity (as in the case of carburetors) or maintain it (as in the case of tires). Figure 6–5 features a tire as it comes from the mold.

Marketing Strategy.   Producers of fabricating materials and parts are usually located near their important customers. The sale of such goods is usually by contract, according to buyer's specifications, and for a long period of time. As a result, marketing is minimal and frequently handled by an executive. The channel of distribution for such goods is generally short, as in the direct channel of producer to user.

Where branding is important in the production of fabricated parts (batteries, fabrics, spark plugs), promotion becomes a significant factor.

Installations

Installations are the major machinery and equipment of an industrial producer which are depreciated over a long period of time. Examples of installations are blast furnaces, factory buildings, and locomotives. Such goods are used in

FIGURE 6–5
Truck tire examined as it comes from the mold. (*Courtesy:* Goodyear Tire & Rubber Company.)

the production of the company's product, and they are so large that they affect the scope of manufacturing operations. Thus, the purchase of twenty adding machines for the office of a large railroad would not be an installation, but the purchase of twenty locomotives would be so classified. Figure 6–6 shows part of a tire producing installation.

Marketing Strategy.   The marketing strategy for the sale of installations is dictated by the size of the individual purchase. These are so large and important

FIGURE 6–6   A segment of a tire installation. (*Courtesy:* Goodyear Tire & Rubber Company.)

that middlemen are rarely used and the channel of distribution is short, usually running from the producer directly to the industrial user. Installations are usually sold on a custom-made basis according to very exact specifications. Negotiations frequently take months or even years. The selling of installations is generally done on a personal basis with a minimum of advertising and sales promotion. The marketing of such products should only be entrusted to high-

FIGURE 6–7
Accessory equipment. (*Courtesy:*
Wang Laboratories, Inc.)

caliber, knowledgeable personnel. Engineers trained in selling are usually found in this position. The marketing of installations is characterized by the high degree of servicing required after the delivery of the product.

Accessory Equipment

Accessory equipment is used to facilitate rather than to perform the basic operations of a manufacturing plant. Typical items are small motors, forklifts, office furniture, computers, and time clocks. Sales of accessory equipment amount to less money than do sales of installations. Accessories are rarely made to order; they are standardized and kept in stock by their manufacturers. Figure 6–7 shows a piece of accessory equipment. The newest addition to this group is the FAX machine, pictured in Figure 6–8, which quickly transfers documents from the sender to the receiver.

FIGURE 6–8   AT&T's FAX 3250D. (*Courtesy:* AT&T Archives.)

Marketing Strategy.   Generally, accessory goods are relatively low priced. Their distribution requires fairly long channels of communications, including retail outlets for such products as typewriters. As is the case with all low-value items, the wide coverage that wholesalers offer is necessary for successful distribution over extensive geographical areas. Advertising and other sales-promoting strategies are commonly used in marketing accessory goods. This is particularly effective with items that may be purchased by both consumer and industrial users, such as batteries and powered hand tools.

The more expensive the accessory product, the shorter the channel of distribution. The reason for this is that the higher-priced articles have a smaller market and their sales are large enough to make it worthwhile for a manufacturer to send a salesperson to a prospective customer. The Hyster Company, for example—a manufacturer of forklift trucks—distributes directly to its customers.

Supplies

Supplies are materials used in the operation of a business that do not become a part of the finished product. Some examples of supplies are lubricating oil, stationery, shipping room supplies, coal, floor wax, and washroom supplies.

Supplies are the convenience products of the industrial market. They are of low value and are frequently bought in small quantities. Supplies are expensed rather than depreciated.

Marketing Strategy. Those industrial supplies that are an important part of the cost of manufacture, such as coal and oil, require special treatment in their distribution. The channel of distribution for these goods is short, and the goods are frequently negotiated in large contract lots by top executives.

Low-cost industrial supplies, like consumer convenience goods, require extensive channels of distribution to provide the broad coverage necessary for success. Wholesalers, by carrying the lines of many manufacturers, are able to have their salespeople call on many users and sell large enough quantities of the goods of various manufacturers to make the call profitable. The standardization of most low-end industrial supplies is so great that there is little difference in the goods of various manufacturers. This results in heavy competition, with price, availability, and speed of delivery among the most important factors. Brand identification of industrial supplies is rare.

Services

It has been estimated that about half of all consumer expenditures are for services. Add to this the very considerable market for industrial services and the tremendous size of the market for services becomes apparent. In recognition of this, many large organizations are moving into the service sector. Sears, for example, now sells insurance (Allstate), Coca-Cola is in the education market, and Gerber, the baby food company, owns nursery schools.

Since the Great Depression of the 1930s, the American economy has been improving. There have been some peaks and valleys, but the overall picture has been a steady growth in wealth. As a result, we are an affluent society with both leisure time and the excess funds to indulge ourselves in the purchase of services.

On the industrial side, the growing complexity of business has reached a point where even the largest manufacturers are unable to fulfill all their needs internally. When problems arise, they turn to highly specialized service companies for help. These may be trained engineering or management consultants, data-processing specialists, or such low-level service specialists as window cleaners, painters, or maintenance service workers. Other service organizations include those providing in-service lunches and piped-in music.

Generally, outside service companies are used when the cost of self-servicing is higher than the cost of buying the service because of special equipment or expertise, or infrequency of use.

The American Marketing Association defines services as "activities, benefits or satisfactions which are offered for sale, or are provided in connection with the sale of goods." There are four characteristics that differentiate services from other products. Services are

1. Intangible.
2. Perishable.
3. Unstandardized.
4. Based on buyer involvement.

Services cannot be seen, touched, tasted, smelled, or heard. They are difficult to display, demonstrate, or illustrate. Because of this they cannot be marketed by normal promotion but require special, imaginative programs.

The perishability of services is obvious. Most services are used up the moment the job is done. When the barber puts down the comb, the hair cut is done. When the movie is over, the service is complete. Moreover, services cannot be stored for later use. An empty hotel room is lost income as is a vacant seat on an airliner.

Services are frequently difficult to standardize. Different hairdressers will give different results. Even the same hairdresser will give varying satisfaction to different customers.

Buyers are very much involved in the service product. Each customer at a travel agency may have a vacation planned to his or her specifications. Income tax specialists give advice on the specific problems of each of their clients.

Marketing Strategy—Consumer Services.   Although all of the principles involved in the marketing of products apply to services as well, the unique features of services require special consideration. In some areas the marketing of services is relatively easy; there are no packaging, styles, colors, or labeling. Brand identification is another matter. Because of the difficulty in achieving standardization, brand identification is difficult to get across. H & R Block promotes its tax service by extensive advertising. The athletic and entertainment industry benefits from free publicity. Travel and real estate agencies advertise. Since sales of services are essentially one-on-one transactions, personal selling is probably the most important marketing feature, and service industries lean heavily on training programs. Some marketers advocate the creation of a tangible product in the minds of their potential customers. Prudential Insurance's "piece of the rock" or the "good hands" of Allstate are examples.

Pricing for service companies can be done in several ways. Repair organizations often use cost-plus and bill their services by the hour. Others charge whatever the traffic will bear, although this is kept within reasonable range by competitors' actions.

Marketing Strategy—Industrial Services.   The most important factors in the success of a service company are speed and satisfaction. To accomplish this, it must be located near its customers, maintain an adequate stock of parts and supplies, and have enough skilled service personnel. Because of the infrequency of use, manufacturers are willing to pay a premium for fast, effective service.

Services are rarely sold through middlemen. The normal distribution channel is from the service company directly to the user. Services of high-level companies such as advertising agencies or management consultants are generally negotiated extensively by important executives of both companies. Compared to personal selling, advertising and sales promotion are unimportant in the selling of services.

Important Points in the Chapter

1. Past experience has shown that certain market mixes are best for specific categories of goods. By classifying goods according to these categories, a producer can benefit from this experience.

2. Consumer goods are produced for the ultimate consumer. Industrial goods are produced for the industrial market, where they will be used to produce other goods. The classification of goods must be based on the type of purchaser, not on the type of goods.

3. Consumer goods are categorized according to the buying habits of the consumers. They consist of convenience goods, shopping goods, specialty goods, impulse goods, and emergency goods. (The last two are special cases of convenience goods.)

4. Convenience goods are those a shopper buys with a minimum of shopping effort. They are frequently bought by habit and brand name and are inexpensive. They must be widely distributed, heavily promoted, and competitively priced.

5. Shopping goods are purchased after comparisons of price, suitability, style, and quality. Characteristically, they are long-lasting, high-priced, and brand-identified. Shopping goods do not require wide distribution but must be well styled, competitively priced, and well promoted (generally by the retailer). Price is the most important factor in the marketing of homogeneous goods, product in the marketing of heterogeneous goods.

6. Specialty goods are products for which customers are willing to make a special effort. These are high-priced, fine-quality products sold at prestigious dealers, and customers will not accept substitutes. Specialty goods are distributed through short distribution channels. The principal elements of the marketing mix are product and promotion.

7. Impulse goods are bought without prior planning. They are inexpensive, and, like other convenience goods, they must be widely displayed, heavily promoted, and competitively priced.

8. Emergency goods must be purchased immediately to fill an urgent need. Place is the vital factor in the distribution of emergency goods. Price is relatively unimportant, and promotion is usually limited to place information.

9. Raw materials are goods that will be used in the production of other goods. Natural-state raw materials require little handling and are sold in large quantities through short distribution channels. Agricultural products, which are subjected to a great deal of handling, require long channels of distribution.

10. Fabrication materials and parts are goods, processed to some extent, that become an actual part of the finished product. Such goods are produced to the customer's specifications and marketed through short channels of distribution.

11. Installations are major items of equipment that affect the scope of a manufacturer's operations. They are produced to the customer's specifications and marketed through short channels of distribution.

12. Accessory equipment is used to facilitate rather than to perform the basic operations of a manufacturing plant. Since accessories are often low-value, standardized items, they generally require wide placement, promotion, and fairly long channels of distribution.

13. Supplies are materials used in the operation of a business that do not become part of the finished product. They are generally low-value products that must be widely distributed (through extensive channels) and are very sensitive to price changes.

14. When the cost of providing internal services is high, institutions turn to private servicing companies. Middlemen are rarely used to sell services. Speed and customer satisfaction are the important factors for the successful marketing of services.

Review Questions

1. Discuss the advantages of product classification to the producer.

2. Define *consumer goods.* Can the same goods be both consumer and industrial goods? How do you differentiate?

3. What are *convenience goods?* Give examples and characteristics.

4. Discuss in detail the importance of place in the marketing of convenience goods.

5. Explain the meaning of *homogeneous shopping goods.* Give examples. How are they marketed?

6. Differentiate between the placing of shopping and convenience goods. Why is there a difference?

7. How are shopping goods promoted? Who is responsible for the promotion of shopping goods?

8. What are specialty goods? What are their characteristics? Give examples.

9. Does overcharging for specialty goods involve dangers? Discuss the pricing of such goods.

10. Discuss the importance of place in the market strategy for impulse goods.

11. Is promotion important in the sale of impulse goods? Why?

12. Define *emergency goods*. Give examples. Compare them with other convenience goods.

13. How should emergency goods be placed? Why? Give examples.

14. Define *industrial goods*. Give examples. Why is the industrial market practically unknown to most people?

15. Discuss the market strategy for the distribution of agricultural products. Why are the channels of distribution different from those of other raw materials?

16. In which way are fabricating materials and parts usually marketed?

17. Define *installations* as industrial goods. Give examples. Differentiate between installations and fabricating materials.

18. Define *accessory equipment*. Give examples.

19. Discuss pricing, placing, and promoting industrial supplies.

20. What are industrial services? Give examples.

Case Problems

Case Problem 1

The Home-Easy Tool Company is the largest producer of electrical hand tools for the consumer market in the United States. The firm has been in operation for over 100 years. Their brand is very well known and is classified as a consumer product in the specialty goods category. This classification has been well earned, since the product line is made up of uniformly high-quality, durable, well-promoted, and conveniently serviced items.

Since World War II the movement of the middle class from inner-city apartments to individually owned suburban homes has resulted in a dramatic spurt of profitable growth for Home-Easy. At present, they are in an excellent financial position.

Management at Home-Easy is interested in expansion to the industrial market. A survey of their potential competitors on the industrial scene has indicated that production facilities, financing, experience, and engineering know-how at Home-Easy are second to none. In addition, several of its most successful consumer products, with minor modifications, would fit the industrial market perfectly.

You have been called in as a marketing consultant. Your job is to prepare a marketing strategy with which the company may successfully enter the industrial field. Your report should touch on the following areas: place, price, and promotion.

Questions

1. How would you classify the product?
2. Suggest areas that might warrant further research.

Case Problem 2

In 1985, Tom Slovak, a chemical engineer, developed a new product for homeowners. The item consisted of a simple device powered by water pressure which, when used with the inexpensive chemicals provided, did an excellent job on cleaning out stuffed drains. The cost of producing the device and chemicals was so low that it could be retailed for $10.95. Considering the rising costs of plumbing services, the product seemed certain to be successful.

Tom patented his invention, built several thousand in his garage, and personally placed them in several neighboring hardware stores. After a brief breaking-in period, the product showed sufficient potential for Tom to quit his job and invest his savings in a small plant for the production of the new product. By the beginning of 1986, Tom was in business. He hired salespeople and began production.

By 1989, Tom had a moderately successful small business. This was disappointing to him, since his was by far the best and least expensive product of its kind on the market. The most serious problem seems to be his inability to keep sales personnel. They rarely stay longer than a few months, and much of Tom's efforts are spent in recruitment. Tom feels that he can solve the problem by hiring a professional sales manager who will be expert at the recruitment, training, and directing of salespeople.

Questions

1. What do you think of Tom's solution?
2. Do you agree that the trouble lies in the sales area?
3. What would you suggest?

7

THE PRODUCT

Learning Objectives _____

Upon completion of the chapter, you will be able to:

1. Define the total product concept.

2. List and discuss six reasons for adding new products.

3. Explain the importance of a properly organized new product department and discuss the duties of such a department.

4. Describe the fashion cycle and discuss methods of reducing fashion risks.

5. Discuss the importance of *fit* in the new product decision.

6. Describe the problems that arise in new product decisions in the area of quality, design, color, size, materials, and performance.

7. Discuss the make-or-buy decision, giving reasons for and against.

WHO'S AFRAID OF MA BELL?

The saying goes, "All good things come to an end." And that's what happened to AT&T when its monopoly on long-distance telephone calls reached the end of the line. Although the company was regulated by the Federal Communications Commission, their rates seemed to increase continuously, much to the dismay and frustration of the user. An alternative was virtually impossible until AT&T was forced to break up and make way for competition. Faced with the possibility of huge losses in revenue, American Telephone & Telegraph had to invest vast sums of money on remarketing their service. No longer would the "If you don't like it, that's too bad" attitude work.

Many new long-distance telephone services appeared on the market. Two of the major companies, Sprint and MCI, undertook major marketing campaigns to capture a significant part of the market exclusively claimed by AT&T. Both Sprint and MCI immediately developed advertising campaigns that blitzed the media. Television, radio, newspapers, and magazines heralded both companies' virtues, the major one being price. The savings promised and delivered were in amounts of up to 40 percent less than the AT&T charges for long-distance calls.

Not about to lie down, Ma Bell, as AT&T is often referred to, countered MCI's and Sprint's cut-rate services with its own marketing strategy in order to maintain its market share. AT&T was unable or unwilling to become involved in direct price competition. Therefore, the company decided to attack with significant promotional devices and advertising that focused on service, experience, and the use of premiums. The caller would now get a "thanks for using AT&T," something which was rarely heard until the devastating blow dealt to the company. Politeness by previously often rude or abrupt telephone operators was accorded great importance. Celebrities were constantly used in commercials to extol the company's virtues. AT&T has involved itself in a tremendous effort billed as AT&T Opportunity Calling, which enables the user to compile credits toward purchases of such merchandise as tools, luggage, bicycles, cameras, and so on, travel by train, plane, and ship, car rentals, and hotel accommodations.

Both MCI and Sprint have countered by using their own armies of celebrities to hammer away at AT&T's overpricing of long-distance telephone calls.

As of this writing, the results are not yet in. Each company is motivating the consumer to come with them. Whether it's the service or premiums which will win or the price that is more attractive, only time will tell. Both camps will have their followings. Naturally, if AT&T's newfound marketing approach doesn't bring the desired results, their fight could also include price incentives to make them more competitive with MCI and Sprint.

The case of AT&T should serve as an example to other companies, whatever their offerings are. Even when it seems that a total hold on the market is presently the case, there is no telling what will undo a company's favorable position. Businesses, or for that matter, nonprofit organizations, cannot afford to sit back and under-utilize their marketing teams. Somewhere out there, even in what seems to be the safest environment, a competitor lurks.

 US Sprint

PRODUCT: NEW WORLD CAMPAIGN
TITLE: "HOMECOMING/II"
CODE No.: GNSP 0023

(MUSIC UP THEN UNDER)

(MUSIC)

(MUSIC)

ANNCR: (VO) Finally, one long distance company gives you late night rates

starting at five,

instead of waiting 'til ten.

Introducing

SPRINT PLUS.

Lower rates than AT&T around the clock.

The lowest rates available after five.

Call now, we'll even switch you for free.

SPRINT PLUS. Late night rates when you can really use them.

Courtesy: US SPRINT

INTRODUCTION

Essentially, the success or failure of a business enterprise is contingent on customer acceptance of its product. It is impossible to select the most important of the four factors of marketing: product, promotion, price, and place. There is no question, however, that product is most basic. It all begins with product. Once product decisions have been made, marketing strategy can be woven around it until a total marketing program is achieved. The success of the final marketing program depends, in large part, on the accuracy of the product decision.

Only on rare occasions does a company market a product that has captured the hearts of Americans to the extent of Coleco's Cabbage Patch kid. The doll was originally produced in 1977 by Xavier Roberts, an artist based in Georgia. In addition to the doll itself, the package included a name, a birth certificate, and adoption papers. At $125 each, about 150,000 were sold between the late 1970s and early 1980s. Coleco licensed the concept in 1982 and marketed the doll as it presently appears at a much lower price. Coleco, in 1983 delivered 2.5 million dolls. Customers have lined up for hours before store openings to purchase the item treasured by every child and many adults. It has been said that people have flown to London, where availability was easier, specifically to purchase the doll. Psychologists and businesspeople alike have yet to explain the enormous popularity. Whatever it is, the marketing mix was on target and the product's success lasted years beyond that of most products of this type.

DEFINITION—THE TOTAL PRODUCT

It should be emphasized that in this discussion, *product* refers to the total product, that is, all the elements that are necessary for customer satisfaction. The total product, in addition to the physical product, includes guarantees, installation, instructions for use, packaging, branding, and the availability of service. The total product is what the customer buys, and frequently the fringe characteristics such as guarantees and servicing are as important as the physical product itself. In the case of a prospective buyer of a home appliance, for example, the fact that Sears, Roebuck offers a one-year replacement, rather than merely service, may be the factor that clinches the sale.

Some years ago Chrysler was on the verge of bankruptcy. It took government financing to bail them out. They hired a new president, took part in a minor redesigning effort, and improved their advertising. It all helped, but the big thing was a 5-year, 50,000-mile warranty. At a time when the public was fed up with poor-quality cars, the warranty showed Chrysler's confidence in their product and offered help if things went wrong. In a few years huge losses became huge profits.

There is much more to a product than the cold, hard facts of its physical properties, warranties, and service. There is a psychological aspect as well. A successful product, indeed the total marketing mix, must be designed to satisfy a buyer's needs. Perfect understanding of those needs is vitally important. The teenager who buys a lipstick isn't buying grease and color. Charles Revson, president of Revlon, says that she is buying hope. Calvin Klein doesn't sell jeans, he sells sex, and Miller beer isn't a beverage, it's macho for the blue-collar trade.

REASONS FOR ADDING PRODUCTS

New products should never be added without a sound business reason. However, there are many situations in which new products are essential to a successful operation.

Market Demand

Perhaps the best reason for a company to add a new product to its line occurs when the market indicates consumer need. While companies try desperately to focus their attention on products with little competition, they often undertake the introduction of an item with no point of difference, or as they are often called, "me-too" products.

Companies are always engaged in the marketing of such products as advertising campaigns point out. They try, through vast promotional expenditures, to extol the virtues of their version of products, although similar ones are already on the market.

A case in point of this type of product introduction is in the caffeine-free soft drink market. While the rest of the industry got on the bandwagon in the distribution of the decaffeinated beverages, the Coca-Cola Company hadn't yet entered the market. With consumer demand reflecting an enormous need, Coca-Cola decided to join the others. It has thus far developed three caffeine-free versions of existing soft drinks, caffeine-free Coke, caffeine-free Diet Coke, and caffeine-free Tab. From every indication, the Atlanta-based Coca-Cola company will once again beat the competition. One danger in the addition of such new products is the possibility of cutting into the sales of existing products. While this might be a risk, Coca-Cola's research indicates a bottom-line total market share increase in soft drinks of 3.1 percent to a total of 34 percent. Figure 7–1 illustrates the Coca-Cola Company's caffeine-free soft drinks.

Mug Root Beer was a strong regional brand that the Pepsi-Cola Company expanded into its bottling system to take advantage of the fastest-growing soft drink segment. This was an immediate success as many of its bottlers had no root beer at the time. Figure 7–2 features both the regular and diet variety of the product.

Recent years have seen a new trend in consumers' everyday living habits. A quick glance at any park or track immediately reveals runners, joggers, and "quick" walkers taking their turns at getting into shape. A look at the restaurant scene across the nation indicates that eating habits have changed as well. Where

FIGURE 7–1   Coca-Cola's caffeine-free soft drinks. (Coca-Cola is a registered trademark of The Coca-Cola Company. Permission for reproduction of materials granted by the Company.)

salads and yogurt were once standard fare only for ladies' lunches, the appetites of many of their male counterparts have moved in that direction too.

Producers of packaged food products have begun to react swiftly to this new-found health kick with the inclusion of many new healthful additions to their product lines. In a $290 billion retail food industry, the segment that is growing fastest is the one that is comprised of "light" and diet foods. Figure 7–3 shows how this $25.8 billion market breaks down.

V8 has been a household favorite for a long time. For many years it had been positioned as something akin to tomato juice, but the commercials tried to impart its zestier taste, with "It sure doesn't taste like tomato juice."

With the market demand for healthful products, Campbell's has tried a new approach to the product's appeal. Figure 7–4 shows V8 in its old package along with the newer carton. The new packaging also helps the product appeal to those who are in need of dietetic balance. The inclusion of the words "The American Dietetic Association says . . ." helps this well-established product seem new.

As marketers know, entry into such a market can result in losses as well as profits. While many small companies have started up specifically to meet the needs of the health conscious, the giants in the industry are treading with caution. Much attention is being paid by the industry leaders to the development of substances on which the new health products will be based such as good-tasting substitute sweeteners and salts.

If the indicators for a health-conscious market continue in a positive trend, many companies will definitely jump in. With a present 6 percent growth rate

FIGURE 7–2   Pepsi-Cola's regular and diet Mug Root Beer. (Reproduced with permission, © PepsiCo, Inc., 1989.)

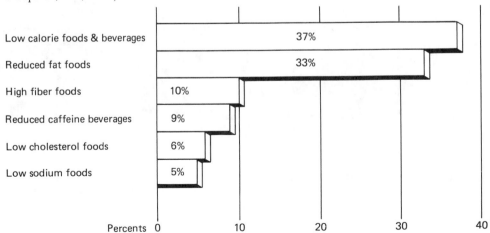

FIGURE 7–3   The light and diet foods market.

FIGURE 7–4   V8 Juice television commercial. (*Courtesy*: Campbell Soup Company.)

annually, it is certain that shelves will be stocked more and more with foods that appeal to the runners and joggers.

Company Growth

Since there is generally a limit to the amount of sales that a given article can produce, company growth may depend on the introduction of new products for an increase in sales. Besides sales volume, profits and capital may also be increased by new products. As a consequence, company growth is the most important or at least one of the principal reasons for introducing new products.

Maximum Use of Resources

Management is charged with the responsibility of getting the maximum use of the resources available. The term *resources available* covers many areas; if they are not fully utilized, profit opportunities may be overlooked.

Idle Plant and Equipment.   When the manufacturing or distribution facilities do not have to work at full capacity to satisfy the demand for existing products, an attempt should be made to use the idle time by the introduction of new products. This will not only increase the potential sales volume of the company but will improve its operating efficiency as well. The cost per unit produced of such fixed overhead expenses as rent is decreased as the number of units produced increases. When new products are produced by existing facilities rather than by specially constructed facilities, the cost of both the new product and the goods presently produced may be drastically cut.

Idle Personnel.   When the personnel of a business is not working at its full potential, the resulting idle time is being wasted. As in the case of idle plant and equipment, new products that can be handled by existing personnel will improve both profits and efficiency.

Idle Capital.   The main function of capital is return on investment. Any company that has more capital than it requires for the operation of its business should try to invest this capital to improve its return on the investment of its owners. New products are an excellent place for such investment, since management knows their impact and can exercise control over them.

Goodwill

An important asset that does not appear on the financial statements of a company is its customer goodwill. In the area of new products, consumer good will may be a factor that enables new products to be introduced with relative ease. Some years ago, the Sunbeam Corporation produced a highly successful electric food mixer. Capitalizing on the resulting goodwill, the Sunbeam Corporation is now a successful marketer of a wide range of household appliances. The Green Giant Company is another good example of effectively using customer acceptance as a vehicle for expansion through the introduction of new products. During the last ten years, this fast-growing company has introduced nearly five new food products a year, most of which were readily accepted by its customers.

Distribution Channels

Another important nonfinancial asset consists of a company's channels of distribution. These are difficult and expensive to set up and maintain. If the distribution channels are capable of successfully marketing products in addition to those already handled, the introduction of new products should be considered.

Replacement of Old Products

Every product has a life cycle. This may be graphically illustrated as is shown in Figure 7–5. This cycle may be divided into four periods:

1. The *pioneer period* of introduction is characterized by slow sales growth as the company strives for distribution and customer acceptance.
2. The *period of growth* occurs as customers accept the product. This is a time of rapidly rising sales volume and profits. If there is a strong period of

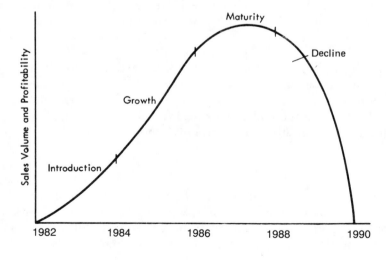

FIGURE 7–5
The life cycle of a new product.

growth, the product is successful, and competitors are attracted. This causes price declines and a movement toward manufacturing efficiency. The competition results in a leveling off of sales and profit. This signifies the end of the growth period.

3. The *maturity period* is marked by a further leveling off and gradual decline of the product's growth and profitability. It is a time of high competition that requires large outlays of promotional expenses that tend to reduce profits. During this period variations on the original product appear that appeal to specific segments of the market. These tend to increase costs and reduce the potential sales market. During the latter half of the maturity period the weaker producers are forced out.

4. The *period of decline* begins when the product is made obsolete by the introduction into the market of a new product that replaces the old. The necessary cutback in promotional expenditures to match the declining sales accelerates the decline. The time comes at which the product must be abandoned.

A study of the product illustrated in Figure 7–5 indicates that a product started in 1982 reaches maturity in 1988 and begins to decline by 1990. If the company wants to maintain its high sales and profit level, a new product must be introduced in 1984. The new product will then reach its maturity (and maximum profitability) by 1988, the date at which the product illustrated begins its decline.[1] Since nearly all products face a growth and decline cycle of one time span or another, management is required to be constantly researching new products to maintain the company's profitability.

Sometimes life cycles can be prolonged. Think of Listerine, Ivory soap, Scotch tape, and others. These have been top items for generations. How did they manage to do it?

Johnson & Johnson did it by repositioning. When the baby boom slacked off, its baby shampoo began to falter. It began to promote it as a total family product. Ads featured a macho professional football player, and sales once again increased.

DuPont found new uses for its synthetic fiber, nylon. During World War II it was used by the military for parachutes. When the war ended, it was used as a silk substitute for ladies' stockings and soon took over the whole market. Now nylon is used for everything from ball bearings to carpeting. Another classic example of new uses for a product is Arm & Hammer baking soda. For over a century, its use was confined to baking, one teaspoon at a time. After being

---

[1]It must be understood that the chart in Figure 7–5 relates to an imaginary product. Specific products will vary greatly.

FIGURE 7–6 IBM Personal System 2 Model 50 with IBM Personal System 2 Monochrome Display Model 8503 and IBM Pro-printer XL24. (*Courtesy:* International Business Machines Corporation.)

promoted as a refrigerator deodorant, the product found its way into some 70 percent of the country's refrigerators. Many also use it as a tooth cleanser.

Texas Instruments extended the life cycle of its pocket calculators by price adjustments. As competitors' products began to flood the market, Texas Instruments maintained its dominance by lowering prices on an almost monthly basis.

Procter & Gamble maintains Tide's dominance by constantly changing the product's formula. In 1947 P&G revolutionized the industry with a low-suds detergent. As washing machines and fabrics changed, so did Tide, more than fifty times since its inception.

One product that seems to go through the life cycle very quickly is the personal computer. With the ever-present new technology in the field, and the expansion of the market, producers must constantly replace the old products with the newer models. Personal computers that seemed to revolutionize the industry a few years ago, have met with obsolescence and have been replaced with newer, more efficient designs. Figure 7–6 features the IBM Personal System/2 Model 50.

THE DEVELOPMENT OF NEW PRODUCTS

A MARKETING PROFILE

Domino's Pizza

Pizza certainly is not a new product, but one that has been around for years and years. Devotees of the product are able to satisfy their appetites by visiting their favorite pizza parlor such as the homegrown individual restaurant or one of the outlets of the national chains like Pizza Hut. Others can stock up on the frozen type such as Jenos and prepare them whenever the urge occurs. Some people even make their own pizzas from scratch.

With the need for convenience and the desire for almost instantaneous consumption, Domino's Pizza, Inc., has taken an old product and marketed it in a most appealing manner. To the delight of the many thousands who crave pizza without the fuss of preparation or the need to leave the home, Domino's has provided just what the pizza lover ordered. In a matter of 30 minutes or less, with a discount of at least $3.00 if the time commitment isn't met, hot pies are delivered to the caller.

The success story that revolutionized the old product began in 1961 when Tom Monaghan traded a Volkswagen to gain controlling interest in a pizza parlor in Ypsilanti, Michigan. The company attributes its success to simplicity—it has only one product, pizza, which is sold along with one cola beverage and service. Not only does it guarantee the 30-minute delivery, but pizza replacement or money back is assured to any dissatisfied customer. With such simple principles, Domino's Pizza has recorded sales of more than $2 billion on delivery of more than two million pies since 1987.

Its success has been remarkable. It sells more pizza than any other delivery company in the world and boasts franchises in the United States and eight other countries, including Australia, Canada, the United Kingdom, and Japan. With 500 stores by 1981, 4,500 by 1988, Domino's expects to reach 10,000 units during the 1990s.

A key to its astounding rate of expansion is the manner in which it chooses its franchisees. While most companies sell franchises to individuals who meet the financial requirements and few others, Domino's rule on franchising requires that units may only be purchased by former store managers or supervisors. A minimum of twelve months of management experience in the company is a rule before application can be made for a franchise. In this way, the company is assured of "selling" its name to those who know the business firsthand.

FIGURE 7–7
Delivery to the home by
Domino's Pizza. (*Courtesy:*
Domino's Pizza, Inc.)

The company's future plans call for a 100 percent average increase in the number of stores for five years, an increase in the number of corporate stores internationally, and expansion into various other countries.

It's amazing how simple dough, cheese, and tomato sauce can be blended to create a dynasty.

As has been indicated, the development of new products is essential to the continuing success of a business organization. That most successful companies accept this idea is evidenced by the fact that some 70 percent of the food products available to today's families were not available ten years ago, and fully 50 percent of the drugs available were not in existence five years ago.

One such group of products centers on the health kick scene. Americans, as never before, are heeding the warnings of the medical profession to lower their cholesterol, reduce sugar intake, and increase their fiber intake. Capitalizing on this is Kellogg. To appeal to adults seeking a healthier breakfast, Kellogg has introduced twelve new "adult" cereals, including as Mueslix, Nutrific, Pro Grain, and Nutri-Grain, and accounts for 50 percent of the market.

Another product classification that was virtually nonexistent ten years ago, save for the sneakers used for tennis and basketball, is athletic footwear. In just a few years, the name Reebok took a market and ran with it.

The need for convenience and the much publicized nutritional boost that Americans are seeking have motivated the food industry to offer a new product group—chilled prepared foods—that are filling the stores' refrigerator sections. Many consumers, especially those in more affluent markets, now take home fresh pasta, gourmet entrees, and sauces that are unavailable anywhere else in the store.

Along with this new entry into the market comes a few problems. One is the relatively short shelf life of the products. Conventionally packaged and frozen foods offer extensive lives whereas chilled foods are usually salable for only a two-week period. Products that are undergoing market testing are Delissio fresh pizza kits, Fresh Nes freshly made entrees, Contadina fresh pastas and sauces, and Pillsbury brownies. Like any other food group, this too will have its successes and failures.

Today, while General Motors, the Ford Motor Company, and the Chrysler Corporation, America's big three automakers, are trying everything possible in the development of new cars to combat the ever-growing imports, and food manufacturers are spending millions in the development of their new goods, some new companies with only one basic product are capturing many marketing headlines. What industry?

If you guessed cookies, you were right! Though not yet nearly as important as the ice cream businesses of Carvel or Baskin-Robbins or the hamburger empires of McDonald's or Burger King, the cookie craze is taking America (and other countries such as Japan, Singapore, Hong Kong, and Australia) by storm. The cookie has been around as long as anyone can remember, so why the fuss? Is the distribution innovative? Are the tastes better? Are cookies being marketed differently? A brief glimpse of the story follows.

Cookies have traditionally been available as prepackaged products in supermarkets and grocery stores or loose in bakery shops. The selection was large in both types of arrangements, with the chocolate chip variety gaining the greatest acceptance.

FIGURE 7–8
David Liederman with his innovative and successful chocolate chip cookies. (*Courtesy:* David's Cookies.)

In 1979, the East Coast witnessed an innovation in the marketing of cookies. David Liederman opened his first "soft" cookie store where freshly baked cookies, primarily chocolate chips, were sold directly to the public. David went on to develop a chocolate chip empire and became a legend in his own time. Figure 7–8 shows David Liederman with his successful product. Just prior to David's debut, a similar enterprise, Mrs. Field's Cookies, was launched on the West Coast, in Palo Alto, California. Here two very young individuals (29 and 20, respectively), with excellent ideas, took the nation by storm. Basically the products were the same and so was their distribution—soft chocolate chip cookies produced throughout the day and sold directly to the consumer. At the present time David and Mrs. Field are not only competing with each other throughout the country but with others who have joined the bandwagon. Estimates of the soft cookie business indicate continuous strong growth. In the late 1980s the reported sales, as shown in Figure 7–9, totaled approximately $145 million.

At this point each company is predicting domination in the field mainly

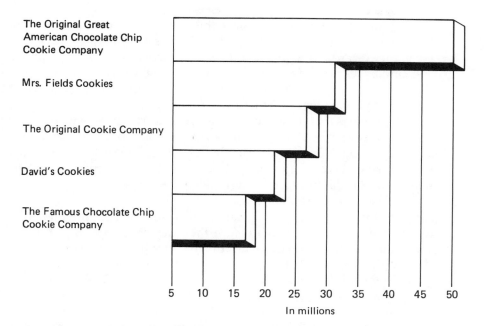

The Original Great
American Chocolate Chip
Cookie Company

Mrs. Fields Cookies

The Original Cookie Company

David's Cookies

The Famous Chocolate Chip
Cookie Company

5   10   15   20   25   30   35   40   45   50

In millions

FIGURE 7–9   Sales of the five leading "over-the-counter" companies.

through two distribution approaches, company-owned stores and/or franchising. Each has added new products—oatmeal, hazelnut, macadamia nut, and so on—to the earlier simple production.

Whatever the industry, be it video recorders, food products, automobiles, clothing, and so forth, marketers must have a plan for the development of new products and must follow it through those stages vital for customer acceptance.

Considering the importance of new product development, it is obvious that product innovation is a top-management responsibility. Despite this, few companies, even the best-managed and most successful, are properly organized for new-product development. A recent survey indicates that four out of five outstanding firms have problems in this area. One author goes so far as to suggest that fewer than one-third of American manufacturing firms have an adequate organization responsible for new products.

The trend among the more aggressively managed American firms is toward formally organized new product departments. These are generally small departments, frequently consisting of not more than four or five people. Typically, the head of the department reports directly to the president.

Duties of the New Product Department

The new product department is responsible for all the steps involved in translating someone's idea into a product ready for production and marketing.

Getting and Screening Ideas.   Since the new product department must depend, to a large extent, on outside sources for ideas, it may be necessary to offer incentive rewards to help generate such information. Sales personnel, customers, employees, and inventors are only a few of the sources of new product ideas that should be utilized. These ideas must be carefully screened to determine the ones that are worthy of further investigation.

New ideas can come from anywhere. An executive's wife thought up the first onion soup mix. A worker in a soap company forgot to turn off his machine at quitting time. By morning air bubbles had worked into the mixture. The floating soap became the biggest seller and longest-running product in the household product industry. They called it Ivory soap.

Analysis of Ideas.   The suggestions that survive the preliminary screening must be put to further tests before they can be placed in the developmental stage. Among these are estimates of customer demand, estimates of profitability, decisions on whether or not the idea falls within the company's goals and objectives, and decisions on whether or not the idea is within the capability of the company.

Development of the Product.   The new product ideas that meet all prior testing satisfactorily must, at this stage, be converted from an idea on paper to an actual physical product. This requires the construction of samples and models in small quantities that can be physically tested and adjusted. In this way, it can be determined what will be the best way to manufacture the article as well as what will be the most salable and profitable product. During the developmental stage the new product department requires the cooperation of the production, engineering, cost-accounting, marketing, and many other departments. The final result of the developmental stage is a product that is ready to be test marketed.

Market Testing the Product.   At this point the consuming public must be brought into the picture. This is generally done in limited geographical areas with the purpose of determining public interest in the product. The information provided by market testing is used to make design and production changes intended to improve the product's consumer acceptability. At the completion of the test marketing program, top management must decide whether or not to go ahead with the project.

Naturally, not all products can be test marketed. Typical of these are real estate projects and machinery whose tooling-up cost would be prohibitive. Other items that fail on the test market can be saved. Procter & Gamble's Pampers tested out as a lemon. The test price, 10 cents each, was simply too high to compete with traditional diapers. When they reduced the price to six cents cotton diapers virtually disappeared and P&G took over a highly lucrative field.

Production and Marketing.   Those new products whose test marketing programs are favorable and that are given a go-ahead signal by top management are now removed from the new product department and turned over to the production and marketing departments as additions to the product line. (This does not mean that cooperation with the new product department should stop at this point.)

It should be noted that the most important steps in the new product development program outlined are the early ones. The getting, screening, and analysis of ideas are the relatively inexpensive parts of the program on which the success or failure of a company's new product development rests. Poor judgment in the early stages results in missed opportunities and costly errors.

The major problem that management faces in new product decision making is the fact that whereas new products are essential to the life of a business, some 80 percent of all new products are costly failures. That these errors are not at all restricted to small, poorly managed companies is evidenced by the fact that even industry leaders whose customer goodwill and promotional facilities are second to none are constantly making new product errors. Giant IBM is a good example. During an eighteen-month period, that company discontinued its operations in microfilm, offset duplicators, voting machines, and production control, all new products that did not make the grade.

Perhaps the most serious problem facing new product development departments is the possibility that failure will be treated so harshly that innovation may be replaced by conservativeness. Top management must expect a great number of new-product failures and not allow such failures to stand in the way of an aggressive search for innovation.

FASHION PRODUCTS

Most consumer and industrial products, as we have seen, go through what are considered the typical stages of study in their introduction or removal from a company's production. Unlike most types of goods, merchandise with fashion orientation requires analysis that is often different. Fashion, with its rapid changes, dictates the need for the continuous introduction of new styles. Not that producers would not be happy with the year-in and year-out success they have with staple products, but change is actually the factor that creates profit in the fashion industry.

Successful fashion producers recognize the fact that the consumer is king in making selections. No longer can costly errors be easily absorbed through the success of the next season's production. In years gone by, designers thought their intuition and signature were all that was necessary to motivate consumers to purchase their creations. In these times of consciousness raising and women's liberation, a new awareness has taken place in the minds of consumers. This, coupled with the fact that the fashion industry is the second largest industry in the United States, makes production of fashion merchandise difficult.

Fashion and Today's Consumer

Today's market is enormously fashion-minded. Years ago, fashion was confined to certain merchandise and a small group of customers. During the last few decades, the ability to copy costly fashion goods on a mass-production basis has made fashion merchandise available to nearly all the population. People become aware of fashion through advertising and, with ever-higher annual incomes, are able to purchase fashion goods during their constantly increasing leisure hours. Fashion has gone far beyond the clothing and automobile industries. Such diverse merchandise as furnaces, shotguns, appliances, and cameras depend upon fashion for sales volume.

The advent of fashion as a requirement for selling has increased producing and marketing risks considerably. For one thing, the costs of advertising and promoting are extremely high. This is particularly true when one considers that such expenditures are frequently made on unproven fashions that are as likely as not to prove poor sellers. The uncertainty of fashion adds greatly to its risk. Figure 7–10 is an example of a fashion risk, the blouson jacket for men. As it turned out, it was successful for the company. The point is that one can never be certain of customer acceptance, and the large sums of money invested in producing and promoting a fashion may be wasted. The automobile industry invests $1 billion each year in retooling (mostly for fashion changes), and a good deal of the retooling is to effect changes that are not acceptable to the public.

Retailers, manufacturers, and middlemen all find that the growing importance of fashion has increased the risk of doing business. The problem is not only the high cost of promotion but the necessity of guessing the *right* fashions as well. Consider the ladies' clothing industry. At the time of this writing, clothing designers still cannot be certain of the skirt length women will prefer. An error would be enormously costly, since wrong styles have almost no value. Problems such as this may force many marginal producers into bankruptcy. In such an industry a great deal of guesswork goes into the ultimate decision making.

Sometimes products get lucky. They find a use for which they never were intended. This, of course, can greatly increase sales volume. Jogging shoes were originally sold only for athletic purposes, and they were very successful. Then, because of their comfort, they were worn for chores, shopping, and other leisure-dress activities. Now, they're being worn to work. It has become quite fashionable for young women to wear a tailored suit or skirt and round out their outfit with color coordinated jogging shoes. They are becoming the "in" thing in large metropolitan areas and are increasing the sales of jogging shoes enormously.

FIGURE 7–10
The blouson jacket, a fashion risk. (*Courtesy:*
Jhane Barnes II.)

The Fashion Cycle

Like all newly innovated products, new fashions follow a definite pattern of stages. The life cycle of new products includes its innovation by the designer, its acceptance by the customer, its peak of customer popularity, and its rapid decline. The life cycle of new products has already been discussed, but it must be emphasized here that although cycles vary in length from a single season to many years, there will eventually be a period of decline. The maintenance of sales volume, therefore, requires that new fashions always be in varying stages of development to replace those that are in decline.

THE BASIS FOR THE MANAGERIAL DECISION

The final decision on whether or not a new product should be included in the line is made at the top-management level. Since the chance of failure is great and the financial result of failure can be massive, this decision must be made with great care. The following are some of the considerations that should be taken into account in making this decision.

Demand

The demand for the item is by far the most important factor that management must consider. No matter how perfectly the new product meets every other standard, it must be discarded if the estimate of the demand is too low to assure profitability. Approximations of a product's demand are based on the results of market testing programs.

Fit

The manner in which the new product fits into the company's operation is important to the success of a new item. Adequacy of fit must be considered in several areas.

Marketing Fit.   Campbell's can sell soups, but it ought to stay out of the paint business. The chance of an item's success is increased if it will be purchased by the same people who buy the company's other products. In some cases, the new product may actually conflict with the old, as in the case of a manufacturer of children's clothing who added a line of teen-age garments only to find that teenagers refused to have any part of a label that was well known in the marketing of children's wear.

Channel Fit.   The existence of a successful distribution channel is an important asset. To set up new channels generally requires a considerable expense and effort, including the cost of establishing a separate sales force. For this reason most companies limit product expansion to those areas that may be handled by their established distribution channels. In this way, General Mills has no trouble introducing several new supermarket products each year.

Promotional Fit.   Promotional activities are both expensive and necessary. If the product under consideration is similar enough in nature to be included in the regular promotion campaigns, considerable savings can be made. In addition, the promotional dollar can be stretched if the promotion of one product helps the sales of allied products.

Production Fit.   Ideally, the capability to produce the new product should be within the capacity of the company's present production facilities. If this is not the case, the production of the new product should, at least, be within the know-how of the company's production experts.

Legal Problems

New products are particularly susceptible to such legal problems as patent infringements. All legal problems must be researched before the decision on adopting a new product is made.

Financial Problems

Before a new product reaches its developmental stage, management must answer two vital questions concerning finances: Does the company have sufficient capital to produce, promote, and maintain an inventory of the product? If so, will the expected profits derived from the product be worth the capital invested?

In conclusion, it appears that the success or failure of a new product depends, in large part, on how well it fits into the existing operation. This includes not only the production and distributional efforts of the company, but its goals, image, and aspirations as well.

DEALING WITH COUNTERFEITS

The development of a winning product can sometimes cost the manufacturer hundreds of thousands of dollars. Besides production costs and the research involved, the advertising and promotional costs to sell it to the user can even exceed that amount.

Manufacturers must always be ready for a fight from other producers who capitalize on successful products with copies or "me-too" versions of the originals. This is expected and accepted as fair game in marketing circles. Sony's Beta format in video recording was improved upon by Panasonic's VCR and others to make Sony a loser in the field; Datril copied Tylenol's lead without similar success; Frigidaire had to deal with the latecomers in the refrigerator business; and so forth. This is competitive, legal marketing.

In the fashion industry, copies of the original, marketed at lower prices, are always a possibility. For the past few years, however, many producers of fashion merchandise have had to face a new troublesome problem concerning counterfeits. Not only are styles being knocked-off, but labels are being counterfeited as well. The situation has reached epidemic proportions. Calvin Klein in his jeans line, Louis Vuitton in his expensive line of handbags, Adidas on shirts and socks, and Izod with the famous alligator symbol have, among many others, been affected. While the various crime investigation units have been busy trying to put a stop to the bogus merchandise that has cost manufacturers millions of dollars, the situation still seems to be prevalent. Many producers have initiated their own investigations to put a halt to the counterfeiting. Louis Vuitton, whose handbags and luggage run upwards to about $1,000, hired a number of ABSCAM investigators to pull off a sting operation in an attempt to uncover the counterfeit ring, and many of the producers of the phony merchandise were arrested. The costs of breaking up such operations are enormous as are the losses attributed to the illegal goods. Louis Vuitton's private investigation is said to have cost over $500,000. Izod's losses of legitimate business run into the millions.

The production of the fakes takes place abroad as well as all over the United States. The ultimate prime selling locations are flea markets as well as makeshift street vending stands. Although careful investigation of some of the phony merchandise will show that it is not the real thing, the price factor will often motivate the customer to purchase.

PRODUCT CHARACTERISTICS

Certain product characteristics require decisions that will affect the profitability of the item. Among these are quality, design, color, size, materials, and perform- ance.

Quality

Naturally, the minimum quality that a product must have is the amount it needs to satisfactorily do the job for which it is intended. Since any increase in quality requires an increase in production costs that must ultimately be passed on to the consumer, the question of how much quality should be built into a product becomes a difficult one. It is possible to include a great deal of quality in a product, but the resulting high price might be more than a buyer is willing to pay. Before the decision on the amount of quality is made, the concept of useless quality must be considered. It is pointless to increase the cost of an item by setting the quality level at a point beyond the customer's desires. Unquestion- ably, General Motors could make a car that would last twenty years, but they would surely find difficulty finding customers willing to pay the cost of such a car. A better example may be found in the high-fashion industries. What wom- an, for example, would be willing to pay the excessive cost of a dress that was constructed to last for ten years? The quality built into a product should be at a level desired by the customer and for which the customer is willing to pay. It should be borne in mind that the quality of most products is determined by their weakest part. It would be wasteful to construct a lawn mower whose body will last for ten years if the motor will break down in five years.

Once a level of quality has been decided upon, it is important that every

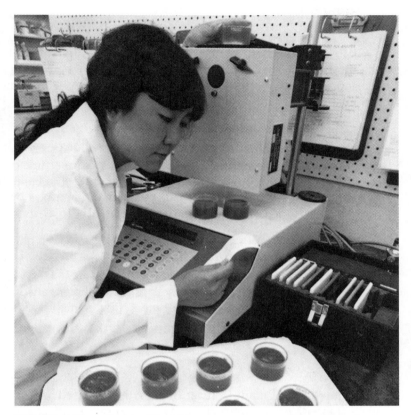

FIGURE 7–11   Beatrice/Hunt-Wesson conducts quality control checks at every step of processing. (*Courtesy:* Beatrice Company.)

unit produced be as close as possible to that level. There is nothing more damaging to the goodwill of a company than a lemon.

Design and Color

Not too many years ago the importance of design and color was limited to a select few fields such as apparel. Today these characteristics are recognized as important sales factors in such widely diversified fields as kitchen appliances and vitamin pills. Decisions on design and color must be customer oriented. That customer opinion must be constantly researched is evidenced by a test made by Rubbermaid, a manufacturer of sink mats, dish-draining trays, soap-dishes, and so on. The company had been successfully marketing its products in bright colors only to find that its customers preferred dull colors. It would seem that the company's success was due to factors that offset the color disapproval by customers.

Size

Size, like the other characteristics of a product, must be fitted to customer needs. Consider the case of Thom McAn shoe stores where some 150 styles must be carried. Each style must be broken down into colors and sizes. Many marketers in similar situations simply do not try to carry all the sizes that customers desire, preferring to lose business in unusual sizes and keep their stock at a manageable level.

The manufacturer's estimate of size is not always correct and requires constant revision. For example, when television sets first came out, manufacturers competed to market the largest sets possible under the belief that the bigger the picture, the wider the public appeal. Most manufacturers produced twenty-seven-inch monsters before they learned that the 19- to 21-inch screen had the widest popularity.

Styles in size vary as much as styles in products. Several years ago, the 25-pound packages of soap powder and 16- to 32-ounce soft drinks, which are popular today, were not available.

Marketers prefer large-package selling, since the expense of selling a large package is no greater than the costs of marketing a small package, whereas the sales volume and profitability are increased.

Materials

Frequently, the manufacturer of an article is faced with a wide variety of available materials. Clothing can be made of fabric constructed of many different natural or synthetic yarns. Other manufacturers must choose between various plastics and metals. The choice of materials should be based on the functional value of the material (the material chosen must be adequate for the use to which it is put), the salability of the material (customers may prefer a particular material over others, for example, nylon stockings), and production problems that might arise from the various materials (it is difficult to manufacture a fine white shirt from pure nylon).

Performance

Here again, the producer must put out an article conforming to the customer's requirements. This is particularly true in the wholesale market, where the customer frequently places performance specifications on desired purchases. Since improved performance raises the cost of the product, manufacturers generally fit performance to customer needs. Thus, most American automobiles are not designed to travel at speeds of 90 miles per hour when they are rarely used at speeds in excess of 65 miles per hour, the legal maximum in the United States.

PRODUCT FAILURE

Although producers constantly engage in the practice of developing new products, in reality many of them will ultimately fail. With all the sophistication of
marketing research, the failure rate is still alarmingly high. Those who are less
knowledgeable might conclude that the unsuccessful products belong to the
inexperienced and lesser known companies. On the contrary, the industrial
giants share the failures proportionately.

Students of marketing, to appreciate new product introduction more fully,
must be aware of the reasons for product failures and the magnitude of the
problem for a company when a new product does not survive in the market
place. In Chapter 8, a full exploration of this area of marketing is presented,
complete with specific examples and the reasons for the eventual withdrawal of
certain products from the production line.

MAKE OR BUY

As the present trend toward expanding the product line continues, management must face the decision of whether to make new products with the company's own manufacturing facilities or to contract for the work. Many firms
compromise by doing part of the work in their own plants and contracting out
the remainder. This is common among apparel manufacturers. In other industries, such as automobile manufacturing, the usual practice is to contract out
almost all the manufacturing and do all the assembling and finishing at company-owned plants. When a company has the idle time and the skills required
for manufacture of the product, it should unquestionably do its own work. On
the other hand, if a company is capable of distributing more goods than it is able
to manufacture, the difficult problem of whether to make or buy must be faced.
That is, should new manufacturing facilities be constructed or should the work
be contracted out? Several questions have to be answered before the make-or-
buy decision can be made.

1. What is the cheapest way to obtain the product? Not too long ago high
   union-labor costs forced low-end ladies' clothing manufacturers to give up
   their New York City area plants. The merchandise could not compete with
   similar goods manufactured in nonunion Southern shops. As a result,
   many manufacturers contracted their goods out to Southern manufacturers. Recent labor increases in the South have forced overseas contracting in
   such low-labor-cost areas as Puerto Rico, Hong Kong, and the Philippines.
2. Does the company know how to make the product? Many companies
   whose personnel does not have the knowledge needed to produce the new
   item prefer to have the work done by experienced, knowledgeable contractors.

3. Is the capital available to set up a new plant? Frequently, the specialized equipment necessary for construction of the new product (or some part of the new product) is beyond the financial capabilities of the company and contracting becomes a necessity.

4. Do the estimated life cycle and profitability of the item warrant the necessary expenditure for plant and equipment? If not, the obvious answer is to contract for the work.

5. Is secrecy important? Particularly among nonpatented items, materials, techniques, and design must be kept secret. This can be best effected by self-manufacture.

6. Can you depend upon outsiders? There is always the possibility of late delivery, price increases, and severed relationships when outside sources are used. This is particularly a problem for small manufacturers who exercise minor control over their contractors. Such giants as Sears, Roebuck—an enormous user of contract manufacturing—are able to enforce rigid control over their contractors.

7. Is the supplier of the merchandise also a customer for the buyer's other products?

Bristol-Myers had the make-or-buy decision solved for it. Management knew its roll-on deodorant product, Ban, was a winner, but design was a problem. The plastic broke down before the bottle emptied. It took six years to design it right only to find that there was no manufacturer equipped to produce the item. Bristol-Myers had to make the container.

PRODUCT DISCONTINUANCE

In the life of each product there comes a point at which decline in terms of sales and profitability necessitates its abandonment. Alert management should be able to milk the declining product until it reaches its nonprofit level. This requires careful planning, since reductions of promotional and other expenses must be timed to coincide with the decline in sales volume.

Many products must be kept in the line despite loss of profits in order to round out the offerings and maintain customer convenience. Most supermarket operators feel that sugar is a losing proposition because its handling costs are greater than its markup. Naturally, they cannot drop sugar from their shelves.

Manufacturers who are considering eliminating a product from their line must keep in mind their obligations to customers who own the product. This may require them to maintain a supply of replacement parts for some time after the last sale of the item.

SERVICE AS A PRODUCT

No discussion of product can be complete without some reference to services, since they form the fastest-growing sector of our economy. The definition of *services* is the performance of activities and accommodations required by the public. The marketing activities related to services do not include any physical goods. They are insignificant and incidental to the services involved. Service industries include professional services (medicine, law, and accounting); recreational services (motion pictures, television, and bowling alleys); renting services (hotels, motels, homes, and offices); personal services (beauty parlors, dry cleaners, and laundries); insurance; finance; and public utilities.

The same principles apply to the marketing of services as to that of other goods. The success of a marketing plan for services depends upon the quality of the service (product), its availability to the consumer (place), and the appeal of its promotion. In short, the marketing mix is as valid for services as products as it is for commodities as products, and the discussions concerning the marketing of products refer to both services and physical products.

Important Points in the Chapter _____

1. To a marketer, the definition of a product includes all the factors needed for customer satisfaction, that is, the physical product plus service, instructions, packaging, and so on.

2. New products are added to the line to get maximum use of manufacturing facilities, personnel, capital, goodwill, and distribution channels. As old products become obsolete, new products must be available to take their place and provide company growth.

3. The life cycle of a product consists of four stages: introduction, growth, maturity, and decline. To maintain a level state of income, new products must approach maturity as older products decline.

4. Well-managed companies set up new products departments that analyze ideas for new products, develop and market test them, and cooperate with the production and marketing divisions to get the product to the market.

5. Management has the final decision on whether or not to adopt a new product. This decision should be based on the probable demand for the new product, the manner in which the new product fits into the company's operation, and the capacity of the company to produce and market the new product.

6. Decisions on a product's quality, design, color, size, materials, and performance must be based on the consumer's desires. It should be neither better nor worse than the consumer demands.

7. The decision to make or buy must be based on comparative costs, capacity to produce, investment required in new equipment, and dependency of the contractor.

8. Products are usually discontinued when they are no longer profitable. As they go into their period of decline, costs should be reduced to prolong the period of profitability as much as possible. The company owes it to its customers to maintain a stock of service parts long after a product has been discontinued.

Review Questions

1. Explain the importance of the product in relation to promotion, price, and place.

2. Management is responsible for getting the maximum use of available resources. Discuss various idle resources that may be utilized by new product development.

3. Discuss the period of introduction and growth in the life cycle of a product.

4. Why are new products important to the life cycle of older products?

5. How should a new product department get ideas?

6. What tests should be put to ideas that seem good before the decision to develop the product is made?

7. Explain the new product department's role in the final production and marketing of a product.

8. Why are the getting, screening, and analysis of ideas the most important steps in new product development?

9. For what reason does the fashion designer constantly create new merchandise?

10. Define *fashion cycle.*

11. List the elements that must be taken into account by management in making the decision for the adoption of a new product.

12. What legal problems may arise with new products?

13. Discuss the quality that should be built into a new product.

14. Why are design and color important to a new product?

15. Why should a company want to contract manufacturing out to other manufacturers?

16. What planning is required when a product reaches the decline stage of its life cycle?

17. Should a company retain an inventory of parts for its discontinued products? Why?

Case Problems

Case Problem 1

Electronic Products, Inc., is the manufacturer of a line of electronic devices. Its alert, engineering-oriented management has been responsible for a steady growth rate during the fifteen years of the company's existence. The product line consists of electronic equipment that sells directly to the Department of Defense and the Atomic Energy Commission. In addition, some 10 percent of the company's sales arise through a subcontracting arrangement with a large manufacturer of household appliances.

Recent cutbacks in defense appropriations pose the threat of a reduction in the principal source of the firm's sales. Like many other companies in the same situation, the company is engaged in a frantic search for new consumer products. They have come up with a ship-to-shore receiver-transmitter radio for boating hobbyists. The consumer market for such equipment is large and rapidly expanding. The test models indicate that the company can profitably produce a better product than is presently available at the $250 price range. The financing, manufacture, and know-how to produce the radio are well within the company's capabilities.

Management understands that it must set up a marketing department to handle the promotion and distribution of the item. A young engineer who has been with the company for five years is anxious to take on the job. She is a graduate engineer with a master's degree in business administration, and is intelligent, innovative, and enthusiastic.

Questions

1. Should the company go ahead with the new product? Why?
2. If they decide to go ahead with it, how should they handle the marketing problem?

Case Problem 2

A leading manufacturer of grocery foods produces a very popular instant coffee. For years the firm has been troubled with the annoying and expensive problem of the disposal of the used coffee grounds that form the waste product of the manufacture of instant coffee.

Several years ago the problem was turned over to the research and development division to determine possible commercial uses for the waste material.

After much testing, it was found that with small additional cost, the coffee grounds could be converted into an excellent mulch for home gardeners and farmers. Cost estimates indicate that the product could be sold at a price competitive with competing brands of similar quality. Although the profitability of the new product would be somewhat below the high return that is typical of the company's other products, it would be acceptable as a return on the investment required to set up a processing plant for the item.

At the present time, the company has no intention of further penetration into the home-gardening or commercial-farming fields.

Questions

1. Should the company go into the product?
2. Are there any other alternatives?
3. If the firm decides to go ahead with the product, outline—in order, the steps that should be followed.

8

PRODUCTS AND SERVICES: FAILURES OUTNUMBER SUCCESSES

Learning Objectives

Upon completion of the chapter, you will be able to:

1. Discuss the rate of product failure.
2. List and discuss eight common reasons for product failure.
3. Compare the Merkur with the Mustang and explain why one was a failure and the other a success.
4. Describe the failure of RJR Nabisco's smokeless cigarette, Premier.

THE SWEET SMELL OF SUCCESS TURNS TO FAILURE

At a time when failure was abounding in many business sectors, the airline industry was no exception. Headlines everyday told us of the troubles of the major as well as minor airlines. It was in 1983 that Continental Airlines was struck by its employees and ultimately had to curtail its operation to avoid total disaster. Braniff declared bankruptcy the same year although a reorganization plan finally came to fruition in 1984 enabling the company to operate on a significantly smaller scale. A couple of years earlier, Freddie Laker with his London Skytrain was being heralded as the champion of the international airways; however his world also collapsed in bankruptcy. Amid these tales of woe, a Newark-based airline had taken the market by storm and had become a major operator.

People Express began its operation April 30, 1981, with three 737–100s purchased from Lufthansa. Their routes were to three cities—Buffalo, Columbus, and Norfolk, fifteen flights per day. Three years later their schedule increased to 116 daily departures from their Newark terminal to eighteen airports in the United States. In addition to the domestic flights, People flew 747 service to London's Gatwick Airport. People had become the number one carrier at Newark Airport and number two in the entire New York metropolitan area. If their plans were realized, this air carrier was destined soon to bypass the area's then top airline, Eastern.

People's record defied everyone's prediction. How could an upstart like People make such enormous inroads into air travel when the giants experienced problems that have made many close up shop?

The company offered as its objectives "high-frequency, low-price service to major markets . . . to be the best provider of air transportation . . . to offer the highest value for the consumer's money," and carried them out with stunning, favorable results. Its marketing strategy utilized a three-pronged approach: frequency, price, service. It selected underutilized markets such as West Palm Beach instead of Miami; went after a broad-based consumer market including business people, college students, and leisure travelers; priced tickets low with no restrictions such as advance purchase, length of stay, or holiday blackouts as required by the majors; initiated in-flight ticketing for all flights; and offered good service but no frills.

The People advertising strategy was noncomparative. It didn't use the other carriers to extol its own virtues. Its advertising, which was in both the print and broadcast media, used an "honest" approach. It regularly featured in some of their newspaper ads a price list of fares, peak and off-peak, to its many destinations. Other typical advertisements featured headlines such as "On People Express you pay for checking your baggage. On other airlines you pay for checking everyone else's"; "There's one airline that profits from charging less"; "The more an airline gives you free, the more you pay for a ticket"; and one that had considerable attention, "Flying that can cost less than phoning" with explanatory copy showing that a one-hour phone call to Boston could cost more than the off-peak fare to the same destination.

People's success was due to the lower salaries paid to their employees (all of whom were in profit-sharing arrangements), the cutting of service to the essentials, and the offering of substantial savings. At a time when Air Florida was in deep trouble,

PEOPLExpress in its prime.
(*Courtesy:* PEOPLExpress.)

Continental and Braniff were still in financial difficulty, People Express was one success in a field of failures.

The darling of the airlines industry was truly "flying high." It was on a roll that saw the acquisition of more planes and more routes. Then, the bubble burst, and People Express joined the ranks of the other airline fatalities. Poor management and financial burdens soon caught up with People Express. As quickly as success was achieved, failure followed even faster.

INTRODUCTION

Marketing strategy and development is perhaps today at a level higher than industry has ever witnessed. The sophistication of the tools available to researchers has never been greater. In the past twenty-five years the advance in technological developments has been tremendous. Comprehension of the consuming population in terms of motivation and needs has continued to improve. Marketers are said to be at a point where just about every bit of scientific and psychological information necessary to ensure product success is available. With the wealth of knowledge that permeates each and every major marketing organization, the rate of product failure seems to remain the same as it was in years when less sophisticated tools of the trade were available to marketers. Practitioners continuously search for the reasons for the failures, but the problem is still very real, with some types of products failing at an unbelievably alarming rate.

It should be mentioned, however, that amid all the gloom hovering over new product introduction, many products are successfully introduced and continue to show profits over long periods of time.

Failure of products is by no means limited to small companies. Many of the disasters have been and will continue to be attributed to the industrial giants. The failure of Scott's Babyscott diapers, Lever Brothers' Vim tablet detergent, Rheingold's Gablinger beer, Bristol-Myer's Resolve, Dupont's Corfam, a synthetic leather that was supposed to revolutionize the shoe industry, Cadillac's Cimmaron, and RJR Nabisco's revolutionary smokeless Premier cigarette baffled marketers.

THE RATE OF PRODUCT FAILURE

When one examines studies that have been conducted in the area of product failure, it is alarming to see that, in some areas, failure has inched up to the 90 percent rate. The information in Table 8–1 shows, according to category, the rate of failure and the group that made the study.

Table 8–1 shows a vast difference in the findings of the various studies. Comparison is difficult because the definitions of *failure* were not universal nor were the markets studied identical. The information is meaningful to marketing students, however, as an illustration that failure is a factor that still plagues even the most prestigious companies.

REASONS FOR PRODUCT FAILURE

The tremendous failure rate has led to all the investigative studies by the major organizations referred to in Table 8–1. Their findings, based on the examination of hundreds of companies, indicate a variety of reasons for nonsuccessful product introduction. Table 8–2 shows a composite of the eight reasons for new product failures that resulted from eight major research studies. Across the top of the chart are indicated the names of the researchers, and at the far right, in the total column, the number of studies that showed the particular reason for product failure. It is interesting to note that while many people suspect high cost to be the likely factor that led to failure, only one study reported the cost factor as the reason.

It should be understood that mistakes made by marketers can be attributed to small and giant organizations alike. In the following section, explanation of the more common reasons for failure are explored, and, where applicable, specific products are indicated to underscore the fact that even household names are affected.

TABLE 8–1. Rate of product failure

Product Classification	Failure Rate (%)	Investigative Study
Food and drug items	53 (1971)	A. C. Nielsen Co.
	50–80	*Business Week*
	Over 80	Charles E. Rosen
	Over 80	John W. Dodd, Jr.
	43	Helene Curtis
	Over 40	J. Walter Thompson
New consumer goods	Over 80	Theodore L. Angelus
	37 (1968)	Booze, Allen & Hamilton
	40	The Conference Board
	80	Ross Federal Research Corporation
New industrial goods	20	The Conference Board
	30–40	Booz, Allen & Hamilton
New products	90	U.S. Department of Commerce

Source: C. Merle Crawford, *Journal of Marketing.*

TABLE 8–2. Reasons for new product failures

	Abrams (1)	Angelus (2)	Booz, Allen, Hamilton (3)	Constandse (5)	Diehl (6)	Hopkins & Bailey (10)	MacDonald (11)	Miles (13)	TOTAL
1. Lacked meaningful product uniqueness[1]	X	X	X	X	X	X	X	X	8
2. Poor planning[2]	X	X		X	X	X	X		6
3. Timing wrong	X	X	X	X		X			5
4. Enthusiasm crowded on facts				X	X	X	X	X	5
5. Product failed	X	X				X			3
6. Product lacked a champion					X				1
7. Company politics					X				1
8. Unexpected high product cost						X			1

[1]In some cases there was, in fact, no difference, but in most cases there was some difference, whose value was overestimated by the marketers to potential buyers.
[2]Includes poor positioning, poor segmentation, underbudgeting, poor overall themes, ovepricing, and all other facets of a plan.

Source: C. Merle Crawford, *Journal of Marketing.*

Poor Market Testing

Included in this category is the inability to predict accurately the demand for the new products. Apparently, even the most sophisticated market research programs cannot always judge the customers' buying habits and product preferences.

Product Performance

With the sophistication of product timing available to marketers today, the percentage of product failures that occur as a result of poor performance is substantially decreasing. Each year more emphasis is placed on prolonged market testing before a company will give the go-ahead for production. This longer testing period affords the producer the chance to uncover product defects.

Although the testing procedures are generally rigorous, products occasionally fail due to unsatisfactory performance that is somehow overlooked during the testing period. In some instances the unique feature of a new product is carefully scrutinized, whereas other product aspects might be less carefully examined. When General Foods nationally distributed Post cereals containing freeze-dried fruits, it eventually cost General Foods $5 million due to the slow reconstitution of the fruit. By the time the fruit was reconstituted, the cereal became soggy.

Most of the products that fail because of poor performance are food products. Essentially, the problem is one of assessing the customer's taste preference. Campbell's Red Kettle and Knorr's initial dry soup failures were the result of the taste problem. Consumers have purchased Lipton's dry soups for many years. Campbell's and Knorr were unsuccessful as a result of their inability to assess the taste appeal of their products in relation to Lipton's.

No Point of Difference

Most new products—about 80 percent—have a point of difference. If not, the new product usually fails. There are, however, exceptions. In some markets where the number of consumers is large enough, many products without particular differences are successful. Cigarettes, hair sprays, toilet soaps, and floor waxes are examples. However, when a market is not large enough, the introduction of the same product with a new name is apt to fail. Kaiser withdrew its aluminum foil because it did not provide any advantages over the leaders, Alcoa and Reynolds. In marketing, new products with basically no point of difference to existing products are often referred to as "me-too" products.

Insignificant Product Differences

Many consumer goods producers try to climb aboard the bandwagon of another manufacturer's successful distribution of a specific product. The mere fact that the new product is just the original in disguise generally leads to the failure of the new product. Container changes, slight formula variation, or presentation of the product in a new form (tablets instead of powders, for example) do not seem to adequately convince the customer to buy the new product. Specifically, the following items failed as a result of insignificant product differences.

Duractin, introduced by Menly and James, was marketed as a painkiller that would provide relief for eight hours. This minor difference (as compared with the other successfully marketed painkillers) proved unimportant to the broad segment of consumers who wanted speedy relief. The cost of failure attributed to the Western region alone is estimated at $1,500,000.

An expected threat to the leadership of Heinz's ketchup was Hunt's introduction of flavored ketchups. They failed to gain the favor of the consumer market. The cost of the failure was approximately $1,200,000. Although Hunt was clearly a loser in this campaign, Del Monte tried to challenge Heinz with a similar idea. It produced a barbecue ketchup, slightly altering the normal ketchup formula by adding onions to the recipe. That, too, failed.

One of the most frequent reasons for failure in this category seems to be that old products are presented in new forms. For example, the production of tablets instead of powder, liquids instead of tablets, and aerosols in place of pastes, does not generally prove to be successful. Formula 409 and Fantastic, both highly accepted and profitable household cleansers, were challenged by the introduction of Easy-Off household cleanser. The former products were in liquid form, the latter was an aerosol foam. Consumers did not see any advantage in the use of Easy-Off. The only difference was in product form. The cost of this failure to American Home Products, Inc., producers of Easy-Off, was estimated at $850,000.

Bad Timing

Often, too many similar products are introduced at the same time. This can alter a company's successful distribution and constitutes a fourth reason for product failure. Usually, the smaller company gets squeezed out of the market first.

A few years ago consumers witnessed the simultaneous introduction of several new toothpastes and mouthwashes. Perhaps best remembered are Vote, Fact, Cue, and Reef. The combined losses to the producers of these products were estimated at better than $40 million. More recently, consumers saw a household-cleaner market explosion. Among the seventeen brands that were introduced in a nine-month period were Easy-Off, Clean & Kill, and Whistle. The estimated losses were between $5 and $7 million.

Presently, explosive situations are much in evidence in the markets for items such as presoaks, phosphate-free detergents, feminine-hygiene deodorants, and sugar substitutes.

During the summer of 1989, fashion trade papers such as *Women's Wear*

Daily, touted the designer collections that featured the "Mao" look in their "Red Guard" supplement. Just as the fashions were being promoted by American companies, the turmoil in China erupted. Given the hysteria that surrounded the deaths of Chinese citizens during the political uprisings, the new Chinese influenced fashion introduction was ill-timed. At any other period, the styles were sure successes.

Poor Product Positioning

Product positioning is categorized into three areas: insignificant, confused, and mismatched. Insignificant positioning is defined as consumer disinterest in the product, confused positioning means that the consumer does not understand the promotional message, and mismatched positioning means that the product's performance does not match the appeal.

Insignificant Positioning.   In most cases this is directly related to insignificant product differences. If a manufacturer produces an unimportant product, it will be reflected in the advertising. In the case of Easy-Off, the basis of the advertising campaign was that it was an aerosol foam. Comparative demonstrations showed that Easy-Off did not run as the liquid did. Although consumer recall of the advertising campaign was extremely high, the fact that the product sold poorly was evidence that consumers did not care for it. If the product difference is a real one, the consumer generally will purchase. Examples of gimmick-free advertising are Head & Shoulders dandruff shampoo and Nyquil nighttime cold remedy.

Confused Positioning.   This is perhaps best illustrated by Revlon's introduction of Super Natural hair spray. The confusion that led to the eventual loss of millions of dollars was directly related to the words *super* and *natural.* In terms of hair sprays, *super* means more holding power, whereas *natural* means less holding power. The consuming public, faced with this uncertainty regarding the product, did not purchase it. Although Revlon, in its own defense, said that hair spray purchases were shifting to lower-priced brands and blamed this as the cause for failure, the confusion left for the consumer to unscramble definitely did not help Super Natural's position.

Mismatched Positioning.   This is generally regarded by marketers as the greatest individual problem in advertising communication. Positioning a new product means determining the most effective combination of the product's features and consumer appeal. An excellent example of a product that was raised to a level of tremendous success by a change in its positioning is Right Guard deodorant. Originally positioned as a man's deodorant, an advertising change was instituted in later campaigns that claimed it to be "the perfect family deodorant because nothing touches you but the spray itself." Sales increased annually by $20 million. Because of a more effective combination of consumer appeal and product performance, Right Guard sales are now at the $50 million mark.

Since there may be many different product characteristics and as many different areas of consumer appeal, the possible appeal–product performance combinations can be almost limitless. The task for marketers is to select the most appropriate combination to ensure product success.

Wrong Market for Company

Although companies may be highly successful with certain product lines, often their ventures into different types of manufacture prove to be disastrous. Marketers sometimes seek to enter markets that do not fall within their capabilities.

Procter & Gamble was unsuccessful when it entered the hair spray market with Hidden Magic and Winterset/Summerset. Colgate also met with failure with the introduction of 007 after-shave lotion. Failures of this nature result from lack of experience necessary to generate a "feel" for certain businesses.

Surveys indicate that companies fail because they try to penetrate a new market, but few marketers readily admit that failure was due to their incomplete understanding of that market.

According to the survey taken by the New Products Action Team, Inc., the failure rate for each category was

Insignificant product difference	36%
Poor product positioning	32%
No point of difference	20%
Bad timing	16%
Product performance	12%
Wrong market for company	8%

(Total is more than 100 percent because some failures were due to more than one reason.)

In addition to the causes of product failures explored, which were based exclusively on new supermarket products, there are others that deserve examination.

Costs

Although this does not happen too often, the costs involved in the production and distribution of a new product may be higher than anticipated. Efficient research should determine the costs of manufacturing, which in turn determine the product's price, but unforeseen variables might invalidate the estimate. For example, between the product's inception and the distribution to the customer a period of three years might elapse. Test marketing at a particular price might have been completed a year prior to production. According to the test market, the product will be successful. After testing of the product, the price of raw materials used in its manufacture increases, as do factory salaries (at an unusual rate because of a strike). These two factors would probably necessitate a price rise. The resulting higher price might attract a smaller market than originally expected, leading to smaller sales volume and eventual product failure.

Inadequate Sales Effort

The giants of industry generally have adequate sales forces, but the smaller producers often spend little time in the training of sales personnel. Insufficient attention paid to formal training or motivation is frequently the cause of the small manufacturer's product failure. It is not the product that is weak, but the selling job that is ineffective.

A MARKETING PROFILE

RJR Nabisco's Smokeless Premier Cigarette

Smoking cigarettes, until recent years, gave the user a feeling of maturity. Young men made the transition from boyhood to manhood by displaying the cigarette pack in their shirt pockets, and young women supposedly achieved an air of sophistication by using the product. For many years, cigarette advertising helped to improve sales until the federal government imposed strict regulations on the industry. With the medical community warning of the cancer and heart problems resulting from cigarette use, the tobacco industry saw a long losing battle ahead.

In 1981 R. J. Reynolds held its first meetings to discuss a revolutionary concept, the smokeless cigarette, and in 1982, the company's research and development division began to work on the project. After five years of preliminary work, the company announced plans for its new product, the smokeless cigarette, Premier, see Figure 8–1. This was to be the product that would stop the campaign against cigarettes. It was not to happen. The new product's failure cost the company an estimated $300 million.

What were the reasons for failure? How could a company of such magnitude commit such a blunder? Some of the following reasons surfaced after Premier was test marketed for five months in St. Louis, Tucson, and Phoenix:

- Igniting the cigarette was no simple matter. The traditional match couldn't do the job, nor could the typical lighter. Only a high-quality

The carbon heats, but does not burn, the tobacco jacket and the flavor capsule to produce a "smoke" that is cooled by passing through a tobacco filter and then a conventional filter.

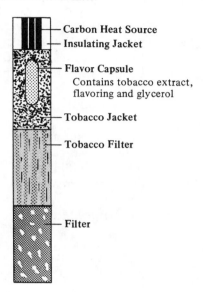

FIGURE 8–1

butane lighter could satisfactorily cause Premier to burn. Consumers just didn't respond to the four-page instruction booklet that was affixed to each pack to direct the consumer to light the cigarette.
- The taste and aroma of Premier were also unpleasant. Some said it smelled like burning plastic.
- Health organizations cited the product as a "drug delivery device." "It could easily be taken apart and reassembled by addicts who wanted it to smoke crack cocaine."

The decision to abandon the product was the first marketing move of Kohlberg, Kravis, Roberts & Company, the new owner of RJR Nabisco, Inc., which owns Reynolds Tobacco.

Since cigarette sales have been declining since 1982, the Premier fiasco was a major setback in the already troubled tobacco industry.

FORD MOTOR COMPANY'S MERKUR—STUDY OF A FAILURE

In 1948 Ford conceived the idea of a new automobile to add to its family of cars, the Edsel. Few people remember it except for some senior citizens and those in the marketing game. Its demise was supposed to serve as a lesson for new company products at Ford, but its recent death of a product, the Merkur, seems to resurrect the ghost of the Edsel along wi   problems. Later in the chapter, attention will focus upon how the Ford Motor Company recouped much of the losses associated with its Edsel, but its latest failure seems to indicate that lessons are not always learned.

The Merkur was not an automobile produced by Ford in the United States, but one that was imported from Germany. In these times of successful imports from Mercedes Benz, BMW, Volvo, and Saab, Ford thought this product would be a natural. Its brief history proved otherwise.

The Product

The automobile was a huge success in both Germany and Great Britain where it was called the Sierra. It was to be renamed the Merkur XR4Ti for export into the United States. The base price was $17,000, affordable when compared to other performance, European automobiles.

The Target Market

The aim of Ford was to appeal to the yuppie market who was having a love affair with BMW and Saab. Those targeted were college graduates, about 30 years old, with incomes of $40,000. With its price tag of about $20,000 (including the extras), it was believed this car could deliver the prestige sought after by this group, at a reasonable price.

The Marketing Approach

An initial investment of $13 million was spent on advertising. Instead of choosing television as the major medium, it elected to use its dollars for print advertising and direct mail. The campaigns centered upon comparing the Merkur to other high-tech, European sports cars such as the BMW 318i and the Audi 4000-S Quatro, both excellent sellers. Comfort and lower sticker price were stressed in the campaigns in addition to status and snob appeal.

A decision was made to feature the Merkur in the same showrooms as Lincoln-Mercury instead of separate showrooms as was done for the ill-fated Edsel. It was believed these sales offices were experienced and already attracted automobile purchasers of Ford products.

After the early indications of problems with sales, the company decided to go the incentive route of discounts to encourage prospective buyers to purchase the car. With discounts of $3,000 in 1988, the Merkur still didn't make its mark.

The Failure of the Merkur XR4Ti

With the decision to discontinue production, Ford had to once again face its critics and stockholders, as it did with the Edsel, and explain the problem.

Among the reasons cited for the failure by the industry were

1. The name of the automobile was difficult to pronounce, and the mix of the letters and number XR4Ti were confusing and jumbled. (The original "Sierra" was abandoned because General Motors complained it was too similar to its Oldsmobile Ciera).

2. The styling was considered too radical for American taste. While it was trying to compete with BMW with its sleek look, the Merkur was "round and bulbous," according to Eric Conn, senior marketing manager for Honda Motor Company. A vast majority of potential purchasers agreed that the styling wasn't to their liking.

3. The use of Lincoln-Mercury dealerships didn't turn up the right market for the car. Their customers were not the purchasers of foreign automobiles but buyers of more moderately priced and conventionally styled cars.

4. The choice of advertising media was wrong, and the allocated budget was insufficient. Network television wasn't used but instead only a handful of ads in a few markets. The print advertising and direct mail didn't have the clout needed to promote sales. "They tried to do it on the cheap, and it didn't work," said Marianne Keller, financial analyst with Furman Selz.

5. The Lincoln-Mercury dealerships didn't understand how to merchandise the Merkur. They were educated in terms of high-volume sales and not the selling of a specialty car. Research showed that the potential buyers of the Merkur knew more about the product than the salespeople.

Perhaps the best explanation is the one given by David Wager, president of Satchi & Satchi Team One, who launched Toyota's latest car, the Lexus. "Ford didn't do its marketing homework. When you launch a car, what you have to do is tell consumers who the car is for, where its from, and where you can buy it."

Inadequate Planning and Testing

It is obvious that many of the reasons for the failure of new products described above are the result of errors of judgment. Although errors like these must occur, they may be kept at a minimum by a careful selection of the personnel of the new-product department. It is not enough to select people with imagination who are capable of innovative ideas; they must also have the proper attitude. Some of the attitudes causing failure of potentially highly successful products are

1. Assumption that everyone looks at a product in the same way the new product department does. To offset this, the new product should be tested among the wide variety of people that will make up its eventual market; this will show the attitude of each class of customers toward the item.

2. Tendency to halt research on new product design too soon, that is, as soon

as what appears to be an adequate design is achieved. The fact is that adequate is not enough. Research and development must continue until the design has been proven successful by careful market research.

3. Attitude on the part of the new product department that the production and marketing of the item is not its problem; in fact, this department should be responsible for the manufacturing specifications as well as for the formulation of the selling pitch. This is a common error that is more the result of faulty organization than of personnel attitude. It can be remedied by a revision of the duties and responsibilities of the new product department.

4. Substitution of the everything-will-be-all-right attitude in estimating the adequacy of the budget for a scientific analysis of the funds necessary to properly launch the product.

6. Failure to have an attorney clear the patent and other legal aspects.

Not all of these errors are the fault of the personnel in the new product department. Generally, the new product department is under considerable pressure from management to get the product out on the market (where it can start earning money) as soon as possible. Giving in to this pressure before the product is ready may result in any of the reasons for failure that were described above.

A number of other reasons for the failure of products, such as poor market analysis, improper determination of consumer motivation, competition, and distribution shortcomings will be discussed in terms of the material that follows.

FORD MOTOR COMPANY'S MUSTANG—STUDY OF A SUCCESS

The 1950s saw the Ford Motor Company introduce a new automobile that was supposed to be one of the century's greatest successes, just like the Merkur. It was given the company's top priority and along with it a great research and development effort. The automobile, called the Edsel, almost disappeared from sight soon after its introduction. Its failure cost Ford enormous sums, and even more than that, its reputation was tarnished. Licking its wounds, Ford was determined to make amends to its stockholders and to regain their once-favorable image.

The outgrowth of this challenge was the introduction of the Mustang. Armed with the all-too-hurtful wounds of the Edsel and a pledge to learn from their errors, they went full speed ahead with plans for what would become the industry's hottest car.

Determining a Market

Before such factors as style, price, and so on, could be estimated, it was necessary to determine whether or not there was a market for a new automobile and, if so, what kind of market it would be. In 1959 the auto industry had introduced its compact cars in response to customer demand for economy transportation. Studying its own Falcon and Chevrolet's Corvair, Ford's research team noted certain important facts. Although customers bought the compacts, many were enthusiastically adding accessories to the basic automobile, thus boosting the price and indicating that perhaps economy was not all that was sought. Additional investigation of the Corvair proved that customers wanted luxury features in their compact auto. Chevrolet dressed up the Corvair with bucket seats and some other sporty features and called it the Corvair Monza. This car was a tremendous success in terms of sales. The study of these two cars brought into view that there was an obvious gap to be filled in the automobile industry. Besides this, there was the success of the foreign sports cars to be considered. At a time when it was believed that nothing but economy was wanted by the public, the European sports automobiles were making an impact on the American auto market. From these observations, Ford's marketing research team set out to discover exactly what the consumer wanted. Seymour Marshak, Ford's marketing research manager, perhaps summed up the situation of the time: "They seemed to want economy, no matter what they had to pay for it."

The State of the Market

Early in 1961 Ford Motor Company observed with considerable interest a number of new, particularly important sociological and economic developments in three distinct areas.

First, the World War II babies were entering the automobile market. According to all indications, buyers aged 18 to 34 would account for more than 50 percent of the increase in sales of new automobiles projected for the coming decade. In addition, this market would account for the majority of the purchases of used cars. It was obvious that the young buyers would be a significant factor in the auto market. Research also showed that youth had certain specialized demands about style and performance. For example, studies revealed that 36 percent of all people under 25 liked the 4-speed floor shift; among those over 25, only 9 percent preferred to shift gears. Another preference of the younger group was bucket seats (35 percent of the young people), whereas only 13 percent of the older group liked such seats. An interesting early study was conducted by Ford to determine whether or not college students considered bucket seats a hindrance to romance. The results of a survey conducted in eight cities throughout the United States indicated that 42 percent preferred them on first dates in comparison with 15 percent preference of couples going steady. It was evident that the young people were seeking an automobile with a sporty flair.

A second development that was affecting the market was education. In addition to the expectation of more young people in the market, there was the certainty that they would be better educated. In 1960 there were 3.5 million students enrolled in colleges. The prediction for 1970 was double that figure.

Bearing this in mind, the company had to be prepared to appeal to a better educated buyer. Ford's market research consistently showed that college graduates purchase significantly more automobiles than less educated people. (A study taken in 1964 substantiates this point. Nineteen percent of the population had some college education; this segment of the population bought 46 percent of all the new cars sold in the United States that year.) Aside from the statistics showing a correlation between car purchasing and education, people in general were becoming more sophisticated through the enormous influence of television.

A third factor leading to Ford's decision to produce the Mustang was the tremendous increase in the number of multiple-car buyers. In 1959 more than one million families owned more than one car, a number that researchers believed would increase in the 1960s. In 1964 multiple-car owners exceeded thirteen million, by 1967, two million families owned three automobiles.

The increasing affluence of the consumer contributed to this growth in multiple-car ownership. Market research went on to predict that this increase in affluence was to continue. This forecast, too, had been substantiated in the last decade and family earnings were expected to keep rising. Women also played an influential role in multiple-auto ownership. Studies showed that the number of women drivers had grown for the period from 1956 to 1962 by 53 percent. They demanded a second car for themselves, and research indicated the type of automobiles they desired. They were interested in ease of parking and handling, a smaller size (because only the first car in the family must be capable of transporting the entire family), and attractive styling.

From the foregoing extensive research, it was obvious to the Ford Motor Company that the ordinary automobile would not suffice. Two criteria, essential to the success of the new car, stood out. The car had to be attractive, with a distinct personality, and the price had to be appropriate for the potential young market.

Creation of the Style

A task force of Ford designers, engineers, and product planners initially set down the concept of an experimental sports car. It was a two-seater, obviously inappropriate for appeal to a mass market. Ford learned with the two-passenger Thunderbird that the market for two-passenger automobiles is too limited to ensure the volume needed to make the new car a success. Research indicated that Ford could not expect to exceed 40,000 units a year for two-passenger models, whereas the figure for a four-passenger auto was as high as 150,000.

A prototype of the original Mustang (see Figure 8–2) was placed on exhibition at the Watkins Glen Grand Prix in the fall of 1962, creating tremendous excitement. Subsequent showings at various colleges drew enormous, enthusiastic crowds. This reaction of admiration, coupled with the research statistics regarding potential sales of four-passenger models, led Ford to believe that it

FIGURE 8–2   A prototype of the original Mustang. (*Courtesy:* Ford Motor Company.)

had the right insights into the production of its new car. The incorporation of the flair of the original two-seater into a four-seater could create a potentially successful car for both personal and family use. While extensive market research continued, spot information and detailed results flowed into Lee Iacocca's (Ford Motor Company vice-president and general manager of the Ford Division) office, where they were questioned, challenged, and digested. In those days it was called the T-5 project, and it was the topic of brainstorming for the entire executive staff. As various T-5 versions came off the drawing boards, market research looked at them through the eyes of consumer panels, asking: Which automotive company would produce a car like this? How much do you think such a car would cost? What don't you like about it? Would you buy it? What would you use it for?

Time was a factor at this point because Ford wanted an automobile ready for display at the World's Fair, scheduled to open in April 1964. It was felt that this setting would provide a dramatic showcase for the première showing of the Mustang.

A crash program was initiated to arrive at an acceptable design. Designers at the corporate projects studio, the Ford studio, and the Lincoln-Mercury studio were given dimensions and desirable features as indicated through research and were asked to engage in open competition, with a two-week limit, for the presentation of clay models of their design ideas. Seven designs were submitted and reviewed at the end of the two-week period. One model stood out distinctly, although many of them were considered to be excellent. After continuous study the Ford planners felt that the car—distinguished by a sporty air—that was produced by the Ford studio (see Figure 8–3) was the one. To satisfy themselves that they had chosen the best model, selected groups of potential customers were invited to inspect the seven models. Careful observations of reactions were recorded and an analysis was made of the opinions expressed. The response confirmed management's decision to produce the design of the

FIGURE 8–3   Mustang's sporty air, as designed by Ford's planners. (*Courtesy:* Ford Motor Company.)

Ford studio. It was felt that this model supplied what the market lacked. The next step was to determine the engineering feasibility of the project. The car stood up well under these tests.

It was determined that the Mustang would offer a wide selection of options and engines. This enabled the automobile to satisfy a large variety of tastes. Luxury buyers could satisfy themselves with a number of extras, whereas young buyers, with more limited budgets, would be able to afford the standard Mustang and would still be satisfied because of its sporty appearance.

Pricing

Having determined through research that the fastest-growing, best-spending segment of the car-buying public consisted of 16- to 24-year-olds, high school and college students, young marrieds, and young working people, the most important question to be answered was how much this group was willing to pay for the car. It was Seymour Marshak's contention that these people would still have low earning power. He felt that a car was needed that would offer the performance and flair of the highly successful Thunderbird and a price tag in the vicinity of the Falcon.

The price was established along lines similar to those used to set the price for the Model-T Ford when it was originally introduced. That is, first determine what the potential customer is willing to pay for the car, then develop the specifications around that price.

Marketing research asked customers how much they were willing to spend on a new automobile. The studies were conducted among young people and young marrieds, the target market. Tabulation and analysis of the data collected indicated that the price could not exceed $2,500. Bearing this in mind, production was organized to create an automobile in that price class.

Consequently, the Mustang was to be priced in an area of the industry that accounted for 22 percent of sales. This figured to almost two million units annually. At this price, it was also within a $200 to $300 range of an area that accounted for 63 percent of the industry. In terms of units, this meant 4.5 million, based on 1963 figures.

Ford, after weighing and measuring the many pricing factors, decided to sell the Mustang as a one-standard model for $2,368, F.O.B. Detroit. The price included many features that are often extras on automobiles, such as bucket seats, padded instrument panel, full wheel covers, wall-to-wall carpeting, cigarette lighter, turn signals, heater, front armrests, and seat belts.

The specifications for the Mustang that evolved from the marketing research data were as follows:

Weight:	Not more than 2,500 pounds
Length:	Not more than 180 inches
Engine:	Peppy 6 cylinders
Seating:	Four passengers, bucket seats in front
Personality:	Demure enough for churchgoing, racy enough for the drag strip, and modish enough for the country club.

Continuous Market Analysis

The research did not cease with the decision to produce the Mustang. There was a continuous study of the potential market. Ford made a series of studies to make sure it was on the right track.

Early in 1963, it conducted a study to check its evaluations of the impact of car sizes and related features on prospective new car buyers. In February and March additional pricing studies were made. These were rechecked with further special pricing studies in August.

Studies to select a name came in mid-1963. These were put off because it was deemed unnecessary to select a name until the actual production of the automobile was completed. Several marketing research studies were used to determine the name of the new car. John Conley of the J. Walter Thompson Advertising Agency collected six thousand names from the Detroit public library. After conducting consumer research to check the image that certain names convey, the list was narrowed to a few finalists. These were Colt, Bronco, Mustang, Puma, Cheetah, and Cougar. Cougar was to be the new automobile's name. It was not until near the end that it was discovered that this name belonged to and was controlled by another company.

The name that Henry Ford wanted, *T-Bird III*, was not acceptable to the other executives. The name *Mustang* was finally chosen by the executive group because of its image established in the consumer research studies. A spokesman for the J. Walter Thompson Agency stated, "It had the excitement of the wide open spaces and was American as all hell."

In September 1963, a special styling clinic was conducted to recheck the styling decision. It had occurred to the Ford people that, although the Mustang was developed primarily to fit the young and multiple-automobile market, it was sufficiently exciting to attract additional prospects from other segments of the consumer market. Accordingly, when a prototype of the Mustang was completed, fifty-two couples who had preteen children and who owned a single standard-sized automobile were selected at random to come to the Ford studio in small groups to see the new car. Although their immediate reactions were enthusiastic in every respect, the observers agreed that the car was impractical for their own needs. When, however, they were asked to estimate the selling price of the Mustang, most of the couples made guesses that were in excess of $1,000 higher than the intended selling price. Upon being told the actual price, by and large they changed their viewpoints. Second looks seemed to bring to the surface many reasons why the car was really practical for their needs, after all. Curiously, none of the fifty-two couples in this aspect of the research questioned the car's performance or handling. The car had the look of good performance about it, and that seemed to be sufficient.

These and other studies helped Ford to pinpoint the buying attitudes toward which a marketing campaign could be aimed. Approval had already been given to the car's styling; it possessed a performance look, the low price appealed to couples with children (who were not previously considered part of Mustang's market), and the wide complement of options made the car suitable for luxury-, sport-, or economy-oriented prospective customers.

The continuous analysis of the market did, indeed, provide wider horizons for the Mustang than were originally anticipated.

Promotion of the Mustang

Introduction day was scheduled for April 17, 1964, approximately three years after the actual planning of the Mustang began. This is considerable lead time in terms of most products; however, it is not uncommon in the automobile industry, where it is essential to determine the needs of the market several years in advance.

Four days prior to the public's introduction to the Mustang, a special press preview took place in the Ford pavilion at the New York World's Fair. The immediate reaction of the press was enthusiastic. Besides just showing the new automobile to the press, Ford did something innovative. One hundred twenty-four reporters were paired and given Mustangs, complete with rally instructions, that took them 750 miles to Detroit. This activity turned the reporters' original enthusiasm into delight, which was soon expressed by the members of the press in their respective publications. The generous praise that ensued is an example of the publicity that can result from an effective promotional campaign. Cover stories were provided by *Time* and *Newsweek* with *Life* and *Look* carrying editorials concerning the new car.

On April 16 the Mustang was shown simultaneously on the three major television networks to twenty-nine million homes. This was the first time that a major automotive company was on all networks at the same time.

Presenting the unexpected...
New Ford Mustang!

This is the car you never expected from Detroit. It is so distinctively beautiful it has received the Tiffany Award for Excellence in American Design, the first automobile ever to be so honored by Tiffany & Co. Mustang has the look, the fire, the flavor of one of the great European road cars. Yet it is as American as its name . . . and as practical as its price. Because Mustang is an amazingly versatile car and can be inexpensively tailored to the widest variety of individual tastes, many very different people will find it surprisingly easy to say: "This is the ideal car for me." Turn the page and you'll see why.

FIGURE 8–4   Mustang announcement as it appeared in U.S. newspapers. (*Courtesy:* Ford Motor Company.)

On the following day the Mustang announcement (shown in Figure 8–4), was printed in more than twenty-six hundred newspapers in approximately twenty-two hundred markets. The theme used, "Presenting the unexpected . . . ," underscored the *unexpected* in styling and low price. Similar to the technique used in catalogs, the ad listed just what the purchaser would receive for $2,368 and what options could be added. The ad was evaluated by the million-market newspapers' reports as having achieved the highest readership score recorded by a full-page color advertisement. It should be noted that successful ads are not just accidental happenings. An enormous amount of effort went into the creation of the ads that were used by Ford for the Mustang's introduction. With the help of the J. Walter Thompson Advertising Agency ads such as the one shown in Figure 8–5 were designed; they were used in the World's Fair Guide, 1964, the *Ladies' Home Journal,* and *Look* magazine. These ads emphasized design, performance, and price.

In addition to the regular newspaper ads, a special announcement directed to the female market was run on the women's pages the same day. This ad highlighted the Tiffany award for excellence in design that had been bestowed upon the Mustang, the first automobile ever to receive such an award. Since Tiffany meant, to most women, the epitome of elegance, the tie-in was extremely effective. It was estimated that 75 percent of all households in the United States were covered through the newspaper medium.

In an effort to capture the attention of as large a part of the reading public as possible, a Mustang announcement was placed in twenty-four of the nation's largest circulated magazines. The total circulation of these magazines was sixty-

FORD MUSTANG HARDTOP

New Ford Mustang—$2368* f.o.b. Detroit

This is the car you never expected from Detroit. Mustang is so distinctively beautiful, it's the first car to receive the Tiffany Award for Excellence in American Design.

*Yet Mustang carries a suggested retail price of just $2368—f.o.b. Detroit, not including destination charges from Detroit, options, state and local taxes and fees, if any. Whitewall tires are $33.90 extra.

At $2368, Mustang includes luxuries like bucket seats, vinyl upholstery, wall-to-wall carpeting as standard equipment. *And* there's a fabulous range of reasonably priced options!

See Mustang while you're at the Fair . . . and ride Walt Disney's incredible *Magic Skyway* at the beautiful Ford Pavilion.

TRY TOTAL PERFORMANCE
FOR A CHANGE!

FORD

Mustang · Falcon · Fairlane
Ford · Thunderbird

FIGURE 8–5   Mustang ads as developed by J. Walter Thompson Advertising Agency. (*Courtesy:* Ford Motor Company.)

eight million. Ford used two- and four-page color spreads to introduce its new automobile to the public.

Although TV, radio, newspapers, and magazines are considered to be the most important advertising media for the introduction of automobiles, Ford felt that no group or promotional device should be neglected in this campaign. The publishing and distribution of a forty-eight-page Mustang introduction plans book recapped the advertising and merchandising plans for the local dealers. It also provided local agencies with a plan to capture their own areas. Included in this package were registration lists of owners of late-model Fords and competitive automobiles. This provided a list of prospects who might be potential purchasers. In order to capitalize on direct-mail advertising, three million color postcards were sent to the dealers for further distribution. It was also suggested, in the plans book, that preintroduction parties be hosted for such groups as service station and independent garage operators. Word-of-mouth advertising from this group would provide other valuable means of getting the message to the consumer.

Dealer showrooms were provided with a variety of Mustang pictures, mobiles, window-trim material, and posters (see Figure 8–6) to be used to attract the customer at the point of purchase. To culminate the promotional campaign, Ford dealers were given materials for use in a Win-a-Mustang contest. With this device, the agencies were able to obtain the names of over three million potential customers who could be contacted after the initial introductory excitement died down.

The major emphasis in the promotion of the Mustang was exposure to as many people as possible. To achieve this, Mustangs were placed at fifteen major airport terminals from New York to San Francisco and at seventy high-traffic

FIGURE 8–6   A totally new kind of total performance car—the new Ford Mustang. (*Courtesy:* Ford Motor Company.)

locations in major cities across the country. Mustangs were on display in two hundred Holiday Inns, either in the lobbies or in their main entrances. Even people traveling by automobile at the time of introduction, who might not be exposed through the other media, were given glimpses of the Mustang on billboards in approximately 170 markets.

Introduction Day

With all aspects of the promotion meshing together, introduction day, April 17, 1964, saw Ford dealers literally swamped with traffic. Approximately four million people visited Ford dealerships to see the Mustang.

Within four months, more than 100,000 Mustangs were sold, making it one of the top five automobiles in sales volume.

Ford didn't rest on its new-found success. It continuously improved the automobile both functionally and esthetically, ultimately adding the Mustang GT to the line and, in 1989, the LX 5.0-liter series to celebrate the car's twenty-fifth anniversary. The convertible model has proven its success by becoming the best-seller in the United States for two consecutive years. Figure 8–7 features the Mustang GT and the LX 5.0-liter convertible.

A MARKETING PROFILE

The Acura Division of Honda Motors

When American Honda Motor Co.'s Acura Automobile Division began operation on March 27, 1986, it marked the first attempt by a Japanese auto manufacturer to enter the highly competitive luxury/performance segment of the U.S. automotive market. What made Acura unique, however, was not American Honda's decision to enter a new market. Rather, it was the decision to form an entirely new division. Not since the Ford Motor Co. formed the Lincoln-Mercury Division four decades earlier had an established automaker successfully launched a new division, complete with a separate dealer network.

By the early 1980s, numerous marketing surveys had predicted rapid growth in the luxury/performance segment of the U.S. automotive market. Dominated by established European imports, these segments stressed performance-oriented automobiles with high levels of standard equipment, luxurious appointments, and outstanding quality. Prestige of ownership was also very important.

The Acura Division was established to participate in the growth of the luxury/performance market segments. Acura would be positioned as an "intercept" product—as new buyers moved into the more upscale market

FIGURE 8–7   The "galloping Mustangs," the Mustang LX 5.0-liter model and the Mustang convertible. (*Courtesy:* Ford Motor Company.)

segment, Acura would provide an alternative to the more established, and often more expensive, European imports.

Marketing surveys revealed that Honda had an excellent reputation for quality, reliability, and value. However, the name was strongly identified with practical, family-oriented vehicles, with an emphasis on fuel economy, primarily in the low to midrange pricing segment. The new vehicles and dealer network would be able to establish their own reputation and image, while maintaining the public's clear perception of existing Honda automobiles.

In just two years of existence, the Acura Automobile Division had clearly demonstrated its ability to provide a viable alternative to the European makes which have traditionally dominated the luxury/performance market segment.

Possibly the strongest assessment of Acura's success came in late 1987, when both Toyota and Nissan followed American Honda's lead and announced plans to establish new divisions to compete in the luxury/performance market segment.

A PLAN BECOMES REALITY

The planning had begun more than four years earlier. Product development had taken over three years. Over a year was spent on the careful selection of the initial dealer network. Then on March 27, 1986 sixty new automobile dealers opened their doors to the public for the first time. Inside the modern sales and service facilities was a new line of luxury/performance cars bearing the name Acura.

Many industry analysts wondered if a Japanese manufacturer, noted for its ability to market low- to medium-priced family cars, could successfully design and produce medium- to high-priced luxury/performance automobiles. But if the industry observers were apprehensive, those within American Honda were not. And for two good reasons.

First, the success of the Acura Division owes much to Honda Research and Development's commitment to developing truly exceptional vehicles. Bringing together a design team of enthusiastic product planners and engineers—many with Honda Formula I racing experience—the challenge was issued to create technically advanced cars built around the single most important element in an automobile, the driver.

Second, was the decision early in the planning process, driven by the new products and the market, to establish the Acura Division as a completely separate entity from the existing Honda Automobile Division. Starting with a concept for a new standard in the way automobiles are sold and serviced, the screening process began for the new dealer organization. From an initial pool of highly qualified applicants, the Acura dealer body was chosen—seasoned professionals dedicated to making the concept a reality.

Two model lines were created: the versatile Integra three-door and five-door sports sedans and the Legend luxury touring sedan. Figure 8–10 features the Acura Legend and Integra. Both lines would be marked by innovative engineering, aerodynamic styling, advanced ergonomics, and quality manufacturing. (See Figure 8–8.)

By the end of 1986, it was clear that the cars and the concept were a success. The national automotive media gave the Legend and Integra excellent reviews. Consumers reacted positively to the vehicles and the Acura dealer network's dedication to customer service.

FIGURE 8–8   The initial Acura product line, the Legend sedan and the Integra three- and five-door sports sedans. (*Courtesy:* Acura Automobile Division.)

As the dealer body continued to grow, the Acura dealer network's dedication to customer satisfaction enhanced the reputation of the new division.

By year's end, any question of Acura's success had effectively been answered. The 1986 calendar year sales totaled 52,869 units and the dealer body had reached 150.

The 1987 calendar year started strong with *Car and Driver* magazine naming the Acura Integra as one of its "10 Best Cars." In March 1987, the Acura Division celebrated its first anniversary with the debut of the exciting Acura Legend coupe.

With such standard features as a 161-horsepower, 2.7-liter, 24-valve, V-6 engine, independent double-wishbone suspension, and a sleek, aerodynamic body, the Legend coupe outpaced 13 competitors to win *Motor Trend* magazine's prestigious "Import Car of the Year" award.

Runner-up to the Legend coupe in Import Car of the Year testing was the Acura Integra.

A new top-of-the-line Legend coupe LS version, offering an Acura/Bose Music System and a Supplemental Restraint System (SRS) with driver's side airbag, was added to the lineup later that summer.

In June, Acura sales passed the 100,000 mark, and by August sales had topped 10,000 units per month for the first time.

The Acura dealer body, which would reach 200 a few months later, was rewarded in August with news of Acura's first place ranking in the

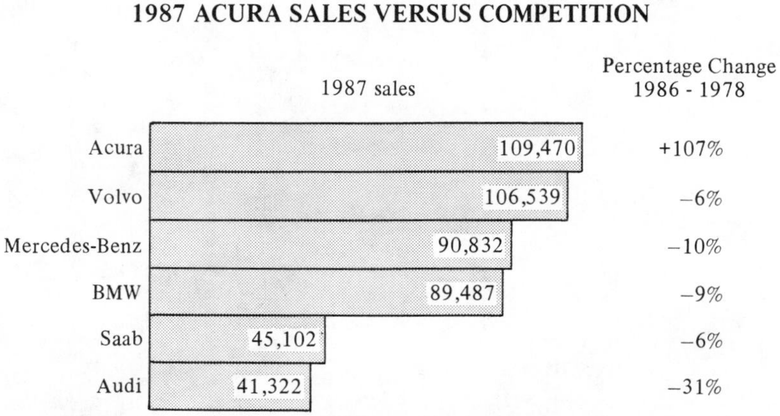

1987 ACURA SALES VERSUS COMPETITION

	1987 sales	Percentage Change 1986 - 1978
Acura	109,470	+107%
Volvo	106,539	−6%
Mercedes-Benz	90,832	−10%
BMW	89,487	−9%
Saab	45,102	−6%
Audi	41,322	−31%

FIGURE 8–9
1987 Acura sales versus competition. (*Courtesy:* Acura Automobile Division.)

annual J. D. Power and Associates Customer Satisfaction Index Survey— an unprecedented finish for a nameplate in its first year. The Acura dealer service score was the highest ever recorded in the history of the survey.

The fall months of 1987 were marked by the introduction of the 1988 Legend and Integra lines. Notable changes were the addition of the Legend coupe's 2.7-liter engine to the Legend sedan, along with the availability of Anti-Lock Braking (ALB) and Supplemental Restraint System. The Integra's horsepower was increased from 113 hp to 118 hp.

As calendar year 1987 came to a close, Acura sales reached 109,470, passing all European luxury/performance nameplates in the U.S. market.

December also saw more media honors, with *Road & Track* naming both the Legend sedan and Legend coupe to its "10 Best Cars Based on Value" list and the Legend coupe to its "10 Best Cars in the World." Then in January 1988, *Car and Driver* named both the Legend coupe and Integra sports sedan to its elite "10 Best" list.

A GROWTH MARKET

The Acura Division was introduced during a time of continuing evolution in market segmentation. While long-term market trends are at best difficult to predict, it was clear by the mid-1980s that the luxury and sporty car segments would be among the fastest growing through the next decade.

The luxury segment, which sold more than 600,000 units in 1980, was projected to more than double to nearly 1,500,000 units by 1990. The sporty car segment, which totaled almost 800,000 units in 1980, was also projected to reach more than 1,500,000 units by 1990. Buyers in these two market

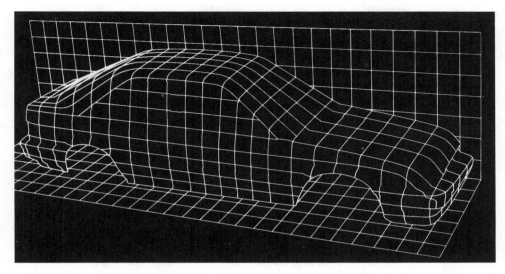

FIGURE 8–10   The Legend and Integra were designed using computer technology. (*Courtesy:* Acura Automobile Division.)

segments are generally more affluent than are buyers in the other segments, making them attractive targets for all auto manufacturers.

The major competitors vying for a share of the luxury import market segment include Acura, Audi, BMW, Jaguar, Mercedes Benz, Saab, Sterling, and Volvo. New entries are expected by the early 1990s, including recently announced new divisions of Nissan (Infiniti) and Toyota (Lexus).

Among the current competition, Acura has shown strong market penetration. In 1987, Acura overtook Volvo to rank as the leading foreign nameplate in the luxury/performance segment with a sales total of 109,470.

PRECISION-CRAFTED AUTOMOBILES

An outstanding dealer organization, effective marketing strategy, and advertising support would all be important in the attainment of the Acura Division's sales success. In the Acura Legend and Integra, the division also enjoyed the advantage of a strong product line, with the precision engineering, quality, and performance demanded in today's market by knowledgeable consumers.

The Acura Integra sports sedan is available in two body configurations, a three-door hatchback and a five-door hatchback. Both feature retractable headlights, a low, sloping hood, near-flush glass and flush door handles, and integrated bumpers. The coefficient of drag is just 0.34.

The 1.6-liter, 16-valve DOHC lightweight aluminum alloy 4-cylinder

Integra engine features tuned intake and exhaust manifolds and computer-controlled programmed fuel injection.

The Integra suspension utilizes an independent strut, torsion bar design in front and semi-independent design in the rear. Power-assisted rack-and-pinion steering and 4-wheel power-assisted disc brakes are standard.

Integra's ergonomically designed cockpit features analog gauges, body-contoured front bucket seats, and an adjustable steering column as standard equipment.

The Integra has been available since introduction in RS and LS trim levels. Limited production Integra LS Special edition three-door versions, with unique exterior and interior treatments and special equipment, have been offered in 1987 and again in 1988.

Since its introduction as a fully equipped touring sedan, the Legend has undergone continuous refinement as befits a luxury/performance automobile.

The first Legend available in the United States was the 1986 4-door sedan model. It featured a 2.5-liter, 24-valve, aluminum alloy V-6 engine rated at 151 horsepower. The suspension utilized an independent double-wishbone design in front and an independent Reduced Friction Strut design in the rear. In 1987, a luxury-oriented L version was added, featuring leather-trimmed seats, leather-wrapped steering wheel, and a four-way electrically adjustable driver's seat.

One year after the debut of the Legend sedan, the two-door Legend coupe was introduced. The coupe features a larger, more powerful engine—2.7-liter displacement rated at 161 horsepower—and a 4-wheel double-wishbone suspension. The Legend coupe L and LS versions offer leather-trimmed power-adjustable seats, standard Anti-Lock Braking system designed by Honda Research and Development, a security system, and a Driver's Information Center. The Legend coupe LS also includes a standard Acura/Bose Music System and a Supplemental Restraint System driver's side airbag.

For the 1988 model year, the Legend sedan received the coupe's 2.7-liter engine and available electronically controlled dual-mode automatic transmission. The sedan L was equipped with Honda's ALB system and security system. A sedan LS version was added to the 1988 lineup, with SRS, Acura/Bose Music System, Driver's Information Center, and automatic climate control.

THE RIGHT BUYERS

One of the auto industry's leading questions in the beginning concerning the Acura Division was "Who would buy an upscale Japanese automobile?" Initially, and as predicted, the largest single group of buyers

TABLE 8–3.   ACURA owners' demographic profile

	Integra 3-Door	Integra 5-Door	Legend Coupe	Legend Sedan
Male	74.1%	69.6%	82.2%	79.4%
Female	25.9%	30.4%	17.8%	20.6%
Median age	33.1	39.0	44.1	45.8
Married/committed relationship	53.5%	78.0%	72.1%	85.7%
College education	89.1%	88.7%	91.1%	89.8%
Median household income	$46,954	$53,854	$90,962	$85,518

Source: 1987 Honda Owner Study.

were Honda owners, for whom the combination of Honda engineering and reliability with Acura performance and luxury fit their growing affluence.

As Acura products established themselves in the marketplace, spurred by excellent third-party endorsements from the leading automotive publications and by strong word-of-mouth from Acura owners, Acura began to "intercept" buyers from other brands. The Legend especially was seen as offering an attractive alternative to more established brands for those entering the luxury car market.

Recent owner studies show both Acura Legend and Acura Integra to have customer demographics high in household income and education. (See Table 8–3.)

TWO CHAMPIONSHIP SEASONS

The worldwide success of Honda in auto racing has played an important role in the development of Acura products and the Acura Division's performance image. Honda's Formula I heritage has been featured prominently in Acura advertising and promotions.

Honda's participation in Formula I Grand Prix competition dates back to 1964. Although the effort was discontinued in the late 1960s, Honda reentered Formula I in 1983, supplying engines and technical development support to the Williams-Honda racing team. The first of many victories came at the 1984 Dallas Grand Prix at the hands of driver Keke Rosberg.

In 1985, Williams-Honda won four events, including the last three races of the season. The next year, the team won nine of sixteen races, including the 1986 Formula I Constructor's World Championship, and narrowly missed the driver's championship.

Honda-powered cars dominated in 1987, with Honda now supplying both Lotus-Honda and Williams-Honda with 1,000-plus horsepower twin-turbo-charged, 24-valve fuel-injected, 1.5-liter V-6s. Williams-Honda drivers Nigel Mansell and Nelson Piquet combined for nine victories, while Avrton Senna of Lotus-Honda added two more.

Williams-Honda repeated as World Constructor's Champion, while Piquet and Mansell finished one-two in the driver's points race. For 1988, Honda will again supply engines for two teams, Lotus and the newly added Team McLaren.

Many of the engineering features found in Acura automobiles can be traced back to the experiences of Formula I racing. Four-valve per cylinder engines, programmed fuel injection, and sophisticated electronic engine management systems are among the systems and technology developed and refined for production from Formula I projects.

Acura products have already established a strong reputation in U.S. racing circles. In 1986, Doug Peterson won the International Motorsports Association (IMSA) Champion Spark Plug Challenge Series Driver's Championship driving a Comptech Racing–prepared Acura Integra.

In 1987, Comptech fielded a two-car team in the renamed IMSA International Sedans series for race-prepared front-wheel-drive sedans. Competing against vehicles from manufacturers such as Dodge, Chevrolet, Mazda, and Volkswagen, Comptech Integra drivers Peterson and Johnstone dominated the series. With a combined eight victories in ten races, Johnstone and Peterson finished first and third, respectively, in the series' Driver's Championship. The domination of the Integras helped to clinch the Manufacturer's Championship for Acura and American Honda.

A SPECIAL DEALER NETWORK

In November 1984, ten months after word of the new luxury/ performance division was announced, a meeting was held in Dallas to brief current Honda dealers on the Acura Automobile Division. On hand were mock-up models of what would become the Acura Legend and Integra.

At this meeting the criteria for selecting Acura dealerships was announced. One item was of primary importance. Acura dealerships had to be separate, stand-alone facilities and not combined with existing Honda dealerships.

The application process began in February 1985. American Honda selected the first dealerships from current Honda dealers, feeling that their familiarity with Honda's corporate philosophy and emphasis on customer satisfaction would prove beneficial in launching the new division. On March 27, 1986, sixty Acura dealerships in eighteen states were ready for business. (See Figure 8–11.)

Dealer body growth was rapid throughout the first calendar year, with 150 Acura dealerships in operation serving the top fifty metropolitan markets in thirty-six states by the end of 1986. During 1978 the Acura dealer total grew to 220 covering forty-four states. The average investment has been well over $25 million, with dealers creating some of the most modern, state-of-the-art sales and service facilities in the business.

FIGURE 8–11
The Acura Division opened with sixty dealerships on March 27, 1986. (*Courtesy:* Acura Automobile Division.)

Facilities are only part of the Acura dealer story, however. Intensive sales and service programs were developed to assist in training dealer personnel. Dealer and customer support systems were established, including the Acura Tech Line to assist service technicians with additional technical information if needed. A computerized parts network was set up to assure rapid location and shipping of any necessary components and a toll-free Acura Customer Assistance Center was created to advise customers in time of need.

The careful attention to dealer selection, training, and support paid immediate benefits to the Acura buyers, who rated Acura number one in the 1987 J. D. Power and Associates Customer Satisfaction Index (CSI) Report—a survey of customer satisfaction with their vehicles and dealers in the first full year of ownership.

"Acura dealers were selected from among the best Honda dealers and were required to make a substantial investment in separate facilities to house their new offspring," the J. D. Power report stated. Figures 8–12 and 8–13 feature the 1989 Acura Legend and Integra.

"The quality of these dealers is apparent from the responses of some very satisfied Acura owners, which gave the new nameplate a people service factor of 186, 9 points ahead of historical people service standard-bearer Mercedes Benz's 177 and 54 points ahead of its sister division Honda."

The report went on to say, "Acura picked a quality dealer network from day one. With a product line that appears to be meeting luxury buyer expectations, Acura's image will soon match that of its more established European rivals."

FIGURE 8–12   The 1989 Acura Integra three-door LS. (*Courtesy:* Acura Automobile Division.)

THE YEARS AHEAD

The Acura Division's first three years have laid a successful foundation on which to move into the next decade. With an outstanding and still growing dealer organization, award-winning products, and a growing body of satisfied owners, the toughest challenges might seem behind the Acura Division.

The next few years, however, will be critical ones for every major automaker. Industry analysts project the U.S. automotive market to become more competitive than ever. New nameplates, eager to emulate Acura's success, are planned for the luxury/performance segment. And the segment should further expand with new models from domestic, European and Japanese manufacturers.

The Acura Division will not stand still. Careful expansion of the dealer body and continued evolution and expansion of the Acura product lineup are planned to more than double Acura sales by the next decade.

True to the original concept, Acura will remain an exceptional name-

FIGURE 8–13   The 1989 Acura Legend coupe L. (*Courtesy:* Acura Automobile Division.)

> plate, dedicated to providing leading edge luxury and performance cars designed around the driver, sold and serviced through dealers committed at all times to outstanding customer service.

SALVAGING THE PRODUCT FAILURE

When a product fails, it doesn't necessarily result in a company's total abandonment of the product. If management continues to believe in the product despite its poor showing, and gets an indication from additional research that a correction will turn the product around, it sometimes makes the decision to remarket the product.

Often, consumers will see an advertising blitz heralding the "new improved" version of a previously marketed product. General Foods' Dream Whip was initially a success but failed to perform properly in warm weather. As the temperature rose, the whipped topping wilted. Initial distribution revealed significant customer acceptance only to find a decline in warm-weather sales. General Foods felt further effort could improve the product to a level customers would find satisfactory. Improvement of the product's performance ultimately was translated into customer acceptance. Dream Whip was saved from the long list of product failures.

Corning Glass Works, manufacturers of such successful product lines as Pyrexware and Corningware, had to make a product design adjustment after Corningware was initially introduced to the consumer. The product was constructed of a new miracle material Pyroceram, which had properties not typical of other glass-type materials. After introduction, the company found that the consumer was totally pleased with the product's ability to be taken from extreme heat to freezing temperatures without damage to the cookware or the food. The problem was with the detachable handles which were to be used to transfer the various pieces from the oven or range. It seemed that while the clip-on type handle was perfectly secure, users complained of the possibility of the handle coming loose. The problem was purely psychological, but Corning Glass recognized that it could turn a potential success into a failure. A redesign of the handle that required the user to twist it into a locked position alleviated the fear of a handle unfastening. After this correction Corningware went on to become an enormously successful product.

Not every product can be saved from failure. Companies must research each problem separately to determine whether salvage is possible or discontinuance of production is more appropriate. Ford decided the Edsel's redesign wouldn't make any difference and moved ahead with the highly successful Mustang.

Postproduction research must be carefully carried out so that the marketing decision makers can choose the proper approach to make their companies profitable.

Important Points in the Chapter

1. The rate of new product failures is alarming, with consumer product failures at about 80 to 90 percent. Industrial products fail at the significantly lower rate of 20 to 40 percent.

2. Products fail for many reasons. Among the most common are
   a. Poor market testing.
   b. Product performance is unsatisfactory.
   c. Insignificant differences in the product in comparison to those that have already been marketed successfully.
   d. Poor product positioning, which can be further categorized into insignificant positioning, confused positioning, and mismatched positioning.
   e. No actual point of difference in the new product. An example is Kaiser's failure in the aluminum foil market because its foil had no advantages over the already successful foils of Alcoa and Reynolds.

f. Bad timing.

g. Product performance does not live up to expectation. This is most relevant in the food industry, although it is not confined to foodstuffs.

h. The wrong market for the company. When a company's capabilities are inadequate for the marketing of a product because it does not belong to the company's usual line of business, the product often fails.

i. When the costs of production and distribution exceed anticipation, thus necessitating a price increase, sales volume might fall. This often leads to failure.

j. When the sales force is inadequately prepared and proper presentation of the product to the buyer is impaired, the product may fail.

k. The effort of the company was insufficient in terms of the need to successfully market the particular product.

3. The study of product failures is essential to underscore the importance of research.

4. The success of the Mustang underscores the need to touch base with every prerequisite of marketing research. Market analysis in terms of need, price, style, and promotion were studied to further ensure success.

Review Questions

1. To what size organization is product failure generally limited?

2. Some new products fail because they are really old products in a changed container or presented in a new form. Under which major heading are such product failures categorized?

3. Define *mismatched product positioning.*

4. To which technical reason was the failure of Super Natural hair spray attributed? Describe what this classification of failure means.

5. Differentiate between insignificant product difference and no difference.

6. What was probably the major reason for the tremendous losses suffered by Vote, Fact, and Cue toothpastes?

7. Why is poor product performance continually decreasing as a reason for product failure?

8. If a firm is successful in the production and distribution of television sets, is it likely that it will also be successful in the marketing of frozen foods? Defend your position.

9. When planning the introduction of a new product, costs are generally

analyzed with great care. For what reasons, then, might cost be attributed to the product's failure?

10. Do you agree that good products can fail because of inadequate sales efforts? Why?

11. Define *corporation loyalty*.

12. Why is it important to study product failures?

13. Discuss how the style of the Mustang was chosen.

14. For what reason was the original early design of Ford's Mustang scrapped?

15. Pricing of the Mustang was set along lines similar to those used for the Model-T Ford. Which system was employed?

16. How was the name *Mustang* finally selected?

17. What unusual role did the press play in Mustang's introduction?

Case Problems

Case Problem 1

For the past twenty-five years Creative Craft, Inc., has been one of the most successful U.S. manufacturers of men's dress shirts. It has consistently been a leader in the market, catering to the conservatively dressed business executive. The shirts, carefully tailored and manufactured from the finest imported and domestic fabrics, retail at prices that range from $50 to $75.

Last year Neil Enesco, son of the company's founder, joined the firm. After six months with the company he presented a proposal to his father and to management that in his opinion would enormously increase Creative Craft's overall sales volume. His idea was to create an additional line of more stylish shirts that would appeal to the younger male. His principal arguments for the new line were that young men were dressing more fashionably and that the firm's regular shirt production was bound to decline once these younger people reached the levels of employment to which Creative Craft catered.

After considerable deliberation the company decided to go after the new market. Prices were to retail from $25 to $35 so that the younger, less affluent male could afford the new product. Creative Craft was to be used as the label for the new line, rather than a new name, since Creative Craft was so well known that it would immediately be recognized in advertisements and in store displays. Similarly, because of their tremendous experience, the same advertising staff and sales force would be used to promote and sell the new line. Production would start at the same plant that produced the regular line of shirts because of the excellent quality control that had been established there.

Soon afterward production was under way, but although it was evident that other firms were successfully selling more stylish shirts, Creative Craft's new line never seemed to get off the ground. The stores did not accept the new line enthusiastically. It was decided that production would cease. The new line was a flop that amounted to a financial loss of $390,000.

Questions

1. In which category would this failure belong according to the general classifications of product failure?
2. Analyzing the situation, what mistakes did Creative Craft make?
3. Could the new product have been successful? How?

Case Problem 2

Clean-Rite, manufacturers of soaps and detergents, decided to promote a new product. Since all existing detergents were either in liquid or powder form and needed measuring when used, it was supposed that the new premeasured product would capture the market. Clean-Rite's product research team developed a capsule that would hold the proper amount of detergent necessary for an average washing load. The capsule (premeasured and filled by the company) was similar to those used for vitamins. When added to the wash, the capsule shell would disintegrate, thus dispensing the detergent. The advantage to the user would be the elimination of measuring the detergent. After sufficient advertising and sales efforts, the new product went into production.

Although the product was enthusiastically received by the stores, consumers rejected it. It was soon withdrawn, with an estimated loss of $750,000 to Clean-Rite.

Questions

1. Which general classification do you believe accounted for the product's failure?
2. What could have been some of the consumers' complaints?
3. How might the company have prevented such a fiasco from the beginning?

9

PACKAGING AND BRANDING

Learning Objectives

Upon completion of the chapter, you will be able to:

1. Explain four factors that must be taken into account before making a packaging decision.
2. Discuss the effect of packaging on sales.
3. Discuss ethics and legality in the area of packaging.
4. Explain the importance of branding.
5. Differentiate between manufacturers' brands and private brands.
6. Compare family and individual brands, indicating the best use of each.

SEVEN DEATHS ALMOST CRIPPLE A COMPANY

In late 1982, Johnson & Johnson and its affiliate, McNeil Consumer Products Company, manufacturers of Tylenol, read the same headlines that frightened consumers all over the country. Someone had poisoned Tylenol capsules with cyanide and seven people from the Chicago area were dead. The tragedy almost meant the death of Tylenol as well.

Almost immediately the companies undertook the enormous task of reintroducing the product to the consumer. The problem was to allay the fears that now were heard all around the world and were threatening the international reputation and sales enjoyed by the producing companies. The promotional approach taken emphasized the triple tamper-resistant seals which would make it impossible for a similar tragedy to happen.

The package designers went to work immediately and created a package that would still employ the colors and descriptive terminology previously used. The package now featured an outer box with all flaps glued shut, a tight plastic band sealing the cap to the neck of the bottle, and a strong inner foil seal over the mouth of the bottle. Additional copy was added to the new packages that clearly warned: "Do Not Use If Safety Seals Are Broken." The additional cost per package was 2 cents and was absorbed by Johnson & Johnson and McNeil. The furor caused the Food and Drug Administration to take a better look at packaging regulations. Tylenol became the first product to adhere to the newly passed packaging requirement.

Six weeks after the incident, Tylenol introduced the new package and embarked upon its marketing. By early 1983, in just five months' time, Johnson & Johnson and McNeil's Tylenol had recaptured 70 percent of the market.

In order to gain maximum publicity regarding the safety of the newly packaged product whose reputation was earlier tarnished by eighty thousand news stories, hundreds of hours of radio and television coverage, and two thousand phone calls from media representatives, the companies undertook numerous activities. Each was directly related to the safety of the product and tamper-resistant packaging. Among them were

> Establishment of a toll-free hot line to answer safety-oriented questions.
> Broadcasts alerting customers to the impending return of Tylenol in tamper-resistant packaging.
> Preparation of a 4-minute videotape covering tamper-resistant packaging.
> The promotion was enormous and ultimately paid off by returning Tylenol to its position as leader in its field.

While companies continue to approach their packaging decisions with attention to how the package will fit on the store's shelf, its attractiveness for the consumer's attention, the requirements of functional storage, and so forth, safety has become a more significant factor.

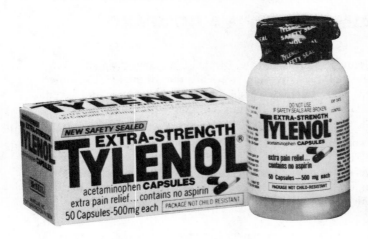

Tylenol product offering. (*Courtesy:* McNeil Consumer Products Company.)

INTRODUCTION TO PACKAGING

The activities throughout the marketing process that are concerned with the design and construction of the container or wrapping of a product are called packaging. Not too long ago, packaging decisions were based solely on the physical characteristics of the product. Goods were moved from the producer to the final consumer in a manner that would ensure product protection at the lowest possible cost. A prime example of this is the old general store, in which merchandise such as flour, sugar, and crackers was received in bulk containers such as sacks and barrels and distributed to housewives in small unmarked containers by the storekeeper.

More recently, the package in which the goods are held has become as much of a sales tool as it is a container. At present, proper package design is one of the most important factors in the competitive battle for sales. The producer with the best package has a decided edge over competitors, and all progressive business managers are constantly researching means to improve their packaging design.

PACKAGING CONSIDERATIONS

The problems of packaging design are not easy to solve. Designing a good package poses many difficulties, and many people are involved whose preferences may conflict. For example, the transportation and storage department may be primarily interested in the safety of the product and the ease with which it can be handled, whereas the main concern of the sales department is the package's eye appeal as a promotional device.

FIGURE 9–1   Distinctively styled, functional packaging. (*Courtesy:* Pillsbury Company.)

Packages must be individualized. That is, each type of goods has its own requirements and the design of the package must be unique to the specific goods involved. Several factors must be taken into consideration when packaging decisions are to be made.

An example of a package that is both appealing visually and functional is the Pillsbury packaging for such products as Pizza Crust, Crescents, Cinnamon Rolls, and so on. Each package is distinctively styled to capture the shopper's attention and is specially packed to ensure freshness during the refrigeration periods of transportation and storage on the retailers' shelves. Figure 9–1 features specially packaged products that have eye appeal and serve a function.

The Retail Store

To design a package for a retail store, the designer must know the kind of store in which the package will be placed and the kind of customer who will buy the package. In a self-service supermarket, or any other self-service store, the package is an important selling device and the design of the package is vital to increased sales. The package must be visually competitive in order to facilitate the undecided shopper's choice.

The designer must keep in mind the location of the store where the pack-

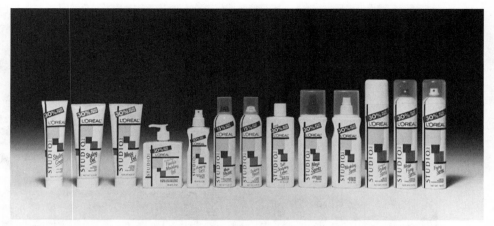

FIGURE 9–2   The attractiveness of the package, the easy use by customers, and the ability to be easily displayed make these excellent packages. (*Courtesy:* Cosmair, Inc.)

age will be placed. Must it fit on a supermarket shelf? Will it be part of a display? How will it be stored in the storeroom? (It must be strong enough to withstand storeroom handling.) Figure 9–2 features packages that fit all the needs of the retailer.

Transportation

Various transportation companies have standards and requirements that must be taken into account in packaging design. In addition, the size and weight of the shipping carton play an important role in the cost of transportation. Some goods require special treatment as to temperature control, moisture, pilferage, and vermin.

Warehousing

Goods that are warehoused may require special treatment relative to the manner of storage. The package design must depend upon the duration of warehousing, the way of handling the goods in the warehouse, the number of pieces that make up a typical shipment, and the method of taking warehouse inventories. There is less wasted space, for example, if square containers are used instead of round containers.

The Consumer

Packages, to be effective, must be designed for home use. A container that is immediately emptied and discarded has different requirements from one that is used to store the product until its consumption. The length of time that the contents will be stored and the method of use are also important. For example, it would be difficult to sell a pound of table salt in a flimsy container without a dispensing device. The packaging designer is also interested in whether or not the package is to be reusable for the same product, reusable for another product, returnable, stored in the kitchen or the basement, and so on.

Safety

While some attention has been given to packaging in terms of the consumer's safety as in the case of aspirin containers which sometimes require proper alignment of the cap for opening, the Tylenol scare significantly underscored the necessity for safer packaging. Johnson & Johnson, faced with the possible demise of the enormously successful Tylenol, spent huge sums to alter the packaging of the product when tampering caused the deaths of some users. This serious problem clearly dictated to their company as well as others that safety must become at least as important in packaging as eye appeal. Figure 9–3 shows an example of the Tylenol safety package.

Convenience

With the increasing number of women in the workplace and the need for people's quick preparation of prepared foods, the microwave oven has become a necessity in many households. Foods can be prepared in a fraction of the time it takes to cook them in the conventional manner. Bearing this in mind, food producers have repackaged many of their items in microwavable containers which virtually eliminate the need to transfer goods from the package to the cooking utensil. The foods are placed on trays or "pans" that are easily popped into the microwave for cooking. Figure 9–4 features a microwavable package of food that is prepared in 2 minutes.

Another convenience package is the "Bowl in the Box." This is not really new, but the reintroduction of a cereal package that was first introduced in the 1940s. Small containers of individual cereal portions into which milk can be poured are finding their way onto supermarket shelves. It allows the user to discard the package, once used, and only wash the spoon.

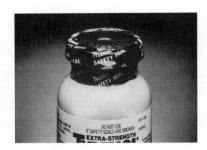

FIGURE 9–3
The new Tylenol packaging features three tamper-resistant seals—an outer box with all flaps glued shut; a tight plastic band sealing the cap to the neck; and a strong inner-foil seal over the mouth of the bottle. (*Courtesy:* McNeil Consumer Products Company.)

FIGURE 9–4   A microwavable package. (*Courtesy:* Campbell Soup Company.)

PACKAGING AND SALES

The expansion of self-service shopping has placed an increased emphasis on packaging. If there is no salesperson to highlight the outstanding features of the product, only the package can be used to convince the customer to buy a particular product rather than that of a competitor. This type of packaging is widely used by food companies. Their packages give such information as recipes, varieties of use, and number of servings in the package.

The use of transparent packaging material permits the supermarket customer to inspect the merchandise visually. Many products that are made of fabric carry a swatch of the goods on the package so that the customer may touch a sample.

Television and magazine advertising have increased the importance of packaging design by visual promotion. Prospective customers who cannot recall the brand name might still be familiar with a package because they have seen it and are more likely to buy it than an unfamiliar product. For this purpose, the package has to be uniquely designed.

Reusable Packages

Many plants package their products in containers designed for reuse. Cheeses, jellies, and similar foodstuffs are packed in containers that are suitable for use as drinking glasses. Many other items, for example peanut butter and mayonnaise, are packed in glass or plastic jars that may be reused for leftovers, home canning, and so on. The aim of such packaging is to increase sales by giving the customer something in addition to the product itself. Packaging in reusable containers may lead to repeat business, since the customer may try to secure a complete set of drinking glasses or a plastic container of a particular size. Of course, the marketing drawback to collecting a complete set is that the customer may switch to another brand upon completion of the set. It is however, effective as a short-term promotional device.

The question that arises with reusable containers is whether or not customers are willing to pay the increased cost. An excellent example of a case in which the package is costlier than the product is a honey jar shaped like a bear, which may be used later as a coin bank. The customer is generally willing to pay far more for such an attractive, reusable container. Candy companies, for Valentine's Day, place more emphasis on the package than on the product.

Multiple Packs

Multiple packaging is the packaging of several units in one container. This practice has been steadily growing, since marketing research indicates that both total and unit sales may thus be increased. Products such as handkerchiefs, beer, golf balls, cereals, dehydrated soups, and pillowcases are generally packed in multiples.

In addition to the obvious increase in sales, there are many other advantages to multiple packaging. For example, it reduces handling and price-marking costs. Many producers find that multiple packaging gives them an opportunity to introduce new products effectively. In this manner a manufacturer of dry breakfast cereals may package an assortment of six products, including a new item. The multiple pack almost guarantees that the new product will be tried by the consumer. Figure 9–5 shows the popular 12-pack of beer.

PACKAGING COSTS

It is obvious that good packaging is expensive. However, good packaging can result in an overall saving by improving product protection, ease of handling, and shipping costs. Moreover, by increasing the total sales volume, the costs per unit may be reduced. It should also be borne in mind that in large part packaging requirements insisted upon by the consumer result in higher costs. The packaging cost of a 100-pound bag of sugar is only 1 percent of its selling price, but most

FIGURE 9–5　　The 12-pack of Coors beer. (*Courtesy:* Adolph Coors Company.)

shoppers prefer to buy sugar in 1- and 5-pound bags and are willing to pay the 25 to 30 percent increased selling price that is involved with smaller lots.

ETHICS IN PACKAGING

One of the harshest criticisms of marketing concerns the misleading use of packaging. Each year the Federal Trade Commission receives an increasing number of complaints concerning the use of unnecessarily large boxes, false bottoms, overly thick walls, and so on, designed to give the consumer the impression that the package contains more of the product than it actually does.

It is true that many producers design their packages to mislead the consumer, but this cannot always be determined by comparing carton size. The cost of packaging is ultimately paid by the consumer. Some producers are able to reduce the retail price of their product by gravity feeding, an inexpensive packing method that results in a considerable amount of air space at the top of the carton. Others reduce packaging costs by volume purchases of single-sized packages, which are then used for various quantities and densities. These usually result in an imperfect fit.

Marketers argue that such packaging is done for competitive reasons rather than to fool the public. They point out that the larger the package, the greater are the customer eye impact and shelf space. For example, the toy industry, in an attempt to attract the eye of a child, often overpackages the product.

Another packaging complaint is that the amount packaged does not lend itself to the arithmetic necessary for comparison shopping. A customer who can easily compare the prices of the products of two manufacturers who package in 1-pound lots cannot so simply make such comparison if one producer markets a 10½-ounce and the other an 11¾-ounce unit.

Some producers, for competitive reasons, reduce the amount in their package without reducing prices. In such cases an attempt might be made to change the container so that the change in quantity will not be noticed. (The law requires that the volume in the container must be clearly indicated on the label.) One large brewer uses an 11-ounce container, whereas the industry standard is 12 ounces. Are the consumers aware of this?

Taking advantage of the fact that most shoppers do not calculate their costs on a price-per-ounce basis, many producers pack in large containers at a price equal to or higher than the sum of the prices of several smaller packages. Since most Americans have been conditioned to believe that savings are made by purchasing in the large "economy" size, this practice may improve profits.

The ethics of the practices described above are a constant source of debate. Truth-in-packaging legislation, to make illegal some of the more flagrant packaging abuses, is constantly being brought up in Congress.

LEGAL ASPECTS OF PACKAGING

Federal legislation has placed certain controls on packaging. One of the most important laws to assist the consumer is the Fair Packaging and Labeling Act of 1966. The act requires

1. Identification of product.
2. Name and address of manufacturer or distributor.
3. Indication of net contents.
4. Indication of weight in ounces and pounds for packages under four pounds.
5. Indication of the exact size of each serving if statements on servings of food product are made.
6. Voluntary, industrywide standards for package sizes.

In addition, through its departments and agencies, the federal government involves itself in other packaging regulation. The Food and Drug Administration is responsible for foodstuffs, nonprescription drugs, and cosmetics; the Federal Trade Commission for nonfood items.

ECOLOGY

In recent years a great deal of attention has been focused on the disposal of waste matter. Since a very substantial proportion of litter consists of discarded packages, the issue is of vital importance to package designers. Chapter 17 addresses itself to ecological problems of packaging.

PACKAGING AND THE UNIVERSAL PRODUCT CODE

Through the cooperation of industry and government, the Universal Product Code has been developed. A series of thick and thin vertical lines is printed on the package. These lines are immediately recorded by electronic scanners. The marks contain the price and code for each item. This eliminates the necessity to mark each item. There has been a great deal of customer resistance to the coding because the prices might not be remembered at home. However, many stores are presently using the system. An illustration of the code is shown in Figure 9–6.

TRENDS IN PACKAGING

Marketers are always researching avenues to improve the total product. As we have already learned, the total product definitely includes the product's packaging. At this time there is considerable effort underway to bring innovative package designs to the marketplace.

Retort Pouches

Kraft has been the food industry's leader in the test marketing of a new food container, the *retort pouch*. The most significant advantage of this foil and plastic container is that it doesn't require refrigeration. Other companies expected to follow Kraft's lead are Stouffer's, General Mills, and Hormel.

FIGURE 9–6
A sample Universal Product Code.

Asceptic Containers

Foil-lined paper cartons are being tested to be used in place of beverage cans and bottles. Two primary advantages are cost and unnecessary refrigeration. If these packages prove to be more cost effective for manufacturers of fruit juices, milk, and so on, than the conventional containers, they would have the added advantage of reducing the need for refrigeration during transportation of perishable drinks.

New Shrink Wrap

The American Can Co. has developed a new version of the presently used plastic material shrink wrap. The new packaging is used in conjunction with vacuum equipment and permits cheeses, meats, and so on to retain their freshness for longer periods of time. Not only will this innovation permit longer shelf life for the food retailer but will also enable the consumer to shop less frequently for perishables.

Modified Atmosphere Packaging

A disadvantage of frozen seafood that has been voiced by household users and food stores is the flavor and texture change that often takes place after freezing. Experimentation is taking place with a process that pumps air out of the package and replaces it with carbon dioxide. Upon sealing the package, bacterial growth is prevented by the presence of the carbon dioxide. In addition to the improved taste and texture of the product, the shelf life will be approximately ten days longer than traditionally packaged frozen fish.

Bag and Box Combinations

In order to prevent air from damaging the flavor and original consistency of some food products such as processed fruits, packagers are testing containers in which bags will "collapse" around the product as it is used. There are packages that have been in use for years employing the bag and box concept, but once opened, air seems to enter and affect the unused portion. This innovation incorporates a device such as a spout, which, when closed, will alleviate the problem of air entrance and spoilage. Fruits such as diced pineapple, packaged in this manner, will not require refrigeration unless the user wants the product chilled.

Packaging innovations such as those just described will not only make the products more convenient for consumer use but could make our homes more energy efficient.

FIGURE 9–7   Brands belonging to the PepsiCo, Inc., family. (*Courtesy:* PepsiCo, Inc.)

INTRODUCTION TO BRANDS

An important factor in marketing success is product identification by customers. Many large firms accomplish this by establishing brands for their products. The American Marketing Association defines *brand* as follows:

> A name, term, sign, symbol, or design, or a combination of them, which is intended to identify goods or services of one seller or group of sellers and to differentiate them from those of competitors.

Figure 9–7 exemplifies the symbols, names, and designs typical of manufacturer's brands.

With the exception of certain bulk, standardized goods, such as cotton, coal, or wheat, almost all goods have an identifying name or brand. For example, Chevrolet is a brand owned by General Motors, and Citgo is the brand name owned by the Cities Service Corporation.

By branding his goods and promoting the brand name, the producer or distributor hopes to develop an attitude in users that will give his goods a better marketing position than that of competing goods. If this acceptance can be achieved, it will result in increased sales and possibly increased selling prices. Frequently, the brand may be the most important asset of a firm and its only asset that cannot be easily reproduced by competitors.

MANUFACTURERS' BRANDS

Since the promotion of a brand requires a considerable amount of financing, usually only the largest companies own important brands. Some of the advantages derived from their established brands are

1. Sales promotion depends upon customer identification with the specific product. Therefore, an established brand can act as a central point around which sales promotion can be built.

2. Branded merchandise is easily recognized by a customer, particularly if the brand is familiar through sales promotion. This encourages repeat sales, since the customer can find the product without searching, nor is the customer likely to make a mistake and take a competitor's product.

3. Brands build up their own customer following, so that it is difficult for a store to replace the brand with another product. A customer who is interested in a particular brand will generally not accept a substitute and will resent being offered one.

4. Customers for present products will potentially buy similar new products with the same brand. Customer confidence in a brand name can be transferred to a new product with relative ease because the customer feels certain that the quality will be up to the same standards.

5. Established brands have a tendency to maintain their prices in a falling market when nonbranded merchandise is likely to require drastic and frequent price cuts.

6. Middlemen in many industries are eager to handle branded merchandise, since customer acceptance of such goods is already high and selling is relatively easy. Wholesale liquor dealers, for example, can rarely exist without including accepted brands in their line.

Manufacturers of branded merchandise face certain disadvantages as well. Some of these problems are

1. A completely successful brand is one whose name becomes synonymous with the product itself. By law, when the "brand name may be identified so completely with an article of merchandise by the consuming public that it becomes the common or 'generic' name for the product itself," the producer's legal right to the brand name is ended. If the brand is too well established, it is no longer a private brand and may be used by all producers. Among the brands that have been lost in this fashion are aspirin, milk of magnesia, cellophane, linoleum, lanolin, and shredded wheat. For this reason, branders must be extremely careful in promoting their brands to emphasize that there is a difference between the name of the brand and

the name of the product. The Coca-Cola Company was not careful enough, and the word *cola* has been ruled to be generic and may be used by any producer of that particular type of drink. Orlon is always advertised as a type of acrylic fiber and has not been declared generic. Borderline cases are Kleenex, Band-Aid, and Frigidaire. Strategies used by companies to protect their brand against being ruled generic are the use of two names, including the firm name (Eastman-Kodak), and the changing of the name of the firm to coincide with the brand (Sunbeam, Sunkist, and Talon).

2. Some retailers resist nationally advertised brands because their profit margin is generally smaller on sales of such items. They either refuse to carry those brands or—if forced by their customers to carry such goods—do not promote them.

3. Branded goods are easily identified, so that any customer unhappiness over the quality of the goods results in immediate sales loss. Effective quality control is absolutely necessary to a branded producer.

4. The advertising and sales promotion required to establish and maintain a brand name are extremely expensive.

CUSTOMERS AND BRANDING

To the customer, the most important characteristic of branded merchandise is that, unlike nonbranded merchandise, a branded item is guaranteed to be of consistently high quality. Manufacturers who have spent large sums of money in establishing a brand cannot afford to allow the quality of their merchandise to vary.

Another advantage of brands to the consumer is that the creation of a brand establishes a certain amount of prestige, which may give added consumer satisfaction.

PRIVATE BRANDS

Not all brands are owned by producers. Private brands are owned by distributors who do not own the manufacturing facilities for the product. Typical users of private brands are Sears, Roebuck, which owns the brands Coldspot, Kenmore, Craftsman, and Homart, and Macy's, which markets a significant portion of its fashion merchandise under private labels. The major supermarket chains also promote a great number of their own brands.

Advantages of Private Brands

Distributors derive the following advantages from private brands:

1. Private-brand merchandise is less expensive than manufacturer's-brand merchandise because the manufacturer does not include the cost of promoting his brand when he produces goods under a distributor's brand. As a result, the distributor may sell his own brand, equal in quality to the manufacturer's brand, at a price below that charged for the manufacturer's brand, and still work at a better profit margin than is made by selling the manufacturer's brand.

2. The private brand is controlled by the distributor. Not only does the distributor control the quality and price, but the brand cannot be taken away at the whim of the manufacturer.

3. It is very difficult for a customer to compare private-branded merchandise with similar goods sold by a competitor because the buyer can never be sure that the products are the same. For this reason private brands are not price-cut as frequently as unbranded merchandise. Private brands are frequently used in retail stores that are faced with discount house competition.

4. High-value private brands can build a following that will increase a dealer's total sales volume. Manufacturers' brands can generally be found at many competing establishments.

5. Private brands can be tailored to the tastes of a dealer's specific customers. Manufacturers' brands, on the other hand, are designed to suit a nationwide clientele.

Disadvantages of Private Brands

1. The private brand requires quality control at a manufacturing facility generally not owned by the distributor. This may result in less consistency in quality than is required of all branded merchandise.

2. The promotion necessary to achieve customer acceptance of private brands is very costly.

3. Owners of manufacturers' brands resent the competition of private brands and may in some instances take their brands away from distributors who sell private brands.

4. Unless the private brander's volume is very high, the material and manufacturing cost may be too high for them to offer a competitive product. In addition, only large distributors have the prestige required to put a private brand across.

Manufacturers' Attitudes Toward Private Brands

Since there is competition between manufacturers' brands and private brands, one would hardly expect manufacturers of their own brands to produce merchandise for private branders. In practice, this is not the case at all. For example, General Electric makes appliances for J. C. Penney, and Whirlpool for Sears. There are several reasons for the brand-owning manufacturers' willingness to produce for private branders.

For one thing, private branders are usually high-volume firms (Sears, Roebuck and Montgomery Ward) whose orders are enormous. The manufacturer knows that if it does not take the order, another will and the business will be lost. In instances where no manufacturer could be found, the private brander may set up its own factory. Sears has done this many times. In short, if Sears wants goods to be manufactured, they will be manufactured. It would be foolish to turn away this business because of fear of competition, which will come about whether or not the order is taken.

Frequently, when the number of units manufactured increases, the cost of all the units manufactured decreases. General Electric, by producing appliances for J. C. Penney, not only makes a profit on the goods sold to J. C. Penney, but reduces the cost of the General Electric goods as well.

Finally, many manufacturers question whether or not the private brand is in direct competition with their own manufacturer's brand. The position they take is that a customer who is interested in a Sears Coldspot refrigerator only rarely considers a Whirlpool refrigerator at the same time.

Battle of the Brands

The competition between manufacturers' and distributors' brands seems to favor private brands. Some of the retailing giants are putting more and more of their offerings under their own labels. In many large department stores 10 percent of total volume is done under the store's own brands. A&P has reached 25 percent and Montgomery Ward is aiming at 80 percent of total sales volume.

Family Brands

A manufacturer or distributor who is interested in establishing a brand must decide whether to set up an individual brand for each item in the line or have one family brand for all products.

Family brands are generally used for products that carry a similar price and market. General Motors uses the family brand Chevrolet for a variety of cars of similar price that are aimed at a similar market. Their Cadillac brand is a separate price range keyed to a different consumer. If both Chevrolet and Cadillac were combined under one brand name, the lower-priced, lower-quality Chevrolet line would damage the image and prestige of the Cadillac models.

Wherever possible, family brands are used, since the advertising and promotion of any item within the family will help promote all the family members. However, the various products in the family must be similar. That is, a successful family brand for canned fruits would not help the sale of appliances.

Many producers package a whole line of similar products in a family of brands. This is done by designing all the packages within the family in a nearly identical fashion. Heinz's and Campbell's soups are typical of family branding and packaging. The advantage of family branding is that new products added to the line reap the benefits of the good will and customer acceptance that has already been established for the old line. For family branding to be worthwhile, the line must have wide customer acceptance and the various items in the line must be similar in cost, use, and quality. The disadvantage in family branding is that customer acceptance goes both ways. Acceptance of the older products will undoubtedly help win approval for the new item, but a weak new product may have a damaging effect on the older, established merchandise in the line. Producers that use family branding are usually extremely careful in their research involving customer approval for new products.

Individual Brands

Although the case for family branding is a very strong one, many manufacturers prefer individual branding. That is, they market identical, nearly identical, or similar products under separate brand names. Procter & Gamble, for example, uses individual branding for such similar products as Tide, Ivory, and Joy. Figure 9–8 features the soft drinks of PepsiCo, Inc. Although Mountain Dew and 7 Up and Slice and Miranda are similar soft drinks, the company elects to

FIGURE 9–8
PepsiCo, Inc., markets its soft drinks as individual brands. (*Courtesy:* PepsiCo, Inc.)

market them individually. Since these are all household soaps or detergents, they could easily be placed under a family brand name. Producers use individual branding for the following reasons:

1. Producers can saturate the market by individual branding. There is a limit to the size of the product market an individual brand can achieve. A consumer who uses Tide to wash work clothes may feel that it is too strong for delicate items; he or she therefore selects Dreft, another P&G product, for delicate laundering.

2. Producers who grant exclusive territories can increase their number of outlets by individual branding. In this way a territory can be saturated without antagonizing the original dealer.

3. To meet price competition without reducing the price of the principal brand, a producer may introduce a new "fighting brand."

4. When there is a chance of failure of a new product, an individual brand will protect the good will of the established brand.

5. Products aimed at different markets should be branded individually. The Gillette Company uses Papermate for pens; Toni, Prom, and Bobbi for home permanents; and Gillette for razor blades. It is doubtful that a woman would be attracted to the brand name Gillette for a home permanent.

6. Different quality levels should be branded separately. General Motors uses different brands for its various price lines. How many people would spend $25,000 for an automobile when the same brand name could be bought for $12,000?

SELECTING A BRAND NAME

Selecting a good brand name can be a very important factor in the success or failure of a brand. The first important feature of a good brand name is that it is easily pronounced, spelled, read, and recognized. If the brand must be sold abroad, these characteristics should hold true for the languages of all countries in which the product will be offered for sale. The simplicity of reading, spelling, and recognition is important if the customer is to be able to find the item on a shelf with a minimum of effort. Since many customers hesitate to ask for a brand name if they are not confident of the pronunciation, the name must be easy. Kodak is an excellent example of a brand name that meets the requirements of pronunciation, spelling, recognition, and the other necessities for success in foreign markets.

Short names are easy to pronounce. They have the additional value that they can be placed in large letters on the package. Major soap companies take advantage of this.

Good brand names are usually unique. Such names are easily remembered and do not run into the problem of being overused, as is the case with General,

United, or National. The use of personal names frequently causes trouble, as in the case of Mr. Gerber's Gerber Baby Food Company having to buy out a furniture manufacturer named Gerber.

A brand name should have the proper relationship to the product. Sears's Craftsman brand of tools is exactly right, as are Frigidaire, Sunkist, and Safeguard (a deodorant soap).

Brand names must be legally protected. Before going into an expensive promotional campaign, a company must make certain that the same name, or a similar one, is not already the property of another firm.

Important Points in the Chapter

1. Packaging consists of the activities—throughout the marketing process, concerned with the design and construction of the container of a product. In recent years packagers are as much concerned with sales promotion as they are with product protection.

2. Since the characteristics of products vary, each package must be designed to fit the needs of the specific merchandise. Complications arise because consideration must be given to a variety of problems, for example, transportation, storage, type of customer, and use in the home.

3. The expansion of self-service shopping has placed strong emphasis on the use of the package as a "silent salesperson." Since in many cases the package must sell itself, it must be designed in an unusual eye-catching fashion.

4. Packaging must perform a wide variety of functions, therefore, packaging costs are high. The customer is willing to pay extra for the convenience of a reusable container, and so on. Multiple packaging is a means of reducing packaging and handling costs while increasing sales volume.

5. Misleading packaging designed to exaggerate the contents in the container or make price comparisons difficult has resulted in legislation that attempts to improve packaging ethics.

6. A brand is a means of distinguishing a producer's or distributor's goods from the product of his competitor. A brand with a good customer following has a marketing edge over its competitors. As a result, companies that are financially strong enough to promote a brand name generally do so.

7. The maintenance of a successful brand requires a guarantee of consistent quality. Failure in this area will offset all the costs and benefits of an established brand name.

8. Customers prefer branded to unbranded goods because they are not gam-

bling when they purchase branded goods. They know exactly what they are getting.

9. Manufacturers' brands are the property of the producers. Private brands are owned by distributors who contract with manufacturers for the production of their branded merchandise. The competition between private and manufacturers' brands is swinging in the direction of private branding among high-volume retailers.

10. Family brands are used for similar items that fall within the same range of price and quality. They have the advantage of carrying each other. That is, when one item in the family is promoted, all the other products benefit.

11. A brand name should be easily pronounced, spelled, read, and recognized. It should also be unusual and related to some quality in the product. Care must be taken in promoting brand names, since they become generic when they are used as a synonym for the product. When a name becomes generic, its use is no longer restricted to the owner.

Review Questions

1. Define *packaging*. Explain the use of packaging as a sales promotion device.

2. Is transportation a problem in package design? Discuss.

3. What factors must be considered in the packaging of goods for home use?

4. Discuss the package as a sales promotion tool. Why is it increasing in importance in this area?

5. Explain the effect of television advertising on packaging.

6. Discuss multiple packaging. What are the advantages of multiple packages? Give several examples.

7. Why are consumers willing to pay for the high cost of packaging?

8. How do distributors and manufacturers respond to the charge that they use large packages to mislead their customers?

9. In your opinion, will the provisions of the Fair Packaging and Labeling Act of 1966 improve packaging ethics? Discuss.

10. What is being done to help the garbage disposal problems partly brought about by discarded packages?

11. Define *brand*.

12. What are the advantages of owning a brand?

13. Discuss the types of businesses that should not attempt to establish their own brands.

14. What type of business is most frequently involved in private branding? Why?

15. Discuss the disadvantages of owning private brands.

16. Why do some manufacturers turn down business from private branders?

17. What is the difference between family brands and individual brands?

18. Why do manufacturers choose to use family brands?

19. List and discuss the characteristics of a good brand name.

20. Explain the use of the term *generic* as it applies to branding. Give examples of brands that have been ruled to be generic.

Case Problems

Case Problem 1

The S&H Kimmel Company is a family-owned and -operated business that has four food markets in high-rent areas in New York City. The stores are partially self-service, with clerks available to make suggestions and offer help when needed. The clientele is wealthy, and Kimmel's carries several well-known brands of gourmet and other high-quality foodstuffs. The service given customers, including deliveries, is excellent and has resulted in a strong, loyal group of customers who provide a handsome living to the owners. The annual sales of the chain are about $8 million and are expanding, both through improvement in individual stores and the opening of new units. Management is conservative about opening at new locations, with a growth rate of about one store every four or five years.

Recently, Quality Foods, a West Coast canner of gourmet foods whose line is not carried by the store, has approached the owners with the suggestion that Kimmel's take in their line under a private label. Quality Foods is a well-established, high-quality producer, whose products are widely advertised and certain to be acceptable to Kimmel's customers.

If Kimmel's decides to go ahead with the offer, it will be able to buy the line at a price about 10 percent less than it pays for foods of similar quality.

Question

1. Discuss the advantages and disadvantages of private labeling in this case.

Case Problem 2

Green Fields, Inc., is one of the giants in the fruit and vegetable-canning industry. Its products are to be found in almost every food store in the country. The company's advertising and promotional policy is aggressive, and it would be hard to find an American family that has never tried a Green Fields product.

There are twenty Green Fields canneries throughout the country, and its four hundred warehouses and distribution centers keep grocery shelves filled in every corner of the land.

At present, the company does not carry a frozen food line. A recent market research study has indicated that there would be wide public acceptance of frozen food packaged under the Green Fields brand name, and the board of directors has authorized construction of the necessary manufacturing facility.

The packaging director has been informed of this development and was instructed to design packages for the new line. To get help with his problem, he has held discussions with the following people:

Production manager
Manager of sales promotion and advertising
Distribution and warehousing manager
Manager of customer relations
His wife

Question

1. What questions should he ask of each of these people?

10

PRICING

Learning Objectives

Upon completion of the chapter, you will be able to:

1. Discuss the importance of selecting a pricing objective and give three examples of pricing objectives.

2. List and describe five considerations that must be taken into account in the pricing decision.

3. Define elasticity of demand and give examples of products that have elastic and inelastic demands.

4. Discuss pricing strategy and define four types of strategies.

5. Explain pricing in relation to a company's marketing policies.

6. Prepare a break-even chart and discuss its findings.

7. List and define four types of discounts.

8. Discuss the effect on pricing of the Robinson-Patman Act.

S'NO RISK

While most of us (skiers excepted) dread the coming of heavy winter snows, the Toro Company of Minneapolis is praying for it. Toro manufactures snowblowers, and its S'no Risk campaign is a price gimmick with a lot of risk attached. The deal is this: anyone who buys a snowblower between May 1 and October 1 can get part of his or her money back if the snow accumulation in the area is below normal that year. If the accumulation is less than 20 percent of normal, the customer gets a full refund, at 30 percent of normal a 70 percent refund, and so on until 50 percent of normal results in a 50 percent refund.

Sales response was great. By the end of October, volume had more than doubled, and snowfall by the end of January was 40 percent of normal in the New York area and had already exceeded normal in many parts of the country. As of this writing, the jury is still out. It's a big country and long-range weather forecasting is notoriously weak.

One important fact: Toro was able to take out an insurance policy against possible refunds. Toro will not reveal the cost of the policy, but claims that it was less expensive than the price it would have paid for a decent promotional campaign. Clever!

There is nothing unusual about cutting prices or offering warranties; just about everybody does it. Toro's innovation was unique, however. Everyone who has ever bought a snowblower has said, "It probably won't snow this winter." Toro's price insurance campaign effectively canceled out this important negative in selling snow-blowers. By combining price reduction with an imaginative promotion campaign it was able to increase sales dramatically. The fact that it could add insurance against excessive losses from the program was to its advantage. The program was so successful that it even generated free publicity, as evidenced by its inclusion in this book.

INTRODUCTION

The success or failure of a business depends on its ability to have available for sale a unique, properly promoted product at an attractive price. This combination of factors is called the marketing mix. The selection of the most important of the four factors (product, promotion, availability, and price) depends on the specific product. However, it is likely that price is the principal factor.

Price, by definition, is an offer to sell for a certain amount of currency. The important word is *offer*, since it indicates that price is subject to change if insufficient buyers can be found at the original price. That is, prices are always on trial, and if they are found to be wrong, they must be immediately changed or the product must be withdrawn from the market.

The Toro model 3521 snowblower.
(*Courtesy:* The Toro Company, Minneapolis, Minnesota.)

PRICING OBJECTIVES

Before prices can be set, it is important that management have an overall marketing goal. A survey of the pricing goals of twenty large industrial corporations
indicated that prices were set with the following targets in mind.

To Achieve a Specific Return on Investment or Net Sales

When prices are set with the purpose of achieving a specific return, the
largest return may be a short- or long-term goal. Targets of this type are generally found among enterprises that are leaders in their field, for example, General
Motors, International Harvester, Aluminum Corporation of America, and Dupont. These firms are generally the price leaders in their industries and as such
are able to set prices without undue worry about competitors. It is important for
these industrial giants to set prices that are "fair and reasonable," since "fair and

reasonable" is the yardstick by which the Antitrust Division of the Justice Department, the labor unions, and the general public measure monopolistic practices or charges of restraint of trade. Smaller firms can only use prices to achieve targets of return on investment or sales if their product is new or unique, because the price of the run-of-the-mill products must be set to meet the competition of the rest of the industry.

To Stabilize the Market—Price Leaders

Another important pricing objective available to industry leaders is price stabilization. Companies that already control a large share of the market are frequently interested in a stability of price that will enable them to maintain their level rather than to increase it. Kennecott Copper, American Can, and Aluminum Corporation of America are typical of price leaders whose target is stabilization.

Price leadership does not indicate that all companies in the field will follow the leader by charging the same price as that set by the price leader. It means, rather, that a relationship is set between the price leader and the others in the industry. For example, minor oil companies generally price their product at 1 or 2 cents a gallon less than the prices charged by the major company in the field.

Price leadership requires careful policing by the leader if it is to be effective. If smaller firms cut their prices in an effort to increase their share of the market, the leader must be ready to keep them in line by means of a drastic, if temporary, price cut which will keep the smaller firm in its place.

As the smaller firms in an industry grow in size, price leadership may shift. In the aluminum industry, the past twenty years have witnessed a gradual decrease in the importance of the Aluminum Company of America as the price leader, with the corresponding growth of Reynolds Aluminum and Kaiser Aluminum.

If a price leader sets price to stabilize the market and achieve a status quo, it does not necessarily follow that conservatism is the rule throughout its endeavors. For example, General Electric, General Motors, and other conservative price leaders are very aggressive in areas of product promotion and research.

PRICING CONSIDERATIONS

Unquestionably, the major objective of pricing is the earning of maximum profits. This may be done by a pricing policy that will attempt to achieve a high return, or by a pricing policy that seeks stability of price while the company seeks to maximize profits by means of research or promotion. Whatever pricing policy is decided on, for maximum effectiveness certain considerations must be taken into account before prices can be set.

Consistency

It is important to bear in mind that pricing is only one part of the marketing mix and that the profitability of an enterprise depends on the total mix rather than on prices alone. For marketing success, all the marketing elements must be handled consistently. For example, Lord and Taylor's (a department store) promotion policy is to establish itself as a high-image prestige operation. Consequently, the product, price, and other factors must be consistent with the high-image concept.

The Long-Run View

Setting prices that will maximize profits requires a long-run point of view. A new product that might be sold at a price that is designed to bring in a very high profit might also result in the attraction of competitors, which would minimize long-run profitability. Frequently, it may be to the long-run advantage of a firm to sell new products at a loss in order to get into a new field or gain customers for the firm's other offerings. New products on which production is limited generally have high production costs. The General Electric Company sets a low introductory price on such items by calculating the production cost of the new item at the estimated cost of full-volume production. This policy may lead to short-term losses that will turn into maximum profits in the long run.

Pricing by Individual Items or by Total Profit

Many organizations find that their overall profits may be improved by varying the profitability of the individual items in their line. This procedure is quite apparent among supermarkets that frequently employ the concept of loss leadership, that is, the drastic reduction of the price of one or more items to attract customers to the store in the hope of selling them more profitable merchandise. Loss leadership can be achieved on individual items as well. Thus, a razor sold at cost will bring no profits, but the associated sale of razor blades may make up for it.

One Price Versus Variable Price

A one-price policy, in which all buyers are charged exactly the same price at any specific time, is the most common type of pricing. However, there may be provision under a one-price policy for varied prices for different classes of customers, quantity discounts, and price changes. The one-price policy has the following advantages:

1. A buyer may be confident that the price he or she pays is exactly the same as the price any other customer must pay.

2. By eliminating negotiation for price, the sales personnel is able to concentrate its selling efforts on the positive qualities of the goods.

3. A one-price policy eliminates possible conflicts with the law.

Despite these obvious advantages, many large industries use variable pricing. Under such conditions, each customer is expected to haggle over price in an effort to make the best deal possible. This situation results in excessive shopping for the best price and loss of good will through favoritism. Variable pricing is much more common on the wholesale market than among retailers, but even at retail, purchases of automobiles and major appliances are tests of the buyer's skill at price negotiation.

Prices and the Standard of Living

During inflationary periods it is considered the responsibility of price leaders to do all they can to keep prices at a stable level. Great pressure is applied by the public and government to influence major industries to forego price increases for the good of the economy. This was dramatically illustrated when an American president applied pressure to the steel industry to achieve the cancellation of a price increase. Since steel is a raw material for many products, any price increase would be inflationary far beyond the price of the steel.

Elasticity of Demand

The term elasticity is used by economists to describe the effect of changes in price on the demand for a product. Merchandise whose demand varies greatly with a small change in price is said to be highly elastic. Many common foods are highly elastic. As the price of tomatoes rises, the demand shrinks and the total sales volume generated by the sale of tomatoes diminishes. A product is considered inelastic if the demand remains fairly constant with a change in prices. Table salt is a product with an inelastic demand. It is doubtful that people would use significantly less salt because of a moderate price rise.

It is frequently difficult to determine elasticity in advance. Automobiles, which had been considered highly elastic, have been selling very well despite large price increases. Similarly, both sugar and gasoline have shown a sharp decrease in demand in response to large price increases. It is likely that all products have a degree of elasticity, depending upon the size of the price fluctuation.

In setting the price of a new product, the producer must weigh the effect of various price levels on the demand for the product and select the price that maximizes sales and profits. This is done with a demand curve, as illustrated in Figure 10–1. The demand curve shown is a simplified example of a curve for a highly elastic product. It indicates that at a price of $60 per unit, only one unit will be sold, producing total sales of $60. By reducing the price to $50, two units

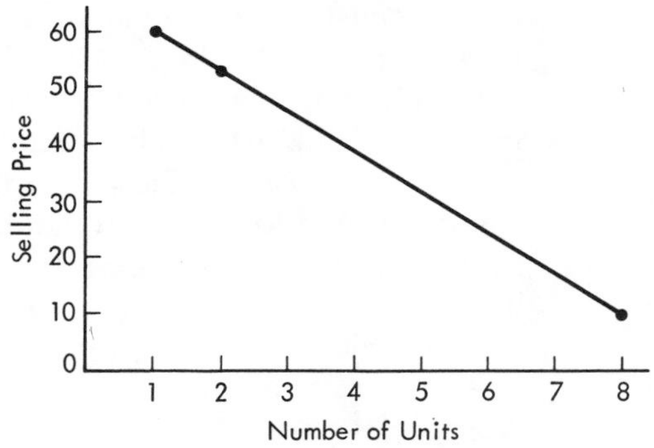

FIGURE 10–1
A typical demand curve.

will be sold, yielding total sales of $100. This information will help determine the price that will generate maximum profits.

PRICING PROCEDURES

Before arriving at a specific price, certain procedures must be undertaken. This is true for new as well as for established products.

1. The demand for the product and the company's share of the market must be estimated.
2. Competitive reaction must be taken into account.
3. A decision must be made on the pricing strategy to be adopted to ensure that the target share of the market will be achieved.
4. Consideration must be given to the company's image, promotion policy, channels of distribution, and a host of other company policies.

The Traditional Price

Customers traditionally expect to pay a certain price for a certain type of article. Lipsticks of a certain grade sell between $3 and $15. A price of more than $15 would probably result in customer rejection, and a price below $3 would cause customers to question the quality of the merchandise. Consequently, for all but completely new products, a definite range must be researched before a specific price is established. The lower end of the price range ($3 in the case of the lipstick illustration) is generally the cost of the product. This does not mean that the cost of the goods must have any effect on the selling price. Rather, if the cost is above the traditional price range, the article must not be included in the company's line of products.

The traditional or expected price can be determined by submitting the product to a knowledgeable retailer or wholesaler who knows the competitor's product. It may also be done by interviews or questionnaires given to wholesale or retail customers. Perhaps the best way to estimate demand at varying price levels is to test the product in a few areas at various prices. This sort of testing, although expensive, provides management with demand estimates at varying prices, which is extremely valuable information for the decision on specific price.

Take the case of Fleischman's gin. It was sold primarily to bars. When the company tried to move it to liquor stores at $4.50 a bottle it didn't do well. The solution? Raise the price and change the bottle (same gin)—and the product became successful. The reason? The buying public considered a cheap price to be indicative of inferior products.

Competitive Reaction

In pricing an article it is vital to estimate the reaction of competitors to the price selected. A highly priced new article may attract competitors in droves. An established article with a low price may force the competition to cut prices, which may result in a price war or in a product with an unrealistically low profit margin. In industries that have price leadership, a price cut by a small firm may result in a sharp, painful response from the price leader.

Competition decreases as the difficulty to manufacture increases. That is, an item that is easily and inexpensively produced is likely to attract competition if the price and consequent profitability make it worth the competitor's effort. Those items that are not easily manufactured must be priced with an eye to the competition available through substitutes. Thus, as the price for steel increases, more use is made of aluminum and plastics.

PRICING STRATEGY

Several marketing strategies are available to management to achieve the target share of the market.

Skim the Cream

The skim-the-cream pricing policy is generally used for new, unique products, such as a television recording device. Ideally, it will get the maximum return from a new product by setting a price at the top of the expected range until all consumers willing to pay that price are used up, and then gradually lowering the price by steps to bring in new groups of buyers. Advantages of the skim-the-cream strategy are:

1. Frequently, errors are made in the selling price of a new item. For example, production costs may be higher than anticipated. The selection of a low selling price that will require an upward revision because of a faulty estimate is poor marketing practice. Consider an appliance that should sell for

$50. It would be better marketing to begin with a $65 price that would eventually be reduced to $50 than to being with a $35 price that would later be raised to $50.

2. New items require high production costs, high promotion costs, and high profits for channel members to stimulate their interest.

3. The production rate of new items is generally low and uneven. A skim-the-cream policy reduces demand while maximizing profits.

4. New items are frequently undercapitalized. High early profits, before the item attracts competition, will enable the producer to accumulate a sound financial base for the article before it becomes competitive.

5. A high opening price on a product frequently has the effect of improving the sales appeal when the price is ultimately lowered.

6. The customers who are willing to buy the new product when it first becomes available are generally not price conscious and are willing to pay a price that will yield high profits to the producer.

A skim-the-cream pricing policy is generally reserved for products that are difficult for competitors to produce. The policy may also be used for short-lived products (fads); in the latter case, the producer expects to be through with the item before any serious competition can develop. Rubik's Cube is a classic example of this situation as is Nikon's F3HP camera, which appeals to customers that do not consider price as a factor (Figure 10–2).

The chief disadvantage of the skim-the-cream policy is that it attracts competition. For those items that are easily produced, excessive competition can be

FIGURE 10–2
Nikon F3HP, top-of-the-line camera. (*Courtesy:* Nikon, Inc.)

disastrous. A case in point is Wella Balsam, which came out at $1.98 when most cream rinses were selling for $1.19. Alberto-Culver jumped in with Alberto Balsam at $1.49 and took over the major market share.

Sony, a company with a large research and development budget, disregards competition. In an attempt to recoup its high research costs, its new products are introduced at the highest price possible to make as much as they can before the competition jumps in. Polaroid does the same. It introduced its SX-70 camera at an exorbitant price and then, after the cream was skimmed, came out successively with SX-70II and SX-70III to increase market penetration. Other examples of skim-the-cream pricing are pocket calculators which opened at $240 and dropped to under $10, ball point pens which originally retailed for $20 each, and digital watches which started at $2,000.

Penetration Pricing

Penetration pricing is the direct opposite of skim-the-cream pricing. Instead of aiming for a market of few non–price-conscious customers, it emphasizes maximum exposure. It is felt that if enough people try the product, its chance of success is excellent. Penetration pricing is effective under the following circumstances:

1. The quantity sold must vary with the selling price. Such products as toothpaste and soap, whose demands vary strongly as prices change, are typically sold under a penetration price policy.
2. For penetration pricing to be effective, the product must have a substantially lower unit cost when produced in high volume, since only reduced production costs will result in profits under penetration pricing.
3. The producing company must be financially strong enough to set up production and carry large inventories prior to the time the product hits the market. This is necessary because effective penetration policy results in an immediate high-volume demand.
4. The competition for the product must be so high that skim-the-cream pricing is impossible.
5. The demand for the product at skim-the-cream pricing must be so low that such pricing is out of the question.
6. Production must be geared to ensure that sufficient goods will be available to satisfy the maximum demand at which penetration pricing is aimed.

Penetration pricing is designed to limit competition. It is generally used for products that are expected to have a long market life and that can be produced easily by competitors.

FIGURE 10–3   A recent model Cadillac Sedan DeVille: A High-Image Product. (*Courtesy:* Paul Conte Cadillac.)

Image Pricing

Image pricing must begin with a strong product. This, coupled with high-image promotion and quality customer service, can result in higher than normal prices. In this way, Saks Fifth Avenue can get more for a product than can a discounter, and the Cadillac division of General Motors can sell at a better mark-up than can the Chevrolet division (Figure 10–3). It should be emphasized that image pricing must begin with a quality product. The finest and most effective promotion cannot sustain an image price if the quality of the product is mediocre.

Image pricing works both ways. Syms, a chain of off-price clothing stores strives for an image of quality merchandise at bargain prices. In this type of operation overpricing a single item might make a customer suspicious of all of the store's other "bargain" offerings.

Once an image has been set in customers' minds, it is very difficult to change. Sears has achieved the image of a medium-priced, quality chain with a low fashion profile. Presently they are trying to add high-fashion designer goods, although the likelihood of success is questionable.

Some producers actively promote the fact that their prices are high. They sell their high prices as an indication of quality. Zenith proudly claims that its high price is proof of high quality. Preference by L'Oreal, a hair dye, is advertised on TV by a model who says, "Sure it costs more, but I'm worth it."

Promotional Pricing

To attract attention to certain products, prices are frequently set to give bargains, or at least to appear as bargains. Promotion pricing should be coupled with a promotional policy in keeping with the product and its price. Nikon's L135AF camera is advertised to appeal to the young, price-conscious buyer (Figure 10–4). Among automobile manufacturers it is commonplace to offer the same basic products under different names with a variety of trims. In this way the lowest-priced model may be available for a promotion price, whereas the more elaborately trimmed models may be regularly priced, that is $400 or $500 higher.

Manufacturer's rebates are a method of promoting a product that became popular in the early 1980s. Chrysler Corporation, for example, gave rebates of $500, $600, and $700 directly to the consumer; today rebates reach as high as $2,500. Manufacturer's rebates have several advantages over traditional price cutting. First, the producer knows that the savings will go directly to the consumer and not be used to increase the dealer's profit. In addition, this sort of price reduction can be easily rescinded, as it always is when automobile sales are favorable.

FIGURE 10–4   Nikon L135AF camera. (*Courtesy:* Nikon, Inc.)

Odd Pricing

Although the evidence is questionable, many retailers believe that customers are more likely to buy if the price is stated in odd rather than rounded-off numbers. They believe that a bottle of salad dressing is more easily sold if it is marked 99 cents than it would be if it were priced at $1.00. This is done at all price levels including autos at $16,990 and houses at $199,900. Nobody really knows whether it works or not, but it is not usually done by prestigious retailers.

THE COMPANY'S MARKETING POLICIES

No discussion of pricing can be complete without reference to the great number of other factors that affect pricing decision. Among these are a variety of company policies that must be taken into account when prices are set. Some of these factors are

1. Relation to other products in the line.
2. Guarantees to the purchaser.
3. Services offered by the company.
4. Channels of distribution.

Relation to Other Products in the Line

Those companies that offer a line of related products must price new products with an understanding of the effect the new product will have upon the other items in their offerings. In other words, General Motors, in setting a price on a newly developed Pontiac, must consider the competitive effect the new item will have on its Chevrolet, Oldsmobile, and Buick divisions. In such a situation, the range of prices for which the new Pontiac must be sold is dependent on the prices that have been set for the other products in the line. In some cases, the same product may bear different labels and different prices to appeal to different segments of the market. The cosmetic industry provides many examples of this situation.

Guarantees to the Purchaser

When product guarantees are made to the purchaser, as is the case with most automobiles and appliances, the cost of fulfilling such guarantees must be included in the price.

Services Offered by the Company

Prices must be high enough to cover any associated services that are offered by the company. For example, Nordstrom is a high-fashion-image specialty store in which the major portion of the selling is handled by carefully trained personnel. Consequently, one would expect to find higher prices at Nordstrom's than at Marshall's, a self-service off-price store. If customer alterations are free in a clothing store, the price must include this cost. The point is that when more than the bare product is being sold, the price must be set to cover such additional expenses.

Channels of Distribution

Prices must be set at a level that offers an adequate profit for each channel member to ensure his or her enthusiastic cooperation. Those channel members who are responsible for the advertising and promotion of the item must have sufficient markup on the product to cover these expenses. In many instances producers set prices not only for themselves but also for every channel member up to the final consumer.

SETTING THE PRICE

After all the various considerations that affect price have been taken into account, the actual setting of the price must be effected. The price must be high enough to cover all costs plus the hoped-for profit.

Markup on Selling Price—Retailers and Wholesalers

Most retailers and intermediary channel members figure their price by using a markup based on selling price. It words this way: an item that costs $1.00 is sold for $1.50. The markup is $0.50. In terms of a percent of selling price, the markup is 0.50/1.50 or 33⅓ percent. In other words,

$$\text{Selling price} \quad \$1.50 \qquad \frac{\text{Markup}}{\text{Selling price}} \quad \frac{0.50}{1.50} = 33\tfrac{1}{3}\% \quad \frac{\text{Markup on}}{\text{selling price}}$$

Selling price $1.50
Cost   1.00
Markup $0.50

Markup is generally based on selling price rather than on cost. For one thing, it is in accord with accounting reports and terminology. In addition, if the average markup percentage based on selling price is known, it can be applied to the sales for a period and an estimated profit can be determined.

In practice, wholesale channel members are generally limited in their pricing by the discounts set for them by prior channel members. For example, in the medical accessory business, the producer or price leader might mark a piece of equipment at the retail price and sell it to a wholesale channel member at 60 percent below retail. The difference between the retail price and the retail price less the 60 percent discount to the wholesaler is the amount of profit to be shared by the remaining channel members.

An important aspect in retail pricing is the number of times the average inventory is sold during the year. This is called turnover. A retail jewelry store that has a turnover of one or two times a year must, of necessity, make more profit per item sold than a fresh fruit and vegetable store that has a turnover of forty or fifty times per year.

The notion that high retail profits result from high markups is erroneous. Low prices can improve the turnover and frequently yield higher profits than the high price resulting from large markups. The growing success of discount retailing operations is proof that profits can be increased by a high turnover caused by low markups and the resulting low prices.

Markup on Cost—The Producer

Most producers compute their selling prices by adding a percentage or specific amount to the estimated cost of product. Various producers use different methods of calculating the selling price, but it is generally done on the basis of cost. For example, one firm may determine the selling price of its product by adding 50 percent to its cost to cover general and administrative expenses (expenses other than those concerned with manufacturing, for example officers' salaries) and profit. Another manufacturer, whose pricing target is to achieve a 20 percent return on investment, would add a specific amount to the cost that would result in the target profit. A producer whose investment is $500,000 and whose target is a 20 percent return on investment, or $100,000, would estimate the number of units he or she will sell for the year and add sufficient profit to the unit price to achieve the desired target. (If estimated sales were 100,000 units, each unit would be priced to yield $1 of profit in order to reach the target profit of $100,000.)

Pricing based on cost is simple and readily understandable. Unfortunately, it has some serious limitations. This can be explained by the following example.

A manufacturer of upholstered chairs decided that he could sell one hundred pieces of a certain style. His workers were paid on a piecework basis, so he was certain of his labor cost. By careful analysis he was able to calculate his material cost exactly. His only other costs were rent, his salary, and other overhead expenses that were easily determined. He set his selling price in this manner:

Total labor cost $60 per chair × 100 chairs	= $ 6,000
Total material cost $40 per chair × 100 chairs	= 4,000
Total labor and material cost	$10,000

By dividing the total labor and material cost by the one hundred chairs that were to be produced, he found his labor and material cost to be $100 per chair

($10,000 ÷ 100 = $100). Since the job would take one month, and his average month's overhead was $2,000, he determined his overhead cost per chair to be $20 ($2,000 ÷ 100 = $20). His total cost per unit was:

Labor and materials	$ 100
Overhead	20
Total	$ 120
Since his profit was to be 25 percent of cost, he added	
($120 × 25%)	30
and determined his selling price to be	$ 150

Let us assume now that he only sold 50 chairs.
His income statement would be as follows:

Sales (50 chairs × $150 selling price)		$7,500
Labor and material cost		
(50 chairs × 100 L&M cost)	$5,000	
Overhead cost for the month	2,000	
Total cost		$7,000
Gain		$ 500

The problem is that there are two kinds of costs: variable costs (that vary with the sales volume), such as labor and materials, and fixed costs (that do not change with sales volume), such as rent and officers' salaries. The difficulty with figuring selling prices based on cost is that whereas the variable cost per unit (materials and labor) remains constant regardless of volume, the fixed cost per unit changes according to the volume. In other words, it is impossible to calculate fixed costs on a per unit basis unless the estimated number of units sold can be accurately predicted.

Marketing specialists construct graphs to illustrate the effect of volume on costs and profits. The graph is called a break-even chart, since it indicates the number of units that must be sold at a particular selling price in order for the firm to break even. Figure 10–5 illustrates the break-even chart of a company with fixed costs of $500, variable costs of $60 per unit, and a unit selling price of $160 per unit.

The chart in Figure 10–5 was prepared as follows:

1. The graph was designed with the number of units that might be sold arranged horizontally, and dollars of sales and costs arranged vertically.
2. The fixed cost of $500, which will remain the same regardless of the number of units sold, was shaded in. (Remember, officers' salaries, rent, and so on, do not vary with sales.)
3. A line was drawn that indicates the variable cost for each number of units sold. Since variable cost must be added to fixed cost to calculate total cost, $500 (total fixed cost) was added to the variable costs. For example, the

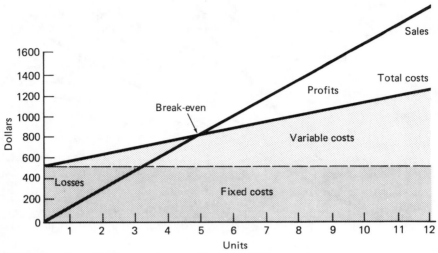

FIGURE 10–5   Break-even chart—selling price $160 per unit.

variable cost of selling three units is $180. In a situation in which three units are sold, the total cost would be $180 variable cost plus $500 fixed cost, or $680. After calculating the total cost for several levels of volume, the total cost line could be drawn on the chart.

4. The sales line was drawn by indicating the total sales volume, which is the result of multiplying the units sold by the selling price per unit ($160). For example, the sale of ten units would yield $1,600 (10 × $160).

ANALYSIS OF THE BREAK-EVEN CHART

The break-even chart indicates the fixed cost, the variable cost, the sales volume, and the profit and loss at every level of sales volume. If three units are sold, the total sales equals $480 (3 × $160), the total cost equals $500 fixed cost plus $180 variable cost, or $680, and the loss equals $200, total cost ($680) minus total sales ($480). In addition, the break-even chart indicates that the break-even point is reached when five units are sold, since total sales (five units at $160 equal $800) and total costs equal $800 (fixed cost of $500 plus variable cost five units at $60 equals $300).

When a pricing decision must be made among several possible prices, the break-even chart can be adjusted to indicate the break-even point, profits and losses, sales, and costs for various levels by adding additional sales lines to the chart. Figure 10–6 illustrates this. The difference between the break-even charts illustrated in Figures 10–5 and 10–6 is that consideration has been given in Figure 10–6 to the effect of various selling prices on profits, losses, and the break-even point.

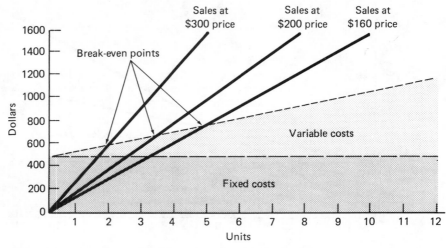

FIGURE 10–6   Break-even chart with different selling prices.

The major difficulty with the break-even charts that have been discussed so far is that customer demand at the various prices has been ignored. The charts are based upon the unrealistic idea that the product can be sold in unlimited quantities at various prices. In other words, although it shows what must be sold to break even, the chart gives no estimate of what can be sold at the various price levels. This can be overcome by estimating the sales of the product at the various price levels.

As we have seen, break-even charts are easy to understand and construct. They are, however, anything but a perfect pricing tool. The problem is that the charts are based upon estimates of future fixed costs, variable costs, and sales levels at several different selling prices. Each of these factors is subject to uncontrollable factors that make accurate estimation very difficult. For example, variable costs tend to decrease at a certain level of production. However, since all pricing must be based on estimates of costs and sales, the break-even chart offers a means of indicating these estimates with maximum simplicity.

Pricing based on cost is widely used among manufacturers and producers. However, the term *cost-plus pricing* is somewhat misused. The price that must be charged for a product is actually the amount the customer is willing to pay. It is ridiculous to assume that a customer would be willing to pay a high price for a product because its cost is high. Cost-plus is used to determine whether or not a business organization should go into the production of a particular product. If the merchandise can be produced at a cost that will result in an adequate profit, the organization might decide to produce it. Once the decision to produce or not to produce is made, the actual price of the product must be based on customer attitudes rather than on the cost of the merchandise.

Geographic Pricing

One important adjustment to price is the cost of freight. When a customer considers the price of goods, the additional freight costs to transport the goods where they are needed must be taken into account. The term FOB (free on board) indicates that the seller will place the goods on the designated carrier, at no cost to the buyer. FOB shipping point means that the goods will be placed on the carrier at the seller's place of business and that all additional costs will be paid by the buyer. FOB destination requires the seller to pay all costs of getting the goods to their destination.

Under *zone pricing* the selling area is divided into separate geographic areas and each customer within that zone pays the same freight cost. This is usually done by averaging all of the freight charges within that zone. An extension of zone pricing is *uniform delivered pricing* in which all of the customers in the country must pay the same freight charge. Occasionally, a seller will pay the freight charges in order to meet competition. This is called *freight absorption pricing*.

PRICE DISCOUNTS

Many sellers permit their customers to purchase merchandise at a reduction from the stated list price. Such reductions in price are called discounts. Although it is rarely obvious, discounts are generally given to channel members in return for their taking over a part of the marketing function. For example, a company that buys merchandise for later sales is in fact taking over the function of carrying inventory for the producer. In return for assuming this important marketing function, it is entitled to a discount. The following are the most commonly used types of discounts:

1. Cash discount—a deduction for prompt payment
2. Quantity discount—a deduction based on the size of the purchase
3. Trade discount—a deduction that is given to differentiate between different types of customers (wholesale versus retail)
4. Seasonal discount—for off-season orders
5. Promotional allowance—to underwrite cost of promotion

Cash Discounts

A cash discount is a reduction in price allowed to a buyer for payment of his bill before it is due. For example, a manufacturer might sell $100 worth of goods, with payment due in thirty days. As a reward for prompt payment, the firm permits the customer to deduct 2 percent if the invoice is paid within ten days. In this manner, the manufacturer is willing to take less money for the merchandise if the buyer is willing to pay the bill before the due date. A 2 percent discount for payment within ten days of a bill that is due in thirty days may be stated as 2/10, N/30 (2 percent discount for payment in ten days, total net amount due in thirty days).

The size of the cash discounts varies from industry to industry. Whereas 2/10, N/30 is common for food sales, dress manufacturers offer their customers 8/10 e.o.m. That is, the customer may deduct 8 percent for payment within ten days after the end of the month in which the purchase was made.

Quantity Discounts

To encourage customers to buy in large quantities, many sellers offer discounts that are scaled to the number of units ordered. As far as the seller is concerned, the larger the order, the smaller the selling and shipping costs and the greater the sales. To achieve this, the seller is willing to offer discounts. To the buyer, quantity discounts offer the opportunity of a reduction of the cost of merchandise.

Quantity discounts may be noncumulative (on a per order basis) or cumulative (over a specific period of time). Noncumulative quantity discounts are based on individual orders. An example of such a discount would be men's shirts sold either at $4 each or at three for $11. At the wholesale level non-cumulative quantity discounts might be offered as follows:

Pieces Ordered	Price per Piece
1–20	$10.00
21–50	9.50
51–100	9.00

Large orders result in savings in such areas as packing, shipping, book-keeping, and production planning. Noncumulative quantity discounts encourage large orders by passing along some of the savings to the purchaser.

Cumulative quantity discounts are based on volume of purchases over a specified period of time. They are a means of encouraging business by offering increasing discounts as the total volume from a customer increases. Cumulative quantity discounts might be offered as follows:

Total Annual Purchases	Cumulative Discount
$0–5,000	1%
$5,001–10,000	1¹/₂%
$10,001–20,000	2%

Trade Discounts

Trade discounts (sometimes known as functional discounts) are a means of reducing the price charged to certain buyers in return for the performance of specific marketing functions. For example, a manufacturer selling to wholesale and retail customers may give a trade discount of 40 percent to the wholesaler (who will have to resell the goods to retailers) and a trade discount of 25 percent to the retailer.

Seasonal Discounts

Manufacturers of highly seasonal products such as toys, furs, and lawn mowers are plagued with the problem of keeping their factories running during the slack season. Seasonal discounts are a means of attracting orders during the slack season by reducing prices on goods sold in the off-season. Frequently, such orders are given forward dating as well. That is, although the manufacturer's regular terms may be 2/10, N/30, much longer terms are offered to those customers that place their orders during the slack season.

Promotional Allowance

Frequently producers offer customers a price reduction in order to encourage the advertising and other promotion of their goods.

GOVERNMENT REGULATIONS ON PRICING

Federal and state governments have been active in passing legislation that affects price. The laws have frequently been poorly written, complex, and difficult to understand or administer. However, some of the laws are important and play a significant role in pricing.

The Robinson-Patman Act

Perhaps the most important type of federal legislation involved with pricing is the government's attempt to limit price discrimination. Any buyer who can make a purchase at a lower price than those of the competing firms has an advantage. The lower cost enables the buyer to increase profits by maintaining the regular selling price or increase his or her share of the market by reducing the selling price without affecting the profit per sale. To protect buyers who do not get a price edge from this sort of discrimination, the Robinson-Patman Act of 1936 (an amendment to the Clayton Act) was passed. In addition, the act states that there cannot be any unfair advertising allowances that would give the larger user an advantage. Advertising allowances should be given in direct proportion to total purchases to prevent discrimination against the smaller business.

Price discrimination is prohibited by the Robinson-Patman Act when

1. "The effect of such discrimination may be substantially to lessen competition or . . .
2. To create a monopoly."

The Robinson-Patman Act does not control all price variations. In the following situations, price reductions may be legal:

1. When the price reduction was made to meet the low price of a competitor.
2. When the price reduction was based upon cost savings incurred in selling the favored customer.
3. When the price reduction was made on goods that were either obsolete or about to become obsolete.

The workings of the Robinson-Patman Act can be illustrated in the following example.

A shoe manufacturer sells to many stores within a certain city. Included among the customers is a member of a large national department store chain. Since the shoe manufacturer is anxious to sell other units in the department store chain, she agrees to grant a 12 percent discount to the department store. This discount enables the department store to undersell its competitors. The discount will be considered in violation of the Robinson-Patman Act unless one of the following defenses can be shown:

1. The discount is based on a reduction in cost. The large sale to the large store resulted in cost savings (delivery, bookkeeping, and so forth).
2. The discount was a response to a similar cut made to the department store by a competitor.
3. The shoes in question had to be sold at once due to style changes.

Important Points in the Chapter

1. Price leaders, who need not be concerned with competitors, fix prices on their products with definite goals in mind. Such goals may be to earn a specific return on investment or to stabilize the market.

2. Pricing is one of many elements upon which commercial success depends. Intelligent pricing requires prices that fit consistently with the other market elements.

3. The procedures used for setting prices include consideration of customer demand, competitive reaction, and other policies of the company.

4. Skim-the-cream pricing is generally reserved for relatively noncompetitive items. This policy attempts to maximize profits by setting high prices that are gradually reduced as the demand at the price set dries up.

5. Penetration pricing attempts to give a product maximum exposure by setting prices at a very low level.

6. Markup is the difference between cost and selling price. When markup is calculated as a percentage, it is generally based on the selling price for retailers and other channel members and on cost for producers.

7. Variable costs are those that change as sales volume changes. Fixed costs remain constant regardless of sales volume.

8. A break-even chart is a graphic way of illustrating the number of units that must be sold at a particular selling price if a firm wants to break even.

9. Discounts are price reductions that are given to channel members in return for their taking over a part of the marketing function.

10. Price discrimination is illegal under the Robinson-Patman Act if it results in lessened competition or monopoly. Price deductions may be legal if it can be shown that the deduction was made to meet competition, from cost savings to a particular customer, or on old goods.

Review Questions

1. Differentiate between the pricing problems faced by price leaders and those faced by smaller firms.

2. Explain the statement, "Pricing must be consistent with other company policies."

3. Discuss loss leadership as a means of increasing overall profits.

4. Compare one price and variable price. What are the advantages and disadvantages of each policy?

5. How can the traditional price range within which the price must fall be established?

6. Why is competitive reaction an important factor that must be taken into account in price setting?

7. Explain the skim-the-cream pricing policy. When is it most effective? When least effective?

8. Explain the penetration pricing policy. When is it most effective? When least effective?

9. What type of product would be suited to image pricing? Promotional pricing?

10. How do company policies such as guarantees or customer service affect pricing?

11. A table that cost $60 is sold at $100. Calculate the markup percentage and the markup percentage on retail and on cost.

12. Differentiate between variable and fixed costs.

13. What information is illustrated by a break-even chart?

14. What are the shortcomings of a break-even chart?

15. How much cash will be needed on July 10 to settle a purchase of $150, with terms 2/10, N/30 dated July 3?

16. Discuss the reasons for which discounts are given.

17. Explain quantity discounts. What is the difference between cumulative and noncumulative quantity discounts?

18. Why are seasonal discounts given?

19. Under which two conditions is price discrimination prohibited by the Robinson-Patman Act?

20. Indicate three instances in which prices may be reduced for special customers without fear of a violation of the Robinson-Patman Act.

Case Problems

Case Problem 1

Prepare a break-even chart from the following information:

Fixed costs	$1,000
Variable costs	$120 per unit
Selling price	$320 per unit

Questions

1. How many units must be sold for the company to break even?
2. Indicate the profits or losses under the following sales assumptions:
   a. None.
   b. 4 units.
   c. 8 units.

Case Problem 2

The Research Department of one of the country's largest cosmetic manufacturers has developed a hair straightener that is far better than any similar preparation presently on the market. The formula is nonpatentable but requires very expensive equipment. It is considered likely that six of the company's competitors have the financial strength to go into the new product. Expectations are that competitive products will be on retailers' shelves within twelve to eighteen months of the time the product hits the market.

The company's marketing division is split over the pricing of the new item. One group favors a low price that will encourage universal acceptance of the product before any of the competitors' products arrive on the scene; the second group feels that because the product is of high quality, the demand will be so great that price will be of little importance and prices should be set to yield maximum early profits.

Questions

1. List all the arguments you can think of in support of the penetration price group.
2. List all arguments you can think of in support of the skim-the-cream price group.
3. As the vice-president in charge of marketing, the ultimate decision is yours. Which policy do you prefer?

11

CHANNELS
OF DISTRIBUTION

Learning Objectives _____

Upon completion of the chapter, you will be able to:

1. Discuss the economic importance of marketing channels and six functions of channel members.

2. Diagram six consumer channels and five industrial channels and for each describe the type of product usually involved.

3. Discuss six factors that should be taken into account before a decision or channel selection is made.

4. Differentiate among intensive, selective, and exclusive distribution.

5. List typical channels for all classifications of consumer and industrial goods.

6. Discuss channel management, including the factors of gravity, push, and pull.

HAS THE PARTY FIZZLED?

Going to a party is considered to be fun by most people. Birthday parties, anniversary parties, engagement parties, and Tupperware parties were regular events that most women looked forward to. Tupperware parties? Are these social events that really excited the housewives of America? By taking a look at sales of close to $900 million in 1982 for Tupperware, the answer has to be a resounding yes! Is it possible that plastic containers with tight-fitting covers could generate such excitement? Another yes!

When the product was first introduced, about thirty-three years ago, the company decided to take the direct marketing approach. Instead of following the conventional method used to distribute consumer goods, that is, to fill the stores with the plastic items and motivate shoppers to come to the retailer for their purchases, Tupperware decided to motivate people to give parties in their homes and sell the products there. And what a successful idea it was! Until 1980, Tupperware's marketing boasted a doubling of sales and profits every five years. In 1983, however, the slide began. Sales dipped 7 percent while earnings fell 15 percent. For the first half of 1984, sales dropped 9 percent with earnings off 21 percent. Why did it happen?

At times like these, when a company seems to be heading toward ultimate failure, action must be taken to correct the situation. But what's the problem? The products haven't changed.

If one carefully examines the marketing of Tupperware, it becomes clear that the party concept sold the product. While just about everyone agreed to the product line's excellence, it was the idea of enjoying a night out that motivated the customer to purchase. When this concept was first implemented, the role of the female was quite different from what it is today. For the most part, women were relegated to the chores of the household with little time off. A chance to get away for a few hours during the evening to have fun with other women was the right prescription for marketing certain products. The party was sponsored by an individual housewife who would invite friends and neighbors. The event meant prizes for the sponsor, the woman whose home was being used as a sales arena, prizes for the guests who answered the "contest's" questions right, commission for the Tupperware dealer whose take averages about 25 percent of sales, and more business for the company.

What happened? Women went to work! It's as simple as that. Being in the work force requires women to spend a great deal of time away from the home. Time spent at home became a valuable commodity; therefore, the prospect of spending an evening at a Tupperware party no longer seemed appealing. The sales seem to bear this out. Instead of leaving the home for what are still considered to be fine products by the user, time-conscious women would be more likely to pick up comparable items during a regular shopping trip. Spending an evening at home now seems more exciting than it ever did. Oh yes, those comparable products, such as those offered by Rubbermaid, sell for as much as 70 percent less than Tupperware.

It should be understood that direct marketing problems are being felt by others. Profits from Avon cosmetics, also sold in the consumer's home, fell off 12 percent in the past five years. To fight the battle, Avon has agreed to sell its cosmetics at retail kiosks where customers can see the products while they are shopping. This is in addition to continuing its former direct market technique.

A Tupperware houseparty. (*Courtesy:* Ellen Diamond, photographer.)

At present Tupperware is sticking to direct marketing. Whether its management believes that the party concept will begin to show positive results, or it is just shortsighted in refusing to change its marketing philosophy, only time will tell. Has the party fizzled?

INTRODUCTION

A channel of distribution is a route over which goods move from the producer to the user. In a simple society producer and consumer are in close proximity to each other. As the society becomes more complex, moving goods from producers to widely dispersed users becomes complicated, and channels must be set up to ensure an economic flow of produced goods from the manufacturer to the market.

ECONOMIC IMPORTANCE OF MARKETING CHANNELS

Market channels play a far more important role than the mere transporting of goods from producers to users. The economic functions of the various institutions that make up a channel are cost reduction, financing, cooperation in setting prices, communications link between buyer and user, promotional assistance, and reduction of the number of transactions.

Cost Reductions

Setting up an efficient, working channel has the effect of reducing costs by establishing automatic systems for supplying goods to customers. For example, a greeting card manufacturer whose channel of distribution includes Party Bazaar, is not required to send salespeople to the store after the channel has been established. When Party Bazaar's greeting card stock is low on a particular item, an automatic reorder is placed via a computerized system. In this way sales calls are restricted to showing new cards that have been added to the line.

Cost reduction also results from established channels through specialization. Essentially, the effect of the marketing channel is that the total distributing effort is broken down into separate functions. Individual channel members who deal in one specific phase of distribution are able to devote all their energies to their own area of responsibility, thereby increasing their efficiency. In general, an agent-middleman who is chiefly responsible for selling can set up a better sales force than an institution that has many other functions besides selling.

Financing

Channel members play an important role in helping to finance the entire product distribution effort. Most successful businesses need financial help in order to expand or to pay a return to their investors. They are required to tie up large sums of money in inventories and accounts receivable (money due from customers). By setting up channels, the producer can share the burden of this capital requirement with the various channel members. In the ladies' shoe business, for example, a large inventory must be carried from which customers' orders may be quickly filled. The manufacturer who sells to a wholesaler, who in turn sells to retailers, shares the financial burden (and risk) of carrying the necessary inventory with the other channel members. Of course, the manufacturer shares the profits from the total operation with them as well.

In some cases, wholesalers buy a manufacturer's total production and pay promptly. The wholesaler then resells the merchandise, giving long-term credit. In such instances, the wholesaler is helping to finance the producer by taking over the financial burden of extending long-term credit to customers and of carrying a large inventory.

Cooperation in Setting Prices

Channel members in a distributive system have an important effect on user prices. The selling of a product is usually cooperatively determined by the various channel members, who are in much closer contact with the customers and more familiar with the competition than is the producer. In addition, the final price must be set at a level at which it will provide each channel member with a fair share of the total profit. In a channel distributive system, the difference between the selling price and the cost of a product is split up among the various channel members.

Communications Link

As a producer grows in size, contact with the final user of the product diminishes. The other members of the channel, particularly those that come in contact with the user, act as an intelligence network for feeding information on style changes, prices, and competitor actions back to the producer. Without this feedback, many producers would lose their competitive position in the market.

Promotional Assistance

Since the retailer is the channel member in direct contact with customers, he or she is generally the most effective advertiser and promoter of goods. Normally, other channel members advertise to achieve product or brand familiarity, but the retailer's advertising display and promotional activities are concerned with the actual sale. Producers are aware of this and see to it that the share of channel profits going to the retailer is adequate to cover promotional costs. In addition, many producers give advertising allowances and outright cash to encourage retailers to advertise their products. In the clothing industry, the cost of the expensive catalogs that department stores send to their customers before the holiday season is often paid for by producers whose merchandise appears in the brochure.

Reduction of the Number of Transactions

If there were no channels of distribution and every producer sold directly to retailers, the number of transactions would be many times greater than it is at present. This would enormously increase the costs of record keeping and transportation, and ultimately the cost of goods to the consumer. The insertion of the middleman into the channel greatly simplifies ordering. This wholesaler may carry the lines of many manufacturers from whom he receives goods in large lots. The middleman's subsequent sale to the retailer will include the offerings of several producers. The retailer then receives the goods from all these sources in a single order and shipment, rather than individually ordering and receiving from each manufacturer.

CONSUMER CHANNELS

There are many choices of channels. Marketers can select the one that is best suited to the characteristics of their products and their other requirements. The seven most widely used channels for distribution of goods to the retail consumer are

Producer ———————————————————————→ consumer
Producer ——————→ producer-owned retailer ————→ consumer
Producer ——————→ franchised retailer ————→ consumer
Producer ——————→ licensed retailer ————→ consumer
Producer ——————→ independent retailer ————→ consumer
Producer ——→ wholesaler ———→ retailer ———→ consumer
Producer ——→ agent-middleman ———→ retailer ——→ consumer

Producer to Consumer

Producers of goods may reach the retail consumer directly by several methods of selling including door-to-door salespersons (Avon, Fuller Brush) and direct mail (many small manufacturers). In another example, Jostens sells high school rings directly to students using a sales force in excess of one thousand persons. Direct selling to the consumer has these advantages for the manufacturer:

1. Ability to control selling since the sales force is directly under the producer's supervision.
2. Close relationship to the consumer makes the manufacturer constantly aware of style changes and other consumer needs.
3. Profits do not go to middlemen.
4. Goods get to the consumer more quickly because they do not have to travel through middlemen.
5. Certainty that the sales force is properly trained if technical knowledge is required to sell the product.

Despite these apparent advantages, it is probable that less than 3 percent of total consumer sales are made in this manner. Some of the reasons for this are

1. The effort and expense of training, maintaining, and supervising a large sales staff.
2. The difficulty of providing and maintaining inventories of goods at many locations to assure prompt delivery to customers.
3. The enormous cost of financing and high risk involved in carrying multiple

inventories and customer credit that would otherwise be shared by channel members.

Producer to Producer-Owned Retailer to Consumer

Manufacturers such as Singer (sewing machines), Castro Convertibles, and
Thom McAn (shoes) maintain their own retail outlets for reasons similar to those
just indicated.

Producer to Franchised Retailer to Consumer

Moving goods to the consumer through franchised dealerships is an old
idea that has grown in importance since World War II. Because of the great
variety of franchising agreements, it is difficult to define a franchise. It is estimated that there are between two thousand and twenty-five hundred companies
offering franchising deals, and each company's contract is different. The broad-
est definition is given by the Small Business Administration:

> A franchise contract is a legal agreement to conduct a given business in accor-
> dance with prescribed operating methods, financing systems, territorial do-
> mains, and commission fees. It holds out the offer of individual ownership while
> following proven management practices. The holder is given the benefit of the
> franchiser's experience and help in choice of location, financing, marketing,
> record keeping, and promotional techniques. The business starts out with an
> established product or service reputation. It is organized and operated with the
> advantage of "name" and standardization.

This definition contains a large amount of information. However, all franchising agreements do not include every item mentioned. For example, many
franchisers make their profit by selling the product to the franchisee; others
profit by charging a commission on all franchisee sales.

The parent company benefits from a franchise operation as a means of
distributing goods in many important aspects.

1. The franchisee, by supplying a large amount of the capital needed for
   building new units, permits rapid expansion without decreasing the
   ownership of the company (as would be the case if capital were to be raised
   by the sale of stock).
2. A serious problem faced by expanding companies is finding management
   with the proper ambition. In franchising, all unit managers are in business
   for themselves with their own capital to protect and futures to ensure;
   thus, they are vitally interested in success and anxious to operate efficiently
   and profitably to protect their cash investment.
3. Overhead is reduced since managers need not be hired, and franchisees do

not require the close supervision that is necessary in units operated by disinterested managers.

4. The chance of success of an outlet owned by a local person is greater than one owned by a distant, impersonal corporation. The community is more likely to accept a product sold to them by one of their own.

An example of the economic advantage available to the franchiser is the fact that in the first three years in which Kentucky Fried Chicken published its quarterly earnings, every quarter showed an increase of 80 to 100 percent over the same period of the preceding year.

Producer to Licensed Retailer to Consumer

Licensing is very similar to franchising except that the licensor doesn't require the licensee to pay for the initial licensing agreement as required in franchising. Benetton licenses its products to retailers who agree to carry only the Benetton label. This arrangement guarantees no competition from other products.

Producer to Independent Retailer to Consumer

Although there are disadvantages involved in a distributive system that runs directly from a manufacturer to an independent retailer, this method is widely used for certain types of products. Among the goods that are frequently sold in this way are

1. Fashion merchandise, for which the time lost in distributing through middlemen is an important factor.
2. High-value goods whose markup offsets the additional distributing costs to the manufacturer.
3. Goods sold in large-quantity individual orders, which minimizes transportation costs.
4. Products requiring installation.

Producer to Wholesaler to Retailer to Consumer

The most common method of distribution is one in which the producer sells to the wholesaler, who, in turn, sells to the retailer, who sells to the consumer. In this channel system, the wholesaler is granted a part of the total profit, in return for which he or she buys, stores, sells, delivers, and extends credit. It is not unusual for a producer who sells through wholesalers to reserve the right to sell directly to certain classes of retailers.

Producer to Agent-Middleman to Retailer to Consumer

The function of an agent-middleman is to buy or sell merchandise for clients. Agricultural products are examples of goods that are bought and sold by agent-middlemen. The buying or selling may be for wholesale or retail clients. Agent-middlemen do not own the goods they sell.

It should be understood that the channels of distribution available to producers are not limited to those listed above. For example, a bushel of apples grown in the state of Washington goes through seven channel members before reaching a New York consumer:

Grower → cooperative → broker → auctioneer → wholesaler → retailer → consumer

INDUSTRIAL CHANNELS

The channels of distribution used for goods sold to industrial users are generally much shorter than the channels required to get merchandise to consumers. Most industrial products follow one of the following four routes:

Producer ──────────────────────────────→ industrial user
Producer ──────→ industrial distributor ──────→ industrial user
Producer ──────────────→ agent ──────────→ industrial user
Producer ──→ agent ──→ industrial distributor ──→ industrial user

Producer to Industrial User

The greatest dollar volume of industrial goods is channeled directly from the manufacturer or producer to the industrial user. This is particularly true for products requiring large capital expenditures such as generators, heating plants, and major construction.

Producer to Industrial Distributor to Industrial User

Operating supplies and accessory equipment are generally channeled through an industrial distributor before arriving at the industrial user's place. These are relatively small, inexpensive products, such as small electric motors, building materials, air conditioning equipment, and maintenance supplies.

Producer to Agent to Industrial User

Producers that do not maintain their own marketing departments frequently turn this function over to an agent. Industrial goods, piece goods, and other textiles and groceries are often marketed in this manner. The agents do not own the goods they sell.

Producer to Agent to Industrial Distributor to Industrial User

This channel also is used by producers who do not maintain their own marketing departments. The inclusion of an industrial distributor is necessary when a wide dispersion of inventory is required to ensure rapid delivery of supplies to users. Industrial distributors are then needed to store the product and service many small-order customers.

Industrial channels are simpler than consumer channels for the following reasons:

1. Since the selling of industrial goods frequently requires technical know-how on the part of the salesperson, the manufacturer must have adequate control over the sales force. The shorter the channel length, the more effective the manufacturer's control over selling.
2. Orders for industrial goods are generally large. This reduces shipping costs, clerical order handling, and the number of salespeople required. Because these are among the most important functions of a middleman, he can be eliminated.
3. Much industrial selling is specially designed to fit the requirements of a specific customer. This reduces the capital invested in finished goods. Inventories and middlemen are not needed for assistance in this function.
4. The industrial market is usually clustered into a small geographic area, which permits the producer to service his or her customers with a relatively small sales force. As a result, industrial channels are generally shorter.

MULTIPLE CHANNELS

It is not unusual for a producer to use more than one channel in its marketing policy. This is required when the products distributed are different. Revlon, for example, sells its expensive line, Ultima II, directly to department stores. Its cheaper products are sold through wholesalers to drugstores. Multiple channels are also set up to reach different target markets. In this way Firestone sells tires to General Motors for new cars, to company-owned retail outlets, to franchised retail outlets, and to wholesalers for distribution to service stations.

Recent years have seen a growth in the sale of the same product by different types of retailers. Hand tools can be bought at hardware stores, lumberyards, drugstores, department stores, auto accessory stores, and so on. Frequently each of these outlets requires a different distribution channel.

When multiple channels are all aimed at the same target market as is the case with hardware, toothpaste, and garden equipment, channel conflicts arise.

This is particularly true if there is a suspicion of price differentiation among competing retailers.

HOW TO SELECT A CHANNEL

There are a number of factors that must be considered when a channel of distribution is to be selected. Many choices are available, so that a careful study is required before a decision can be reached that will fit the problems of the specific institution to the best channel of distribution. Some of the guidelines are

1. Study the channels that are available, particularly those used by competitors.
2. Determine the channel that will best match the characteristics of the product to be marketed.
3. Estimate the probable demand for the product.
4. Consider the available financial resources.
5. Approximate the costs, sales, and profits for each available channel.
6. Determine the size of the product line and the amount of a typical order.

Selection of the proper channel may be crucial to a new product. Welch's grape juice is a good case in point. It was originally sold through food brokers who delivered exclusively to warehouses and only replenished retailers' shelves once a month. This led to poor display and frequent out-of-stock situations. By replacing food brokers with distributors who delivered the beverage to stores several times a week, Welch Foods transformed a marginal product into a highly successful one.

Study of Available Channels

It is rare to find a product so new that no similar product is being distributed. Before making a distribution decision the channels of distribution being used by similar products should be studied. The distribution procedures used by competitors require careful analysis to determine their adequacy, profitability, cost, and effectiveness.

The present trend toward broadening retail offerings has complicated channel selection. There are no longer clear indications of product channel requirements. Twenty years ago, a drug manufacturer distributed through channels whose sales force called on drugstores. At present, drug items are sold in supermarkets, variety stores, department stores, and door to door. Since each system requires a somewhat different channel, it is common to move the same item through several different distributional channels.

Characteristics of the Product

Goods may be broadly classified into two areas, wholesale and retail. Within each classification further breakdowns may be made into more specific categories. In the determination of the type of channel to be used, the distributional requirements of the specific item to be sold are perhaps most significant. The characteristics of each product are unique, and the manner in which it is distributed should be based on its requirements. For example, perishables must get to the consumer quickly. The same is true of fashion merchandise. Heavy equipment, whose installation requires a technology that only the manufacturer can provide, must be sold directly. Seasonal goods, which require large investments in inventory, may need middlemen to help with the financial burden.

Although the nature of the goods dictates their channel treatment, other considerations must also be taken into account. The financing of large inventories can be done through wholesalers, but this is not mandatory for a manufacturer with ample funds. Again, it is not impossible for the producer of heavy equipment to find a distributor-middleman whose staff has the know-how to handle the installation problems, or perhaps the middleman can sell the equipment and the responsibility for installation can remain with the manufacturer.

Estimate of Probable Demand

Since the function of the channel is to get the goods to the customer, the channel must be based upon customers, their habits, and their convenience. A product that is retailed only in hardware stores *must* be sold in hardware stores, and if manufacturers are unable to sell economically to such stores, they must set up a channel that will include wholesalers who distribute to hardware retailers. On the wholesale scene, manufacturers who habitually buy manufacturing supplies, along with other merchandise, from supply houses, are unlikely to change their procedures to buy a particular type of supply directly from the producer.

The geographical location of the market is important. The producer of a product that is to be distributed nationally must weigh the decision to market through wholesalers or to set up and maintain a nationwide network of distribution centers.

Financial Resources

The system of distribution used by many firms is dictated by their financial resources. Small firms, of limited financial strength, are often forced to select channels by cost rather than by effectiveness. Frequently, weak producers select channels for the financial help they get in carrying inventories and extending credit. It is not unusual for a financially strong wholesaler to lend money to a manufacturer to ensure the continuation of high production.

Approximation of Costs, Sales, and Profits

In a highly competitive market, the price the final user of the product will pay depends more on the market than on the wishes of the producer. The channel profit, the difference between the producer's cost to manufacture and the selling price paid by the user, is available for distributing the product and for return on investment for the producer as well as the various institutions that make up the distributive channel. Various channel members demand various shares of this profit. Consequently, the makeup of the channel depends in large part on the approximate amount of profits available from the product. For example, if the difference between the cost to produce the item and the selling price to the user is 40 percent, the channel selected must be one whose members are willing to perform their functions for a share of the 40 percent. Each channel member is paid according to the function he or she performs. A food broker, whose responsibility is limited to selling, is paid 2 to 5 percent of sales. General-line grocery, wholesalers who store goods, give credit, deliver, and sell, operate on approximately 10 percent of sales. Which channel the product can afford can be determined by approximating the cost, selling price, and profitability of the item.

Size of the Line and Amount of a Typical Order

As a rule, middlemen can be eliminated when a salesperson can make a living carrying the product. A salesperson can make only a limited number of calls per day. If the typical order is too small to pay for his or her salary, middlemen, whose sales force carries many products, must be used. Orders increase in size as the size of the line and the selling price per unit increase. Manufacturers of extensive lines of merchandise or high-priced merchandise are more likely to have their own sales force than single-product, low-priced producers.

INTENSITY OF DISTRIBUTION

After the channels of distribution have been determined, a manufacturer must decide upon the number of members that should be installed at each level of distribution. This can be thought of as the degree of intensity with which the manufacturer wants the product to be marketed. Although there are many degrees in between, this topic can best be discussed in terms of intensive (mass) distribution, selective distribution, and exclusive distribution.

Intensive Distribution

Highly competitive convenience goods—for which customers will not go out of their way to buy and for which substitutes are readily available—require maximum exposure and mass distribution. Goods such as cigarettes, candy, and toothpaste should be placed in every available outlet. Since the extent of distribution is vast, merchant wholesalers are an absolute necessity.

The Coca-Cola Company has achieved intensive distribution for its products. By using over one thousand wholesalers it has placed its product into close to two million consumer outlets.

Selective Distribution

Selective distribution is the practice of distributing through a carefully selected channel in each geographical area. By carefully choosing the institutions through which the goods reach the consumer, many advantages may be effected:

1. The placing of goods in certain high-reputation stores can increase sales. A manufacturer whose goods are handled by the R. H. Macy chain of department stores stands a good chance of getting excellent market exposure. (It should be noted that Macy's does not successfully promote every one of the lines it carries.)
2. Selectivity can reduce credit risks by limiting sales to those stores that are financially secure.
3. By limiting the accounts to be sold, marketing costs are reduced. Since the shipments are larger and fewer, transportation costs drop. In addition, fewer customers mean fewer salespeople. Selling only to retail leaders who advertise extensively reduces the producer's advertising costs.
4. Most firms that distribute their products on a selective basis feel that the small loss in gross sales resulting from this system is more than offset by a considerable increase in profits.

The chief disadvantage of selective distribution is the difficulty most firms have in getting the desired high-volume, prestigious retailers to handle their lines. Obviously, all household appliance manufacturers would like Neiman-Marcus of Dallas to handle their products, but not every line can be accommodated by them.

Another problem faced by producers who distribute exclusively through major retailing outlets is loss of control. The producers who sell to the R. H. Macy chain must be prepared to extend maximum service, give prompt delivery, make large advertising allowances, adopt a liberal returned-merchandise policy, and perform all the special services demanded by a powerful channel member.

Exclusive Distribution

Exclusive distributorships are granted by some manufacturers to wholesalers and retailers as in the case of Benetton products. Wholesalers guarantee that they will not sell their products to any competitor in the area. Exclusive distribution has the effect of including the dealer as part of the producer's organization. Generally, exclusive distribution either on the wholesale or retail level is awarded to the channel member in compensation for a specific service performed. For example, an automobile agency requires a large capital investment. It is doubtful that anyone would make such an outlay without exclusive distributional rights. Other exclusive distributions are given in return for large advertising guarantees or the right to be carried by a high-volume distributor.

The following are some of the advantages to dealers who are granted an exclusive distributorship:

1. The product is carried in their areas only by them, so all benefits of promotion and advertising accrue to them.
2. The service and repair-parts inventory is set up exclusively for one product line. As a result, the service department is efficient, which adds to the goodwill enjoyed by each dealer.
3. The absence of competitors carrying the line minimizes competition and price cutting.
4. The importance of each dealer's business to the producer is so great that dealers generally receive maximum cooperation.
5. The total inventory is reduced, since only one line is carried.

The disadvantages of being granted an exclusive dealership are loss of business in competing products and the possibility of losing the line, after heavy investment, if the sales volume does not satisfy the granter of the exclusive distributorship.

The granter of the distributorship has the advantage of placing the product in the hands of a dealer who does not handle competitive goods. The result is more aggressive selling, better customer service, and retail price maintenance. Moreover, since the number of accounts that must be serviced is reduced, marketing and clerical costs are also smaller.

Obviously, not all goods can be marketed through exclusive distributorships. Some merchandise is not important enough to be granted exclusive rights. Convenience goods, for example, need maximum exposure. Generally, at the retail level, specialty merchandise, men's clothing, and products such as automobiles that require special services or large investments are marketed exclusively. Industrial goods that are sold under exclusive dealerships are those that require installation and service, such as farm equipment, turbines, and furnaces.

MERCHANDISE AND TYPICAL CHANNELS

Although the producer has many variations of channels available, the specific channel used is generally determined by the type of goods being marketed. The following is a broad classification of merchandise and the typical channels through which such goods are marketed.

Convenience Goods and Staples

Since convenience goods, particularly staples, require intensive distribution over a widely dispersed market, middlemen are always found in the channels that distribute such goods. The goods are generally uncomplicated and require no installation or service. Intensive promotion of such goods is usually taken up by the producer. Various middlemen store, break bulk, and sell to retailers, who, in turn, sell to consumers with little more sales effort than shelf arrangement and display.

Impulse Goods

Impulse goods are those products that are bought on the spur of the moment, without previous planning. A soft drink or an ice cream cone is typical of such merchandise. Impulse goods must be prominently displayed and promoted to be sold. They require aggressive middlemen and retailing activity. Frequently, middlemen cannot be found to push the article to a producer's satisfaction, so they will use their own sales force to sell direct to retailers.

Emergency Goods

Emergency goods, since they must be available at all times, require wide distribution and availability. The channels of such goods must include all-night service stations, vending machines, and other outlets that stay open late and on holidays.

Shopping Goods

Items such as clothing, furniture, and appliances, which are subject to price and style comparisons by shoppers, are called shopping goods. As is the case with all goods that require aggressive selling and promotion, the channel must be designed to keep the producer as close as possible to the retailer. At best, shopping goods should be channeled directly from the producer to the retailer. This close contact results in better retail promotion, feedback on styling, and technical information to the retail sales force.

Industrial Equipment

Industrial equipment is usually channeled directly from the producer to the user. The sales are few and large and the technical training required for selling, installation, and service requires the sales force to be controlled directly by the producer.

Agricultural Products

Agricultural products require many middlemen. The harvests of many small farmers must be collected, sorted, and in some cases processed before they can be sold at retail. This requires the efforts of many brokers and agent-middlemen.

Raw Materials

Raw materials generally have few producers and users; both are large and well financed. Consequently, there is no necessity for middlemen in the marketing channels of these goods. They are usually marketed directly from the producer to the user.

Maintenance Supplies

Essentially, maintenance supplies are industrial convenience goods. There are many widely dispersed customers, who buy in relatively small quantities and rarely require technical help. Middlemen such as office supply stores and mill supply houses are very active in this field.

MANAGING THE CHANNEL

The success or failure of a marketing channel depends not only on the choice of channels and the effectiveness of the channel members but on certain channel policies as well.

Gravity

Gravity is a policy of putting goods into the channel and then letting nature take its course. It is based on the theory that there is an economic need for the goods and that after the product is placed in the channel, it will find its way to the consumer. This policy is typically used by the small producer. The farmer sells his wheat to a wheat elevator and forgets it. The small manufacturer sells to a jobber and drops out of the picture.

Pull

A better operation may result when pull is added to gravity. Pull is a policy in which the product is pulled through the channel by applying suction at the consumer end. Branding, consumer advertising, and premiums are examples of pull. The successful use of consumer advertising can result in demand for a product that will make retailers and wholesalers extremely anxious to handle the product. This may increase the channel opportunities open to the producer and improve control over the channel members.

Push

Push is a policy of improving channel operation by putting pressure on the channel members to sell more effectively. Unlike pull, which appeals to the ultimate consumer, push is directed at channel members. Push may be applied through cooperative advertising, "missionary" personnel to aid the distributor's sales force, manufacturer's representatives called *detailers*, sales promotional materials, and window trimming. In the pharmaceutical field detailers visit doctors and hospitals distributing samples and literature to influence prescription writing, even though the product will be sold through wholesalers.

Channel Cooperation

The effectiveness of any channel of distribution can be improved by the amount of cooperation the producer gives the channel members.

Consumer Goods.   The following are instances typical of the manufacturer's cooperation with channel members.

1. Johnson & Johnson maintains a sales training program for drugstore sales personnel.
2. The Maytag Company has a program designed to aid customers in reconditioning and selling trade-ins.
3. General Electric conducts a school for repair personnel.
4. Rexall Corp. gives their retail outlets (drugstores) help in store design, fixture planning, merchandising, and financing.

Industrial Goods.   Manufacturer's assistance to channel members in the marketing of industrial goods is generally limited to advertising and training programs such as service, installation, and sales.

The Channel Captain

It should not be assumed that the channel captain of every distribution line is the manufacturer. The strongest institution in the channel generally assumes all interchannel responsibilities. When Sears selects a factory to manufacture a line of appliances to be sold under the Kenmore brand name, that manufacturer has no responsibility other than production. The Kenmore image belongs to Sears and they can change producers, but the manufacturers cannot replace Sears.

Frequent Channel Evaluation

The changing business environment requires frequent channel evaluation. Not only must the individual channel members be checked in terms of costs and sales quotas, but the total system must be studied as well. New types of wholesale and retail establishments and the services performed by old ones are always changing. It is not uncommon for marketers to work diligently to set up an excellent channel and stay with it long after it has become obsolete.

CHANNEL CONFLICTS

A *channel of distribution* may be defined as a series of companies cooperating to move goods from the producer to the consumer. While the definition is a good one, it does not describe the conflicts involved. What sounds like a peaceful group working together toward a common goal, is often a group of individual firms fighting among themselves for a larger share of the pie, each certain that they are getting less of the profit than they deserve. These conflicts are rarely publicized for several reasons. One is that kicking up too much of a fuss might jeopardize the whole operation, and few people really want that. Another reason for the silence is the difference in size between the channel leaper and the other channel members. Consider the futility of a small gas station operator taking on a major oil company. Occasionally, channel conflicts do surface. Here are some examples:

FIGURE 11–1   A Winnebago. (*Courtesy:* Winnebago Industries, Inc.)

FIGURE 11–2   Itasca by Winnebago. (*Courtesy:* Winnebago Industries, Inc.)

When 25 percent of Coca-Cola's bottlers and distributors decided to add Dr Pepper to their line, Coca-Cola muscled them into replacing Dr Pepper with Mr. Pibb, Coke's cherry-flavored soft drink.

Winnebago's new line of trailers, Itasca, is being distributed through Itasca dealers, in direct competition with the established Winnebago dealers. See Figures 11–1 and 11–2.

Chicken Delight franchisers were required to buy their product directly from the franchise. They felt they were overpaying and went to court. The court agreed. Now, franchisers merely offer their principal products to their franchisees.

When Sylvania felt that several of its dealers were out of line, it revoked their credit lines.

At one time a group of large retail discount chains refused to buy appliances from General Electric because they thought GE was selling to catalog stores at a lower price.

Important Points in the Chapter

1. A channel of distribution is a system through which goods move from the producer to the user. The channel serves an economic need, since it re-

duces marketing costs, helps to finance the marketing system, and acts as a communications link between the producer and the user.

2. There is a wide variety of channels available; the type selected depends, in large part, on the characteristics of the goods and the financial strength of the producer.

3. Generally, the more expensive, technical, and highly styled the goods, the shorter the channel. The reason for this is that such goods require the producer to be in close contact with the user. Industrial goods usually have shorter channels than do consumer goods.

4. The choice of a specific channel must be based upon distinctive qualities of the merchandise; estimates of the probable demand; channels available; approximation of sales, costs, and profits; number of items in the line; size of a typical order; and financial resources.

5. The intensity of distribution (the number of channel members at each level of distribution) can be intensive, selective, or exclusive.

6. The producer can influence the flow of goods through a channel by a policy of gravity (put the goods into the channel and let nature take its course), pull (promote the goods to the final consumer and have demand act as suction to pull the goods through the channel), and push (apply pressure to the channel members to improve their selling and promotion efforts).

7. The changing economic scene requires frequent review of channel operations.

Review Questions

1. Define *channels of distribution* and explain the reasons for their existence.

2. Explain the part channels of distribution play in the financing of a marketing system.

3. Discuss channels of distribution as a communications link between the producer and the user of the merchandise.

4. Producers who sell directly to consumers use one of three methods. Discuss and give examples of each method.

5. Define *franchising* and give examples of franchisees.

6. What are the disadvantages of direct producer-to-consumer selling?

7. Discuss the types of goods that generally go directly from the producer to the independent retailer.

8. Explain the function of an agent-middleman in the buying and selling of agricultural products.

9. Why is an estimate of the demand for a product important to the selection of the channel that is to distribute it?

10. Discuss the importance of the size of the product line to channel decisions.

11. What effect does a company's financial condition have on its choice of channels?

12. Explain the effect on distributive channels of such changes as the sale of drugs in supermarkets.

13. Why is the approximation of a product's profit an important consideration in channel selection?

14. Define and discuss *exclusive distribution*.

15. What are the advantages and disadvantages to the dealer of selective distribution?

16. What are the advantages and disadvantages to the retailer of exclusive distribution?

17. What channels of distribution would you expect to find for distributing raw materials? Agricultural products? Why?

18. Define the policy of *gravity* as the term is used in marketing.

19. Give examples of the type of cooperation one might expect to find between a producer and other channel members.

20. Why should channels of distribution be constantly evaluated?

Case Problems

Case Problem 1

The Cure-All Manufacturing Company manufactures a line of non-prescription medications, such as aspirins and cold remedies. The company has been in business for many years with great success, and the brand name is important in the industry. The product is channeled through wholesale and retail druggists.

Because the brand is well known, most supermarkets carry the product. To obtain the product line, supermarket buyers are forced to go to wholesale druggists, since their normal suppliers, the food wholesalers, do not carry Cure-All products. This is an inconvenience to the supermarkets; they could cut down on their transportation, handling, and clerical costs if they were able to order the line with their regular merchandise from their regular suppliers.

Women seem to prefer buying the products at supermarkets because they are there often. Drugstore purchases frequently require an extra trip. It is apparent that the line should be distributed through food wholesalers. This would probably increase sales, since many small grocers who do not carry the product now would take them in the line.

Questions

1. What channels of distribution should be set up to reach the food trade?
2. It has been suggested that the most promising one hundred food wholesalers out of the two thousand available in the directory should be chosen and given exclusive territories in which to sell the line. What is your opinion?

Case Problem 2

The Wing Ski Corporation is a manufacturer of metal skis. When the item was first produced, it was exclusively distributed through the major ski shops in every geographical area. This worked out very well, since metal skis were a new idea requiring the promotional help that only the leading retailers could supply. Both Wing Ski and its exclusive retailers prospered.

As the sport increased in popularity, many new ski shops opened. They needed a metal ski line and turned to Wing, the leader in the field. Wing remained loyal to its dealers who had helped build its success and refused to sell to the new retailers. This gave Glide-Ease, a competitor in metal skis, the opportunity to take over a large share of the market. Glide-Ease manufactures a somewhat lower-quality line that is sold at a price that makes it an excellent value.

The sport has become even more popular in recent years and Wing Ski has increased its volume and profits each year. Naturally, this profit is considerably less than it would be if Glide-Ease were not in the picture.

Questions

1. Did Wing Ski make an error?
2. What alternatives are available to Wing Ski?
3. Does Wing Ski have a responsibility to its dealers?

12

WHOLESALING

Learning Objectives

Upon completion of the chapter, you will be able to:

1. Define wholesaling and differentiate between wholesaling and retailing.

2. Discuss service wholesalers, enumerate three types, and discuss the products they carry.

3. Discuss limited-function wholesalers, enumerate five types, and discuss the products they carry.

4. Describe the differences between agents and brokers and other wholesalers, list six types, and discuss their functions.

GET RID OF THE MIDDLEMEN

They are responsible for high costs. They add as much as 50 percent to the cost of some products without changing the merchandise in any way. For a while it looked as though this would happen. During the 1930s and 1940s wholesaling went into a decline, but it was only temporary. By 1950 wholesaling had regained its earlier level of importance and it has been growing ever since. Why? Consider the following example:

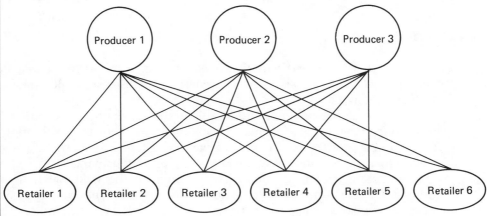

Without middlemen, three producers need eighteen transactions to service six retailers. Note the difference when a middleman is inserted into the channel:

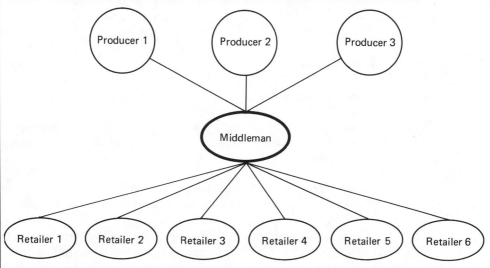

Now there are only nine transactions, with savings in handling, packing, selling, shipping, bookkeeping, and so on. And this is only a part of the service supplied by middlemen. The fact is that middlemen provide a vital function. Certainly, we can get rid of middlemen, but somebody will have to replace them, and the cost of their function cannot be eliminated. It's true that they add nothing to the product, and they certainly add a substantial amount to the cost, but they are as important to getting the product into use as anyone in the channel of distribution. They have been with us for a long time, and their continued function is assured.

INTRODUCTION

The size of the wholesale market is staggering. It is estimated that there are about 400,000 wholesalers in the United States whose gross sales are about $1.3 trillion annually.

Wholesalers play an important role in the distribution of goods. Although it has often been suggested that elimination of the wholesaler will bring greater profits to the producer and perhaps lower prices to the consumer, statistics show clearly that the activities of wholesalers are continuously increasing. Obviously, the marketing experts do not wish to eliminate the wholesaler. In order to understand the significance of wholesaling for the marketing of goods, it is necessary to study the various types of wholesalers and the services they provide for producers and consumers alike.

This chapter shows charts provided by the Bureau of the Census that incorporate both consumer and industrial goods. However, wholesaling principles and methods in this chapter apply strictly to consumer classification of goods and services. The industrial market was covered in Chapter 5.

DEFINITION OF WHOLESALING

The American Marketing Association defines *wholesaler* as

> a business unit which buys and resells merchandise to retailers and other merchants and/or to industrial, institutional, and commercial users but which does not sell in significant amounts to ultimate consumers.

Wholesalers are primarily middlemen who buy for the purpose of resale. Technically, however, retailers whose main function is to sell to the ultimate consumer, may be classified as a wholesaler if the goods they sell are not intended for personal use of the buyer. For example, a retail stationery store that sells ledgers to other retailers for their record keeping is engaged in a wholesale activity. Thus, the *purpose* of the sale determines whether it is a wholesale or a retail transaction.

DIFFERENCE BETWEEN WHOLESALING AND RETAILING

Wholesalers differ from retailers in many ways. Neither group is involved in manufacturing goods, and they both engage primarily in selling, but to separate and distinct markets. Basic differences are

1. *Markets served.* Retailers sell goods and services to ultimate consumers for their own use. Wholesalers sell primarily to retailers (or other wholesalers), whose purpose it is to resell the goods.
2. *Size of purchases.* Wholesalers buy in significantly larger quantities than retailers. One of the wholesaler's main functions, in fact, is to afford the retailer the opportunity to buy in small quantities.
3. *Methods of operation.* Wholesalers generally operate in lofts and warehouses, which are typically located in out-of-the-way places. This is possible without being detrimental to business because they sell their goods either by means of orders placed with salespeople who make retail store visits, or via telephone or mail orders. Retailers, on the other hand, generally operate from stores located in areas that are easily accessible to the ultimate consumer.
4. *Area served.* The trading area of the wholesaler is typically larger than that of the retailer. There are exceptions to the rule. For example, by way of mail or telephone orders, the retailer's trading area can increase enormously.
5. *Cost of goods.* Although wholesalers and retailers can often purchase from the same manufacturer, the wholesaler generally is charged a lower price because of the nature of the business. Of prime importance is the fact that the wholesaler buys in much larger quantities than does the average retailer. Giant retail chains are able to place orders larger than those of wholesalers. They frequently buy directly from the manufacturer, bypassing the wholesaler, and obtaining a price advantage. Examples of such retailers are Sears, Roebuck and R. H. Macy.

HISTORY OF WHOLESALING

Wholesaling of goods dates back at least five thousand years. At that time the Chinese emperor Shen Nung established "the practice of holding markets for the exchange of commodities."[1] Early wholesaling was also in evidence in such far-off lands as Sumeria, Egypt, Babylonia, Phoenicia, Greece, and Rome. Much of the trade, wholesale as well as retail, took place at fairs.

During the Middle Ages, great fairs were held in Russia, France, Italy, and China. Manufacturers and merchants from distant lands came to these fairs to

---

[1] H. H. Gowen, *An Outline History of China* (Boston: Sherman, French & Co., 1917), p. 26.

buy and sell merchandise. In the thirteenth and fourteenth centuries the fairs were held at intervals of three to twelve months and often lasted a full month.

From 1500 to 1800, wholesaling activities in foreign countries increased. Exchanges were organized to trade commodities, auctions flourished as means of selling certain goods, and the number of wholesale middlemen multiplied greatly.

In the United States, wholesaling activities expanded following the Civil War. Before that time the general merchandise wholesaler was busy servicing the needs of the general store. The decline of the general store and its eventual replacement by the specialty retailer (limited-line store) prompted wholesalers (who heretofore carried wide assortments of general merchandise) to specialize also. Large-scale production helped to change the complexion of the wholesalers' wares. Formerly, they dealt substantially in imported merchandise, but now their goods were primarily domestic.

Since 1929, a more accurate appraisal of wholesaling has been possible. In that year the wholesale trade was made part of the first census of distribution. Periodically, censuses of business are taken. They offer invaluable statistics with regard to the various trends of wholesaling.

CLASSIFICATION OF WHOLESALING IN THE UNITED STATES

The census of business classifies wholesalers into two major categories (see Table 12–1): merchant-wholesalers and other operating types.

Merchant-Wholesalers

By a wide margin, the merchant-wholesalers comprise the most significant of the wholesaling classifications. Aside from their importance in terms of the mere number of establishments, they account for greater sales volume than any of the other categories. Basically, the merchant-wholesalers buy, take title to, and store goods for the purpose of resale.

Merchant-wholesalers are separated into two basic types and are further subclassified as follows:

1. Service wholesalers
    a. General merchandise wholesalers
    b. General-line wholesalers
    c. Specialty wholesalers
2. Limited-function wholesalers
    a. Cash-and-carry wholesalers
    b. Drop shippers
    c. Mail-order wholesalers

TABLE 12–1. Wholesale trade, by type of operation and kind of business, 1977 and 1982*

Type of Operation and Kind of Business	Establishments (1,000)		Sales (mil. dol.[1])		Annual Payroll (mil. dol.)		Paid Employees[1] (1,000)	
	1977	1982	1977	1982	1977	1982	1977	1982
Wholesale trade	**382.8**	**415.8**	**1,258,400**	**1,997,895**	**58,290**	**95,209**	**4,397**	**4,985**
Merchant wholesalers	307.2	337.9	677,550	1,159,334	42,067	69,936	3,368	3,918
Other operating types	75.6	77.9	580,851	838,561	16,223	25,273	1,029	1,067
Durable goods	**226.2**	**256.1**	**608,756**	**831,212**	**34,998**	**57,368**	**2,539**	**2,913**
Motor vehicles, automotive equipment	38.9	39.5	147,112	187,607	5,148	7,524	423	433
Furniture, home furnishings	11.1	12.5	22,032	32,452	1,445	2,367	110	126
Lumber, construction materials	15.7	17.0	46,179	50,694	2,502	3,429	180	184
Sporting, recreational, photographic goods[2]	6.6	7.3	16,521	26,980	1,024	1,646	77	85
Metals and minerals, except petroleum	9.4	10.1	80,298	102,690	2,178	3,359	133	148
Electrical goods	24.9	29.2	69,999	120,062	3,922	7,462	277	357
Hardware, plumbing, heating equipment	18.6	20.8	30,605	43,529	2,576	4,051	194	217
Machinery, equipment, supplies	84.0	99.2	165,057	263,309	14,350	24,804	986	1,192
Miscellaneous	17.1	20.5	30,952	53,889	1,852	2,726	160	171
Nondurable goods	**156.6**	**159.7**	**649,644**	**1,116,683**	**23,292**	**37,841**	**1,858**	**2,072**
Paper, paper products	11.7	13.9	32,509	53,493	2,103	3,586	149	187
Drugs, drug proprietaries[3]	3.6	3.9	19,445	33,987	1,148	1,975	89	106
Apparel, piece goods, notions	13.0	14.3	39,895	55,897	1,830	2,897	131	144
Groceries and related products	38.0	38.5	182,905	288,659	7,469	12,269	602	674
Farm product raw materials	14.8	13.9	110,332	153,419	1,273	1,839	135	136
Chemicals, allied products	8.5	10.7	51,661	76,103	1,603	2,902	100	124
Petroleum, petroleum products	22.6	18.7	116,780	296,995	2,249	3,433	179	188
Beer, wines, distilled alcoholic beverages	6.7	6.4	26,979	42,122	1,841	3,091	122	141
Miscellaneous	37.8	39.4	69,138	116,008	3,778	5,849	351	372

*See *Historical Statistics, Colonial Times to 1970*, series T 274–287 and T 352–369 for similar but not comparable data.

Source: U.S. Department of Commerce, *Statistical Abstract of the United States, 1989* (Washington, D.C.: U.S. Government Printing Office, 1989).

[1]For pay period including March 12.

[2]Includes toys, hobby goods, and supplies.

[3]Includes druggists sundries.

Source: U.S. Bureau of the Census, *Census of Wholesale Trade, 1977*, Geographic Area Series, WC 77-A-52, and *1982*, Geographic Area Series, WC 82-A-52.

     d. Truck-and-wagon distributors

     e. Rack jobbers

Service Wholesalers.   As the name implies, service wholesalers, often known as regular or full-function wholesalers, in addition to goods provide a host of services for both their customers—the retailers, and for manufacturers. Limited-function wholesalers, on the other hand, provide relatively few services. The following is an extensive list of services; not every wholesaler provides every service discussed.

Services afforded the retailer

1. By carrying a sufficient supply of merchandise, the wholesaler makes it possible for the retailer to operate with a limited inventory. Since one of the major functions of the wholesaler is storage, the retailer can feel confident that stock replenishment will be quick and easy.

2. In order to make certain that the proper merchandise will be offered, ultimately, to the consumer, the wholesaler attempts to ascertain the needs of the retailer. Thus, the wholesaler actually gets involved in the forecasting of consumer demands and plans purchases accordingly. With the wholesaler researching the needs of the ultimate consumer, some of the burden is taken away from the retailer. Wholesalers are successful only when they make certain that retailers' shelves are stocked with the appropriate goods.

3. The prompt delivery of goods is often vital to retailers. Service wholesalers generally provide transportation at nominal costs plus quick delivery. The importance of quick delivery can be better understood with a practical situation. When a retailer advertises an item of merchandise that sells better than initially anticipated, the inability to replenish the item quickly becomes the store's loss. Reliance upon immediate direct shipment from the manufacturer is often impossible. Wholesalers, who have little to offer except service, often provide delivery within twenty-four hours. In the case of the advertised merchandise, customers can almost immediately be satisfied.

4. Merchandise is offered in small quantities and in various assortments. The retailer, when purchasing directly from the producer, might be confronted with minimum orders and must spend significant time seeking the best merchandise for customers. Service wholesalers ease these two areas of purchasing for the retailer. Restrictions concerning the size of the order are generally nonexistent. The purchase of any quantity is usually permitted. In addition, the time and effort involved in selecting from many producers' lines are eliminated because the merchandise has been collected by the wholesaler from several sources of supply. Just as the consumer is afforded the luxury of one-stop shopping in department stores, so is the retailer when purchasing from the service wholesaler.

5. Wholesalers, by and large, provide better credit assistance to retailers than producers do. Traditionally, periods ranging up to several months are commonplace. Small retailers with insufficient amounts of capital could not function without the extension of credit. Although manufacturers often provide credit for their customers, wholesalers are generally more lenient. Perhaps this reason, more than any other, is the basis of the popularity of wholesalers with small retailers.

6. The prompt delivery of a large assortment of goods affords the retailer a faster stock turnover. This is a great advantage to the retailer, in that it allows for a continuous fresh supply of merchandise with much less working capital. Retailers often measure their success on their turnover rate, that is, the number of times the inventory has been completely sold out and repurchased during one year.

7. By purchasing through a wholesaler, the retailer gets a guarantee concerning the quality of the goods. Since wholesalers buy in very large quantities, it is important for them to make certain that the merchandise will live up to expectations. Through trained and knowledgeable buying personnel, the wholesaler is able to ascertain the quality of the goods and the reputation of the manufacturers from whom they purchase. The small retailer who is neither able to make the investment of time nor of money to determine the value and quality of merchandise, depends on the wholesaler's ability to make sound judgments. It might be said that the purchase of goods through the wholesaler provides the retailer with a double guarantee, one from the wholesaler and the other from the producer.

8. Complaints are more easily adjusted through the wholesaler. If the retailer had to contact the many hundreds of manufacturers personally whose merchandise is stocked, the task could be monumental. Purchasing through a wholesaler affords the luxury of having the middleman act as a clearinghouse for complaints.

9. The wholesaler's success is completely dependent on the success of the retail outlets serviced. Thus, to ensure maximum success, the wholesaler must see to it that the retailer succeeds. Continuous advice and counsel is an important role played by the wholesaler. This assistance is almost completely provided by the wholesaler's sales force. Since the salespeople are technically oriented to the merchandise they offer for sale, they are invaluable sources of aid for the retailer. Among the areas of information and assistance provided by the wholesaler are

    a. *New-product development.*

    b. *Inventory checks.* Salespeople may actually take a physical inventory of goods in order to advise properly about stock replenishment.

    c. *Merchandise planning.* This may include special store promotions, advertising, and display.

    d. *Markup.* Suggestions are made concerning the proper markups to arrive at proper pricing levels in order to meet competition adequately.

e. *Store modernization.* Complete assistance may be given regarding store fixtures, lighting, layout, service managements versus self-service, and so on.

f. *Training.* Through the use of brochures, manuals, films, and even in-person lectures and discussions, proper training of sales clerks and other personnel is supplied to improve the efficiency of the operation.

10. The use of salespersons to call upon retail customers is a very definite service. Without such visits, it would be necessary for the store buyer to go to the market. Aside from being considered a convenience for the retailer, this also serves as a way of reducing expenses. That is, if retailers had to visit wholesalers when purchasing was necessary, they might need additional store personnel in their absence.

Services afforded the manufacturer

1. By providing the sales force to seek out and service retail customers, the wholesaler makes it possible for the manufacturer to employ fewer salespeople. Store contact is now the wholesaler's task, so the manufacturer's salespeople have only to solicit wholesale business.

2. Wholesalers purchase in large quantities, thus decreasing considerably the manufacturer's shipping and packing problems. Manufacturers need only to ship the larger orders to the wholesalers, who in turn break down the goods into smaller orders for the retailer. This enables the manufacturer to save on shipping, packing, and billing expenses.

3. Through the maintenance of storage facilities for the manufacturer's goods, the wholesaler helps to alleviate many warehousing problems. In peak-production seasons, for example, it is likely that producers would have to lease additional space for their manufactured goods if it were not for the wholesaler's warehouse facilities. Purchasing and maintaining permanent additional storage space for the peak-production periods is unsound, since the premises would be likely to remain empty in times of low production. Thus, the wholesaler aids the manufacturer by providing the warehousing function. It should be noted that public warehouses constitute an alternative for the manufacturer. However, wholesalers continue to serve manufacturers in this capacity.

4. Wholesalers typically purchase well in advance of the usual retail purchasing, thereby giving manufacturers business soon after the goods are produced and simultaneously affording them the necessary money for continued production. Thus, a manufacturer's working capital is reduced.

5. Because they are closer to the consumer, wholesalers are able to make meaningful market information available to the manufacturer, resulting in

less involvement on their part in marketing research than would otherwise be required to determine consumer demand and reactions.

6. The number of transactions is tremendously reduced when manufacturers deal with wholesalers; therefore, their bookkeeping is simpler.

7. Because manufacturers have fewer customer contacts, their credit risks are reduced.

As indicated, service wholesalers are subclassified according to the product lines they carry.

General merchandise wholesalers.   As the name indicates, this group of wholesalers offers for sale an assortment of unrelated merchandise. They carry such items as appliances, drugs, cosmetics, sporting goods, farm implements, and other nonperishable goods. Occasionally, they sell limited assortments of groceries. The importance of this wholesaling group has decreased significantly to a position of less than 1 percent of sales accounted for by wholesalers. Once general merchandise wholesalers satisfactorily served the needs of general stores that stocked numerous unrelated items, but the waning importance of general stores led to the decline of general merchandise wholesaling as well.

General-line wholesalers.   Unlike the preceding group which handled an unrelated assortment of goods, general-line wholesalers carry a wide assortment of a specific type of merchandise. One might limit the lines stocked to groceries, and carry a complete selection of canned goods, coffee, sugar, cheeses, soap powders, and so on. Another might confine merchandise stocked to hardware and sell, for example, pots and pans, conventional tools such as hammers, power equipment such as rotary saws and lawn mowers, home electrical appliances such as coffee makers and toaster ovens, and other related items. Whereas the general merchandise wholesaler serves the needs of the general store, this group of wholesalers sells primarily to limited-line stores. Among others, hardware stores, stationery stores, groceries, and delicatessens patronize the general-line wholesaler.

Specialty wholesalers.   The general-line wholesaler specializes more than the general merchandise wholesaler, but the specialty wholesaler is involved in the highest degree of merchandise specialization. Wholesalers of coffee, tea, canned goods, fabrics, millinery, or some other specific line are considered to be specialty wholesalers. This classification of wholesalers offers the narrowest range of goods. Consequently, the specialty wholesaler offers the most complete assortment of the particular line.

A comparison of the three kinds of service wholesalers facilitates understanding:

1. Wholesaler A sells all kinds of merchandise, including fabrics, hardware,

sporting goods, furniture, and canned goods. He or she is a *general merchandise wholesaler.*

2. Wholesaler B operates on a more specialized basis and carries only furniture. In this assortment are chairs, beds, sofas, lamps, tables, and mirrors. He or she is a *general-line wholesaler.*

3. Wholesaler C specializes to the fullest. Lamps are carried exclusively. In the assortment are featured French, Italian, Spanish, oriental, and contemporary lamps. He or she is a *specialty wholesaler.*

Limited-function Wholesalers. Unlike service wholesalers, limited-function wholesalers make few wholesaling services available to their customers. They are not numerous and they deal primarily in a few product lines. The major types of limited-function wholesalers will be examined to show the role that each plays in the wholesaler market.

Cash-and-carry wholesalers. Typically, cash-and-carry wholesalers, aside from operating on a cash basis (that is, no extension of credit), do not deliver the goods they sell to the retailer. Probably the most important product line offered by this type of wholesaler is the grocery line. They sell to small grocers who are often unable to purchase from service wholesalers because the amounts they buy are too small. Some service wholesalers operate cash-and-carry departments specifically to serve the small retailer. These departments provide immediate cash for the wholesaler.

Drop shippers. Often referred to as desk jobbers, drop shippers do not perform warehousing. Their function is to obtain orders from retailers (or other wholesalers) and to process these orders through producers. The producer then ships the merchandise directly to the customer. Although drop shippers do not physically handle or store the goods—as do most wholesalers—they nonetheless take title to the goods, which makes them the owners. With the elimination of warehousing and reassembling the goods for shipping, their operating costs are reduced. Most drop shippers deal in coal and lumber—products that sell in carload quantities and carry high freight costs.

Mail-order wholesalers. Very much like the mail-order retailer, the mail-order wholesaler operates through the use of catalogs, with orders placed by mail. The only difference between the two kinds of mail-order houses is the type of customer being served. The former sells to the ultimate consumer, whereas the latter sells to retail stores. Merchandise wholesaled in this fashion includes jewelry, novelty items, sporting equipment, and piece goods.

Truck-and-wagon distributors. Immediate delivery and cash payment are generally characteristic of the truck-and-wagon distributors. These wholesalers are actually a combination of sales and delivery people. They deliver both perishable and nonperishable products, such as candy, cheeses, tobacco products, and processed meats. The delivery of goods is immediate because they are carried right on the truck.

Rack jobbers.   The newest type of limited-function wholesaler is the rack jobber. Rack jobbers sell merchandise other than food items primarily to supermarkets. Products such as toys, housewares, greeting cards, paperbacks, toiletries, and stationery, found in ever-increasing numbers in supermarkets, are usually merchandise maintained and owned until sold by the rack jobber.

The store provides space in which rack jobbers set up racks for the display of merchandise. They are responsible for the display and the replenishment of the merchandise and get paid only for the merchandise that has actually been sold. Supermarkets, on the whole, have experienced greater success in the merchandising of these nonfood items when handled by a rack jobber than when handled by their own staff.

Rack jobbers are sometimes considered to be service wholesalers because in recent years the services provided by them have increased in scope. However, since they are generally paid on a cash basis when the merchandise is sold by the retailer they are technically considered as limited-function wholesalers.

Other Operating Types

The remaining wholesale establishments are categorized by the United States Census Bureau in their census of wholesale trade as operating types. They include manufacturers' sales branches and offices and merchandise agents and brokers. The two classifications are then further separated to underscore their distinct differences.

Manufacturers' Sales Branches and Offices.   Although they comprise only about 10 percent of the total number of wholesale organizations in the United States, manufacturers' sales branches and offices account for approximately one-third of the total wholesale industry in terms of sales.

The establishment of these types of branches and offices has cut substantially into the traditional methods of wholesaling. Examination of statistics since 1929 shows a significant periodic increase in manufacturers' determination to wholesale their own products. One of the major reasons for bypassing the traditional wholesaler is the belief that lower marketing costs will be incurred. Moreover, the fact that some wholesalers do not satisfy all the requirements of manufacturers regarding the distribution of their goods makes this kind of wholesaling popular. For example, the Japanese camera manufacturers Minolta, Pentax, and Canon, dissatisfied with the job that American wholesalers were doing, dropped them in favor of their own sales force.

Typically, the branches and sales offices are located away from the production point, at various places throughout their market. Customers may go there to write orders and some branches also maintain inventories to facilitate the filling of orders. Typical of manufacturer-owned branches is the General Electric network which maintains sales branches in all major cities that provide overnight delivery to retail and industrial customers.

Merchandise Agents and Brokers.   Aside from the various ways in which they perform their wholesaling functions and the different types of services rendered, all merchant-wholesalers take title to the goods; this is not true of merchandise agents and brokers. The principal service rendered by this group of wholesalers is the facilitation of buying and selling.

There are several kinds of agents and brokers. They are characterized by the customers they serve and by the products in which they deal. A brief examination follows to underscore their different roles.

Manufacturer's agents.   The manufacturer's agent—or *manufacturer's rep* (representative) as he or she is commonly called, works for a manufacturer on a commission basis. Agents are assigned specific territories in which to transact business. Their work is not to be confused with the job of regular salespeople (although they are primarily engaged in selling); manufacturers' representatives are in business for themselves. Generally, they carry a number of different, noncompeting lines of merchandise. Manufacturers usually enter into contractual agreements with several reps because each is assigned to a limited geographic area.

Manufacturers and customers alike seem to enjoy this kind of arrangement, as is evidenced by the growth in this type of wholesaling. It affords the manufacturer the advantage of larger orders (because the reps accumulate orders of many small customers), and it gives the buyer the convenience of purchasing many items from one location rather than having to be inconvenienced by visiting each manufacturer's showroom for individual lines of merchandise.

Manufacturers' agents deal in many different types of goods; included are home furnishings, electrical appliances, fashion apparel, sports equipment, and piece goods.

Buying from a manufacturer's agent does present some disadvantages as compared with purchasing from other wholesalers. Significant among the disadvantages are the possibility of slower delivery (this wholesaler does not stock merchandise) and the inability to obtain repair services on some technical merchandise that wholesalers frequently supply.

Selling agents.   Selling agents usually provide more marketing services than do other agents and brokers. For the manufacturer, they normally take the place of an entire marketing department. Unlike the manufacturer's rep, who primarily sells, the selling agent guides the manufacturers along styling lines (where pertinent), establishes prices, and often supplies financial aid to the manufacturer. In addition, they are a manufacturer's only agent without territorial restrictions. Selling agents deal in textiles, coal, lumber, some food products, and clothing.

Brokers.   Dealing mainly in information, the broker's role is to bring buyers and sellers together. They are strictly concerned with the needs of buyers and the offerings of suppliers. The majority of brokers work for sellers, although some do work for buyers. Their fee is based on a commission paid by the party that engaged their services after the terms of the sale have been negotiated and the deal has been consummated. Brokers work for a variety of producers, most often in the food industry. They might represent a small canner during the canning season and then move onto another industry in need of their services. It should be noted that unlike manufacturers and selling agents, brokers do not enter into lasting or permanent relationships.

Commission merchants.   Generally confined to agricultural markets, commission merchants serve producers who do not wish to dispose of their goods through local auctions. Since farmers do not accompany their goods to the big cities, the commission merchant is engaged to sell the goods and make all the necessary arrangements in connection with the sale.

These merchants have some latitude as to the eventual price the goods will bring but are usually governed by a minimum price determined by the producer they represent.

Auction companies.   Auctions are commonplace in a number of industries. They provide a place at which buyers and sellers can come to negotiate sales. For furs, used automobiles, tobacco, livestock, and produce, auctions are the usual means of sale. The prices of merchandise sold at auctions vary considerably, depending on supply and demand. The auction company is paid either a flat fee or a commission for the use of its premises and the auction services supplied.

Farm products assemblers.   Small producers of farm products employ the services of assemblers, who, as their name implies, accumulate and sort the farmers' offerings into a large unit that is more economical for shipping. Local farmers use assemblers because they are then often paid cash for their products. The local assembler ships the assembled farm products to central markets for disposal. Raw fish from fishermen are also handled in this fashion.

Producer's co-ops.   Small growers of agricultural products often band together to form cooperatives that are owned and operated for the benefit of their members. These, in addition to the traditional middleman functions of gathering, sorting, and shipping also carry heavy promotional budgets to help increase member sales. They are frequently the largest advertisers in their field and their names are familiar to everyone. Among them are Sunkist (oranges), Land-O-Lakes (dairy products), Diamond (walnuts), and Sun-Maid (raisins).

FUTURE OF WHOLESALING

In recent years there has been a steady growth in both the number of wholesale establishments and the total sales volume done by wholesalers. This has occurred despite the fact that many large distributors have taken over many functions that had previously been assigned to middlemen. The fact is that middlemen perform

TABLE 12–2.   Wholesale trade—service industries, by state, 1982

Division and State	Estab-lishments	Sales (bil. dol.)	Paid Employees* (1,000)	Division and State	Estab-lishments	Sales (bil. dol.)	Paid Employees* (1,000)
U.S.	415,829	1,997.9	4,985				
New England				WV	2,380	6.1	26
ME	1,654	4.2	18	NC	10,234	39.6	116
NH	1,487	4.1	16	SC	4,539	12.7	46
VT	800	1.9	9	GA	11,322	56.1	140
MA	9,709	49.8	132	FL	19,537	65.6	212
RI	1,549	5.0	18	East South			
CT	5,329	32.7	69	Central			
Middle Atlantic				KY	5,278	19.2	60
NY	39,106	261.2	430	TN	7,853	37.8	102
NJ	14,739	89.4	211	AL	5,913	19.6	68
PA	17,873	78.4	221	MS	3,633	10.8	38
East North				West South			
Central				Central			
OH	16,965	79.6	221	AR	3,769	10.7	39
IN	8,953	31.5	99	LA	7,678	36.1	98
IL	21,722	131.1	287	OK	6,167	28.1	71
MI	12,999	59.8	146	TX	31,978	205.0	417
WI	8,159	27.4	91	Mountain			
West North				MT	1,809	4.9	16
Central				ID	2,026	5.1	22
MN	9,020	47.4	104	WY	1,091	3.3	10
IA	7,393	25.8	69	CO	6,357	26.9	77
MO	10,149	49.4	122	NM	2,123	5.1	21
ND	2,109	6.0	19	AZ	4,555	13.9	52
SD	1,803	4.9	16	UT	2,585	8.7	31
NE	4,073	17.4	42	NV	1,233	3.9	14
KS	5,607	24.5	58	Pacific			
South Atlantic				WA	7,889	31.3	90
DE	819	7.3	14	OR	5,180	26.9	58
MD	5,507	25.8	77	CA	43,278	217.7	548
DC	495	2.6	9	AK	706	2.7	7
VA	6,960	28.7	91	HI	1,737	4.1	17

*For the pay period including March 12.

Source: U.S. Department of Commerce, Statistical Abstract of the United States, 1989 (Washington, D.C.: Government Printing Office, 1989). U.S. Bureau of the Census, 1982 Census of Wholesale Trade, Geographic Area Series, WC82-A-1 to 51.

a function that is vital in the distribution of goods. For example, when Perrier decided to move its carbonated water into supermarkets in addition to gourmet shops, there was simply no way to do it without the help of soft drink wholesalers.

To ensure their place in the channel of distribution, progressive wholesalers offer a host of new services to their customers. These include location analyses, store layout and design, sales training, and promotion help. Some wholesalers like Foremost-McKesson (drugs) provide electronic ordering equipment to its customers to cut down on delivery time. The Berger Brunswig Drug Company and its wholesaler offer many nonmerchandise services including price stickers, shelf labels, ordering terminals, and management reports.

GEOGRAPHIC DISTRIBUTION OF WHOLESALING

The location of wholesaling establishments is influenced by the available transportation facilities and the nature of the products to be marketed. This is unlike retailers who must locate where the population is concentrated. Examination of Table 12–2 shows the heaviest wholesale concentration in the Middle Atlantic region followed by the East North Central region. California enjoys its status as the most important wholesaling state. Although the two previously mentioned regions continue to lead in sales at wholesale, we see significant wholesale volume in some of the other regions, such as the Pacific states, New England, South Atlantic, East South Central, West South Central and the Mountain states.

Important Points in the Chapter _____

1. Wholesalers are basically middlemen who act as intermediates between producers and retailers or other commercial users.

2. Wholesalers differ from retailers with regard to the markets and areas they serve, their purchasing power, and their methods of operation.

3. Most important of the wholesalers is the merchant-wholesaler. Merchant-wholesalers are classified according to their services and are called either *service* or *limited-function* wholesalers. They are further categorized according to the product lines they offer.

4. Some of the services supplied by wholesalers to retailers are quick delivery, credit assistance, handling of complaints, operation with a smaller inventory, and advice.

5. Wholesalers afford manufacturers such services as a complete sales force, warehousing, market information, and simplified bookkeeping.

6. Some manufacturers engage in wholesaling through the operation of their own sales branches and offices.

7. Merchandise brokers, unlike other wholesalers, service producers but do not take title to the goods they sell.

Review Questions

1. Define *wholesaling* in your own words.

2. Which group serves a larger market, the wholesaler or the retailer? Explain.

3. How does the method of operation for the wholesaler differ from that of the retailer?

4. Why have marketers been able to more satisfactorily appraise wholesaling since 1929?

5. According to the listing of the Bureau of the Census, which wholesaler is most important?

6. In which case is the service of quick delivery, available through the service wholesaler, extremely meaningful to the retailer?

7. Compare the consumer's one-stop shopping in department stores with the retailer's one-stop shopping at wholesalers' establishments.

8. How does purchasing from wholesalers affect the retailer's rate of stock turnover?

9. Discuss the importance of the storage service for manufacturers as provided by wholesalers.

10. What is the major difference between the general-line wholesaler and the specialty wholesaler?

11. General merchandise wholesalers are declining in popularity. Why?

12. Differentiate between the drop shipper and the rack jobber.

13. Should the manufacturer's sales branch be considered a wholesale establishment? Why?

14. Compare the major function of the manufacturer's agent and that of the selling agent.

15. What is the role of brokers in the transfer of goods?

16. What is another, more popular title for the manufacturer's agent?

Case Problems

Case Problem 1

Louis Blank and Mel Weinstein have been equal partners of Glo-Gems for the past ten years. Glo-Gems is a jewelry business where semiprecious stones such as amethyst, aquamarine, coral, and quartz are made into pins, necklaces, rings, and so on. Since the company's inception, Mr. Blank has been responsible for the purchase of the stones, a task that frequently takes him to the Far East and Europe. Mr. Weinstein, on the other hand, is responsible for production and also supervises the sales.

For the past few years, selling has been under the direction of Mr. Weinstein, with the bulk of sales attributed to his personal efforts. Mr. Blank, when not away on his foreign buying trips, has helped with selling, too. As the business continued to grow, Glo-Gems hired salespeople; the firm now has three. The salespeople work exclusively for Glo-Gems, each in his or her own assigned area. The regions covered are the Middle Atlantic states, the New England states, and the East North Central states.

At this time Glo-Gems has a tremendous market. Its products include school rings, which are sold to students from junior high school through college. Expansion of the presently covered territories seems to be a perfect way to transform the business into a large operation. Both partners agree to the expansion, but they are in disagreement as to how they should sell their products. Mr. Weinstein insists upon hiring twelve additional full-time salespersons to work exclusively for Glo-Gems. Fifteen salespeople could adequately cover the United States. Mr. Blank's opinion is that sales should be the responsibility of outside agents, specifically manufacturer's agents or representatives. Mr. Weinstein argues that company salespeople could be better trained and supervised under his direction and would devote their efforts to Glo-Gem's products exclusively. Of equal merit is Mr. Blank's argument that, with the anticipated growth, Mr. Weinstein would be needed to supervise production on a full-time basis.

Questions

1. Compare the advantages of each partner's recommendation.
2. With whom do you agree?
3. Is there still another method they could employ to distribute their goods? Discuss.

Case Problem 2

Sherry Kuhn and Estelle Barish have made all the necessary arrangements to open a retail store called Party Boutique. Their business will be located in a suburban shopping center approximately ten miles from New York City. Having signed the lease and selected the necessary fixtures, they expect to open in eight weeks. Their working capital is limited, owing partly to the fact that they underestimated the costs involved in starting a retail business. Nonetheless, they plan to go ahead as scheduled with a complete assortment of merchandise.

After thorough investigation of similar stores, they have decided on the type of inventory to carry. Initially, they will sell party goods (plates, tablecloths, napkins, cups), greeting cards, gift-wrap (paper, ribbons, bows), and packaged chocolates. Arrangements have already been made with suppliers for the purchase of the greeting cards, gift-wrap, and chocolates. Although this merchandise is available through wholesalers, traditionally it is bought directly from manufacturers; they want to follow this rule. Party goods, however (which they expect to account for about 50 percent of their sales), are often purchased from wholesalers.

The partners have looked around everywhere for a supplier for their party goods. Ten of the best-known party goods manufacturers are located in New York City. About fifty miles from their shop is a service wholesaler who could serve them at a price about 5 percent higher than that of the manufacturers.

Questions

1. List all important factors that the partners should consider before coming to a conclusion.
2. From whom should they purchase? Why?

13

RETAILING

Learning Objectives

Upon completion of the chapter, you will be able to:

1. Describe the differences between discounters and traditional retailers.
2. Discuss the operation of four types of large retailers.
3. Explain franchising giving advantages and disadvantages of the system to the franchisee and franchisor.
4. Define catalog stores, multimerchandise marts, leased departments, warehouse operations, and flea markets.
5. Discuss future concepts in retailing.

COPING WITH THE NIGHTMARE OF SHRINKAGE

Finding the solution to one of the most serious problems that continues to plague retailers is a major topic for discussion whenever and wherever retailers gather. Whether it's an informal meeting of local merchants or the annual conference of the National Retail Merchants Association, the topic of shrinkage and how to curtail the ever-increasing problems associated with it, seems to capture everyone's attention. The NRMA reports that its member stores report shortages to average approximately 2.5 percent of sales with estimates for some stores running as high as 8 percent. Translated into dollars the losses add up to billions.

Which slice of shrinkage pie is the largest? Is it the shoplifter? Is it the salesclerk who fails to ring up a sale or takes something without paying for it? Is it the middle manager who authorizes fraudulent refunds? Is it the accounts payable manager who adjusts the books? There doesn't seem to be any stereotypical situation. Shoplifters and dishonest employees are generally reported to be culprits of equal proportion with the store's employee being the greater offender when one outweighs the other.

If the losses continue to accelerate, the consumer will ultimately bear the burden with higher prices. Is anything being done to cope with the nightmare? The answer, to varying degrees and with different approaches by retailers all over America, is definitely yes!

Dealing with shoplifters takes any number of approaches. Many stores have employed the services of reformed shoplifters to assist them. Some of these individuals have admitted that stores that have sufficient salespersons to approach customers to offer assistance do not provide a fertile ground for shoplifting. Surveillance systems are also reported to work efficiently enough to discourage the would-be thief.

An additional problem that confronts the merchants is the cost involved in beefing up security. Do the increased costs justify the investment? Obviously, there isn't one right answer to this question.

Specifically, how are some retailers coping with the shrinkage problem? The Gap, a chain of 550 stores in forty-four states does a number of things, such as teaching better interviewing skills to those involved in recruitment. By employing district managers and regional managers each store is within easy reach for problem solving in terms of specific shortage problems attributed to personnel. County Seat, another chain, has installed a hot line for anonymous reporting of internal theft. This, coupled with better customer service to deter shoplifting, has resulted in a reduction in shortages. Hart Schaffner & Marx reports enormous strides through electronic surveillance.

Whatever the approach, merchants are starting to cope with the shrinkage nightmare. With the advent of "open-front" stores in malls their problems will continue to grow. Using fewer employees in these units will certainly contribute to the problem. Only through concentrated and well-organized programs will success be achieved and the profit picture be meaningfully improved.

One method of coping with "shrinkage."
(*Courtesy:* Securax Enterprises, Inc.)

INTRODUCTION

Retailing is the aspect of marketing that is most familiar to the ultimate consumer. The goods purchased by household consumers are bought through various retail institutions. *Retailing*, simply defined, is that form of business that starts with purchasing goods from vendors and ends with reselling them to the ultimate consumers. The activities included in this transfer of goods from the producer to the user (sometimes called merchandising) are buying, advertising, display, promotion, and selling.

Retailing has changed considerably since its inception. A brief overview of its history will enable marketing students to appreciate its fantastic growth.

HISTORY OF RETAILING

Retailing as we know it today, with its sophisticated research methods and such decision-making devices as the computer, had its meager beginning in the United States at the trading post in the early 1600s. Instead of purchasing goods from retailers by means of money, a barter system was employed. Merchants would exchange their own goods for those brought to the post by others. More specifically, fur trappers and farmers would exchange their merchandise for imported wares.

In the mid-1700s the trading post began to expand its operation to better serve the needs of the colonists. With large amounts of new merchandise desired, the trading post could no longer fulfill these needs. To accommodate the settlers, the general store was established. Unlike the trading post, which was dominated by an exchange system, the general store operated on a cash basis.

The variety of goods in the general store was much larger than that in the trading post. The general store carried fabrics, manufactured clothing, shoes, cattle feed, harnesses, and so on. Contrary to the orderly arrangement in modern retail stores, merchandise was haphazardly placed wherever there was sufficient space. Today, general stores are still found in rural areas, but they are no longer important retail establishments.

In the mid-1800s the number of manufacturing establishments increased rapidly, resulting in a larger quantity and variety of merchandise. The general store could no longer stock everything that was produced in the United States. This necessitated the beginning of specialization in retailing and the introduction of the limited-line store. The limited-line store—or specialty store, as it is frequently referred to—carried a particular category of merchandise exclusively. Shoe stores, ladies' specialty shops, jewelry stores, groceries, and so on are examples of limited-line stores. Today, the limited-line store remains an important retail enterprise. Although initially these businesses were established by families or individuals as single-unit shops, a great number have grown into prestigious and successful chain operations. Among the most familiar nationally are Lerner's, A&P, Friendly Ice Cream, and Thom McAn Shoe Stores.

The chain organization, the first venture into large-scale retailing in the United States, began in the late 1800s. It is generally defined as two or more stores similar in nature and having common ownership. Many operators of successful limited-line stores opened second, third, and more units in other areas. Among the early chain organizations were J. C. Penney Co., A&P, and F. W. Woolworth Co.

In the late 1800s and early 1900s Americans also witnessed the beginning of the department store, which was to become one of the most popular and successful organizations in retailing. It carried a full complement of hard and soft goods under one roof, so that the customer no longer needed to shop in many limited-line stores. It might be said that the department store provided the unrelated items offered by the earlier general store (with many more lines) and the assortment afforded by the limited-line store. The merchandise was arranged in an orderly fashion, in separate departments. In addition to the usual merchandise, modern department stores also have departments that specialize in travel, gourmet foods, baked goods, optics, pets, entertainment arrangements, and garden supplies.

Branch stores, smaller units of the department store carrying a representation of the main store's offerings, became popular as the population moved to the suburbs. Today, in the retail field, few new department stores are being established; instead, we see a great expansion of the established stores through additional branches.

In an effort to better serve the needs of those people unable to patronize the existing retail institutions, either because of their distance from the stores or their lack of time to buy in person, the mail-order retailer came into existence. At first, in the late 1800s, little was available to the mail-order customer. Therefore, extensive catalogs—since then enjoying great popularity—were prepared and sent to customers. Thus, the mail-order business became an important part of retailing. Montgomery Ward and Sears, Roebuck were early mail-order houses. Even with mass transportation, the extensive chain organization, the branch store, and so on, mail-order retailing continues to flourish.

Most mail-order retailers agree that their present-day success is directly attributable to the increase in the number of working women. Households in which the wife works continue to increase in number. Although many of these women prefer to shop in stores, the time limitation often brings them to the mail-order house.

The supermarket, a large departmentalized food store, became popular in the late 1930s. In addition to the large variety of foodstuffs, it carries an abundance of miscellaneous items, such as drugs, toys, accessories for men, women, and children, plants, hardware, and so on. Just as the department store provides one-stop shopping for the consumer, the supermarket affords shoppers the luxury of being able to purchase all food needs at one location instead of having to make separate trips to the grocer, the butcher, the baker, and the produce dealer. Although the great majority of supermarkets are chain organizations, many independent markets are in operation.

The late 1940s and early 1950s witnessed yet another retailing innovation, the discount operation. At its inception, discounters offered price as their most important ingredient at the expense of comfortable surroundings and customer services. This method of doing business spread rapidly throughout the country and cut across all types of retail organizations such as chain stores, department stores, and specialty stores. Stores like John's Bargain Stores and E. J. Korvettes became household names with their numbers rapidly multiplying. As fast as these stores flourished, however, their popularity waned, and ultimately they ceased to operate. Today, their popularity seems relegated to household appliances, stereos, televisions, and so on. As they were originally conceived, discount stores didn't fare well in soft goods.

The early 1980s saw the introduction of a new type of retailing. Off price retailing, as it is generally referred to, is making serious inroads into the traditional retailer's market. In this type of operation, the retailer purchases merchandise, "off-price" or at prices normally lower than the manufacturer sells, and resells it to the consumer at below the traditional price. The popularity of the concept is obvious with the examination of such rapidly expanding off-price merchants as the Melville Corporation's Marshall's, Zayre Corporation's Hit or Miss, and F. W. Woolworth Company's Brannam stores.

OFF-PRICE VERSUS TRADITIONAL RETAILING

A question that seems to be gaining more attention today is, How will off-price retailing eventually affect the traditional retailer? Many traditional merchants fear that there will be serious competition from the off-pricers. Most agree that the new merchandising concept is something to be reckoned with.

The element that seems to be a key factor in the survival of traditional retailing is timing. Stores throughout the country like Macy's, Bloomingdale's, Saks, Neiman-Marcus, and Jordan Marsh provide their customers with goods early in the season. Their customers want the merchandise prior to the time it is to be worn, and often, price is not a serious consideration. These companies buy early, at the top price but provide their customers with early availability. On the other hand, the off-price store must wait until the traditionalist receives the goods and for the manufacturer to cut prices for quick disposal of the remaining inventory. By the time this happens, the traditional retailer has had sufficient time to sell. Customers of traditional stores who want the goods early, pay the "penalty" of a higher price; off-price customers are willing to wait for the "bargain."

Can the two coexist? So far the answer is yes! Evidence of this is the fact that companies like Lord & Taylor, Abraham & Straus, Sears, and J. C. Penney are operating traditional stores as well as off-price operations.

Table 13–1 focuses upon the ten off-price leaders in retailing.

TABLE 13–1.   The off-price leaders in retailing

Company	Sales in Millions	Number of Units
Marshall's	$830	137
T. J. Maxx-Hit or Miss	525	353
Loehmann's Inc.	260	61
Pic-A-Dilly	165	250
Syms, Inc.	147	8
Burlington Coat Factory	128	31
J. Brannam	85	30
T. H. Mandy	80	52
Dress Barn, Inc.	32	49
Ross Stores	15	6

MARKETING PROFILE

Nordstrom

How does a major department store maintain its image, increase sales, and compete with the off-pricers and discounters who are quickly proliferating in the retail marketplace? According to the success of Nordstrom, it's three simple words: service, service, service!

The Seattle-based retailer that now has invaded the east with its Tyson Corner store in Virginia serves as the benchmark for customer service. While others resort to continuous sales promotions and special price incentives, Nordstrom continues to achieve its traditional markup. According to retail analysts, the company's per square foot sales figures are at twice the industry average.

The Nordstrom philosophy for customer treatment begins as soon as the new employee begins an orientation program. "Do whatever it takes to make the customer happy." The service is individualized. Many salespersons keep records of their customers in areas such as style preference, sizes, and so on. When something of interest arrives at the store, the customer might then be personally contacted. Clerks have been seen helping customers with bundles to cars or serving refreshments to those who seem to need a pick-me-up. Some employees write thank you cards to their customers after the sale has been consummated.

Why has Nordstrom been so successful in customer relations while others have resorted to moaning and groaning? The key seems to be commission sales. The rate of commission varies from department to department, but earnings typically range from $30,000 to $50,000 annually. By comparison with the typical straight hourly wages common to retail, the earning potential is at least double that of other stores' sales personnel.

Another motivating benefit that makes Nordstrom a winner is that salespersons have the opportunity to move into management positions. Few executives are hired from outside sources. Most retailers have a two-track system where salespeople destined for sales and management personnel begin as trainees headed for the managerial team.

The Nordstrom touch has finally made an impression on other retailers. Bloomingdale's opened its Chicago branch as an all-commissions store and has now introduced the plan to its other stores. It is Bloomingdale's management's hope that it too will be able to transform its high-fashion emporiums into service environments that will establish customer loyalty.

With the Nordstrom success, it seems as if service is about to be returned to the customer.

MAJOR CLASSIFICATIONS OF RETAILERS

The era of the trading post belongs to history, but the other types of retail institutions that have been organized since then are still very much in evidence. Except for the general store, they are all flourishing throughout the United States.

Retailers may be classified in many ways. They can be grouped according to merchandising activities (activities in the buying-selling cycle), merchandise carried, dollar volume, number of employees, and so on. Although the study of each classification may be valuable, we feel that the investigation of small retailers and large retailers as separate categories, with further expansion into the variety of large retailers, presents the most complete overview of retailing institutions.

The Small Retailer

The small retail business usually grosses under $200,000 annually. Typically, there is very little job specialization. The owner is generally responsible for the overall management and merchandising tasks. He or she buys, sells, sets work schedules, plans sales promotions, secures personnel, and so on. The "larger" small retailer, doing business at the $200,000 level, has more specialized personnel working in the organization. There might be a person responsible only for merchandising duties which include the entire buying-selling cycle. A part-time display person might be hired for window decoration. Or a store manager might be responsible for the management of the physical layout of the store and the supervision of personnel. In stores of limited gross sales, it is obvious that the owner must perform all activities.

The majority of small retail operations are individual proprietorships. However, included in the group are partnerships and corporations. The general store and the specialty store are the typical types of small retail operations, with the latter accounting for the vast majority of small retailing institutions. In addition to these conventional small retail operations, another type has afforded the small businessperson the opportunity to enter the retail market. It is the stall operation in flea markets.

The General Store.   The age of specialization, the success of the chain organization, movement to urban and suburban communities, the automobile, and the continued growth of the mail-order house are some of the factors that have contributed to the decline of the general store.

In rural areas the general store is still in operation. Management is generally haphazard. The sophisticated tools and aids of modern retailers are rarely employed. The proprietor engages in purchasing merchandise, the variety of which is so great as to include cracker-barrel goods and ready-made apparel. The owner's knowledge in any single area is sometimes so limited that he or she lacks the ability necessary to make the right decisions. How can one individual have the product knowledge for so diversified an inventory?

The limited floor space does not allow for wide assortment within a merchandise classification. The general store has the questionable distinction of being the most mismanaged type of retail organization. Retailers, although reluctant to agree on many things, usually concede that the general store will never regain its popularity.

The Specialty Store.   The limited-line store or specialty store—most retailers use the terms interchangeably—is an establishment carrying one line of merchandise. Stores specializing in jewelry, furs, shoes, hardware, groceries, baked goods, and broader classifications of women's clothing, men's accessories, and so on, are examples. The greatest number of successful small retailers operate specialty stores. Some of the factors that have led to the success of this type of operation are

1. Personalized service.
2. Wide assortment of merchandise.
3. Knowledgeable buying—the buyer must only be educated in certain lines of merchandise.

The chain organization is the major competitor of the small specialty store. The chain is actually a retail organization, with many units carrying specialty merchandise. The chain's wider advertising to the consumer and its ability to offer lower prices because of greater buying power pose the greatest threat to the small retailer.

In an attempt to meet the "unfair" competition of the chain, many small merchants have informally united. The combining of small orders to qualify for quantity discounts—particularly in groceries, small hard goods, and staple menswear (shirts and other accessories)—has enabled the small merchant to become more competitive by lowering prices. Lately, advertising—an area that the small retailer often avoids because of the costs involved—has become popular as a group activity. Instead of one merchant spending a large sum for an advertisement, the group now shares the costs. A complete listing of all the stores involved in the advertisement indicates to the consumer which merchants offer the advertised merchandise. In both group-buying and group-advertising activities, noncompeting stores are generally involved.

More formalized groups of small retailers are evidenced by the voluntary chain or the cooperative chain. The former is usually organized by a wholesale firm that enters into contractual arrangements with the individual retailers, requiring that all purchases be made from them. In that case, promotional plans, point-of-purchase display arrangements, advertising materials, merchandising advice, counter and shelf setup, and location selection are typical aids provided by the wholesaler. The cooperative chain is different in that the retailers join

TABLE 13–2. Retail trade sales by kind of business, 1970 to 1987[1]

Kind of Business	1970	1975	1980	1982	1983	1984	1985	1986	1987
Retail trade, total	**375.2**	**588.1**	**957.3**	**1,069.3**	**1,168.4**	**1,282.6**	**1,367.3**	**1,437.5**	**1,510.6**
Durable goods stores, total[2]	**114.8**	**185.9**	**300.2**	**338.0**	**391.0**	**454.0**	**497.0**	**538.6**	**559.1**
Automotive dealers	65.2	107.3	164.7	193.5	229.2	271.2	299.5	320.3	326.9
Motor vehicle, misc. automotive dealers	59.2	97.3	146.2	172.4	206.9	247.7	273.6	294.4	299.8
Motor vehicle dealers	57.2	89.5	137.7	162.9	197.0	234.1	258.7	277.7	280.3
Motor vehicle dealers, franchised	54.3	84.9	130.5	154.7	187.0	224.2	248.7	266.0	267.1
Auto and home supply stores	6.0	10.1	18.5	21.2	22.3	23.6	25.9	25.9	27.0
Building materials, hardware, garden supply, mobile home dealers[2]	18.1	27.3	50.8	51.0	58.5	66.6	70.4	75.8	78.0
Building materials, supply stores	11.3	17.9	35.0	35.1	40.8	46.1	49.1	54.1	57.9
Hardware stores	3.0	5.2	8.3	8.7	9.5	11.0	11.6	12.3	14.1
Furniture, home furnishings, equipment[2]	17.0	27.0	44.2	46.8	55.3	63.0	71.3	80.3	84.1
Furniture, home furnishings stores	10.4	16.5	26.3	27.1	31.1	35.2	37.6	41.9	44.2
Household appliance, radio, TV	5.6	8.2	14.0	15.8	20.1	23.7	29.2	33.3	34.5
Nondurable goods stores, total[2]	**260.3**	**402.2**	**657.1**	**731.2**	**777.4**	**828.6**	**870.3**	**898.9**	**951.5**
Apparel and accessory stores[2]	22.1	32.4	50.4	57.8	60.0	64.0	69.6	74.8	79.1
Men's, boys' clothing, furnishings	4.5	6.6	7.7	7.8	8.0	8.4	8.7	9.0	9.0
Women's clothing, specialty stores, furriers	8.2	12.4	18.7	22.3	22.0	24.2	26.9	29.7	31.2
Women's ready-to-wear stores	7.1	11.4	17.0	20.4	20.1	21.6	24.3	26.7	28.2
Family clothing stores	4.4	6.7	10.8	13.7	15.1	15.8	16.8	17.8	19.5
Shoe stores	4.5	5.8	10.5	11.4	11.8	12.1	12.7	13.4	14.6

Drug and proprietary stores	14.6	20.0	31.0	36.4	40.8	44.5	47.9	51.6	56.0
Eating and drinking places	30.5	51.1	90.1	104.6	112.5	119.6	125.1	135.3	147.6
Eating places	25.5	44.4	80.4	95.1	102.7	109.4	114.2	123.6	135.1
Food stores	90.0	138.7	220.2	246.1	257.1	274.2	288.6	301.8	314.3
Grocery stores	82.6	129.1	205.6	230.7	241.1	258.0	271.9	284.1	296.1
Gasoline service stations	28.9	47.6	94.1	97.4	101.8	105.2	109.6	97.3	103.2
General merchandise group stores	49.1	73.7	106.6	120.4	135.1	148.7	155.9	165.1	175.9
Department stores[3]	37.4	57.5	86.2	99.2	112.0	123.8	129.4	137.2	146.5
Variety stores	6.1	7.9	7.8	8.2	8.6	9.1	9.1	8.3	8.4
Misc. gen. merchandise group stores[4]	5.7	8.3	12.6	13.0	14.5	15.8	17.3	19.6	20.9
Liquor stores	8.4	11.9	16.9	18.1	19.1	18.1	19.3	19.6	19.5
Nonstore retailers	9.1	13.4	22.8	23.8	24.3	25.7	25.0	25.7	26.5
Mail-order houses (department store merchandise)	1.8	2.8	4.3	4.3	4.3	4.8	4.2	3.7	3.6

[1]In billions of dollars. Based on 1972 Standard Industrial Classification. See headnote, table 1328. Based on Current Business Survey, see Appendix III. See also *Historical Statistics, Colonial Times to 1970*, series T 245–271.

[2]Includes kinds of business, not shown separately.

[3]Excludes leased departments.

[4]Includes catalog showroom stores.

Source: U.S. Department of Commerce, *Statistical Abstract of the United States*, (Washington, D.C.: U.S. Government Printing Office, 1988). U.S. Bureau of the Census, *Current Business Reports, Revised Monthly Sales and Inventories, January 1978 through December 1987*, (BR-13-87S) and unpublished data.

together and operate their own warehouse. They, too, are involved in many group activities that tend to lower the cost of individual operations and increase individual efficiency.

In retailing today, with the giant chain and department store organizations, small retailers can compete more effectively through group activities. Of paramount importance in the field is knowledgeable advice on management and merchandising. The large retailer can afford the luxury of specialists. Through their combined efforts, the small merchants avail themselves of an exchange of ideas. One store owner may be expert in designing the best store layout, another might excel in the buying activity, still another might have a talent for writing advertising copy. In this way, the exchange of information and ideas provides the special knowledge so necessary for success in retailing. Since the merchants are not direct competitors, this free exchange can be open and beneficial to all. The nature of some small stores dictates a different type of management. Therefore, retailing today still includes completely independent retailers who are not involved in any group arrangement.

The Flea Market Stall.   Unlike the general store and specialty store, which conduct business in a conventional retail manner at a "store" location, another avenue has become available to the individual wishing to pursue business as a retailer.

FIGURE 13–1   Flea market.

Flea markets have cropped up all over the country where, for a very small rental fee (approximately $15 to $40 per day per stall), individuals have been able to set up shop to sell their wares. Not to be confused with junk merchandise from the garage, the goods offered at these markets range from inexpensive tools to expensive fashion merchandise and home furnishings. The individual is provided with a space (most often it is regularly assigned and sold on a yearly lease) in which he or she sets up tables, racks, counters, and so forth, to carry on business. Selling is generally conducted on a cash-and-carry basis. The retail prices are considerably lower than those at the conventional stores because the overhead is very low.

So successful has this form of retailing become that many vendors have simultaneous operations in different flea markets, much the way conventional retailers have units in many shopping centers.

The magnitude of this type of retailing can easily be appreciated by paying a visit to any of the major flea markets. On any Sunday (they usually operate one weekday and on weekends) there can be as many as 100,000 customers eagerly moving from vendor to vendor to make their purchases. Figure 13–1 pictures a large flea market.

MARKETING PROFILE

Ralph Lauren

Initially making his mark on the world of fashion as a tie designer, Ralph Lauren has gone on to become one of America's leading designers of clothing and home furnishings. His distinctive styling and the ever-present polo pony logo is part of the wardrobes of millions of people all over the world. Design ability, alone, however, isn't Mr. Lauren's only genius. His keen sense of merchandising has made him one of the world's finest specialty retailers.

Most retailers restrict their businesses to a specific type of operation and aim for a specific market. Not Ralph Lauren! His approach to capturing the consumer's dollar is virtually unparalleled in a field fraught with competition and significant failure.

The goal of the Lauren organization, obviously, is to sell to people in a variety of places and at different price structures. His outlets are both company owned and private retail organizations. The customer is presently reached by way of four different types of stores.

The major department and specialty stores across the United States such as Macy's, Bloomingdale's, and Saks Fifth Avenue, have long been Lauren's major retail outlets. With the enormous popularity of the label and the company's clout in the marketplace, it has placed new demands on those retailers who carry the line. All menswear, for example, must be housed within a "small shop environment" within the store that delineates its merchandise from the rest. The shop is visually merchandised by using the typical antique props that enhance all of Lauren's merchandise in the company's displays and advertisements. Stores not willing to follow Lauren's "small shop" edict simply must give up the line.

Ralph Lauren owns and operates what is the flagship store in the old Rhinelander mansion on Madison Avenue, New York City. All of the Lauren designs including clothing, accessories, home furnishings, furniture, and children's wear fill this enormous retail environment. Lauren operates other wholly owned shops, but this is the quintessential, opulent retail operation devoted to one designer.

Ralph Lauren franchises, too, are found all across the country in prestigious malls and upscale shopping centers. These outlets carry anywhere from a limited assortment to the entire Lauren collection.

Recognizing the need to dispose of slower-selling goods or styles that are about to be removed from the "regular" stores, the company has invaded a new market. In outlet or closeout centers, in places like Freeport, Maine, or North Conway, New Hampshire, all far from the traditional stores so as not to offer unfair price competition, Mr. Lauren has opened his outlet stores. Selling at prices that are as much as 50 percent lower than the conventional retailers, customers buy the Lauren "bargains" in unparalleled quantities. In order to handle the crowds who want the "polo pony" but are unwilling to buy at the regular prices, many of these units remain open until midnight.

With the invasion of so many retail markets, Ralph Lauren has shown the retail world that business, with the same goods, can be successfully merchandised in many ways.

The Large Retailer

Today retailing is dominated by the large organization. Department stores, chain organizations, supermarkets, and mail-order houses provide the majority of retail sales.

The Department Store.   The department store is a departmentalized retail institution that offers a large variety of hard goods and soft goods and numerous customer services. It has huge sales volume and employs a great number of people, specializing in various tasks.

The merchandise assortment varies according to the size of the store. Organizations such as Macy's, Woodward & Lothrop, and Bloomingdale's offer enough types of merchandise—in a range of prices—that a consumer family can satisfy just about any of its needs, for example, men's, women's, and children's clothing apparel; accessories; musical instruments; sporting equipment; toys;

furniture; hardware; perfumes; toiletries; gourmet foods; liquor; floor covering; bedding; draperies; and appliances. In many stores optical goods, beauty salon services, precious jewelry, religious articles, meat and poultry, silverware, and so on are available through leased departments. These departments are operated by independent or chain owners generally because the nature of the goods or services warrants unusual specialized ability. The department is usually leased on the basis of a square-foot rental or a percentage of sales. Department stores have found that a greater profit for the store can be realized this way than if they operated these departments themselves. An important reason for offering these specialized goods and services is to provide the customer with one-stop shopping.

The department store offers the greatest variety of services in retailing. Free delivery, gift wrapping, charge accounts, return privileges, extended credit plans, and provision of meeting rooms for clubs are among the usual services. Unusual ones include personal shoppers for people speaking a foreign language, babysitting for shopping mothers, special openings for children shoppers before holidays, and procurement of tickets for theatrical and sporting events.

One of the most highly regarded, upscale department store organizations in the United States is Bloomingdale's, whose flagship store is featured in Figure 13–2, continues to spread its wings all across the United States. Its first venture

FIGURE 13–2   Bloomingdale's flagship store in New York City. (*Courtesy:* Bloomingdale's.)

FIGURE 13–3   Bloomingdale's salutes California. (*Courtesy:* Bloomingdale's.)

into the Midwest has been in Chicago, where it opened on the fashionable "Magnificent Mile" on North Michigan Avenue. Bloomingdale's has long been a leader in unique promotions that feature regional merchandising extravaganzas. Figures 13–2 and 13–3 depict the store's facade during the company's salute to California entitled "California: The New International Style."

Department stores are individually owned, belong to ownership groups, or are chains.

Branches and twigs.   In view of the increase in the number of families leaving the cities and moving to the suburbs, the almost hopeless traffic congestion, the shortage of adequate parking facilities, and the development and growth of suburban shopping centers, department stores have opened additional units away from the city.

The branch is a store usually smaller than the main store, carrying a representation of the parent store's merchandise. It is geared to the needs of the community in which it is located. Some branch stores have exceeded the sales volume of the main store. Twigs, relatively rare in retailing today, but still in existence, are very small units belonging to a department store, which, unlike the branch, carry only one classification of merchandise. For example, a department store might operate a shop in a college town featuring merchandise worn on the campus. This sort of operation is called a twig store.

The Chain Store.   The chain store may be defined as a centrally owned and managed organization with two or more similar units, each carrying the same classification of merchandise. It should be known that the Census Bureau disagrees with two as the number of units that constitutes a chain. They consider a chain to be more than ten. If this be the case, what would a nine-unit centrally managed retail organization be called? Perhaps a small chain could be considered as having from two to ten units with large chains having more than eleven.

Merchandise categories carried by chain stores include drugs, hardware, shoes, jewelry, variety goods, groceries, baked goods, and so on. For example, F. W. Woolworth is a variety chain, A&P a supermarket chain, J. C. Penney a general merchandise chain, Edison Brothers a shoe chain, The Limited a women's apparel chain, and so on. Each unit in these chains is similar in nature to the other units. The management of all chain operations is similar enough in nature that it does not necessitate separate investigation into the different kinds of chains according to merchandise sold.

The department store considers the main store its base of operations; it plans its purchases there. The chain organization operates from central headquarters, a location that houses merchandisers, buyers, personnel administrators, advertising executives, and so forth. Large chains have regional offices in addition to central headquarters. The units of the chain are generally charged with the responsibility of selling merchandise, whereas the central team is the decision-making body of the organization. Store managers usually do not formulate policy. Instead, they carry out the policies of the central staff.

The Supermarket.   The supermarket is a large departmentalized, self-service retail organization selling primarily food but also other merchandise. The merchandise assortment has grown from the usual grocery, meat, poultry, and produce categories to include hardware, toys, hosiery, drugs, books, greeting cards, and so on. Supermarkets are independently owned, operated individually, part of voluntary or cooperative chains, or part of regular chain organizations. The greatest number of supermarkets belongs to the latter category. Emphasis on lower prices, parking facilities for customers, and the luxury of one-stop food shopping are some of the more important factors that led to their success.

The Mail-order Retailer.   This operation, although not as important as the chain or department store, does contribute enough to warrant further discussion. Selection of merchandise through the use of a catalog, ordering through the mail, and delivery by similar means are the major characteristics of the mail-order house. The merchandise offerings of some mail-order houses are so large and diversified that as wide an assortment can rarely be found in a merchandise-stocking store. In addition to those retailers that sell exclusively by mail, a large percentage of the total sales of department and specialty stores can be attributed to this method of retailing. Montgomery Ward, Spiegel, and Sears, Roebuck are leading mail-order retailers. The more than 140,000 items now sold by Sears include mink stoles and sculpture priced as high as $39,500. With the exception of liquor and automobiles, almost any article can be bought from Sears.

The chain has moved retail stores closer to the people and has perhaps made buying through catalogs not as necessary as it was in earlier times, when farmers and others in isolated areas depended heavily on mail order for merchandise. However, this method of doing business has not disappeared from the retailing scene. The large number of women in the work force probably results in less time for shopping and encourages mail-order purchasing. Judging from the great sales volume of mail-order houses, this form of retailing is still important.

CURRENT TRENDS

While many of the retailing procedures and practices of the past are still in evidence today, no period in history has seen the number of innovations and trends being explored by today's merchants. Through the investigation of these trends, one can realize how diversified retailing is today.

MARKETING PROFILE

Sears, Roebuck and Company

For one of the nation's largest retailers to change its merchandising philosophy is enough to make newspaper headlines, but to get the message out successfully in a few days seemed to be an impossible task. Through a series of newspaper, television, and radio advertisements, Sears told the world of its plan to rollback prices on 50,000 products.

Sears has been a household name across America for as long as anyone can remember. Business comes from more than 800 stores and a catalog that features just about anything a consumer could need. To reach the enormous number of Sears customers regarding this change was no simple task. The new merchandising approach, prompted by sluggish or lagging sales, had to be done swiftly and carefully to notify its market.

To get the message across, and tell the world that its doors will close for forty-two hours to make price adjustments, Sears used a multimedia approach. The television blitz consisted of an eight-commercial campaign, the first of which was entitled "Glow" (see Figure 13–4). In it the empty

FIGURE 13–4   The sears "Glow" television commercial announcing the change in merchandising philosophy. (*Courtesy:* Sears, Roebuck and Co.)

Sears parking lot symbolized the store's closing for forty-two hours to prepare for the everyday low-pricing launch. Following that ad, which was used for two days, others included "Smoking Gun," which humorously traced the reactions to the new Sears philosophy, and "1,000 Brands," which in rapid fire, showed 1,000 name brands that would be reduced in price. More than 100 national spot commercials were used to reach the automobile and home listening audiences. More than 900 newspapers carried full-page ads during the week of the launch.

While the consumer was taken by surprise with this new merchandising arrangement, Sears had studied the reasons that led to the change. The results in a Sears-commissioned Yankelovich report left little choice but to make the change. The report noted that "consumers don't want to wait for sales and want more consistency in the pricing of merchandise." Sears' customers were always waiting for periodic price reductions unless the purchase was a necessity. This made the retail operation more difficult to merchandise.

Early reports from the company, once the plan was in place, showed a better spread of business and more total sales volume.

By reacting to consumer demand, Sears has shown that the consumer is king, and must be listened to.

Franchising

In the arrangement known as franchising, an organization (the franchiser) that has developed a successful retail product or service sells to individuals (the franchisees) the right to engage in the business, provided that they follow the established pattern. Because of the expertise of the franchiser, the probability of success for the individual opening such an operation is greater than if he or she ventured into a completely new independent enterprise. Most retailers agree that inexperience and incompetence account for the great majority of retail store failures. The franchiser offers such services as location analysis, tested managerial techniques, knowledgeable merchandising, training plans, financial instruction, and counseling in other pertinent areas. With these services provided by the franchiser, the risk of failure is greatly reduced. Franchising got its major start in 1898 by General Motors; today it accounts for 10 percent of the gross national product through 300,000 to 400,000 outlets. Carvel, Howard Johnson, Chicken Delight, International House of Pancakes, AAMCO Automotive Transmissions, Rexall, Hickory Farms, and Baskin-Robbins 31 Ice Cream Stores are examples of franchise operations that bring to the consumer a variety of goods and services.

In addition to these traditional franchises, a new generation of these businesses is growing by leaps and bounds. Unlike the fast-food ice cream and hamburger joints, this new breed is catering to the yuppies and "dinks" (double income, no kids). Dunhill Personnel Systems supplies office and household workers, Great Expectations provides haircuts, Minutemen Press International offers printing services, and Decorating Den offers decorating advice from a decorator driving a van who comes to the client's home with interior design plans and sample materials.

Owning a franchise is often the best route to success, particularly for an individual lacking experience. However this type of business has its drawbacks. For one thing, the lump-sum payment required to get into business is likely to be high. While a franchise for Augie's, Inc. industrial catering truck is only $1,000, a Good Taco Co. restaurant can run as high as $1.5 million. In addition, most franchisers require royalty payments based on sales. This has the effect of reducing the profit margin of the franchise compared to that of a conventional outlet. Perhaps the biggest complaint of franchisees is the dictatorial direction of the parent company. When disputes arise, and they often do, the individual franchisee feels like a pigmy against the giant corporation. To overcome this, some franchisee organizations (like the Midas Dealers Association that represents approximately fourteen hundred dealers) have been able to exert considerable power. When Midas decided to expand, the association was able to protect its member's territories.

Automation

The purpose of automation in retailing is to reduce costs by saving personnel. Some examples of automation follow.

Automatic Vending Machines.   Coin-operated machines can now dispense many products that were originally sold over the counter. Today, in addition to the usual merchandise found in these machines, such as newspapers and cigarettes, one may purchase cooked foods, flight insurance, women's hosiery, sandwiches, and other goods. The machines are particularly successful in areas where stores are unavailable—for example, at railroad stations and movie theaters. The vending machines offer the customer the opportunity to purchase at any time, whereas in the conventional retail store the hours for purchasing are limited. Since the consumer usually requires service for expensive merchandise, the vending machine is most successful for selling inexpensive commodities.

Automatic Stores.   Today, automatic checkstands have been installed in some supermarkets. The bill is determined more quickly, and the tally is more accurate. Better inventory control will result in automatic orders being placed with the warehouse for the replenishment of stock. In addition, customers are, in some cases, able to have money automatically withdrawn from their checking accounts and transferred to the store's account when they present an identification card to the store's computer. Today, some stores automatically move the goods along a conveyor belt until they reach the customer's car. With the introduction of the new automatic services, the supermarket is certainly moving toward more complete automation.

In Tokyo, an automatic computerized supermarket is in operation. It has ended shoplifting, mistakes by cashiers, and the long line of customers waiting at cash registers. Shoppers push their carts, with plastic cards attached to them, and do their purchasing by inserting their cards into slots located near the merchandise in the windows. Automatically, after each insert, the food is released and the computer adds what has been purchased. When the shopper is finished, he or she is given a bill that itemizes all purchases made.

Electronic Video Kiosks

The craze of the video game has now moved into the business arena. Retailers, in increasing numbers, are installing video kiosks in their stores to promote their items and take orders. Florsheim is installing the kiosks in all its stores that feature every shoe style. The merchandise may be ordered without the assistance of a salesclerk.

Sears has entered this new market with kiosks that are placed outside of the store. In strategic locations such as office building lobbies, customers are able to order specific Sears products.

Computerized Inventory Control

In retailing, the merchandise inventory on hand is probably a store's most important asset. In dollars, it requires a very large part of the enterprise's capital. In terms of profits and losses, the makeup of the inventory is critical. Having the wrong merchandise is disastrous. Having the correct merchandise but too little quantity loses sales. Too much of the right merchandise results in markdowns. In addition to this, a large store has an inventory of thousands of items, frequently kept at a large number of locations. The problems of inventory control are so vast in a large organization that decisions on what to buy, how much to buy, when to buy, and from whom to buy require a considerable amount of up-to-date information. These problems match perfectly the capabilities of the computer:

1. Its capacity is so huge that it can collect data from many departments and locations.
2. Its speed is so great that it can process an enormous amount of data rapidly.
3. It has the ability to print out reports in easily understood form.

It must be borne in mind that the computer cannot think through a problem by itself but can follow instructions to the point where the results are the same as if it had. For example, the computer itself does not know whether or not the inventory is low. However, it can be programmed so that when 80 percent of the stock previously on hand has been sold, it can type a reorder of those sizes, styles, and colors that sold most effectively. Thus, the result is the same as it would have been if the machine could think.

Since the end product of the computer is the informational report, it is vital that the computer be given all the information that is required to construct such a report. Basically, the required information consists of the merchandise on hand, the merchandise sold, and the merchandise on order. Moreover, to be usable, the data must be presented to the computer in a language the computer can understand. The following is the input necessary to the computer for comprehensive merchandise inventory control. (It should be pointed out that many department stores are moving toward the following systems, but that most stores have considerably fewer information categories.)

1. Style number
2. Vendor
3. Sales
4. On hand
5. On order
6. Receipts from vendors
7. Returns to vendor
8. Cost
9. Selling price
10. Color and size

11. Markdowns
12. Customer returns
13. Shipment to branches
14. Shipment among branches

From this information, the computer can be instructed to provide, as output, a wide variety of reports at required time intervals. A particular department store furnished its buyers with the following informational reports:

1. Information on sales of high-fashion merchandise every three days. Such reports allow buyers to make decisions on reordering or transferring stock between branches while the style in question is still new, available, and in demand. Since this report is to be used by a buyer for reordering, it would include the following information for each style: price, color, three days' sales, week's sales, sales to date, sales in the various branches, number of pieces on hand, number of pieces on order, date the order is due, and so forth—in short, all information needed by the buyer to make the reordering decision.

2. Reports on staple-type goods, for example, men's black socks, need not be nearly so detailed or frequent. Since staples do not run "hot," the decision based on the reports is merely to reorder when the number of units on hand falls below a certain level. In many operations, the computer is actually instructed to print out a reorder automatically whenever the stock on hand falls below a certain level.

3. Weekly unit reports are frequently presented to the buyer, merchandise manager, and department manager. They include sales for the week, prior week, and month to date, as well as the on-hand figure for each style. From this report, trouble spots can be seen earlier and remedial action, such as transfers between branches and special promotions, can be implemented before markdowns become necessary.

4. A dollar report furnishes information every ten days on the current total inventory, this month's and this year's sales, and markdowns for each store in the chain. From this the buyer can determine trouble spots, the amount of inventory in each store, and the financial success of each store.

5. A monthly report showing the relative importance of each price line in the various units making up the chain. This report compares the prior year's units and dollars of sales with those of the current year. Future merchandising trends for each unit can be established from these monthly reports.

6. The vendor's analysis presents the buyer every six months with information on total purchases, returns, markdowns, and gross profit for each vendor. Excessive returns, markdowns, and so on, that turn up in such reports are important for future purchasing.

7. Special reports constantly flow from the computer to the buyer in addition to the reports already mentioned. These might include size and color analysis and the aging of the inventory to indicate the amount of time each unit has been in the store. In fact, almost any information that the buyer requests and for which computer time can be found can be produced.

Although large retail establishments have been operating successfully for many years and the computer is relatively new, it is difficult to understand how buyers could ever have performed effectively without them.

Multilevel Enclosed Shopping Centers

In an effort to add to the customer's comfort and accessibility to more stores, many shopping centers have enclosed their malls if they weren't initially built that way. The stores have the appearance of a huge unit selling a wide variety of merchandise under one roof. Customers can park their cars, enter the enclosed center and move freely from store to store without being bothered by extreme hot or cold weather.

Today the trend is toward even larger enclosed malls. All over the country two-level and three-level malls have become commonplace. The multilevel malls not only increase the number of stores in the malls but incorporate as many as six movie theaters in one structure. The anchor stores in these multilevel situations generally have entrances to their stores at each level to benefit from the traffic on each floor.

Downtown areas are jumping on the bandwagon with the vertical mall concept. In these areas where land space is at a premium, the only place to go is up. Many cities are now boasting malls that rise up to ten stories and feature hotels in addition to the obligatory movie theaters and restaurants. One of these is the upscale Water Tower in Chicago, which houses such retailers as Marshall Field and Lord & Taylor, a large number of famous specialty shops, and a hotel as an attached neighbor, the Ritz Carlton. The Herald Center in New York City, as seen in Figure 13–5, is another highrise mall.

Shift in Hours

Since most shopping is done by women, the fact that many of them are working has caused a shift in retail store hours. Many retailers open later in the day and/or add evening hours to the schedule. In many stores two shifts of employees are necessary to run the operation. In states where local laws permit, Sunday openings are common. Throughout the United States some operators of supermarkets are open twenty-four hours a day. This arrangement allows people to shop at any convenient time.

FIGURE 13–5
Herald Center in New York
City. (*Courtesy:* The New
York Land Company.)

Research

The retailer, to meet competition and satisfy the customer's needs more efficiently, is greatly involved in research. Questionnaires, interviews, and fashion and traffic counts are some devices used to bring pertinent data to the retailer. By better understanding what the consumer wants, management should be more efficient and thus more productive.

It should be evident that retailing is in a state of flux, and perhaps only those willing to accept and make the necessary changes will be successful in future retailing.

Flea Markets

Throughout the country part-time retailing has become extremely popular in the form of flea markets. Owners of large pieces of land, such as drive-in theaters, are renting space to sellers and charging entrance fees to buyers for the right to engage in retailing activities. What started out to be a place for individuals to dispose of accumulated merchandise from their garages has mushroomed into a regular business for individuals who buy from producers to sell to the flea market consumer.

Multimerchandise Marts

With the success of the flea market, realtors are developing giant enclosed stores that are subdivided into ministores which feature a wide variety of household goods. Many now-defunct supermarkets are being converted into this type of retail operation. For a fixed fee, independent merchants are offered space, electricity, security, and so forth. The hours are generally restricted to evenings and Saturdays so that people with other daily occupations can be part-time merchants. So successful is this type of operation that many of the independents are expanding into "stores" at more than one mart.

Noncompeting Cooperative Advertising

Many retailers agree that success is dependent upon continuous advertising. Small retailers who wish to participate but cannot because of budget limitations have started to advertise cooperatively with noncompeting merchants who specialize in identical merchandise. A prime example of this is in the retail liquor operation in New York. Liquor stores have organized solely for the purpose of sharing advertising expense. Only one store in an area becomes part of the group, to avoid direct competition. The members decide upon the advertisement in terms of merchandise and price and share equally the advertising expense.

Warehouse Outlets

In certain product lines, retailers have begun to move in a direction other than what is considered traditional or conventional. Until 1980 the operations have centered upon food and furniture. Levitz, a major furniture retailer, has opened multimillion-dollar warehouse operations from coast to coast. These operations offer customers immediate delivery at lower prices and are beginning to compete heavily with popularly priced furniture retailers, in particular, that take months to deliver and charge higher prices. The success of these operations has prompted many regular furniture merchants to operate warehouses similar to Levitz in out-of-the-way locations that do not necessarily compete with their more conventionally operated units.

More recently, the trend is moving into soft goods and other merchandise. Since the start of the 1980s, warehouse outlets have opened in record numbers throughout the United States. The Warehouse Club in Niles, Illinois, broke every marketing rule in 1983 by opening in an out-of-the-way location in less than attractive surroundings. Annual sales for the first year of operation approached $25 million. With such stores as R. H. Macy & Co. seeking to appeal to the more affluent customer, warehouses are seeking to fill the void with bargain prices aimed at the less traditional shopper. Secaucus, New Jersey, and Reading, Pennsylvania, are two areas which boast warehouse centers featuring scores of such outlets. It is expected that this form of retailing will soon become a major force in business.

Catalog Stores

Sears and Montgomery Ward have successfully operated catalog stores, in addition to mail order, for many years. It is noteworthy, however, that catalog stores are springing up all over the country. Instead of merely ordering from catalogs (which many of these operations also offer to their customers), individuals can come to the store and actually see what the merchandise looks like. Usually, the goods can be taken home immediately by the purchaser. On identical merchandise, the prices at the catalog store are generally at least 20 percent lower than the prices at the traditional retail outlets. Two of the fastest-growing catalog chains in the East are Consumers Distributing and Service Merchandise, which offer a wide variety of goods, including appliances, toys, precious jewelry, cameras, and housewares.

Private Labeling

For years, retailers have concentrated their merchandising efforts on filling their shelves with nationally advertised and easily recognized brands and labels. With the recent success of the earlier mentioned off-price merchants, many traditional retailers have experienced difficulty in achieving the high markups associated with the manufacturers' labels. In an effort to counteract the adverse effects caused by selling the well-known brands at discounted prices, many major retail organizations have embarked upon the development of private-label programs.

Under this concept, stores are making arrangements for manufacturers to produce goods strictly for the particular store's own use to be identified by the store's private label. In that way the consumer's ability to comparison shop is eliminated. As one major retailer stated, "Private label is our number one option for coping with off-pricers."

The trend has been steadily gaining with many stores adding more private-label goods to their merchandise mix. Dayton's (Minneapolis) private-label "Boundary Waters" has been setting records. Such giants as The May Company, Allied Stores, Macy's, and Saks are just a few who have gone all out in the introduction of private-label programs for their stores.

FUTURE RETAILING CONCEPTS

Not yet actually operational, but more than merely dreams, are many new concepts that retailers will be using in the near or distant future. The expected changes necessitated by both increases in operational expenses and shortages in qualified personnel may be any or all of the following.

Automatic Fund Transfer Machines

Living in a cashless society is no longer a myth but a theory that is going into practice. Diebolt, Inc., a North Canton, Ohio–based company that manufactures automatic teller machines for banks, is experimenting with a similar machine for retailer usage. The device, called a *convenience center*, is a computer terminal which would automatically transfer customers' monies from a personal bank account to the store's account. It would involve the use of a personal card, much like the bank cards now used, to complete the transaction. This system would enable the retailer to gain immediate access to the customer's bank account for the entire purchase. It would eliminate the time needed to gain the dollars now generated by store credit cards and third-party cards. It could encourage the customer who is fearful of carrying cash to make cash purchases more readily.

Shopping by Computer

More than $800 million has been spent by companies in the research and development of systems which would enable customers to shop at home. American Bell as well as IBM are busily engaged in the activity. American Bell is experimenting with the Video Frame Creation Terminal which will enable artists to draw detailed color pictures with a quality similar to the home video games. These computerized networks would permit the shopper to buy a store's current offerings without leaving the house.

Joint Training Centers

Aware that it is expensive to train retail personnel properly and dangerous to place untrained people on selling floors or other store areas, merchants are beginning to talk about the creation of cooperative training centers. The plan is not really far-fetched and is operational in the advertising field. In this way, stores could continue to train employees while reducing their training expenses.

Main Street Mall Conversion

It is obvious to knowledgeable merchants that consumers are flocking to malls for the conveniences they offer. Small merchants who occupy locations on

main streets are, in surprising numbers, discussing the conversion of their locations into malls. Retailing seems to be moving even closer to developing areas
resembling the giant enclosed malls. It is expected that merchants will alter their
shopping streets not only to prohibit auto traffic but also to provide interstore
connections for easier access. This will eliminate to some degree the need for
complete enclosure under one roof, while affording the shopper the luxury of
shopping in areas that are free from the discomfort caused by cold, rain, extreme
heat, and so forth.

Employee Sharing

As impossible as it might seem to many retailers, there are indications that
a sharing of employees, particularly salespeople, might become a reality. The
arrangement is conceivable for two reasons. First, peak sales hours are not the
same in all stores—sales personnel in one store may not have much to do while
at the same time another store desperately needs more help. Thus, an employee-
sharing plan could be arranged to accommodate two or more employers' needs.
Second, with the cost of transacting business becoming increasingly higher, this
new arrangement could minimize expenses while maximizing profits. It might
be suggested that part-time employees working exclusively for one retailer could
accomplish the same goals as would be found in an employee-sharing plan.
Most experienced retailers will agree, however, that those guaranteed full-time
work for which they can earn a full salary are more committed than is the part-
time employee.

These innovative ideas, along with many others that will eventually be put
to the test, will continue to assist retailers in the challenges they have to face in
the future.

Important Points in the Chapter _____

1. The growth of retailing in America can be traced from colonial trading
    posts, where barter was used as the process for exchange, to modern
    retailing giants.

2. The history of retailing parallels the growth of American consumer de-
    mand. As society became wealthier and more sophisticated, retailers re-
    sponded by offering a greater variety of goods and enlarging the size and
    the number of locations at which such goods could be purchased.

3. To satisfy consumers, goods are presently offered at retail in a great variety
    of stores, featuring an enormous range of goods and services.

4. Currently, retailing is characterized by an increase in franchising, wider
    use of automation, and the prevalence of shopping centers.

5. Research to prevent unnecessary risk in retailing has expanded in recent years and will gain importance in the future.

6. Flea markets, multimerchandise marts, and warehouse outlets are new retail outlets available to the consumer.

7. In the not-so-distant future, there are indications that retailers will operate joint training centers as well as share the services of some employees.

8. Off-price retailers are challenging the traditional retailer with identical merchandise at 20–50 percent below the regular price.

9. Many retailers are featuring private-label merchandise as a means of competing with off-price merchants.

Review Questions

1. Define *retailing* in your own words.

2. Compare the trading post with the general store. How did the two retail institutions differ?

3. What is another name for limited-line store? What contributed to the need for this type of retail enterprise?

4. How many units comprise a chain organization?

5. Discuss some advantages of department store shopping for customers.

6. The department store offers a wide variety of goods, but so did the general store. Are they basically the same operation? Defend your answer.

7. The mail-order business flourished as soon as it began. What market did mail-order retailers seek to service?

8. Define *branch store.* Why are these stores established?

9. The department store and the supermarket afford the same convenience for customers. Which convenience?

10. What lines are sold in supermarkets in addition to foodstuffs?

11. Discuss what is meant by *leveling off* pertaining to discounters and traditional retailers.

12. By what other name are discounters known?

13. Aside from the typical management responsibilities performed centrally by chain organizations, a rather unusual, important task is often executed centrally. Name and describe the procedure.

14. What attractions do supermarkets hold for their customers?

15. What is the reason for the steady increase in mail-order sales aside from new lines of merchandise?

16. For what reasons are individuals attracted to franchising rather than to establishing their own retail stores?

17. Describe the automatic checkstand.

18. To increase sales, some major controlled shopping centers have altered their physical structures. Describe the procedure and discuss it in terms of sales.

19. What are some of the ways retailers might enter joint ventures in the future?

20. Discuss the relatively new types of retail outlets available to consumers.

Case Problems

Case Problem 1

Supermarkets continue to grow because of their popularity with the consuming public. Endover, a small city in the Northeastern part of the country, has seen several supermarket chains establishing units in the community. Large parking fields, competitive prices, and wide assortments of food items have contributed to the supermarkets' success.

While this supermarket boom has taken place, Bill's Grocery has slowly declined. Many of his regular customers have moved away, and many have switched to the supermarkets for their needs. Although Bill has thought about closing his doors and giving in to big business, at the present time he still wants to fight. His encouragement comes from travel to other communities where he has witnessed the same supermarket explosion, plus the existence of some small produce stores, delicatessens, and grocers.

On the other hand, his family is trying to persuade him to close his business and take a job with one of his large competitors. With his experience, a job is a certainty.

Question

1. Should Bill fight or switch? Defend your answer.

Case Problem 2

For twenty-five years Steinway Stores has operated as a chain, specializing in hardware and automotive productions. Among the products carried are tires, automotive batteries, car accessories, paint, conventional and power tools, small appliances, and plumbing supplies. Business has been excellent for most of the time. Recently, an opportunity has materialized that would direct Steinway Stores into a new field of endeavor.

Bartlett Associates, realtors and developers of large and small shopping centers, has offered the Steinway organization a two-story structure of 100,000 square feet. The building plans call for sufficient space for a full inventory of hard goods and soft goods. The location is adjacent to one of Steinway's existing units, the second largest in the chain.

Steinway Stores is interested for a number of reasons. The most important is that if it decides against the new location, a competitor of its already established business could affect the success of this unit.

After a good deal of negotiation, management decides to accept Bartlett's offer and to proceed with the new enterprise. One by no means simple problem facing the executives is how to operate this new store and turn it into a successful venture.

Questions

1. What roads are available to Steinway Stores?
2. If you were to make the decision, how would you operate the new business? (Keep in mind that the merchandise offerings must be expanded past what is in the realm of management's knowledge.)

14

TRANSPORTATION AND STORAGE

Learning Objectives

Upon completion of the chapter, you will be able to:

1. Discuss the relative position of the railroads in the American transportation system, including innovative ideas they use to improve their position.

2. List the advantages and disadvantages of the use of trucks to transport merchandise.

3. Give the advantages and disadvantages of pipelines, waterways, and air carriers and describe the merchandise best suited to each.

4. Discuss the factors that affect transportation rates.

5. List six reasons for the storage of merchandise.

6. Define five types of warehouses currently in use.

7. Enumerate the services offered by public warehouses.

8. Explain the relationship between warehousing and transportation costs.

LET'S GO PIGGYBACK!

It's unusual to find two such fierce competitors as truckers and railroaders cooperating in the same advertisement, but the senior vice-president of a major trucking company was featured in an ad placed by the Association of American Railroads. The message is that truckers can often save money by shipping their trailers piggyback on railroad flat cars.

Piggyback traffic is the fastest-growing segment of the rail freight industry. It has grown at a rate that is significantly higher than overall freight traffic.

Intermodal transportation, the technical name for piggyback, is most cost effective when the run is long and nonstop, when it may be less expensive than trucks. Rail deregulation in 1981 allowed individual railroads to negotiate rates with individual shippers and thereby supplied the impetus that spurred the growth of piggyback shipping. Another factor is the growth of mergers in the railroad systems which sets up longer lines of individual railroads and does away with the necessity of transferring from one railroad to another.

Due to competition, piggyback is not as profitable as it should be. This has led to the development of new equipment to reduce costs. Lighter flat cars to reduce fuel costs

Piggyback transportation via the railroad. (*Courtesy:* Association of American Railroads.)

and containers that can be stacked on top of one another are being produced. The Bi-modal Corp. has developed a trailer than has both tires and railroad wheels.

Continued growth of piggyback seems assured since it benefits the railroads, the trucking industry, and the customers in terms of reduced shipping costs.

INTRODUCTION

From a business manager's standpoint, transportation has the function of moving goods from the place of production to that of consumption. To be effective, a system of transportation must be able to deliver the correct quantities at the right time at a reasonable cost.

In marketing, transportation is essentially a tool for carrying out the place function. As such, it is extremely important, since it affects both the time and price functions: time because transportation must ensure that the product is in the proper place when it is needed and price because the additional cost of transportation must be taken into account in determining price. The importance of transportation to marketing cannot be overemphasized. Physical distribution of goods accounts for nearly 50 percent of total marketing costs.

The wide variety of methods by which goods may be transported at different costs creates rather complicated transportation decisions. Success or failure of the product may depend in large part on selection of the most suitable transportation method. Naturally, the type of goods involved is the most important factor in this decision.

TOTAL COST APPROACH

The alternatives available for the distribution of goods are many and complicated. The type of carrier, the number and location of warehouses, and the type of warehouse are only the beginning. In addition, the effect of the distribution system on the amount of inventory that must be carried and its associated costs and the effect on customer service and lost sales due to out-of-stock situations must be taken into account. For example, providing two-day delivery service to customers might improve sales dramatically, but it would require carrying a huge inventory, employing additional warehousing locations, and using air freight more frequently. Would the additional expense offset the benefits provided by the extra sales? Solving such problems always involves trade-offs. Carrying a smaller inventory would save space, insurance, and labor, and there are other uses for the money, but how would it affect customer service?

TABLE 14–1. Volume of domestic intercity freight traffic, by type of transport, 1970–1987*

Type of Transport	1970	1973	1975	1978	1979	1980	1981	1982	1983	1984	1985	1986	1987[1]
Freight traffic (bil. ton-miles)													
Total	1,936	2,232	2,066	2,467	2,573	2,487	2,430	2,252	2,337	2,515	2,458	2,501	2,673
Railroads	771	858	759	868	927	932	924	810	841	935	895	889	976
Motor vehicles	412	505	454	599	608	555	527	520	575	606	610	634	666
Inland waterways[2]	319	358	342	409	425	407	410	351	359	399	382	393	435
Oil pipelines	431	507	507	586	608	588	564	566	556	568	564	578	587
Domestic airways[3]	3.3	4.0	3.7	4.8	4.6	4.8	5.1	5.1	5.9	6.5	6.7	7.3	8.7
Percent distribution													
Total	100.0	100.0	100.0	100.0	100.0	100.0	100.0	100.0	100.0	100.0	100.0	100.0	100.0
Railroads	39.82	38.44	36.74	35.18	36.03	37.47	38.02	36.00	35.99	37.18	36.41	35.55	36.51
Motor vehicles	21.28	22.63	21.97	24.28	23.64	22.32	21.69	23.11	24.60	24.10	24.82	25.35	24.91
Inland waterways[2]	16.48	16.04	16.55	16.58	16.52	16.37	16.87	15.60	15.36	15.86	15.54	15.71	16.27
Oil pipelines	22.26	22.72	24.54	23.75	23.64	23.64	23.21	25.16	23.79	22.58	22.95	23.11	21.97
Domestic airways[3]	.17	.18	.19	.19	.18	.19	.21	.23	.25	.26	.28	.28	.34

*A ton-mile is the movement of 1 ton (2,000 pounds) of freight for the distance of 1 mile. A passenger-mile is the movement of 1 passenger for the distance of 1 mile. Comprises public and private traffic, both revenue and nonrevenue. See also *Historical Statistics, Colonial Times to 1970*, series Q1–22.

[1]Preliminary

[2]Includes Great Lakes and inland waterways, but not coastwise, traffic.

[3]Revenue service only for scheduled and non-scheduled carriers, with small section 418 all-cargo carriers included from 1978. Includes express, mail, and excess baggage.

Source: U.S. Department of Commerce, *Statistical Abstract of the United States, 1989* (Washington, D.C.: Government Printing Office, 1989). Transportation Policy Associates, Washington, DC, *Transportation in America*, March 1988, with periodic supplements. (Copyright.)

METHODS OF TRANSPORTATION

Railroads

Despite the growth of various competitive means of transportation, the railroads are still the major carriers of goods, as shown in Table 14–1. The reasons for this success are

1. Fairly quick service.
2. Fairly low cost.
3. Fairly extensive coverage (there are in excess of 400,000 miles of track in the United States).

Although the railroads do not lead in any of these respects, their combination is unique and enables them to maintain superiority. For example, waterway carriers are less expensive than railroads, but they offer far less speed and geographical coverage; trucks give more extensive coverage, but at a higher cost.

The rates charged by railroads vary considerably with the size of the shipment and the distance the goods must travel. Thus, the full-carload (CL) rate is much lower than the less-than-carload (LCL) rate and the through rate (relatively long distance) is less expensive than the local rate (short distance). These characteristics of railroads make them ideally suited to the transportation of heavy, bulky goods, such as coal, sand, and ores, over long distances.

In recent years, shippers have been inclined to bypass the railroad carriers in favor of other means of transportation. To offset this, the railroads have instituted certain innovations designed to keep old customers and attract new users.

Piggyback Services.   One of the disadvantages railroads face is the fact that they are limited to tracks. As a result, a shipper using the railroads frequently must allow the time and bear the expense of unloading a freight car and loading the merchandise on a truck before it reaches its destination. Piggyback service entails loading the goods on a truck trailer, which in turn is loaded on a freight car. When the freight car reaches its destination, the truck trailer can be quickly attached to a truck cab and the delivery can be completed. In this way the shipper is not bothered with unnecessary unloading of the freight car and loading of the truck trailer.

Pooling Shipments.   To try to overcome the competition offered by other carriers for LCL shipments (with a relatively high railroad cost), the railroads have developed procedures for LCL shippers to pool their shipments into CL quantities. This results in lower shipping rates and faster service. One requirement for pooling LCL merchandise into CL quantities is that the goods must have the same point of origin and destination.

In-transit Privileges.   In another attempt to make rail transportation more attractive to customers the railroads permit their customers, at no extra cost, to change destinations while en route. In this fashion a shipment of oranges from California to Omaha may be diverted to Kansas City and be charged as if the shipment were made directly from California to Kansas City. Another in-transit privilege permits goods to be processed en route, with a rate from the point of origin to the ultimate destination (a longer haul, therefore a cheaper rate). Under this provision, wheat may be shipped from Kansas City, converted to flour in Detroit, and shipped on to New York, with a freight rate based on the through rate from Kansas City to New York.

Specialization of Equipment.   Railroads are able to attract business by specializing their equipment to the needs of specific customers. Triple-deck carriers for automobiles, refrigerator cars, and tank cars are typical of the types of equipment used by railroads to suit the needs of certain target customers.

Fast Freight.   To compete with carriers who move goods more quickly than the conventional freight service, many railroads offer fast-freight service. This is a nonstop 60-miles-per-hour freight service designed to compete with trucks for shippers of perishables and goods that require rapid transit.

Trucks

The enlargement of the American network of roadways and the technological improvement of motor vehicles has brought about a tremendous expansion in the use of trucks as means of transporting goods. There are three types of motor transportation:

1. *Common carriers* serve the public at large. They move any type of goods to any part of the country. Generally, common carriers specialize in particular types of vehicles, such as refrigerated trucks and moving vans.
2. *Contract carriers* serve particular customers by entering into formal contracts with their customers for specific periods of time.
3. *Private carriers* are owned and operated by individual firms for the transportation of their own goods.

The reason for the competitive success of motor vehicle transportation is that it offers the following advantages over transport by railroad:

1. Trucks are not restricted to railroad tracks. Unlike railroads, they can go to any place that has available roads. The network of roads in America is vastly more extensive than is the network of railroad tracks.
2. Goods shipped by truck sustain less damage, since their handling is lim-

ited to loading at the shipping point and unloading at the destination. This results in savings in expensive packing materials and in insurance.

3. Merchandise can be picked up at any time and delivered directly to the customer. There is never any unnecessary unpacking and repacking.

4. Railroads cannot begin a trip until a full load of freight cars has been assembled. Trucks, on the other hand, can leave at any time.

5. Transportation for short distances is considerably cheaper by truck than by railroad.

6. Motor carriers offer great flexibility. Their size range, from very small to huge tractor-trailers, permits customers to select the specific design needed to accommodate specialized products such as air-conditioned trucks, freezer trucks, tank trucks, and so forth.

Disadvantages of Trucks.   As is the case with all forms of transportation, motor carriers have their disadvantages:

1. Trucks are frequently loaded on their outgoing trip but often empty or only partially loaded for the return trip. This is particularly true in the case of shipments to out-of-the-way destinations. While other forms of transportation suffer from the same problem, it is more serious for motor carriers. This results in increased costs to the shipper.

2. Traffic congestion and the need for drivers to make rest stops tends to increase delivery time by truck.

3. Since even the largest trucks are too small for such high-bulk products as ores or grain, they lose out to railroads and water transportation on this type of transporting.

4. Less-than-full truckload shipments require a great deal of handling and are very expensive.

No comparison of trucks with railroads can be complete without mentioning the fact that trucks benefit from the building and maintenance of highways by public funds, whereas railroads must build and maintain their own tracks. Therefore, in part at least, motor transportation receives governmental subsidy in its competition with railroads. This puts the railroads at a significant disadvantage, which is apparent in their reduced profits and increasingly less effective passenger service.

Many businesses operate their own fleets of trucks. These private carriers received a boost in 1978 when the ICC ruled that private carriers could act as common carriers. Now, Nabisco's trucks that carry their goods to distant warehouses need not return empty. They are able to contract a paying load for their trip home.

Pipelines

Although rarely noticed by travelers, pipelines rank third in America as a means of transporting goods. They are used chiefly for the movement of natural gas and crude oil and derived products. Continued improvement in the construction and operation of pipelines has considerably increased their efficiency and extended their use to other types of liquids.

For suitable products, pipelines offer an economical way of transportation. Like railroads, pipelines are limited in their use by the availability of facilities; railroads and trucks are still widely used to transport goods that could be more efficiently handled by pipelines. Presently, there is widespread construction of pipelines; this will further increase their use at the expense of other means of transportation.

Waterways

The cheapest transportation available to American industry is via the coastal and inland waterways. Regrettably, the waterways are also the slowest means of transportation. However, there are many industries to whom price is more important than speed. They locate their facilities to take advantage of the low freight cost offered by the waterways. Typical of this is the location of steel mills in the Great Lakes area, where the barge rate for iron ore is about one-tenth of the rail rate.

The construction of the St. Lawrence Seaway resulted in important savings to Midwestern shippers and increased the use of the waterways for shipping goods. At the same time, the St. Lawrence Seaway points up one of the serious disadvantages of waterway transportation—freezing, floods, or drought increase the risk of delay. Despite these drawbacks, the petroleum, chemical, sugar, coffee, cotton, and grain industries use the waterways extensively for transportation of their products.

Fishyback.   Water transportation suffers from the same disadvantage as does rail transportation: merchandise must be unpacked from the barge and repacked on a truck before reaching its destination. This is made unnecessary by the "fishyback" method of packing, which involves packing the goods into a truck trailer and the truck trailer onto the barge. At the end of the waterway the truck trailer is attached to a truck cab; this eliminates unnecessary packing.

Air Carriers

Although recent years have seen enormous growth in the use of the air carriers for transporting merchandise, they are still relatively insignificant in terms of total ton-miles shipped. The most important features of air transport are

1. They are much faster than any other means of transportation. As a result, the air carriers are excellent for the shipment of perishables, high-fashion goods, small, high-value industrial goods, and rush deliveries.

2. Thanks to their speed, air carriers have opened markets never before available because of the perishability of the product. This is particularly true for overseas shipments. For example, Hawaiian orchids, too perishable to be sent to the continental United States by boat, are now being flown in.

3. The careful handling given freight by air carriers reduces damage and packaging costs. One California producer of equipment merely wraps his product in paper for air freight. In the past, when his goods were shipped by rail or truck, costly wooden containers were required.

4. Many shippers who previously maintained warehouses at central points throughout the country to assure prompt delivery to customers are finding that air freight can get the goods to the customer as fast without the expense of maintaining warehouses.

FIGURE 14–1   Air freight offers special advantages. (*Courtesy:* Delta Air Lines, Inc.)

Despite the high cost of air freight, many companies have turned to air carriers for certain classes of their goods and were able to realize considerable savings. They used to use forty warehouses to stock parts and surplus. An analysis indicated that 80 percent of the supplies were rarely ordered. Thirty-seven of the warehouses were closed. The time lost by shipping from a distant warehouse to customers was offset by using air freight. The net savings was counted in millions.

Undoubtedly, air transportation of merchandise will continue at an enormous growth rate.

Containerization

In recent years, there has been a promising attempt to reduce transportation costs by shipping all goods in standardized containers. If a group of small packages going to a single destination is packed into one container, considerable reduction in the amount of handling, pilferage, and time will result. In addition, specially designed merchandise handling equipment can be used, which will further reduce costs.

Regrettably, the packaging requirements of shippers and the preferences of carriers have made agreement on standardization difficult. Consequently, containerization is less widespread than would be expected, although it is used extensively for overseas shipping.

Parcel Post

In 1912 the federal government established parcel post under the Post Office Department to stimulate transportation by mail. As is the case with UPS, parcel post is generally used for small consumer articles. Parcel post puts some restrictions on size, weight, and perishability that are not in force for UPS. Mail-order companies make considerable use of parcel post.

United Parcel Service

The United Parcel Service (UPS) is a privately owned delivery system that has grown dramatically in recent years, in large part at the expense of the U.S. Postal Service. Unlike the Postal Service, for a small fee UPS will make pickups as well as deliveries. Moreover, they guarantee delivery in three days. If the difficulties the Postal Service has been plagued with in recent years continue, UPS and similar companies will continue to grow. Apparently, customers are willing to pay a premium for better, quicker delivery service. This is particularly true if pickup service is included.

Overnight Delivery

When time is of the essence, companies often resort to the overnight delivery services. Federal Express is the leader in this field, with others such as

Purolater Courier providing the same service. The United Postal Service offers its own speedy service that guarantees next-day delivery by three P.M. or the fee is refunded. Costs are extremely high for this express delivery, but in emergency situations, the delivery is worth the price.

TRANSPORTATION RATES

As we have seen, the shipper can choose from several competing transportation facilities; each performs a somewhat different service for a different rate. The cost depends chiefly on the amount and type of goods to be shipped and the travel distance. However, numerous factors within those two classifications affect the cost of transportation.

Type of Goods

1. Loading problems. The difference between the loading cost of, for example, canned foods and iron ore affects the total cost of their transportation.
2. Carrier's liability for loss or damages.
3. Volume and frequency of shipments.
4. Special requirements of the goods and type of equipment needed.

Travel Distance

1. Longer hauls are relatively less expensive.
2. Switching from one line to another and reloading (for LCL) increases the cost.
3. The amount of other traffic in the same direction has an effect on costs. Generally, the more heavily traveled routes have a lower rate.
4. Competition among carriers frequently results in considerable price variations.

FREIGHT FORWARDERS

Freight forwarding is a service industry specializing in handling LCL shipments. By appealing to a wide variety of small customers, freight forwarders are able to consolidate small lots into full-carload or full-truckload shipments and to reduce freight costs. For customers with occasional export business they offer the know-how and paperwork for combining train, truck, and transoceanic shipments. They also provide the technical skill and traffic management services for small shippers. It is estimated that about 75 percent of the general cargo shipped from U.S. ports to foreign countries is handled by freight forwarders. Their expertise in processing the required export paperwork makes them valuable to even the largest exporters. As a result, the vast majority of exporters use freight forwarders.

FUTURE TRENDS IN TRANSPORTATION

During the past thirty years there has been a consistent trend in the relative importance of the various types of transportation available to shippers. There is no reason to believe that this trend will not continue.

The future of transportation will probably be along the following lines:

1. Railroads will continue to lose their relative importance as freight movers while continuing to increase their ton-mileage.
2. Waterway traffic will continue to increase both in ton-mileage and relative importance, despite the construction of new pipelines for the petroleum industry.
3. Pipelines will increase in relative importance, owing to continued increase in the consumption of the products they serve and the construction of new pipelines.
4. Motor trucks will be used more and the relative importance of the trucking industry will expand.
5. Air freight will have the most dramatic growth, both in terms of ton-miles and in relative importance.
6. Martin-Brower, a distribution specialist whose customers include McDonald's and Baskin-Robbins, has a gross income in excess of $1 billion. They perform the service of inventory carrying and transportation for their customers. Relying heavily on computers and other up-to-date equipment, they offer a savings for their clients while making a handsome profit for themselves. Because of the complexity of the distribution process this sort of independent distribution service is certain to grow in importance.
7. Aerojet-General maintains an automated warehouse in Frederick, Maryland. One person at a computer is able to operate the entire system. Orders are read, picked, and moved to loading docks and paperwork is generated.

TRANSPORTATION AND THE COMPUTER

As has been discussed, the variety of carriers and rates can pose a complicated problem to a shipper. As for many problems in which a wide variety of factors must be considered, modern business is turning to the computer for rapid solutions. By putting all pertinent data into the memory banks of a computer and requesting information as to the best route between two points, many firms have succeeded in simplifying an otherwise knotty transportation problem.

STORAGE

The time function is created by storage. Storage is involved with the holding of goods from the time of their production to that of their final sale. Some of the reasons for storage are

1. Agricultural products and other seasonally produced goods must be warehoused between the production and final sale or use.
2. Goods that are produced regularly throughout the year but sold seasonally, such as sporting equipment, toys, furs, and so on, require storage.
3. Excess goods, that is, goods bought in excess of immediate needs of the purchaser because of quantity discounts offered by producers and the transportation savings that result from full-carload shipments, require storage.
4. Goods not purchased for current use must be stored. Frequently, price increases can be anticipated. In such cases, it is common for buyers to place large orders prior to the price increase.
5. Some products, such as tobacco, liquor, meats, and cheeses, require an aging period after they are produced to improve their quality.
6. When the selling price of goods can be increased by withholding them from the market, storage becomes necessary.

Methods of Storing Goods

Since the types of merchandise that require storage differ widely as to their physical requirements, their storage requirements differ as well. Storage facilities include cold storage (for meats, fruits, and vegetables), grain elevators, and warehouses.

Warehouses are the most common type of storage facility. These may be privately owned by industries who maintain, control, and supervise the storing of their merchandise to suit their own specific needs, or they may be public warehouses. Public warehouses are regulated by the government and are found throughout the country. For a fee they provide all the services required in the storage of goods. There are five types of public warehouses:

1. *General merchandise warehouses,* used to store a variety of goods for a relatively short time. General merchandise warehouses may be bonded, in which case they control merchandise on which a tax must be paid before the goods are released. There is, for example, a tax on whiskey. Rather than pay the tax during production and storage, the producer sends the finished product to a bonded warehouse that provides for the payment of the taxes only when the goods are shipped to customers.
2. *Special commodity warehouses,* designed for the specific requirements of such merchandise as grain, tobacco, and cotton.

3. *Furniture warehouses,* specially designed for furniture, household goods, and other personal property.
4. *Cold storage warehouses,* for goods such as dairy products and furs whose preservation requires carefully controlled, low temperatures.
5. *Field warehouses,* set up on the premises of the owner of the goods, but completely controlled by an independent warehouse owner.

Services Offered by Public Warehouses.   Public warehouses generally offer their customers the following services:

1. Receipt, unloading, and placement of goods in storage
2. Inspection of all incoming goods in accordance with the standards set by the owner
3. Packing, shipment, and performance of the necessary paperwork of goods sold by the owner

These services are generally performed in well-constructed, often fireproof buildings, provided with sprinkler service and twenty-four-hour-a-day guards. (These provisions reduce insurance rates.) Public warehouses are generally used by manufacturers who lack storage space or whose requirements for storage are too small to make owning or leasing private warehouse facilities practical. Another important reason for public warehousing is to secure a warehouse receipt.

Warehouse Receipts

When goods are stored in a public warehouse, the owner of the merchandise is given a warehouse receipt. This receipt is proof of ownership of the goods, and its importance lies in the fact that it is negotiable. That is, the warehouse receipt may be transferred to a third party. The significance of the negotiability is that because the warehouse receipt carries with it the title to the goods, it may be given as collateral for bank loans. Each year banks lend hundreds of millions of dollars on inventory secured by warehouse receipts. In this way warehousing provides an important source of working capital to American business managers.

Warehouse receipts that are later used as collateral for loans are the most important reason for the maintenance of field warehouses. Because the merchandise stored in such a facility is controlled not by the owner but by a warehouse operator who is completely independent of the owner, the banker making the loan on a field warehouse receipt may be confident that security (the inventory covered by the field warehouse receipt) will remain intact.

WAREHOUSING AND TRANSPORTATION

Many manufacturers who do business on a national scale maintain warehouses throughout the country. This results in savings in transportation and improvement in customer services. Many large supermarkets maintain distribution centers (in effect, large warehouses from which shipments are made) in or near every large population center that is served by their retail outlets. This enables them to replenish stock on the store shelves within a day or two. Similarly, manufacturers locate warehouses near their markets, guaranteeing their customers improved delivery service.

The savings in transportation costs described above can be effected because businesses using distribution centers for shipping to customers are never forced to send expensive, small lots from the factory to far-off customers. Instead, they send inexpensive, large-volume shipments to their distant warehouses, store the merchandise there, and make small, expensive shipments only for the relatively short distances between the distribution center and its local customers.

Since transportation and storage are closely related, they must never be considered separately. Instead, the overall picture must be carefully studied in terms of the effect on timely delivery and transportation costs before the location of distribution centers can be decided.

Improvement in the speed of transportation, particularly air freight, has led many companies to reconsider their warehousing systems. Some examples of this are

1. Raytheon replaced four New England warehouses with one large distribution center. By relying heavily on air freight and using a computer for filling orders, they were able to reduce the amount of capital tied up in inventory, cut their distribution costs by 20 percent, and improve customer service.

2. Libby, McNeill, and Libby replaced 214 warehouses with five distribution centers as a result of a careful study of their warehousing and transportation needs. The savings led to increased profits and lower customer prices.

3. The Borden Company replaced 136 warehouses with eighteen distribution centers. This resulted in a huge savings in inventory carried—labor, rent, insurance, and so on.

Progressive management is constantly studying its warehousing and transportation problems. The present trend seems to be away from small warehouses and toward major distribution centers. This pattern has been followed by the Whirlpool Corporation, Bigelow-Sanford, and many others.

REDUCING TRANSPORTATION COSTS

Considering the fact that transportation costs are almost half of the total cost of marketing, it is strange that many firms ignore the opportunity to cut their transportation costs. Even those firms that employ the most scientific methods of shaving pennies from their manufacturing costs are frequently blind to the important savings opportunities resulting from improved transportation planning. Some suggestions follow:

Proper Location of the Manufacturing Plant and Warehouses

The location of the manufacturing facility of a business organization has an effect on both the transporting of raw materials into the plant and the movement of finished goods out of the plant. Thus, the geographical site picked for manufacturing is most vital with regard to transportation costs. In general, it is wise to manufacture as close to the raw materials as possible, because raw materials frequently contain waste whose transportation should be minimized.

Warehouses and warehouse distribution centers should be located near the markets they must serve. Transportation facilities at the warehouse sites should be adequate to their needs both in terms of incoming bulk shipments and outgoing small shipments.

Proper Use of Inexpensive Transport

Not all shipments require rush service. This is particularly true if production planning takes shipping problems into account. Production should be completed early enough so that inexpensive bulk rates can be used wherever possible.

The opening of the St. Lawrence Seaway provided the opportunity for tremendous savings on transportation to many businesses. However, some business managers, unaccustomed to this form of transportation, have not yet made a proper survey of the effect of using the waterways to reduce their transportation costs.

The pooling of small orders into carload lots is another frequently ignored method of reducing transportation costs. Businesses that have occasional opportunities for pooling should turn to freight forwarders for help in arranging such pools.

Proper Packaging

Too often businesses use specific packaging containers that are unwieldy and expensive to ship. Studies should be made of the possible transportation savings that can be made by a change in the packaging design.

Proper Authority for the Traffic Manager

In most firms, the responsibility for transportation and warehousing is divided among many individuals who are under the direction of various executives. When the importance of traffic in terms of the total cost of the product is considered, it becomes obvious that transportation is as important as any other major business function. Transportation and warehousing should be under the control of a distribution manager who reports directly to the president and who is equal in rank to the sales manager, the factory manager, and similar executives.

Important Points in the Chapter

1. Transportation is a tool for moving goods from the place of production to the place of consumption. As such, it creates the place function. Since transportation constitutes about one-half of the total cost of most goods, it is a vital element in the price function as well. In addition, the time function (that is, availability of the goods at the right time) depends largely on the effectiveness of the system of transportation used.

2. Transportation problems are complicated by the large variety of methods of transportation, each of which has a great number of advantages and disadvantages.

3. Technological advances have reduced the relative importance of railroads while improving the relative significance of other means of transportation. In an attempt to keep their competitive position, the railroads have instituted certain innovations, such as piggyback and specialized equipment. Although they are still the transportation leaders, particularly for long-distance bulk shipments, the importance of railroads for transportation of merchandise is decreasing.

4. Trucks are steadily becoming more important. Our enormous network of roadways permits trucks to go almost anywhere. Trucks dominate the short-haul transportation market.

5. Pipelines are growing in importance as a means of moving petroleum products and other liquids.

6. The waterways, though slow, are the cheapest means of transportation. The opening of the St. Lawrence Seaway resulted in their increased use. Bulk shipments for which speed is not vital are frequently shipped by boat.

7. Air freight, although still relatively small in volume, is the fastest-growing method of shipping. The airways are very expensive, but their speed makes them attractive for high value, perishable, and urgently needed goods.

8. Transportation rates, controlled by governmental agencies, are based on the characteristics of the goods and the travel distance.

9. Storage creates the time function. It is involved with the holding of goods from the time of their production to that of their final sale.

10. A wide variety of public warehouses is available for storing merchandise; warehouses also provide other services, such as unpacking and shipping.

11. Warehousing and transportation must be considered jointly, since the proper location of a warehouse may result in important savings on transportation costs.

12. Large distribution centers are replacing groups of smaller warehouses. The large distribution center, coupled with rapid means of transportation such as air freight, can be located farther from the markets without a loss in customer service, but with considerable savings in distribution expense.

13. It is important that all storage and transportation functions be combined into one department; its manager should be the equal of other executives.

Review Questions

1. Explain the effect of transportation on the place, time, and price functions.

2. Discuss the use of railroads for moving goods, indicating its advantages and disadvantages.

3. What are pool shipments? Why are they used?

4. Railroads offer specialized equipment to their customers. Discuss fully.

5. Why are trucks able to compete successfully with railroads?

6. Compare the effect of governmental subsidy on the trucking and railroad industries.

7. What are the advantages and disadvantages of shipping by waterways?

8. Describe the type of merchandise that is likely to be shipped by air freight.

9. Define and discuss UPS as a way of moving goods.

10. Discuss some of the characteristics of goods that would have an effect on transportation rates.

11. Give instances in which the travel distance will affect transportation rates.

12. Discuss the future of trucks and of air freight.

13. Define *storage* and differentiate between private and public warehouses.

14. What types of services are offered by public warehouses?

15. Field warehouses are located on the premises of the manufacturer; why are independent warehouse managers brought in to control them?

16. Explain the relationship between warehousing and storage.

17. What is the effect of the location of manufacturing and warehousing facilities on transportation costs?

18. How can packaging affect the cost of transportation?

19. Discuss the use of a computer for the solution of transportation problems.

20. Why is it important for the person in charge of transportation and storage to be equal to the sales and production managers?

Case Problems

Case Problem 1

The Royal Company is a large, well-established manufacturer of household appliances. It boasts nationwide customers and maintains twelve warehouses throughout the country to store goods, reduce transportation costs, and provide quick customer service.

A survey of transportation and warehousing costs has indicated that the expense involved in physical distribution exceeds the amount considered normal for the industry. The organization chart of the company indicates that the responsibility for transportation is divided among departments as follows:

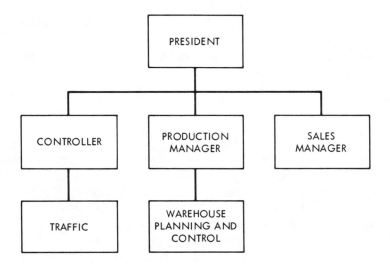

Inventory is carefully controlled by a computer that provides weekly information on low-inventory items. Production schedules are based on the indicated inventory shortages.

A management consulting firm called in to study the distribution problem proposes that the organization of the firm be changed as follows:

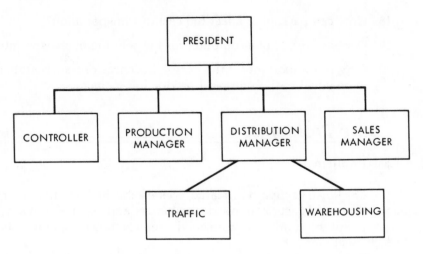

Questions

1. Why should all matters of transportation, both incoming and outgoing, be handled by the same department?
2. Why should both traffic and warehousing be placed under the responsibility of the distribution manager?
3. Why should the distribution manager be equal to the controller, the production manager, and the sales manager?
4. Comment on the effect of the system of production planning on transportation costs.

Case Problem 2

Sunflower Stores, Inc., is a large, rapidly expanding supermarket chain. At present, Sunflower Stores operates at 712 locations throughout the country.

The method of expansion used by Sunflower Stores is to construct six to eight large outlets in a specific area and to support these stores with a centralized warehouse. There are now 102 warehouses throughout the country, providing rapid service in keeping the supermarket shelves filled. This system works very well, as is evidenced by the fact that a store rarely has to wait more than three days after a request for merchandise until the goods arrive.

There is a proposal before management to replace the 102 warehouses with twelve large distribution centers. It is felt that considerable savings can be effected by this move.

Questions

1. What would be the effect of the change on transportation costs to the distribution center? To the stores?

2. What would be the effect of the change on warehousing costs?
3. What would be the effect of the change on the amount of inventory that Sunflower Stores would have to carry?
4. Since the distribution center would generally be located further from the existing supermarkets than the present warehouses, how could delivery time be speeded up?
5. Comment on the importance of a computer to a distribution center.
6. What would be the effect of this new system of warehousing and distribution on expansion into lightly populated areas that cannot support more than one or two stores?

15

SALES PROMOTION

Learning Objectives

Upon completion of the chapter, you will be able to:

1. Explain budgeting for sales promotion, defining three methods of accomplishing this.

2. Describe and give the advantages and disadvantages of seven types of advertising media.

3. Explain the importance of measuring advertising effectiveness and give four methods of evaluation.

4. Discussion fashion shows, demonstrations, and sampling and indicate the type of merchandise best suited for each.

5. Explain the importance of visual merchandising.

CAMPAIGNS FOR SUCCESS

Without question, General Foods, manufacturer of such successful product lines as Maxwell House coffee and Birds Eye foods, continues to be one of the dominant American forces in the processing and marketing of convenience grocery goods. The company believes that in order to maintain its enviable position there must be a considerable advertising effort. It considers advertising to be "an effective, economical and necessary tool for developing a large and dependable volume of sales."

At General Foods an advertising campaign begins approximately six months before any print space or broadcast time is purchased. Product managers consider such factors as sales targets for the product, geographical differences, target markets to whom the product is to be presented, and statistics on the nature of the audiences reached by the available media. The media used are television, radio, newspapers, magazines, newspaper supplements, billboards, and point-of-purchase advertisements. The actual media selected for each campaign depends upon the company's objectives for the product.

Once the foregoing factors have been evaluated, the product manager for the particular product or product category meets with the in-house media services staff to develop an outline for the promotional media program. Upon completion of this preliminary stage of planning, the information is fed into the computer for estimates on advertising reach, frequency of exposure for beneficial results, and possible areas of weakness. If any weaknesses are indicated by the computer printout, the product manager and the media staff make the necessary revisions. Not until all the kinks are ironed out does the campaign plan move to the next step. The ultimate decision for the type of media to be used comes from a computer-generated detailed list of media recommendations. This list is the basis for the final decision management makes.

At this point all of the needs of the various product groups at General Foods are considered at the corporate or top-management level. Advertising funds are then translated into the most economical and efficient use for maximum exposure to the consumer market.

While the research indicates a particular approach, each campaign is subject to regular review. If competition or other marketing considerations indicate a need to change, the change is initiated. The policy at General Foods in terms of advertising is a flexible approach. No decision is cast in stone.

Among the approaches successfully used in the introduction of a new product is the store coupon which provides incentive to try the product. Another is to advertise a product in the newspaper featuring a recipe in which the product is a major ingredient. Such ads are clipped for future reference and serve as a reminder, whenever used, of the advertised product.

At General Foods there is a constant attempt to conform to high standards. Their campaigns are based upon strict policies for accuracy of representation. Realistic household situations are used, and there is equal representation of minorities. General Foods always attempts to avoid showing their commercials on sex- or violence-oriented programs.

General Foods' International Coffees entries. (Advertisement and photograph reproduced with the permission of General Foods Corporation. GENERAL FOODS is a trademark of the General Foods Corporation.)

Through careful planning, General foods effectively and economically presents their product offerings in advertising campaigns that more often than not bring positive results and help them to continue as one of America's leading processors and marketers of grocery products.

INTRODUCTION

There are about as many different definitions for the term *sales promotion* as there are textbooks concerning this area of marketing. In the context of this chapter, *sales promotion* refers to such mass communications media as advertising, special promotions, visual merchandising, and publicity. Personal selling, which some might consider logical to include as part of sales promotion, will be discussed independently, in Chapter 17. The primary reason for this separation is that the forms of promotion presented here, contrary to those in personal selling, appeal to groups rather than to individuals.

Marketers, as we have learned earlier, spend about as much in the marketing of goods as they do in their manufacture. Often the costs of marketing exceed those of actual production. A large portion of the marketing dollar goes for promotion of the product. This is not only true for new products but also for established ones.

BUDGETING

The actual sum a company should spend for adequate promotional coverage constitutes a problem that continues to plague even the most sophisticated marketers. Agreement is unanimous among knowledgeable marketers that in order to bring a successful product into being it must be promoted, but the amount to set aside and the method to employ in establishing the amount is not standard procedure. Unfortunately, most budgets are made by executives who are not directly involved in day-to-day expenditures. This often leads to unrealistic budgeting. Many barometers are used, some of the most popular of which will be discussed next.

Percentage-of-Sales Method

In this approach, companies use a percentage of the past year's sales in determining the amount to set aside for promotion. Some companies vary this technique by substituting an average of several previous years' sales. Although this may be thought of as a logical base upon which to set the budget, many promotion experts consider the system to be illogical. Advertising people believe that sales result from advertising and other promotional devices rather than the opposite. Expenditures for promotional purposes should not be decided as a result of sales. Certain companies who effectively use the percentage-of-sales approach in budget determinations have found that it makes more sense to use anticipated sales as a base than to use previous sales figures. This technique seems to be most logical in that it takes into consideration company growth and the value of sales promotion in achieving this growth. Tables 15–1 and 15–2 show specific products and their percentage of sales in terms of promotion.

Units-of-Sales Method

Instead of basing a budgetary decision on total dollars, some companies expend sums for the promotion of their goods based on the number of individual units of merchandise they sold in the past year (or hope to sell in the coming year). A determination is then made as to how much an individual article will cost to promote. This sum is then multiplied by the total units of production to arrive at the actual budget.

TABLE 15–1.   Promotional costs as percentage of sales of consumer goods:
by individual companies

Note the wide variations in the promotional mixes used by different firms. Compare the cosmetics
firm (3) and the insurance company (62). Also note the variations in total promotional appropriations. A paint company (12) devoted 27 percent of sales to promotion, while the promotion budget of
an appliance company (43) was only 8 percent of sales. How do you account for these differences?

Number	Type of Product	Advertising Budget[1]	Advertising	Sales Promotion	Sales Force
1.	Toiletries and proprietaries	A	30.0	4.0	10.0
2.	Package goods	AA	25.0	8.0	8.0
3.	Cosmetics	C	24.0	5.0	7.0
4.	Cosmetics	AAA	22.0	2.0	10.0
5.	Housewares	B	20.0[2]	—[2,3]	3.5
6.	Perfumes and cosmetics	B	16.0	3.0	21.0
7.	Drug sundries	A	14.0	3.0	5.0
8.	Drugs	A	12.0	8.0	7.0
9.	Books	A	11.0	6.0	5.0
10.	Food	AAA	11.0	6.0	—
11.	Mail order	AAA	10.5	0.2	0.3
12.	Paints	B	10.0	2.0	15.0
13.	Housewares	B	10.0	2.0	6.0
14.	Beer	AA	9.5	6.4[4]	—
15.	Food and feed	AAA	8.1	3.2	6.1
16.	Food	AAA	7.0	5.0	3.0
17.	Food	AAA	7.0	4.5[4]	—[4]
18.	Small housewares	B	6.0	1.3	12.5
19.	Appliances	AAA	5.0	1.0	—
20.	Soft drinks	B	5.0	3.0	1.0
21.	Soft goods	C	5.0	6.0	12.0
22.	Nonferrous metals	AA	5.0[5]	—[5]	—
23.	Salt	C	5.0[5]	—[5]	—
24.	Packaged grocery products	AAA	4.8	0.7	1.2
25.	Beverages	A	4.6	1.4	—
26.	Tool manufacturing	C	4.0[5]	—[5]	10.0
27.	Paper converting	C	4.0	4.0	—
28.	Soft goods, textiles	A	4.0	1.0[6]	17.0
29.	Tires, foam rubber	A	4.0	4.0	—
30.	Pianos	C	4.0	0.3	5.0
31.	Chemicals	D	3.5	1.0	—
32.	Automotive parts	C	3.5	—	10.3
33.	Photographic equipment	C	3.3[5]	—	3.0
34.	Food	A	3.5	1.7	6.0
35.	Appliances	A	3.0	3.0	—
36.	Textiles	B	3.0	0.7	3.6
37.	Shoe manufacturing	A	3.0	0.3[6]	4.5
38.	Marketing cooperative—fresh produce	C	3.0[5]	—[5]	10.0
39.	Baby foods	A	2.7	2.6	6.0
40.	Hand tools	B	2.5	0.9	7.1
41.	Home furnishings	B	2.5	2.0	6.0
42.	Power tools	C	2.5	—	—

(continued)

TABLE 15–1.   (*Continued*)

Number	Type of Product	Advertising Budget[1]	Advertising	Sales Promotion	Sales Force
43.	Appliances	A	2.5	1.5	4.0
44.	Airline	AA	2.2	0.7	—
45.	Building materials	A	2.2	1.9	4.8
46.	Liquors	A	2.0	—	—
47.	Basic metals	A	2.0	1.0	—
48.	Heating and air conditioning	A	2.0	0.5	4.5
49.	Soft goods	C	2.0	2.5	4.5
50.	Floor coverings	A	2.0[5]	—	—
51.	Plumbing and heating	A	2.0[5]	—	—
52.	Shoe manufacturing	D	2.0[5]	—	5.3
53.	Steel equipment	C	2.0[5]	—	16.0
54.	Transportation	AA	1.8	0.2	6.0
55.	Building materials	AA	1.5	0.7	8.0
56.	Automotive	D	1.5	—	3.0
57.	Rubber	C	1.5	1.5	4.5
58.	Rubber products	C	1.3	1.0	—
59.	Water pumps	D	1.3	1.3[6]	5.0
60.	Photographic equipment	B	1.3	0.7	3.0
61.	Food	A	1.0	0.3	—
62.	Insurance	A	1.0	0.5	17.5
63.	Textiles	B	1.0	1.0	0.5
64.	Petroleum	C	1.0	—	—
65.	Retail food chain	AAA	1.0[5]	—[5]	—
66.	Oil	A	0.7	0.3	—
67.	Petroleum	A	0.6	0.3	—
68.	Domestic pumps and water systems	C	0.6	1.0	—
69.	Over thirty industries	A	0.5	1.5	—
70.	Glass manufacturing	A	0.5	0.2	—
71.	Steel manufacturing	D	0.2	0.5	0.5
72.	Iron and steel	D	0.1	—	—
73.	Aluminum	B	0.1	0.1	—
74.	Building industry	A	0.1[7]	—[7]	—[7]

[1]AAA, $10,000,000 and over; AA, $5,000,000–9,999,999; A, $1,000,000–4,999,999; B, $500,000–999,999; C, $100,000–499,999; D, under $100,000.
[2]Advertising, sales promotion, and marketing research combined.
[3]Dash (—) indicates data not given.
[4]Sales promotion, marketing research, and sales force combined.
[5]Advertising and sales promotion combined.
[6]Sales promotion and marketing research combined.
[7]Advertising, sales promotion, marketing research, and sales force combined.

Source: Dale Houghton, "*Marketing Costs: What Ratio to Sales?*" Printers' Inc.

TABLE 15–2.   Promotional costs as percentage of sales of industrial goods: by individual companies

Sales force expenditures are typically much higher than advertising appropriations. In the promotional mix, marketers of industrial goods usually emphasize personal selling to a much greater degree than firms selling consumer products. Why? Compare this table and Table 15–1; note that the total promotional budget for industrial products is typically a smaller percentage of sales than that for consumer goods.

Number	Type of Product	Advertising Budget[1]	Advertising	Sales Promotion	Sales Force
1.	Paint	D	10.0	—[2]	—
2.	Road construction and agricultural	D	4.0[3]	—[3]	7.0
3.	Industrial fasteners, steel shelving, and shop equipment	B	2.8	—	—
4.	Office equipment	C	2.5[4]	—[4]	—
5.	Instrument	C	2.0	0.9	9.0
6.	Tool manufacturing	C	2.0[4]	—[4]	10.0
7.	Paper converting	C	2.0	2.0	—
8.	Instruments and controls	C	2.0[3]	—[3]	15.0
9.	Electrical control	C	1.8	3.8	—
10.	Metalworking machinery	C	1.8	0.2	—
11.	Graphic arts	C	1.5	0.5	16.0
12.	Metalworking	C	1.5[4]	—[4]	5.0
13.	Metal cutting tools	C	1.2	—	5.6
14.	Industrial machinery	D	1.0	2.0	7.0
15.	Package grocery products	B	1.0	0.9	4.8
16.	Metal product—foundry and machining	C	1.0	0.8	5.5
17.	Automotive parts	C	1.0	0.5	4.5
18.	Building materials	B	1.0	0.3[5]	4.0
19.	Nonferrous metals	A	1.0[4]	—[4]	—
20.	Die cutting	D	1.0	—	10.0
21.	Basic metals	AA	1.0	—	—
22.	Aluminum	A	0.8	0.4	—
23.	Petroleum	B	0.8	0.3	3.0
24.	Chemicals and plastics	A	0.8	—	—
25.	Chemical and food processing, steel mill, and construction equipment	A	0.7	0.2	6.0
26.	Iron and steel	A	0.6	—	—
27.	Hand tools	C	0.5	0.2	2.4
28.	Materials handling	B	0.5	0.5	—
29.	Soft goods—textile	C	0.5	—	12.0
30.	Automotive	D	0.5	—	0.5
31.	Plate steel fabrication	D	0.4	0.5	0.5
32.	Foundry	C	0.3	—	—
33.	Iron and steel	C	0.3	—	—
34.	Rubber products	D	0.3	—	—
35.	Photographic equipment manufacturing	D	0.2	—	—
36.	Food and feed	C	0.1	0.3	2.5
37.	Chemicals	B	0.1	—	—

(continued)

TABLE 15–2. *(Continued)*

Number	Type of Product	Advertising Budget[1]	Advertising	Sales Promotion	Sales Force
38.	Glass manufacturing	D	0.1	—	—
39.	Oil	C	0.1	—	—
40.	Aircraft	C	0.1	—	—
41.	Heavy manufacturing and aircraft accessories	C	0.1	—	9.3
42.	Manufacturing conveyors and pneumatic tube systems	C	—	—	—
43.	Building industry	C	—	—	—

[1]AAA, $10,000,000 and over; AA, $5,000,000–9,999,999; A, $1,000,000–4,999,999; B, $500,000–999,999; C, $100,000–499,999; D, under 100,000.
[2]Dash (—) indicates data not given.
[3]Advertising, sales promotion and marketing research combined.
[4]Advertising and sales promotion and marketing research combined.
[5]Sales promotion and marketing research combined.

Source: Dale Houghton, *"Marketing Costs: What Ratio in Sales?"* Printers' Ink.

Task Method

Use of this technique requires complete research of the product and its potential markets. The company using this method defines its objectives, such as the number of units to be sold, total sales, and profit expectation. After careful consideration of the costs involved to reach these objectives, a budgetary figure is reached. Sometimes called the task-and-objective method, this technique is considered by many marketers to be the soundest approach in the determination of the promotion allocation.

Although businesses can get scientific in the planning of the budget, some organizations leave the amount to be spent for the promotion of goods to chance. Unsophisticated approaches such as whim or whatever amount happens to be available at the time often determine the amount allocated for advertising. Little logic is associated with this kind of thinking, but there are business managers who will confide that this is the tactic used by their companies. Little can be said for the validity of such an approach.

ADVERTISING

Advertising as defined by the American Marketing Association is "any paid-for form of nonpersonal presentation of the facts about goods, services, or ideas to a group." A breakdown of the definition and comparison with the other areas of sales promotion makes it more easily understandable. Publicity is free and advertising is paid for; display actually shows the goods, whereas advertising only

A SIMPLE LESSON IN ECONOMICS FOR ANYONE WHO BELIEVES ADVERTISING RAISES PRICES.

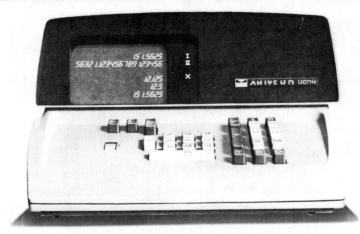

1965 calculator – Over $2000.00

1984 calculator – Under $10.00

FIGURE 15–1 Ad in defense of advertising. (*Courtesy:* American Association of Advertising Agencies.)

tells the facts about them; and selling (as noted, considered by some to be included as a sales-promotion activity) is personal, but advertising is nonpersonal or to a group.

By and large, companies feel that the greatest return for the promotion dollar comes as a result of advertising. Hence, advertising warrants and is afforded the lion's share of the promotion budget by most marketers.

Marketers make use of two classifications of advertising: product and institutional. The former stimulates the market regarding the product or services, whereas the latter is designed to create a proper attitude toward the seller and to build goodwill.

The Cost of Advertising

Marketers will readily admit that advertising expenditures for the promotion of products and services run into billions of dollars. Consumers often voice the opinion that the advertising expense significantly contributes to higher prices. The debate is one which promises to continue forever. The community of professionals which constitutes the advertising world contends that the end result of the costs of advertising is beneficial to the consuming public. That is, as advertising spreads the word about a product's benefits, sales increase. As production increases to meet the demand, the price per unit decreases. Ultimately, the consumer is the winner. The advertisement pictured in Figure 15–1 exemplifies the American Association of Advertising Agencies' defense of advertising benefits to the consumer.

The Major Marketing Advertisers

The marketing institutions responsible for the majority of advertising are manufacturers and retailers. Although the media employed by both groups are the same (the amount of emphasis in each of the media will differ), the messages they convey are not. Manufacturers make every effort to arouse the customer's desire to purchase their product. Where or how the purchase is made is often immaterial. Retailers, on the other hand, concentrate their efforts on convincing the public to buy products from them. With the tremendous amount of competition at both marketing levels, manufacturers and retailers alike expend enormous sums to garner their share of the market. It is estimated that marketers are currently spending well over $20 billion a year for advertising.

Advertising Agencies

Although companies often have their own advertising staffs, the advertising agency plays the major part in the advertisement of goods and services. The agency is an independent business charged with responsibility for the preparation of ads and the selection of appropriate media for presentation. Remuneration generally comes from the media. This is usually 15 percent of the cost of the ad. If a company goes directly to the media to place an ad, the cost will be the same as that charged by the agency. The agencies actually receive a better price for advertising space or time because of their purchasing power. Thus, the cost of employing an agency to carry out the advertising task virtually does not contribute any additional expense to marketers.

Advertising Media

The advertising media available to marketers include newspapers, magazines, radio, television, direct mail, hand-distributed circulars, signs and billboards, car cards, and shopping publications. Few companies utilize all media. A discussion of each type follows to indicate the various advantages of each classification for the marketer.

Newspapers.   There are two distinct types of newspapers for the promotion of goods and services. They are the consumer newspapers (the ones we read as consumers) and the trade papers, which are carefully scrutinized by business managers.

Both types of papers are directed to specific audiences; when properly executed, both reap the rewards sought. From this point, *newspaper advertising* is to mean the consumer newspapers. Traditionally, retailers spend the larger part of their promotional dollar on advertising. Patronized by retailers are the giant dailies such as *The New York Times*, the *Miami Herald*, and the *Chicago Tribune.* Not neglected, but nonetheless not as widely used in terms of overall dollars, are the publications that cover smaller, local areas. Most newspapers have numerous data on hand to enable the advertisers to determine which newspaper is best suited for their needs.

Of the advantages of newspaper advertising, the following are most significant:

1. The newspaper's offerings are so diversified that they appeal to almost every member of the family. For example, a young adult, not prone to newspaper reading, might be attracted by an advertisement while looking for the television section.
3. Although advertising space might be considered costly upon initial examination, closer inspection shows its cost to be lower per reader than the cost of all other media.
3. The newspaper can be examined at leisure, and therefore its life is longer than that of broadcast advertising. A moment away from the television set means that the commercial will not be seen.
4. Being brought home by the working members of the household (many read the newspapers on the train ride home) or delivered directly to the home by newspaper carriers, the newspaper is readily available on a daily basis.

Newspaper advertising also has its disadvantages.

1. Longer distance from the stores sometimes prevents the interested reader from shopping the advertised merchandise.
2. The life of the message may only be very short. Sometimes it is for only part of the ride home.
3. The quality of the stock (paper) used often limits the attractiveness of the item being offered for sale. For this reason, color is rarely used.

Figure 15–2 shows an example of an institutional newspaper ad.

To Our Dear Customers:

Rule #1 at TSS-Seedman's:
There must never be
a dissatisfied customer.
So I, personally, want to know
about any unsatisfactory experience
you may have had with us.

Despite all training—
human error sometimes occurs.

If you write your complaint to me
and mail on or before Nov. 8, 1984,
I will send you a Gift Certificate
for your kindness.

When I say. . .
Your complete satisfaction
is guaranteed always—
I mean it, and so do all our Executives.

Please address me at:
104-01 FOSTER AVE.
BROOKLYN, N.Y. 11236

G.J. Seedman, Chairman

TSS *Seedman's*
TRUTH IN ADVERTISING   CONSUMER PROTECTION
D e p a r t m e n t   S t o r e s
Better Quality at Lower Prices—Test Us!

FIGURE 15–2
Institutional advertisement. (*Courtesy:* TSS Seedman's.)

Advertising rates.   The rates charged for space vary according to size of the advertisement, location (placement), circulation, and newspaper in which the ad is placed. Although it is common practice to sell space on a full-page, half-page, and so on, arrangement, the cost is actually figured on a line basis. The actual size of the line varies from newspaper to newspaper, but it is one column wide and usually $\frac{1}{14}$ inch deep. The number of lines multiplied by the cost per line indicates the cost of the space. The cost for the same ad in two newspapers may vary considerably. To find the true value, that is, the cost per reader, the milline rate formula is applied as follows:

$$\frac{\text{rate per line} \times 1{,}000{,}000}{\text{circulation}} = \text{milline rate}$$

If the rate per line is $0.40 and a paper's circulation is 400,000, the milline rate is

$$\frac{0.40 \times 1{,}000{,}000}{400{,}000} = \$1.00$$

By applying this formula to the various newspapers' rates and circulation, an advertiser can determine whether a higher line rate might actually cost less per reader.

As indicated earlier, in addition to the cost per line in newspapers, the costs vary according to placement or position of the ad. The least expensive method of advertising placement is called "ROP" or "run of press." This means that the advertisement will be placed at the discretion of the newspaper. "Regular position" guarantees that a store's advertisements will be placed in the same position all the time. It is costlier than ROP, but readers eventually know where to find a store's advertisements. "Preferred position," the most costly, locates the advertisement in the most desirable spot in the newspaper for that particular ad. The position may be adjacent to a pertinent newspaper column. For example, men's sporting goods' advertisements would be more effective if placed next to a sportswriter's daily column. This positioning guarantees exposure to the appropriate readers.

Taking all these factors into consideration, a retailer is often wise to run a smaller advertisement positioned in the best location in a newspaper with a larger circulation than a larger ad without these important features. After careful examination of all the variables, the actual rate per line might not be the most important consideration.

Consumer Magazines.   On an overall basis, the magazine is extensively used by marketers, although retailers are not major users. Since magazines' trading areas generally extend beyond the bounds of the retailer's trading area, the cost per reader who is actually able to patronize the retail store is very high. Stores are

FIGURE 15–3
A cooperative advertisement. (*Courtesy:* Macy's.)

usually involved in advertising promotions that are planned in considerably less time than is necessary to meet a magazine's advertising deadline, therefore stores tend to avoid this form of advertising. Stores such as Saks Fifth Avenue, Lord & Taylor, and Macy's do spend some money on magazine advertising, but this can be considered an effort to gain prestige. Figure 15–3 features a magazine advertisement cooperatively sponsored by Macy's and Villeroy & Boch.

Magazine advertising may not be the retailers' medium, but it is the one consistently employed by manufacturers. The magazine has many advantageous features for them. First, the life of a magazine is longer than that of any other written medium. It is frequently passed from household to household, enabling it to reach many readers in addition to the actual subscriber. Second, each magazine has a clearly defined audience. Thus, specific markets are easy to reach. Rolls-Royce can advertise in a magazine that boasts an affluent readership. Magazines specializing in sports, hobbies, travel, and theater, for example, will appeal to manufacturers of merchandise that is of interest to their particular readers. Third, magazines frequently offer to their advertisers markets more limited than their total circulation by running ads only for specific regions. For example, marketers wishing only to appeal to the Northeastern part of the country may do so by having their ad run only in the issue distributed to this particular region rather than in every copy printed. In this case, the cost is less than for full coverage.

The magazine offerings around the world have expanded more than any other medium. Marketers no longer have to be restricted to the likes of the old general audience variety of the past. Magazines of every type and description and earmarked for specific audiences are being born everyday. *Lear's* is marketed to the over-40 female, for example, who has the dollars to spend but whose presence has sorely been neglected. Others such as *Interview,* a publication that features celebrity profiles, *Metropolis,* aimed at architects, *Taxi,* an Italian fashion format, and *L. A. Style,* a fashion magazine, enable the advertiser to reach a more delineated market.

Television.   Television advertising has enjoyed the fastest growth of any advertising medium. With the vast number of receivers in operation today, marketers can easily and quickly reach a very large audience. For almost every product the visual impression on television cannot be duplicated by any other medium. With the popularity of color (and the increase in color sales), marketers continue to expand their television advertising budgets. Only actual in-person viewing of the product, coupled with expertise in personal selling, can be more effective in the promotion of a product. The high cost of network television has restricted its use to the giants of the marketing industry. Manufacturers of automobiles, household products (e.g., detergents, toothpaste), and foods, as well as public utilities (e.g., AT&T) are the principal users of TV for advertising. Smaller retailers often use TV for promotion limited to their geographic area. Figure 15–4 shows an example of the California Raisin Advisory Board advertising program for television.

Radio.   The very nature of the radio today has changed its position in advertising. Once, the family congregated around the radio for entertainment, but their attention has shifted to television. Thus, the radio listening audience is now generally relegated to the automobile driver, the person at home tending to chores, and the teen-age market.

Although the medium is perhaps not as frequently employed by national

FIGURE 15–4   Television advertisement. (*Courtesy:* Foote, Cone & Belding.)

advertisers as it once was, it is still an excellent outlet for the small, local advertiser who wants to cover the immediate area but cannot afford the high cost of television. The teen-age segment of the population is an avid listening audience. Whether it is in an automobile, at the beach, or just at home, the teenager spends a good deal of time listening to the radio. Marketers of teen-age clothing, records, entertainment places, and so on, are able to get their messages across to potential customers through radio at a cost that is compatible with their advertising budgets.

In comparison with other media, broadcast advertising—radio and television—has been used sparingly in retailing. Some firms do invest a small portion of their sales promotion dollars in these media. Since the costs are very high and the audiences are spread across the country, advertisers do not sponsor entire programs; instead, they make use of a spot commercial either when a station identifies itself during program changes or as one of a great number of sponsors on various shows. By using the media in this way costs are minimized and messages are restricted to that segment of the viewing and listening audiences that is pertinent to the particular store. Spot commercials generally go only to preselected local audiences. This type of advertising is generally employed by stores wishing to announce special one-day sales, special events, or news of that nature.

Direct Advertising.   Direct advertising is the delivery of advertising materials such as merchandise brochures, sale announcements, letters, catalogs, booklets, and circulars by means of mail or hand distribution.

Marketers, both large and small, use direct advertising extensively. Among many of the benefits derived from the practice are that

1. Direct advertisements are often included in billing statements of both manufacturers and retailers. The manufacturer might send to the wholesaler or retailer a brochure that features new items. Retailers similarly whet their customers' appetite in this fashion. Without additional delivery expense, the advertisement can be distributed among all customers.
2. The company can appeal to a particular group of people. Mailing lists can be compiled from names of satisfied customers or purchased from commercial list houses that categorize the population according to such classifications as occupation, income, education, and religious background.
3. Direct advertisements, in comparison with other media, give the advertiser the prospect's undivided attention. Periodicals contain many advertisements in one issue, all of which compete for the prospect's eye.
4. Costs of direct advertising can be as varied as the budget allows. This is not true for newspaper, magazine, radio, and television rates. A simple message, for example, about a change in the manufacturer's discount allowances, can reach the customer at minimal expense via a postcard.

FIGURE 15–5
Direct-mail advertising.   (*Courtesy:* The Toro Company, Minneapolis, Minnesota.)

A serious disadvantage of direct advertising is that some pieces go straight into the wastebasket without being read. Another of the pitfalls is poor maintenance of mailing lists. If these lists are not continuously updated, a percentage of the mail will not be delivered. With guaranteed postage, the post office will return all undeliverable mail to the sender. Thus, if the company makes use of this service, it can easily clean up its mailing list. In an attempt to solicit new customers, businesses often prepare a mailing addressed to "occupant." This directs mail to a particular address but to no particular person. This system is used, for example, when a new company begins operation and wishes to announce its opening. Figure 15–5 is an example of a direct-mail piece.

The computer has had an enormous impact on direct-mail marketing. This has come about as a result of the following three capabilities of the machine:

1. The computer's tremendous capacity for storing information from which exact combinations can be selected allows the direct-mail piece to be sent to exactly the right prospect. Where in the past a direct-mail piece might have been sent to all homeowners in an area, it may now be sent only to those homeowners who have college-age children.
2. The computer's speed, analytical ability, and report-producing capacity provide means of correctly checking the effectiveness of the direct-mail promotion.
3. The computer's ability to personalize a direct-mail piece improves the chance of success of the direct-mail effort.

The trend in direct-mail is toward size and selectivity. Generally, the lists are compiled by specialists into massive data banks that are available for customers. For example,

1. R. L. Polk offers its customers a magnetic tape of all automobile owners, including the total dollar value of the cars owned by each family.
2. The Reuben H. Donnelley Corp. controls the Donnelley Quality Index master file, which contains fifty million names taken from auto registration lists and telephone directories.
3. By interviewing twenty-four million homeowners, R. L. Polk compiles its Household Census List, in which sixteen separate factors are supplied.

The foregoing examples represent merely a few of the many data banks that are available. A marketer with a plan for a direct-mail promotion aimed at a specific segment of the population is able to pinpoint from these massive lists the likeliest customers. This is one reason why the computer is increasing direct-mail response above the expected 2 percent level. Another effect of better selectivity in direct-mail promotion will be a considerable decrease in the amount of junk mail received by householders, since their receipt of promotional mail will be limited to those areas in which the computer has indicated an interest.

FIGURE 15–6
Cooperative advertisement.
(*Courtesy:* Institute of Out-
door Advertising.)

Billboards.   Marketers make relatively little use of billboard advertising. Billboards are permanently painted, or covered with prepared advertisements that
can be changed frequently, or they offer an illuminated and often animated
presentation. Billboard space is generally available on a rental basis. The cost is
dependent on size and location of the billboard. It is inexpensive to advertise in
this manner, as the cost per observer is little, but the audiences attracted are
usually moving quickly (in an automobile, for example) and are not selected on a
scientific basis. Magazines, on the other hand, have particular audiences and a
company can select the most appropriate one. The billboard medium does not

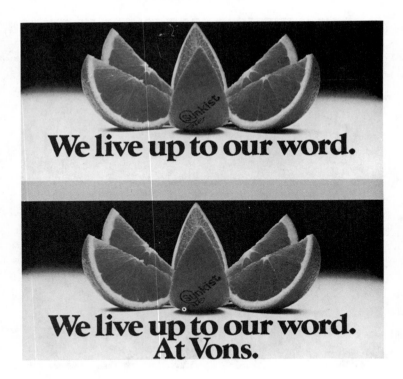

FIGURE 15–7
Billboard advertisement. (*Courtesy:* Institute of Outdoor Advertising.)

allow for such precise selection. The reader is aware of the billboard for only a limited period, so that the message must be very brief. Although there are certain disadvantages to billboard advertising, marketers do find it more or less valuable for the promotion of certain goods and services, such as automobiles, gasoline, motels, and restaurants. Figure 15–6 shows cooperative outdoor billboard advertising. Figure 15–7 shows billboard advertising.

Car Cards.   Travelers on public transportation witness a great number of advertisements during their rides. Colorful posters or cards occupy a great deal of space on train and bus walls. With the great number of riders using public transportation daily, businesses make extensive use of this form of advertising. Cigarette manufacturers, loan companies, local retail shops, and entertainment establishments such as theaters spend large sums on this medium.

In New York City, a producer of Broadway plays might select a railroad from a nearby suburb in which to place car-card advertisements, in order to gain new, distant audiences.

Car-card space is purchased in runs: full, half, quarter, and often double runs. A full run would place one card in each car of a train. A half run would place one card in every other car, and so on.

Messages must be brief, printed in color, and lettered sufficiently large to be seen by most people in the car. Since passengers usually remain in one place

FIGURE 15–8
Blimp advertising for Slice beverages. (*Courtesy:* PepsiCo, Inc.)

for an entire trip, careful planning is necessary to guarantee a maximum amount of exposure.

Planes and Blimps.   Some marketers have taken to the skies to advertise their goods and services. Beaches have long been places where sun worshippers have looked skyward to find planes pulling banners extolling the benefits of sun-screen preparations. Goodyear, with its long-time use of blimps, are regular features hovering over sports stadiums to the excitement of the spectators. Figure 15-8 features a blimp used by PepsiCo, Inc., to advertise Slice beverages.

Independent Shopping Publications. In many cities advertisers have been publishing independent periodicals primarily for the purpose of retail advertisements. The *Pennysaver* is an example of such a publication. It is almost completely devoted to the advertisement of the local retail store. It is extremely attractive for this segment of retailing in that it is less expensive than regular newspaper or broadcast advertising and reaches a clearly defined market in which the store's customers live. These publications are either mailed to prospects in a particular area or hand-delivered to the home, free of charge. Their success can be evidenced by the increasing number of shopping publications now in print. The *Pennysaver* is very successful on Long Island. Local merchants find it their best and least expensive advertising investment.

Testimonial Advertising

The use of personalities in the promotion of products is not new to marketers. The youth market has always had a penchant for using products that were endorsed by their heroes. What baseball glove would ever sell if the star athlete's signature weren't affixed to it? In both the print and broadcast media, a host of household names are endorsing the use of specific products. Senior citizens are told the virtues of products that may appeal to them by Art Linkletter, a former television celebrity with whom the retirees can relate. Yogi Berra, to the delight of kids of all ages, "drinks" Yoo-hoo and has made sales soar.

FIGURE 15–9 Michael J. Fox. (*Courtesy:* PepsiCo, Inc.)

The last few years have witnessed a high-tech look to television commercials that utilize many recognizable stars. Among the leaders in this form of promotion has been PepsiCo. Michael Jackson reportedly received $10 million for his role in promoting Pepsi-Cola, and Michael Tyson, large sums for his efforts in trying to stem Pepsi-Cola's slip in the diet soda market. Madonna has also performed for the company as has Michael J. Fox, whose entertaining commercials have significantly aided PepsiCo. Figure 15–9 features Michael J. Fox and Diet Pepsi.

Types of Advertising

Marketers employ two specific types of advertisement to promote their companies and products. One is promotional advertising, which tries to sell a specific product; the other is institutional advertising, which emphasizes the company name and promotes goodwill so that future sales will be generated for the company.

Promotional Advertising.   Manufacturers and retailers place the vast proportion of their advertising dollars in campaigns that promote specific products. The promotional ads are in both print and broadcast media. The intention of these ads is to boost sales on the products which are advertised. Figure 15–10 features a print promotional ad for BMW's 5 series, the family size, four-door car. Sales results are easily measured with the use of promotional advertising.

Institutional Advertising.   Many companies use a portion of their budgets to present a favorable image to their consumer markets by underscoring the company's awareness and concern for social issues. Figure 15–11 depicts one of the numerous institutional ads Coors uses to show that it is more than merely bent on making beer sales. Figure 15–12 features a television commercial by the Dupont Company that centers upon the plight of Vietnam veterans. In Figure 15–13 a retail institutional advertisement features a change in company policy.

The success of the institutional advertisement cannot be measured as easily as can that of its promotional counterpart. Its effectiveness to the company can be determined over a long period of time.

Advertising Effectiveness

The effectiveness of its advertising is vital to the growth of a company. Evaluating the effectiveness is usually the task of the marketing research department or of an outside research agency. Although it is important to receive advice from experts concerning the effectiveness of advertising, this source alone is not sufficient for a truly scientific measurement.

Advertisements and their effectiveness may be measured at three distinct periods: prior to publication, while shown to the potential market, or after presentation. There are a number of tests to measure effectiveness. They are

The typical BMW engineer is a **THE BMW 5-SERIES.** (AutoWeek Magazine). This athletic-family man with a genuine **THE PERFECT RECONCILIATION** ically-shaped BMW coddles passion for building and driv- **BETWEEN LOVE OF FAMILY** the senses with rich leather ing extraordinary automobiles. **AND PASSION FOR DRIVING,** seating, and ride comfort So it's not surprising that BMW's 5-Series deemed the new standard in its class. And it is the family-size four-door that "effectively re- reassures the mind with superior anti-lock calibrates the performance sedan benchmark" disc brakes and a unitized steel body that is

© 1988 BMW of North America, Inc. The BMW trademark and logo are registered.

designed to absorb 35 percent more impact en- suspension mate your tires to the curving pave-ergy than Federal law requires. ment—all this must be experienced.

But what this car does best is exalt the The experience is yours by contacting your spirit. The sweet song of its in-line 6-cylinder BMW dealer and test driving the 5-Series sedan. engine, the feel of the road transmitted through The car you need, reconciled with its precise power steering, the pull of gravity the car that you really want. as its 50/50 balance and patented independent **THE ULTIMATE DRIVING MACHINE:**

THE ST. FRANCIS YACHT CLUB.

FIGURE 15-10 Magazine promotional advertisement. (*Courtesy:* BMW of North America.)

Unemployment is also hell.

At Coors we feel a strong commitment to the veterans of this country. And we believe it is both our responsibility and our privilege to provide an opportunity for them to attain the kind of life they fought so hard to preserve.

In addition to being this year's American Legion's National Large Employer of Veterans, Coors has been honored by the Veterans of Foreign Wars, the Disabled American

© 1988 Adolph Coors Company, Golden Colorado 80401 · Brewer of Fine Quality Beers Since 1873.

Veterans, and received the Secretary of Labor's Recognition Award for being top employer in the United States in veteran hiring.

We hope other companies will follow in Coors' footsteps and make jobs available to our veterans. After all, we counted on them. Why shouldn't they count on us?

Coors

Getting together with Veterans.

FIGURE 15–11   An institutional print ad. (*Courtesy:* Adolph Coors Company.)

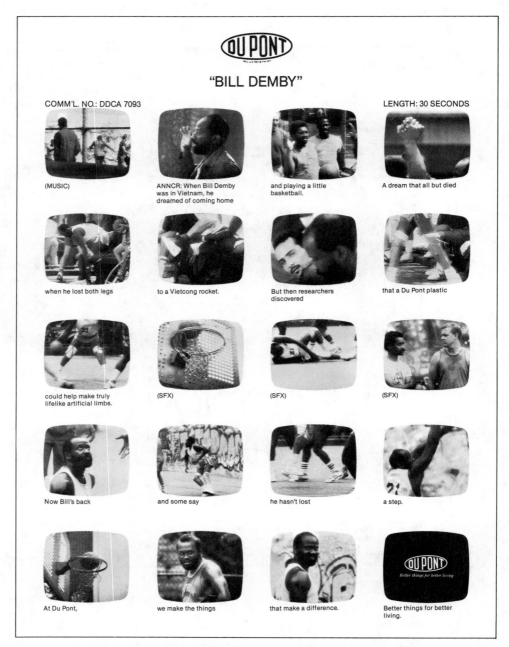

FIGURE 15–12 An institutional television commercial. (*Courtesy:* DuPont Company.)

Tomorrow, every Sears in America will be closed to make the biggest change in our history.

We're lowering prices on over 50,000 items in our stores and catalogs.

On Wednesday, March 1,
Sears will open at noon
with a whole new way to shop.

SEARS
*Your money's worth
and a whole lot more.*

FIGURE 15–13
Retail institutional adver-
tisement. (*Courtesy:* Sears,
Roebuck, and Company.)

1. *Sales results tests,* which try to measure the sales volume that will directly result from the advertising campaign that is being tested.
2. *Readership tests* (sometimes known as recall tests), which involve showing all or part of an advertisement to the reader in an attempt to have him or her recall all or part of the ad, such as the sponsor's name.
3. *Coupon measurement,* tests in which readers are asked to return a coupon from an advertisement if they are interested in more information, a free

sample, and so on. Count of the returned coupons shows whether or not the ad was effective.

4. *Comparison measurements,* which use consumer panels to select the best possible ads for a company.

Only scientific measurement will guarantee the effectiveness of advertising, which is both expensive and valuable to the marketer.

SPECIAL PROMOTIONS

As the title of this section implies, special promotions are events that take place for special reasons or purposes. A food producer might choose to introduce its product to the consumer via taste sampling at supermarkets. The cosmetic manufacturer often chooses makeup demonstrations and applications at major department stores as a means of product introduction. Some of these promotions are annual events that prove to result in regular increases in business for that time period. Whether it's the one-shot deal of fashion shows, demonstrations or sampling programs, or regular periodic presentations whose success warrants repeat performances, special promotions are being utilized with more frequency by marketers than ever before.

The Annual Event

Many companies, most notably retailers, elect to present promotions that are truly special events whose arrival is eagerly awaited by consumers. One of

FIGURE 15–14
Macy's Herald Square main floor flower show display. (*Courtesy:* Macy's.)

EVENTS IN THE CORNER SHOP ON 9
DURING MACY'S 15TH ANNUAL FLOWER SHOW

Sunday, March 19:

Elvin McDonald takes you on a visual tour of the BROOKLYN BOTANIC GARDENS, at 1:00 P.M.

Bunny Williams discussess interior decorating, followed by tea, at 3:00 P.M.

Monday, March 20:

Artist Margo Davis autographs her floral posters at 1:00 P.M.

Tuesday, March 21:

Deborah Reich, author of *The Complete Book of Topiary,* discusses and demonstrates topiary, at 1:00 P.M.

Wednesday, March 22:

Ken Druse, author of *The Natural Garden* and Garden Editor at *House Beautiful,* speaks on American gardening, at 1:00 P.M.

Thursday, March 23:

Allison Kyle Leopold, author of *Victorian Splendor,* discusses Victorian interiors and Victorian houses open to the public, at 1:00 P.M.

Friday, March 24:

Susan Feller, of Garden Works Design Associates, discusses urban gardens, 1:00 P.M.

FIGURE 15–15   Calendar for Macy's flower show, 1989. (*Courtesy:* Macy's.)

Saturday, March 25:	Lecturer Marvin Schwartz, of the Metropolitan Museum of Art, discusses French and English Victorian furniture, at 3:00 P.M.
Sunday, March 26:	Macy's will be closed on Easter Sunday.
Monday, March 27:	Abbie Zabar, author of *The Potted Herb,* discusses herb topiaries and demonstrates their use in recipes, at 1:00 P.M.
Tuesday, March 28:	Terry Sideman, author of *Decorating Rich,* discusses decorating around a single piece of antique furniture, at 1:00 P.M.
Wednesday, March 29:	Katherine Whiteside, author of *Antique Flowers,* discusses the use of old fashioned flowers in contemporary settings, at 1:00 P.M.
Thursday, March 30:	John Earl, of the flower boutique "By Special Arrangement," will demonstrate how to arrange fresh flower topiaries.
Friday, March 31:	Jim Morgan, of Ireland-Gannon Associates, presents creative ways to use perennials in window box displays, at 1:00 P.M.
Saturday, April 1:	Sara Slavin, author of *On Flowers,* presents a multitude of nontraditional uses for flowers.

FIGURE 15–15 *(Continued)*

the retailing giants who sponsors a host of these presentations is Macy's. Along with the nationally famous Thanksgiving Day Parade is Macy's Flower Show, an annual in-store feature that is used to herald the spring season. Not only does the store transform itself into a garden of flowers, but it also prepares numerous events that add to the customer's pleasure and interest. It should be kept in mind that this special promotion and others are for the purpose of increasing customer awareness and ultimate purchase of the company's offerings. Figures 15–14 and 15–15 feature Macy's Herald Square decorated for the flower show and an events calendar for the 1989 promotion, respectively.

Holiday Celebrations

Every holiday season holds the promise of a shopping surge if the event is properly promoted. Christmas, Easter, Mother's Day, and Valentine's Day are times when businesses capitalize on the occasion. Figure 15–16 depicts Macy's Valentine's Day Pink Panther promotion.

Fashion Shows

The display of fashions on live models has been a regular sales promotion device for manufacturers as well as retail stores. Executives may express the opinion that the presentation of a fashion show is primarily for prestigious purposes; however, companies do achieve immediate business from them. You need only watch the audience rise from their chairs to rush to the racks of clothing after a showing of fashions to realize the instant success of the show in terms of sales. Retail store buyers spend a great deal of time attending the season's openings, both here and abroad, in preparation for their buying needs. Even if a fashion show does not result in immediate sales, it is valuable in that it exposes fashion merchandise to potential buyers in a lively and exciting manner unobtainable through any other medium. With properly conceived and executed production, appetites are likely to be whetted for future sales.

Demonstrations

Demonstrations are not new to business managers. What can better sell typewriters than to show how they can be utilized? Business shows dramatize the use of the computer by demonstrating the remarkable amount and variety of data that it can instantaneously sort and feed to executives. These demonstrations are often a result of the combined efforts of manufacturers, wholesalers, retailers, and other businesses. Some are only one-day events; others are major special events, requiring a large amount of space and a number of demonstrators. Very often, Abraham & Straus, a leading Eastern department store, participates with local restaurants and fine bakeries in week-long baking demonstrations. At the main store and all the branches customers are invited to see outstanding demonstrations and taste the end results. This technique is suc-

FIGURE 15–16
Pink Panther promotion. (*Courtesy:* Macy's.)

cessful in drawing throngs of shoppers to the stores. The cooperation of all the companies involved guarantees a successful event. Store sales usually increase, which sometimes means new customers and increased sales for the participating restaurants and bakeries. Figure 15–17 shows a demonstrator showing a consumer Tylenol's new tamperproof package.

Sampling

A method of promoting sales very closely related to demonstrating is to attract prospective customers through the use of samples. Sampling is similar to

FIGURE 15–17
Demonstrator showing consumer Tylenol's
new tamperproof packaging. (*Courtesy:* Mc-
Neil Consumer Products Company.)

demonstrating, in that it shows the customer how actually to use the merchandise. The major difference between the two methods is that in the one case the
merchandise is used by a company representative and in the other by the customer personally. The decision as to whether to sell by demonstration or sample
is based on the characteristics of the merchandise. Expensive merchandise that
requires skill to operate is sold by demonstration. Products that can be inexpensively sampled, and the use of which requires no previous training, can be very
effectively sold by means of samples.

   The importance of the sample method is that it allows the customer to
actually touch the product. Depending on the merchandise, sampling can effectively take place in the store or in the customer's home. Food products, stationery, candies, and yard goods are generally given out by salespeople in the stores.
Soap powders, razor blades, and swatches of material for shirts, bedclothes,
sheets, and so on are frequently mailed to the customer's home. As long as the
cost of the sample is relatively low, sampling is a very effective way to sell
merchandise and get publicity.

FIGURE 15–18
Coupon promotion for Tylenol. (*Courtesy:* McNeil Consumer Products Company.)

Premiums

The use of premiums, that is, the process of giving special merchandise (products that are not regularly offered for sale) as an inducement to buy goods, is not as popular as it used to be. When used, premiums may be free or offered at substantial savings, for example, a $3 pair of pantyhose may be purchased for 50 cents plus one coupon from a producer's package. Whatever the premium plan—and there is a constantly growing variety of plans—when properly handled, it can offer a means of stimulating sales. Figure 15–18 shows a coupon promotion for Tylenol.

Trading Stamps

Although trading stamps have lost much of their popularity, they are sometimes used as an inducement to buy. Stamps are given at the time merchandise is purchased. The rate varies, but the general practice is ten stamps for each dollar's worth of merchandise. In slow periods, double the regular number of stamps is offered as means of further motivation. Stamps are pasted in books and redeemed for premium merchandise that may be inspected in catalogs, or even more closely at redemption centers.

The cost of trading stamps to the retailer is about two-hundredths to three-hundredths cent per stamp, plus the time involved in handling. This can be a fairly high cost to large-volume stores, but the use of trading stamps builds sales volume by attracting customers who might otherwise shop at a competitive store.

To the consumer, trading stamps offer a means of savings to get premium merchandise in a somewhat painless fashion. That the books of stamps have a definite value has been proven by many studies, which show the books to have a value of $3.21 in traditional stores or $2.82 in discount stores.

The question most often raised among customers of stores that feature trading stamps is, "Am I paying for these stamps in terms of higher prices?" The answer, of course, is yes. On the other hand, the customer pays for all store promotions (such as advertising) with no questions asked.

Whether or not a store should handle trading stamps is a problem that requires careful analysis. However, it is likely that of two otherwise equal stores, the one handling trading stamps will attract more customers.

VISUAL MERCHANDISING

Visual merchandising, unlike advertising, is a visual presentation of the goods to be sold. Manufacturers play an important role in the preparation of point-of-purchase display materials for the retail outlets to whom they sell. In some industries, for example the liquor industry, manufacturers (or wholesale distributors) take care of display services. Display personnel travel from store to store to put up the displays. Other manufacturers make the display materials, complete with easy-to-follow instructions and photographs, available to the retailer. For example, Russell Stover, a manufacturer of packaged chocolates, prepares such a package. To the new marketing student, the displaying of merchandise might seem to be the sole responsibility of the retailer. This is not true, because the manufacturer, to sell merchandise, must make certain that all outlets are successful. By becoming involved in display, the visual presentation of the product to the consumer is improved.

In the highly competitive and profit-producing cosmetic industry, manufacturers spend vast sums on point-of-purchase displays. Figure 15–19 features a self-contained product and display unit that offers Performing Preference by L'Oreal.

Nevertheless, the retailer plays the major role in visual merchandising. For many years retailers have considered windows (and counters) to be silent salespeople. With the practice of self-selection in stores throughout the country, greater emphasis is now placed on display, or visual merchandising, than ever before.

The display must attract the attention of the buying public. This may be achieved by exciting use of color, dramatic lighting effects, or motion. The great annual event at Lord & Taylor's in New York at Christmastime (dancing dolls in the window, or a live Santa coming down the chimney) is an example of an in-motion display.

In addition to attracting attention, a satisfactory display must hold the individual's interest in much the same way as does a newspaper or magazine advertisement. It is not enough to stop the reader; it must make him or her investigate further. Interest is held by the timeliness of the display, the appeal of the merchandise, or the information contained in the message on the accompanying show card.

Next, the display must be exciting enough to arouse the desire to further

FIGURE 15–19
Point-of-purchase display by L'Oreal. (*Courtesy:* Cos-mair, Inc.)

examine the merchandise (by asking to see it, try it on, and so on). Marketers have long argued over whether display creates or arouses desires. They should settle for the awakening of the individual's interest.

Finally, with the enormous increase in shoplifting, retailers must pay attention to securing the merchandise in their interior displays. Figure 15–20 shows an interior display that employs an antitheft locking display system.

When window display is effective, the customer will enter the retail store. Then, either creative interior displays will take over, or perhaps the salesperson will answer questions unanswered by the window display alone.

PUBLICITY

According to the American Marketing Association, "publicity is the nonpersonal stimulation of demand for a product, service, or business unit by planting com-

FIGURE 15–20
An interior display that employs an antitheft
locking display system. (*Courtesy:* Securax Enterprises, Inc.)

mercially significant news about it in a published medium or obtaining favorable
presentation of it upon radio, TV, or stage that is not paid for by the sponsor."

The issue is promotion without cost. For example, a new automobile might
be produced that is so outstanding that the local newspaper or automotive
magazine will review it. A retail store's holiday parade might get attention on a
television news broadcast. The larger companies employ public relations staffs
charged with the responsibility of preparing releases about their offerings that
might attract the media and, therefore, customer interest. The free publicity a
business receives is not always kind, and could work adversely. For example,
recent newspaper coverage of the effect of disposable containers on the environment could hurt the sales of a company that utilized this type of packaging.

POINT-OF-PURCHASE MEDIA

The retail establishment has become a battleground where manufacturers are vying for their share of the consumers' dollar. Now, more than ever before, marketers are trying unique methods to attract customers to their products. While the mix used involves display, advertising, and special promotions, the promotional creativity has reached new heights.

For many years, food distributors, for example, resorted to gaining maximum exposure through the best shelf space and aisle displays for their products. Signs featuring their products were mainstays in the stores. Today a host of new point-of-purchase media have settled into the supermarket arena. Along with the signs and banners have come the next generation of promotion.

Video displays on shopping carts are in evidence at supermarkets throughout the country. Each cart is equipped with a monitor that focuses the shopper's attention to specific products.

Kiosks are placed at checkout counters that offer recipes, promotional coupons, and other attention-getting devices.

In-store radio features a commercial network. Consumers hear a variety of product announcements as they walk through the store aimed at specific products.

Major food producers are spending enormous sums on the point-of-purchase media. Thomas J. Lipton is currently using Actmedia's Aisle Vision, which features ads mounted on supermarket aisle directories. Campbell Soup Company has interactive video kiosks that display recipes utilizing Campbell's products and maps directing shoppers to their aisles. Kraft, Inc., is experimenting with the "Checkout Robot," which involves do-it-yourself checkouts that feature numerous computerized promotional materials.

Supermarkets are not the only retail environments with point-of-purchase media. Major department and specialty stores have long been the users of devices to attract customer attention. In-store video is perhaps the tool that is bringing the best results to this retailer group. Designers spend enormous sums that present their lines on videotape and send the tapes to the stores for use in the departments. A customer can watch these presentations, spot an item of interest, and find it on the rack. Some major designers of expensive couture merchandise prepare videos of their entire collection for store showings. Since the garments are so costly, and impossible for retailers to stock in complete selections, the customer can view the tape and have the store order a sample. In this way, inventories are kept to a minimum.

Liz Claiborne's magic mirror, which enables a customer to stand in front of a special mirror that superimposes outfits on the viewer saves a great deal of time. Instead of trying on each style, the customer only tries those that appeal to her in the mirror.

Point-of-purchase displays of this new generation have passed the $500 million level. With the success already realized, the industry hopes to double that figure.

Important Points in the Chapter

1. Sales promotion refers to such mass communications media as advertising, special promotions, display, and publicity. Personal selling is excluded, since its appeal is to individuals, whereas the others appeal to groups.

2. Promotion budgets are based on three measurements. They are percentage of sales, units of sales, and task to be performed.

3. Newspapers receive the largest part of the retail advertising dollar; magazines account for the largest part of the manufacturer's advertising allocation.

4. Television is presently accounting for the fastest growth in advertising.

5. Manufacturers spend large sums for special promotions such as fashion shows, demonstrations, samples, premiums, and trading stamps.

6. Visual merchandising is the visual presentation of goods to be sold. Although retailers play the major role in the display of merchandise, manufacturers become involved in the preparation of point-of-purchase display materials for retailers.

7. Publicity, unlike the other forms of promotion, is free. It comes as the result of effective advertising, visual merchandising, or special promotions.

Review Questions

1. What other forms of sales promotion are there besides advertising?

2. On what bases do companies plan their advertising budgets?

3. Discuss the term *task method*.

4. Define *advertising*. How does advertising differ from personal selling?

5. In what principal way does retail advertising differ from that engaged in by the manufacturer?

6. How does the advertising agency receive its remuneration?

7. Which of the advertising media is used most commonly by retailers? What advantage does this medium offer to retail stores?

8. Determine the milline rate if the rate per line is $0.35 and the newspaper's circulation is 500,000.

9. Differentiate between *ROP* and *preferred position* in newspaper advertising.

10. Why do manufacturers generally limit their newspaper advertising expenditure? Why do they extensively invest in magazine advertising?

11. Which of the media has had the greatest growth in recent years? Why?

12. Billboard advertising is infrequently used by marketers. Why?

13. Define *full run* and *half run.*

14. Which marketing institution uses the sampling method in the promotion of new products? What characteristic must a product have in order to be promoted via this method?

15. Discuss the importance of trading stamps in marketing.

16. Cite some examples of the use of premiums in the promotion of goods.

17. How do visual merchandising and advertising differ?

18. To what extent do manufacturers become involved in display?

19. Define *publicity.* How does it differ from the other sales promotion techniques?

Case Problems

Case Problem 1

Childcraft, Inc., has just started business as manufacturers of a full line of toys. Areas of concern, such as the number of different items to produce, the prices to charge for each item, and the consumer market to be reached, have been discussed. In fact, just about all the pertinent questions relating to the marketing of a new line have been examined, and plans are under way for the start of production.

Ms. Santos, marketing manager for Childcraft, has been unable to come to a decision concerning the promotion of the line. Specifically, she is uncertain about where and how to promote the line and about exactly how much should be set aside for the promotional budget.

The company is new, so it would be impossible to make use of past company experience. Also, budgeting is difficult, since the firm's newness eliminates the percentage-of-sales and units-of-sale methods for the determination of an appropriate budget.

Questions

1. Where should Ms. Santos look for help in deciding how to promote the line?

2. Where would you suggest that Childcraft advertise? Why?

3. Which technique should be used in determining the promotion budget? Discuss the areas to be investigated.

Case Problem 2

David's Department Store has been in operation for twenty years. It is a conventional-type business, with a main store located in a downtown shopping area and five branch stores in suburban shopping centers. For the past few years, David's has suffered a steady decline in business. The problem seems to be attributable to the number of discount operations that have opened in competition with David's. Since the store is service oriented, management has decided that it would be both inappropriate and unprofitable to lower prices in order to regain lost sales.

Mr. Clements, senior vice-president in charge of operations, has charged the store's promotion departments with the responsibility of reattracting old customers and motivating new business.

Questions

1. Which promotion departments should be involved in the new assignment?
2. Since price cannot be stressed, what should their advertising appeal to?
3. What kinds of special events could the store plan in order to attract customers?

16

DIRECT MARKETING

Learning Objectives

Upon completion of the chapter, you will be able to:

1. Define direct marketing and differentiate between direct and traditional marketing.

2. Discuss databases, including their importance and methods of accumulating and enhancing.

3. Describe the various media available to direct marketers, including the importance of each and their advantages and disadvantages.

4. Explain the importance of business-to-business direct marketing, emphasizing the reason for its importance.

5. Write a short essay on the fit between direct marketing and research. Include examples and their importance.

SHARPER IMAGE

When Richard Thalheimer graduated from college in the early 1970s he moved to San Francisco where he thought an opportunity for success could be found. Unfortunately, the West was not the land of opportunity for him. He couldn't find a job. Finally, he landed one selling office supplies door to door. Someone suggested mail order and he started a company, The Ribbon House, that sold office supplies through mail order. This was somewhat successful, but despairing of ever making big money in office supplies, he went to law school at night. Upon graduation he practiced law for a year.

He still liked the possibilities of mail order and attended a consumer electronics show in Las Vegas to look for items to merchandise. Richard Thalheimer was a jogger, and at the show he found an item that he liked. Seiko made a digital runner's watch that sold for $250.00. Richard found a knock-off that he could sell for $69.50. He selected *Runner's World*, a monthly magazine for joggers for his direct-response advertisement. He ran a half-page ad for a year. The first month brought in three thousand orders—$90,000 in profits.

He was off and running. In the following year he organized the Sharper Image Company. In 1979 the first catalog showed twenty-five items including the runner's watch. In his first year, the catalogs plus some direct marketing ads grossed $9 million.

Today the catalogs advertise 150 sophisticated novelty items and go to 2.5 million homes monthly.

Sharper Image opened its first retail store in 1983 and has been averaging about ten openings a year since then. The combined store and catalog sales volume exceeds $100 million annually. Not bad for an ex–door-to-door salesman barely 40 years old.

INTRODUCTION

The American Marketing Association's committee on definitions describes marketing as the performance of business activities that direct the flow of goods and services from the producer to the consumer or user (customer). Direct marketing provides the same service but includes the use of a database. This additional provision requires the following:

1. The accumulation of lists of customers and prospective customers and a history of their purchasing activities
2. An analysis of the effectiveness of the results of advertising in a variety of media, particularly direct advertising
3. Provision for continuing interaction with customers usually by mail or telephone

The principal difference, then, between marketing and direct marketing is the building and maintenance of a constantly updated database. Part of the database takes the form of lists of customers and their sales histories and purchasing habits. This provides for one-on-one interaction between salespersons and customers, usually by direct mail or telephone. The database also carefully analyzes the results of advertising by measuring the response in terms of inquiries and sales to advertising in various media, and even to the wording used in the various advertising pieces.

The Direct Marketing Association provides the following definition:

> Direct marketing is an interactive system of marketing which uses one or more advertising media to affect a measurable response and/or transaction at any location.

To clarify this definition, it is necessary to understand certain key words and phrases. Interactive means one-on-one communication between buyer and seller. Measurable response requires that the response to the sales pitch can be studied and analyzed, so that the product or the pitch can be adjusted, improved, or if necessary, discarded.

Essentially, direct marketing involves selling which may result in a one-on-one discussion between seller and customer. Here's an example: General Electric dominates the light bulb market, and therefore retail shelf space. Sylvania, a competitor, cannot improve their market share the traditional way, the shelf space is simply not available to them. To offset this, they designed a kiosk requiring two square feet of shelf space. It contains a catalog showing all six thousand of their lighting products, and a toll-free telephone number. The customer can thumb through the catalog, select an interesting lighting system, and call to place an order or get more information. As a further inducement to retailers, Sylvania does not require the store to carry an inventory of its products and pays a commission of about 25 percent on every sale.

Direct marketing is often referred to as direct-response marketing; that is, the customer responds to the offer by telephone (usually an 800 toll-free number), letter, preprinted card, coupon, or catalog order form.

Since the 1950s direct marketing has grown enormously in importance on the marketing scene. It is no coincidence that a comparable growth in the use of computers by marketers has taken place, since direct marketing requires the accumulation, manipulation, and storage of masses of data, a chore perfectly matched to a computer's capabilities. The increasing success of direct marketing ensures its continued growth. Another important reason for the continued increase in the growth of direct marketing has been the widespread use of the 800 telephone number. This ability of a prospective customer to call the seller free of charge not only reduces the cost of purchases, but also allows the salesperson the opportunity to talk to a mildly interested customer who might not have called at all were it not for the toll-free feature offered by the 800 number. It is interesting to note that Sears, in an attempt to reverse the sagging fortunes of its $4 billion catalog business, has begun testing toll-free 800 telephone numbers.

The growing number of working women has also helped the growth of direct marketing. Women, traditionally the principal buyers in the family, no longer have the time or inclination to spend their now-limited free time to shop. It is much easier to buy from a catalog, a home-shopping TV show, direct-mail piece, and so forth.

DATABASES

The principal reason for the success of direct marketing is that they know their customers. They have a database. They have names, addresses, size of purchases, how much they spend, when they buy, how often, and so on. In contrast, supermarkets, department stores, in fact most retailers know little other than the addresses of their charge customers. The more the direct marketer knows about the customer, that is, the more data in the database, the greater the chance of success.

Customer Databases

The information required of a successful database depends upon the characteristics of the product to be sold and will differ with each type of business. However, there are certain universal basic requirements. These are

> Name
> Address
> Telephone number
> Manner in which the prospect was found (media used, etc.)
> Date found
> Sales made
> > Date
> Items sold
> Amount of each sale
> Total sales
> Cost of acquiring customer

Once this basic information is stored in a computerized database, a world of information is available. For example, the information can be manipulated by the computer to provide

1. The effectiveness of various types of media in getting prospects or sales.
2. The cost comparisons of various methods of obtaining leads.
3. The frequency and size of purchase that were the result of various media advertising.

4. The success of the product by geographic area (Zip codes). Where specific Zip codes are particularly successful, a direct-mail piece to that area might be considered.

5. By knowing the specific items a customer purchased, follow-up sales might be in order. For example, someone who purchased a how-to book on wiring might be interested in a how-to book on carpentry. A direct-mail piece to such people might be considered.

6. The profitability and total sales to each customer give an indication of customer loyalty and confidence. This can be used for special sales, bonus offerings, and similar sales drives.

This list could go on and on, and as more information is accumulated in the database, the manipulation of data and possible uses available to the marketer increase as well. If a life insurance company knows the age of its policyholders, it can send a direct-mail piece to those approaching age 65 advising them of its supplementary Medicare insurance policy. This is called cross-selling, and it is very important to direct marketers. What better source of leads can a computer software company have than a list of recent computer purchasers? Moreover, if the software company's database includes information on the ages of the purchaser's children, the chances of developing a successful direct-mail piece to sell educational software programs to computer owners with small children are greatly increased.

Enhanced Databases

As the basic database is expanded with more and more information, it is called an enhanced database. The material added to the basic database is usually that which is specifically required for the direct selling of the particular product involved. For example, if the product involved is a luxury item such as a Mercedes Benz automobile, the database should include potential customers who can afford such a car and whose life-style might make them a likely target.

MAILING LISTS

So far our discussion has been confined to the importance and uses of databases. We must now turn to the problem of accumulating the information. The raw database information is called a list, that is, a list of potential customers who have a characteristic in common. Thus, a group of people who earn over $100,000 is called a list. Lists can be divided into two categories, internal and external.

Internal Lists

Internal lists or house files consist of customers, former customers, prospects, and people who have made inquiries. They are the most important part of the total list because people who have already bought are the ones most likely to buy again. Where the internal list is large enough, it should be further broken down into such areas as type of product and cost of purchase on the theory that the buyer who buys expensive merchandise is likely to continue to buy expensive items and one who buys tools is likely to buy more tools.

External Lists

In addition to the internal lists there are thousands of external lists available for rent to the direct marketer. These are generally obtained through list brokers and may contain millions of names and addresses of individuals having in common a specific interest, characteristic, activity, or life-style. For example, lists are available of individuals who have the following characteristics in common:

Age	Entertainment preferences
Income	Reading preferences
Family size	Ethnic/religious background
Hobbies	Frequent mail-order buyers
Sex	Just about any other characteristic

In other words, if a product is to be targeted to a single woman, living alone, aged 30–40, who jogs, likes serious music, eats gourmet foods, earns over $50,000 per year, there is a list or combination of lists available. The possibilities are almost endless. It is even possible to buy a competitor's list. Incidentally, research has shown that the loss to the renting company of renting a list to a competitor ranges from none at all to very little.

Why do companies rent lists? There is a lot of money to be made by doing so. Consider a magazine that has a million subscribers. It charges $85 per thousand for list rentals, that is, $1,000 \times \$85 = \$85,000$ per one-shot rental, and it may rent their list 20 or more times per year.

Lists usually are rented under the following terms:

1. Rented lists may be used only once. They may not be copied or kept.
2. The mailing piece for which the use was obtained must be cleared by the list owner. No changes may be made without approval.
3. If the list is to be broken down in any way such as by sex, Zip code number, and so on, there are extra charges.

When lists are combined, as in the case of using more than one external list or adding external lists to internal lists, care must be taken to avoid the duplication of names. This will avoid the unnecessary cost of mailing, telephoning, and so on. Also, the person on the list will be annoyed at receiving the same mailing piece more than once. Elimination of duplication is a fairly simple computer operation, but has the effect of increasing the cost per thousand of the list since duplicates cannot be used.

External lists are used once in accordance with the rental agreement. Internal lists, on the other hand, are used over and over again. This leads to another problem because lists constantly change over time. People die, move, get married, and change their buying habits. This necessitates that lists be constantly monitored and updated. The use to which the list is put is usually very expensive, and a stale list can be costly.

List Testing

The costs of catalogs, direct-mail pieces, telephone calls, and the like can be considerable. Therefore, it is common to test the effectiveness of a list before it is used in total. Generally this is done by testing a portion of the list before the major thrust and carefully analyzing the results. Then if the results prove successful, the full campaign is begun.

CATALOGS

As has been discussed, direct marketing has witnessed considerable growth in recent years. Nowhere has this been more evident than in catalog sales. Industry experts estimated that ten thousand companies will mail about eleven billion catalogs to retail customers this year, almost three times the amount sent ten years ago. Many factors are responsible for this, including the importance of convenience shopping, reduced cost of toll-free telephone calls, widespread credit card use, and improved mailing lists. In addition, catalog retailers have a cost advantage over traditional retail stores. Rather than an expensive downtown or suburban location, Lands' End's distribution center is in a cow pasture and L. L. Bean is located in Freeport, Maine.

While total industry sales have been booming, individually many are feeling a competitive pinch, and many giants like General Mills are bowing out. The problem is that anything the successful operators can do can be easily copied, and hundreds of smaller, lesser known companies are jumping in. The result is that consumers are being drowned in catalogs, and many simply discard them, unread.

One outstanding example of success in consumer catalog selling is Lands' End. (In an early catalog the printer put the apostrophe in the wrong place and the company went along with it.) The major portion of its business is casual clothing and luggage. It is located in Dodgeville, Wisconsin, from there it sends out about eight million catalogs (one in ten households nationwide), and has been increasing its mailing list by about one million each year. On a good day it receives 30,000 calls, of which 1,500 are taken between midnight and 6:00 A.M. On its best day 1,350 operators took 78,500 calls. Each operator has a computer terminal and can give information in less than 2 seconds on the inventory status of the order—whether it is on hand, if not when it will be, and if necessary suggest alternative merchandise. Lands' End, like many catalog merchants, is a specialty cataloger offering a limited line of goods. L. L. Bean is another specializing in camping gear and outdoor clothing.

The nation's largest catalog retailer is Sears, Roebuck and Company, which does about $4 billion of business annually and has been facing tough times in recent years. It still sends about 15 million catalogs annually, but has been slow to face the competitive challenge of its more aggressive competitors. For example, it is just now converting to 800 toll-free lines, and until now catalog buying has been handled by traditional store buyers. Management is finally beginning to use special buyers. Sears's catalog is a full-line rather than a specialty one. There are very few full-line catalogers, among them Spiegel and J. C. Penney.

One type of catalog widely used by major retailers is the vendor catalog. In these catalogs the company that produces the goods permits the retailer to deduct an "advertising allowance" from its bill in return for having its goods displayed in its catalog. The advantage of this widely used idea is that the vendors pay the cost of the catalog. The disadvantage is that the vendors end up with too much say in the makeup of the catalog.

The catalog area of direct marketing is in an extremely treacherous position. It is very competitive, and as more and more catalogs overstuff consumer mailboxes, less and less attention is paid to them. The market is becoming oversaturated. One way to offset this is by opening traditional retail outlets. Many large catalogers have owned retail outlets to dispose of their slow-moving goods for years, but now there seems to be a trend toward traditional retail outlets. It started with Sears, which began traditional retail stores in the late 1920s and now does some 80 percent of its business through these stores. Now, such catalogers as Sharper Image, Brookstone, Banana Republic, and Royal Silk are opening retail stores. Banana Republic sells its khakis, fatigues, and bush jackets in forty-nine stores, while Brookstone shows its unusual and hard-to-find tools in sixty-four outlets. It works nicely since the catalogs advertise the stores and the stores provide mailing lists for the catalogs. Brookstone's indicates that 25 percent of its mailing list is obtained through its retail outlets. It should be understood that there are considerable differences between mail-order and traditional retailing, and not all stores opened by catalogers are successful. Successful catalogers do not automatically become successful traditional retailers. R. S., Inc., a mail-order retailer of old-style hardware and lighting fixtures, recently closed six of its eighteen stores.

DIRECT MAIL

Direct mail is an advertising medium and perhaps the most important of the communications media available to direct marketers. Once a database is established, direct marketers find that it can be the least costly means of communicating with their customers or prospects. The mass media such as newspaper or magazine reach huge numbers of mostly disinterested readers. Direct mail, on the other hand, permits individual selection of consumers whose characteristics are those that have been targeted. This results in a lower cost per actual prospect.

There are other advantages to the use of direct mail as well.

1. Direct mail allows for creativity. Unlike other media advertising, which must conform to specific formats, the direct-mail package can be as simple or elaborate as desired. The choice size, style, colors, or format are completely up to the user.
2. The scheduling of a direct-mail piece is up to the user rather than the amount of time or space that is available in the mass media. This flexibility is valuable. Marketing plans need never be adjusted to the availability of media space.
3. The use of direct mail is private. Competitors do not immediately become aware of promotions and cannot move quickly to counter them. In other words, a "hot" scheme or product is less likely to be "knocked off" quickly.
4. Mass media contains a host of other advertisements, stories, and editorial comments. An advertisement can be missed or its importance diluted. Direct-mail pieces cannot be ignored. They may not be read, but they will be noticed.

Zip Codes

When Zip codes were introduced twenty-five years ago, everybody howled in anger. They were unwieldy, difficult to remember, and another sign of government regimentation. In fact, the use of Zip codes revolutionized mail-order marketing. Based on the old adage, "Birds of a feather flock together," Zip codes provide marketers with geographic locations of people with similar characteristics. Instead of segmenting their targets by city, county, or state, which included people of vastly different interests, marketers can now subdivide by Zip codes. This provides for a much more specific target. As a result a person whose address bears the Zip code 90210 (Beverly Hills, California) or 48013 (Bloomfield Hills, Michigan) will receive direct-mail advertising world cruises or Mercedes Benz automobiles while those whose Zip code is 05401 (Burlington, Vermont) will find mail selling snowmobiles.

There are presently some forty-three thousand Zip codes in the United States. They change frequently as local populations change. Each Zip code is made up of an average of four thousand families.

Companies like the Claritas Corporation and CACI International analyze these zip codes and offer a great deal of information about the consumers to be found in each Zip code number. For example, Claritas Prizm System divides the nation's Zip codes into forty groups. One includes small towns and rural areas whose consumers are characterized by large families with school-aged children. The head of the household is a blue-collar worker with a high school education. This is just some of the information given. Obviously, areas such as this provide targets for outdoor gear, four-wheel-drive vehicles, and so on.

As important as Zip codes are to direct mailers, they still have the problem of not being sufficiently specific. The total 4,000 or so families that make up a Zip code is too large and diversified to be really efficient. Zip code 60043 (Kenilworth, Illinois) signifies what is considered a high-income area. However, not all households in the area are wealthy. Sending applications for gold credit cards to each of the 4,000 or so families would be wasteful. CACI International offers a more refined system. By analyzing the results of the U.S. Census, CACI has narrowed down the groupings into lists of about 350 addresses that have many more characteristics in common than do the total 4,000 addresses of that Zip code. For example, they have found that Zip code 07728 (Freehold, New Jersey) consists of twenty different market types of households. This permits much more sharply defined targeting. These narrowed groupings are called *census blocks* and are likely to replace Zip codes for the same reason that Zip codes replaced city, county, and state groupings. Two CACI clients, Dreyfus Corporation, a large securities broker, and Resort Condominiums, Inc., a time-sharing organization, have recently switched from Zip codes to census block systems.

MAGAZINES

Of the print media, magazines are by far the most important to the field of direct marketing. Whatever the reason, magazine readers are prone to respond to advertisements. However, great care must be taken in the selection of an appropriate magazine. Some do much better than others. Among the more successful magazines from the viewpoint of the direct response advertiser are the *National Enquirer, Parade, T.V. Guide,* and *Better Homes and Gardens.*

Most of the larger, national magazines publish regional issues. By using regional issues, advertisement can be limited to a particular region rather than be run nationwide. Although the cost per reader is greater than it would be if the piece ran nationally, there is still a considerable cost saving.

1. This is valuable in the testing of a new product or of the effectiveness of the media itself. In this way the response can be tested before the entire investment is made.
2. Some areas like the West Coast do appreciably better than others like New England. Regional editions can save money by permitting the weeding out of areas of questionable success.
3. The characteristics of certain products limit their appeal in certain areas. For example, snowmobiles will have little appeal below the Mason-Dixon Line.

The selection of the particular magazine to use offers a problem because of the huge number available to choose from. However, they can be broken down into groups thus narrowing the possible choices. For example, if the product is a fashion item, the choices might be *Mademoiselle, Vogue, Glamour,* or *Harper's Bazaar.* Within this relatively narrow group, the one selected might depend on such product characteristics as the price or age group to which it appeals.

Insert cards are both expensive and effective. For one thing, the reader can't miss them—the magazine opens automatically to them. In addition, the reply card saves the reader the annoyance of writing and addressing a letter plus postage. The cost of insert cards includes the cost of the space, printing the card, and binding. This can be very expensive.

The particular place in the publication that an advertisement is placed is of considerable importance. Right-hand pages do better than left-hand pages. The first few pages do better than the last. In fact, the first right-hand page is considered twice as good as the back pages. Naturally, better placement is more expensive.

HOME SHOPPING TV

The most dramatic direct marketing story of the 1980s has been the spectacular growth of home shopping shows with a sales volume of $9 million in 1985 to a level of $4 billion by 1990. Unfortunately, the last few years have shown a shakedown in this branch of direct marketing. Of the peak of fifty shopping channels, only thirty are left at the time of this writing. Such retailing giants as K-Mart, Dayton Hudson, and Consolidated Stores have dropped out. But a look at the statistics indicates that the future of this medium is safe. Close to six million people are customers of the various home shopping TV shows, averaging $300 of average purchases. As the number of subscribers to cable TV increases, the number of home shoppers will as well.

Originally, these TV shows sold closeouts and other off-price merchandise. Lately, they have been turning to name brands and staples. Electronics and fashion goods are taking the place of jewelry and collectibles. Perhaps the recent hard times are the result of these people learning their business, and things will start picking up again as the know-how is achieved. A medium through which Telshop, a service of the Financial News Network, was able, in one weekend, to sell 107 diamond tennis bracelets at $2,000 each has to have a future.

NEWSPAPERS

The use of newspapers by direct-response advertisers is generally restricted to weekend magazine supplements and preprints, advertising supplements printed in advance and given to the newspaper for insertion with their regular edition. Preprints offer a great deal of space to the advertisers as well as a perforated, preaddressed response card. The wide use of preprints, fifty-five billion circulated in 1986, testifies to the success of this direct-response method.

USA Weekend and *Parade* are syndicated sections that appear in the weekend editions of many newspapers. Both have wide circulations and contain many direct-response advertisements. In the case of *Parade*, 60 percent of its advertising includes coupons for direct consumer response.

CO-OPS

A co-op mailing is one in which the offerings of two or more advertisers are contained in the same package and provides for a sharing of the cost. Most co-op mailing consists of price reduction coupons. The main figure in this system is Donnelley Marketing, publisher of the Carol Wright mail co-op, which sends packets to thirty-five million addresses nine times per year.

Marketers use the coupons for the following reasons:

1. To introduce new products.
2. To move goods that are overstocked.
3. To aid in the revival of old products.
4. To get retailers to stock a product by increasing consumer demand.

According to Donnelley, virtually all persons who receive coupon packages go through them, and they are used by 92 percent of the recipients. Curiously, they are more widely used by people with over $25,000 of annual income than by those with under $10,000 of annual income.

Not all co-op advertising is done by such organizations as Donnelley/Carol Wright. Sometimes direct marketers solicit other direct marketers to join them in their mailings. This, of course, reduces the cost to each participant.

Somewhat similar to co-op mailing is ride-along mailing. It is a system of including a direct-mail piece with another mailing sent out by another business to its customers. For example, when a department store sends its monthly statements to its charge account customers, it is common to find a separate direct-mail piece included in the envelope. This reduces the mail cost of the ride-along user while providing income for the major mailer. Personalized stationery and perfumes are often sold in this way. The major mailer is usually very careful about these enclosures because their image and reputation are at risk if the mail along is of questionable quality.

TELEMARKETING

Another marketing medium available to direct-response marketers is telemarketing, that is, marketing by telephone. Telemarketing includes cold canvassing, canvassing from lists by telephone, and answering the telephone in response to a prospect calling to inquire about an ad that supplied an 800 toll-free number, direct mailing, or coupon. It is particularly effective when combined with other media, as is the case when a toll-free number is shown on a TV ad.

Care should be taken to use the telephone sensibly. Calls that are made at inconvenient times often result in angry responses that can turn a prospect away forever. This widespread misuse of the telephone as a selling tool has resulted in legislation being considered in many areas that will seriously affect the future of this medium for canvassing.

The cost of getting leads by using a telephone as opposed to the cost of sending out salespersons is extremely low. This is particularly true in the case of high-tech products or complicated services. Where orders must be customized, as in the case of industrial users, the person making the sales call may be required to have an engineering background and command a high salary. It would be prohibitively expensive to send such an individual to seek out leads.

Cross-selling is another advantage of selling by telephone. Consider a woman using an 800 toll-free number to order a pair of slacks being told that there is a beautiful blouse that would go well with the slacks or being reminded of this week's special. Catalog directors find that orders by telephone average 20 percent higher than those that are mailed in.

Obviously, telemarketing offers many advantages, but this is true only if the operator answering the call has the right qualifications for the job and has been properly trained. When hiring telemarketing operators the following characteristics must be sought:

1. Good diction, with a clear, easily understood voice.
2. Well organized.
3. Must not be thrown by immediate rejection.
4. Should be able to adjust to a variety of types of customers.
5. Must be friendly, kind, and enthusiastic.

Since the skills of the operator are a vital consideration to successful telemarketing, training programs are generally worked out and can last as long as three weeks. This is followed up by shorter programs in the months ahead. During that time the operator is taught the following:

1. The nature of the company and the image it seeks to project
2. The product line
3. The use of the computer terminal from which inventory information and cross-selling possibilities are determined
4. Selling skills, including the ability to identify customer's needs and suitably fill them or offer substitutes

Role playing is an important teaching method in these training programs and is widely used.

Once hired and trained, operators should be periodically checked and given an efficiency rating. This is particularly true for those whose rating declines or whose volume does not meet expectations.

BROADCAST MEDIA

While the major portion of radio and television advertising takes the form of general advertising, there is a growing use of this media for direct-response advertising. These advertisements take the form of supplying the address of the advertiser for a mail response from the prospect as well as a toll-free 800 number for prompter service. Cable TV is uniquely suited for direct-response advertising since, unlike general TV which broadcasts to the total population, cable television is directed to specific audiences. By using this information, sporting goods, outdoor clothing, and how-to sports cassettes can be advertised on a sports channel while cassettes of classic films would appear on a movie channel.

BUSINESS-TO-BUSINESS

The field of direct marketing is in rapid growth. In no segment of it is this more apparent than business-to-business direct marketing. The continued growth of business-to-business direct marketing is assured since the high cost of sales calls is the main reason for this increase and these costs are likely to grow. Research indicates that a sales call by a salesperson presently exceeds $200. Moreover, it takes an average of five calls to get an order. It is obvious that the use of telemarketing, catalogs, and direct mail in the industrial market are important.

Business-to-business direct marketing serves many purposes, the most important of which is to seek out leads. Typically, the first step in a lead generation program is a direct-response advertisement, telephone call, or direct-mail piece to which the prospect will respond with a request for further information. Internal or external lists are widely used for this purpose. When the prospect responds, printed data or catalogs are sent. Then about two weeks later, a telephone call is made to supply more information and, hopefully, set up an appointment with a sales representative.

Much business-to-business marketing is done through channels of distribution. The producer of the goods sells to wholesalers or distributors that, in turn, sell to the ultimate consumer. As a result the middleman receives a significant share of the total profit. Marketing directly, that is, from the producer directly to the consumer, cuts out the middleman and that share of the profits goes to the producer. This is not always feasible since middlemen serve a definite economic function. Where this is the case, the leads are turned over to the distributor.

Areas that are too small or insignificant to be served by salespersons can only be reached by direct-response marketing. This is due to the fact that the cost is much less. In the same way less promising leads can be handled by telephone or direct mail. A lead generation program provides a wide variety of prospects. "Hot" ones require a salesperson's visit. For others, a phone call or direct-mail piece might be more logical.

When a major industrial sale is made the product frequently requires a constant stream of supplies. The supply business, though profitable, is generally of too small a dollar volume to make visits by salespersons economically worthwhile. Catalogs, phone calls, and direct mail can ensure the continuation of these small, but lucrative, orders.

Media Available

The media available to business-to-business marketers are somewhat different from those used in direct-response consumer marketing. While direct mail and telemarketing are used by all direct-response advertisers, business-to-business direct-response marketers also use trade papers and periodicals as well as trade shows.

Trade periodicals and newspapers are publications that are targeted directly at specific industries. All the articles, discussions, and advertising are specifically aimed at industry interests. As a result, these publications are widely read. The advertising that appears in them can be institutional, direct response, or a combination of the two. The purpose of the institutional advertisement is to promote the company's name and image. Direct marketing advertising searches out prospects or actual sales. It is not unusual to find a full page institutional advertisement that includes an 800 toll-free number and a mailing address for readers who want more information.

Many industries hold periodic trade shows. These provide sellers with the opportunity to show their products and make contacts with buyers. Buyers attending trade shows are given the opportunity of comparing the offerings of many suppliers simultaneously and seeing what is new in the industry. Perhaps as important as the sales written up at trade shows are the contacts made there. It is the place for arranging sales calls, distributing catalogs, and accumulating material for mailing and telemarketing lists.

Telemarketing is uniquely suited for the industrial market. Business-to-business telephone calls are made to people who are accustomed to doing business by telephone. They are always made during business hours and are never resented. Telemarketing may be the most expensive of the direct-response media on a cost per person reached, but it is very low in terms of cost per sale.

RESEARCH

Perhaps the most important characteristic that differentiates direct marketing from general marketing is its potential for accurate research. Tests are available to direct marketers that can be used to make accurate predictions. If an advertisement is placed with a response card or a toll-free number is included, the number of calls received or cards returned can be calculated and the cost per inquiry or per individual sale can be calculated. In this way, various advertising media can be compared. Similarly, if a program of 500,000 direct-mail pieces is to be made, it can be tested by sending out groups of 5,000. Each can have the offer presented in a different way to determine the most effective wording or they can be sent to different mailing lists in order to decide the one that is most likely to succeed.

Consider this offer:

1. Half price
2. Buy one, get one free
3. 50 percent off

Each statement is exactly the same offer as the other two. One would expect them to do equally well in the marketplace. The fact is that statement number two was 40 percent more successful than the others. It is doubtful that this could have been predicted by anyone without research. Incidentally, this does not mean that buy one, get one free will always win. It might for men's shirts, but probably wouldn't for pianos.

Important Points in the Chapter

1. Direct marketing differs from regular marketing in that it includes the use of a database, testable results, and direct-response advertising.

2. A database is an accumulation of information about customers or prospects. It may include economic, social, life-style, and buying habits of customers and prospects.

3. Mailing lists may be internal or external. Internal mailing lists are those generated by the company itself. External mailing lists are those rented or acquired from outside sources.

4. There are thousands of mailing lists available to direct marketers. They are usually rented on a one-shot basis and must be used strictly in accordance with the wishes of the list owner.

5. Lists should be tested for effectiveness before expensive, full-scale use is made. Duplication, erroneous addresses, and so forth should be eliminated.

6. Convenience of use, toll-free telephone numbers, and wide-spread credit card use are among the reasons for growth of catalog sales volume.

7. Vendor catalogs are those in which suppliers pay for the right to have their merchandise included in the catalog.

8. Many catalog merchants have opened traditional retail outlets. The store gets the benefit of the catalog's good name, while providing the catalog division with many additional names for its database.

9. Direct mail is the most important media for direct marketers. It has benefited greatly from the use of Zip code numbers which permit more specific targeting.

10. Magazines are the most important media for direct marketers. The use of regional issues and insert cards improve their efficiency.

11. Home shopping TV has leveled off after a spectacular start. Its future, however, seems assured.

12. Telemarketing, while the most expensive in terms of cost per person reached, is probably cheapest in terms of cost per sale.

13. Direct marketing is widely used by business-to-business marketers. As the cost of a salesperson's call becomes more and more expensive, the use of direct marketing in this area will grow.

Review Questions

1. Differentiate between traditional marketing and direct marketing.

2. What is a database?

3. List ten customer/prospect characteristics that may be included in a database.

4. What is an enhanced database?

5. Define internal and external lists. Which are more important? Why?

6. Why do businesses rent lists?

7. Why should a list be tested? How should this be done?

8. Give three reasons for the increase in catalog sales.

9. Discuss the cost advantage catalog marketers have over traditional retailers.

10. What is a vendor's catalog? What are the advantages and disadvantages of this kind of catalog?

11. Why are some catalog marketers opening traditional retail stores?

12. Give four advantages of direct mail as an advertising media.

13. Discuss the importance of Zip codes to direct-mail advertisers.

14. What is a census block? Why is it important?

15. Give three advantages of the use of regional issues of national magazines.

16. Why is placement important in magazine advertising?

17. What is the past, present, and future of home shopping TV?

18. What are the advantages of the use of coupons?

19. What is cross-selling as it applies to telemarketing?

20. List five characteristics of a good telemarketing operator.

21. How do you account for the growth of direct marketing in the business-to-business field?

Case Problem

Lednam Industries, a family-owned business based on Long Island, manufactures a full line of quality office furniture. Founder Max Lednam has proved to be a savvy marketer since he started the company in 1959. His first-year sales of $90,000 have mushroomed into a record $5.1. million in 1989.

He contributes his long-term business success to a number of factors. Among them are a computerized sales/inventory program, an outside sales force who visit office complexes, continuous newspaper/trade publication advertising, and a once-a-year mailing of a color catalog to Long Island business firms.

As Max plans for retirement, he has delegated day-to-day business responsibilities to each of his three college-educated sons. The oldest, Jason, holds a B.B.A. degree in management and is in charge of production and traffic management at the factory. His second son, Joshua, is an accounting major who minored in computer technology. He handles inventory control and financial matters. His youngest son, Jordan, specialized in marketing at college and currently manages showroom sales.

Max is confident in the ability of his sons to carry on the business. However, he wants to ensure that upon his retirement, Lednam Industries will continue to be innovative and keep ahead of his competition. He has read several articles about telemarketing in trade publications. He believes that the time may be right to institute a telemarketing program at his firm.

Questions

1. What advantages and disadvantages do you foresee in implementing a telemarketing program at Lednam Industries?

2. After careful consideration of your answers to question 1, if you were Max Lednam, would you use telemarketing?

3. When Max retires, which of his sons should be responsible for the telemarketing program? Why?

17

PERSONAL SELLING

Learning Objectives

Upon completion of the chapter, you will be able to:

1. Enumerate five important personal qualities that are necessary for successful selling and indicate why each is important.

2. Explain why a salesperson's knowledge of the company, the product, and the competition are important to successful selling.

3. Discuss prospecting and methods of obtaining leads.

4. Describe the proper method of approaching a customer and presenting the merchandise.

5. Describe the proper method of handling objections, closing the sale, and promoting future business.

6. Discuss five methods of compensation for salespeople.

THE CHAMP COMES OUT FIGHTING

One has only to turn on the television set or read a newspaper to discover the battle taking place for the customer's dollar for soft drinks. The competition has reached such proportions that the companies are spending millions of dollars in the hope of gaining a bigger share of the market. Most of the expended dollars go for promotional campaigns which utilize all of the available media. The Pepsi-Cola Company has beefed up the promotional route with such events as the "Big Boom in Cincinnati" which centered upon an enormous fireworks display and for the annual "Pepsi Challenge 10-Kilometer Races" it entered into a relationship with Burger King which now uses Pepsi products exclusively. These and a multitude of other innovations, employed by the Pepsi-Cola Company indicate that the company has decided that the challenge of today's soft drink business can best be met by improving their ability to sell.

A few years ago Pepsi's management education committee introduced the *Champ* program which was based upon two years of research. Champ is a sales training program which utilizes videotapes and hands-on training. It was developed for training new people and improving the performance of someone who has been in the business for a quarter of a century.

Involved are twenty sessions which incorporate in-plant and on-the-job training. Included are segments on the overall requirements of the salesperson's job, the company's history, and the various products in the line. Merchandising sessions place emphasis on distribution systems, vending services, management of shelf space, and so forth. Pepsi-Cola believes that videotaping is a key element to the program's success since it can provide the flexibility needed without interrupting employee schedules.

The term *Champ* was decided upon by the company president who defined a champ

PepsiCo's "Champ" sales training program utilizes videotapes and hands-on training. (*Courtesy:* Pepsi-Cola USA.)

as "someone who has what it takes to go the distance, to outperform the competition, and stay out in front."

The final sessions of the Champ program incorporate seven steps which Pepsi considers necessary in order to sell successfully. They bear the name "P.R.O.F.I.T.S. Selling System" which stands for *P*repare to sell, *R*elate to the buyer, *O*pen the presentation, *F*eature the benefits, *I*nteract, *T*ackle the objections, *S*eal the deal.

The Pepsi-Cola Company has been making significant strides in their competition with Coca-Cola and the others. They seem to consider a successful sales team to be the backbone of their approach.

INTRODUCTION

When marketing management's attention is focused on sophisticated aspects of present-day marketing (research, computer applications), personal selling is too often treated as the company's stepchild. However, whether it is selling for a manufacturer, showing a wholesaler's complete line, or approaching the customer in a retail store, selling is vital to today's business organization. The lifeblood of the distribution of goods is still in the hands of the trained salesperson. Paying attention to the other functions in the marketing mix, such as product and price, and not to personal selling, can lead to the failure of even the most promising product.

Often, a person considering a marketing career must begin at a lower level before gaining a position of authority such as sales manager, marketing research director, or transportation manager. To make a career in marketing, a salesperson's job is the usual port of entrance. Only excellent preparation will make the salesperson sufficiently effective to go out and turn prospects into purchasers and purchasers into regular customers. Without regular customers and their continuous orders, the company may eventually run out of prospective buyers. Satisfied customers, who demonstrate their satisfaction through repeat business, are the end result of effective selling.

Among the aspects of selling considered to be the most important are the customer, competition, knowledge of product, pricing policies and practices, prospecting, planning the sales presentation, handling customer objections, and closing the sale. Prior to a discussion of these key points, those qualities necessary for successful careers in personal selling will be examined.

PERSONAL QUALITIES FOR THE SALESPERSON

Too often when recruiting salespeople, management does not stress sufficiently the importance of selling ability. When two companies offer similar or identical merchandise (as is possible through two wholesalers), the impression projected by the salesperson might influence the prospective customer. The image of the company is usually projected by the salesperson. It should be kept in mind that, in most instances, the salesperson is the sole representative with whom buyers negotiate. To the prospect, the salesperson *is* the company. To make certain that the company is properly represented, marketers must carefully scrutinize their sales staffs and adequately prepare them for the prospective buyers.

Appearance

Initially, the only tool for the salesperson, upon meeting the prospect, is appearance. It is of paramount importance that the impression is satisfactory. When the two parties are to meet for the first time, appearance is about the only factor that the buyer can measure and by which he or she can be motivated. It is unlikely that shoddy dress will be well received.

Enthusiasm

Being enthusiastic should not be confused with being pushy or overly aggressive. If the salesperson dominates the prospective customer, the transaction (if it does materialize) might not really be appropriate. The wrong merchandise might be ordered, which could prove to be a misfortune for the customer. This could lead to termination of a business relationship that otherwise would have been fruitful to both parties. Being enthusiastic, on the other hand, often transfers from the salesperson to the customer. Proudly displaying and demonstrating a line of merchandise in a real and stimulating manner often meets with a warm reception.

Voice and Speech

To be able to project the voice sufficiently and to use proper diction is a must for successful personal selling. This does not mean that professional training is essential for a proper sales demonstration. Care should be exercised as to the words the salesperson chooses to use. Proper speech is certain to produce an image that should make the buyer more attentive and receptive.

Tact

Being tactful is essential to all levels of selling, in particular to retailing. The retail salesperson's job is helping to satisfy the customer's needs. Should he or she allow the customer to purchase something that is wrong, even though the customer wants to make the purchase? Allowing this purchase to be made might lead to the possible loss of future business. On the other hand, a suggestion that the buyer's choice is a poor one might be an affront. Tact must be used to guide the customer toward goods that are more appropriate. Tactfulness comes only with care and experience.

Self-discipline

Losing patience is very possible for almost every salesperson. Prospective customers' personalities and attitudes are not all the same. A salesperson must remember that if one is to be successful, there must be control over the emotions, even when the situation seems intolerable. Abusing the customer will only lead to loss of the sale. The individual who is easily excited by the shortcomings of others should not pursue a salesperson's job.

In addition to the previously mentioned essentials for good selling, a prospective salesperson should show initiative, sincerity, cheerfulness, knowledge, and resourcefulness. Although it seems unusual for all people interested in sales positions to possess all these qualities, the more they have, the greater will be their chance for success.

ESSENTIAL KNOWLEDGE FOR SELLING

In addition to knowing the customer (no two customers are exactly alike) the salesperson must have knowledge in three specific areas: the company, the product, and competing companies. Only when armed with this knowledge can an effective sales presentation be made.

Company Knowledge

It is safe to assume that the prospective customer is most often interested in what is being offered for sale, but it is presumptuous for salespersons to believe that only they have the goods that can adequately satisfy the customer's needs. Merchandise from one wholesaler will probably come from others as well. Also, at the retail level, the same merchandise is certainly available at different outlets. Even the manufacturer's creations are offered in forms similar enough to accommodate the most discriminating buyer. Consequently, often the company itself, its background, and its policies, not just the specific goods, appeal to buyers. Among the points that might be stressed during a presentation are the growth and development of the company; its merchandising practices, such as policies regarding merchandise returns and allowances; credit arrangements; key personnel involved; production features; discounts and other price advantages; and service facilities, such as repair depots. The characteristics of the company to be stressed can be determined individually for each prospect. For example, a buyer might be sold on the merchandise but could have doubts about punctuality of deliveries. For this purchaser an overview of production facilities and shipping practices, coupled with the elaboration of key people involved in the specific activities, might overcome the uncertainties. Similarly, if a salesperson represents a wholesaler whose goods are the same as those of three other local wholesalers, it might be stressed that this company has the most liberal credit policy. Whatever the situation, delving into the background of a company can often supply the answer that is needed to make the sale.

Product Knowledge

To sell any merchandise successfully without prior product knowledge is rather difficult for the salesperson. To sell goods or services in a manner that will gain the customer's confidence, an understanding of what is for sale is required. The inability to answer specific product questions tends to make salespeople bluff or avoid the queries. The extent of product knowledge needed to complete a sale varies according to the complexity of the goods. For example, salespeople of technical objects (dentists' apparatus, lease of computer equipment) must be better acquainted with their products than representatives selling paper supplies to retail stores. Similarly, the manufacturer's salesperson must generally be better informed than the retail salesperson simply because the former's customers are certainly more knowledgeable about products than the latter's. Specifically, salespeople must be prepared to discuss the product's construction, the servicing that is required, the justification of its price, the exact manner in which the product will meet the buyer's needs, and perhaps other uses for the product that would make it more salable. A closer examination of these points should clarify their importance.

Meeting the buyer's needs is of utmost importance. For example, sellers who represent the manufacturer of a new type of paint, stucco paint (which gives a three-dimensional look to a wall), must have at their fingertips information that will make other, conventional paint used to achieve this effect seem obsolete. The salesperson must extract, from the available information, the knowledge that the customer (the retailer) can in turn use on the ultimate consumer. By simply putting the pertinent information in logical order and presenting it in comparison to competing paint, the salesperson can approach the prospective customer with confidence. Many manufacturers supply their salespeople with training manuals that include this type of information in similar arrangements:

COMPARISON STUDY FOR THE ACHIEVEMENT OF TEXTURED WALLS

Stucco Paint	*Conventional Paint*
1. No base application	1. Application of plaster (irregularly applied)
2. Regular brush or roller	2. Specially designed roller or brush to apply paint over plaster

Stucco Paint	*Conventional Paint*
3. One-step application	**3.** Two-step application
4. Fast-drying	**4.** Plaster must dry before painting can begin

Clear and logical information will enable the salesperson to present a factual and meaningful demonstration.

The manufacturing processes often make the difference between closing a sale and losing a sale. Single-needle tailoring (an example of fine sewing) might prove to be the deciding point for the prospect. A knowledge of steel and its advantages over wood is probably a must for the salesperson trying to promote steel tennis rackets. Being able to discuss knowledgeably the manufacture of fiberglass boats and their advantages over wooden boats would certainly be necessary for the salesperson of fiberglass vessels. Whether the product is food, machinery, fashion merchandise, or general office supplies, knowledge of the product's materials and construction will make for a more convincing presentation.

Servicing and facilities for servicing are factors that often turn prospects into buyers. Buyers of machinery, either consumers or industrial purchasers, are concerned with servicing. Factors such as the number of centers for servicing, the costs involved, the expertise of the service departments, and the company's promptness in answering service calls are extremely important to buyers. All things being equal, the company providing the best service will probably make the sale. The consumer can easily understand this when considering the purchase of an automobile. Cadillacs can be purchased at a variety of agencies, at prices that almost always are identical. The consumer is therefore influenced by something other than cost. Frequently, the service afforded by the particular agency affects the buying decision.

Aside from remembering the price, the salesperson should be able to justify it. The explanation of "you get what you pay for" is not likely to satisfy the industrial purchaser or, for that matter, the shopper in a retail store. Most frequently, the salesperson relies upon the quality aspect in justifying price. The distributor of a line of television receivers whose price is higher than the rest of the market might justify the additional cost by indicating that the line has a handwired chassis or that the cabinets are hand-rubbed for added beauty. The explanation of the product's salient features and the translation of those features into user's benefits is the most intelligent manner in which to convince the buyer that the price is warranted.

Most products are only usable for the function for which they were intended. However, in some cases, a salesperson might promote the sale of a line of merchandise by being able to suggest additional uses for the products. The vacuum cleaner that can also be used as a spray-painting device and the power drill that adapts as a polisher or buffer are examples of products whose different uses can be promoted.

The area of product knowledge to be stressed depends on the individual buyers. The salesperson, through study and experience, can quickly determine which to use in the presentation.

The Competition

Rarely will a salesperson have the opportunity of approaching a prospective buyer who has not either actually purchased from the salesperson's competition or heard about it. Professional purchasing agents of consumer and industrial goods are knowledgeable individuals who are highly paid to carry out their jobs. They seldom make purchases without being fully aware of the entire market for the goods that they purchase. They must be familiar with such factors as prices, delivery, services, and quality. Keeping this in mind, it is unlikely that a salesperson can successfully sell to one of these prospects without thorough knowledge of the competition. Much merchandise is sold merely by underscoring the advantages gained by purchasing from a particular company rather than the competition. Every salesperson must be prepared to offer some of these advantages. Although price can be an important factor, not every company offers the lowest price. It is the salesperson's job to be prepared with the point that beats the competition. Presenting misinformation to the buyer regarding the competitor's company or product is dangerous. In addition to the fact that misrepresentation is unethical and dishonest, it is also risky. It could prove disastrous for a salesperson to alter the truth in order to sell the product, since most buyers are experts in their fields and are generally aware of prices, availability of merchandise, and quality. The buyer who hears false information from salesperson will lose confidence and will not purchase. Even if he or she could be fooled once by a less than truthful salesperson, repeat business will not be forthcoming.

Salespeople who are well prepared through formal college education, on-the-job training, or actual experience will concur that there is no substitute for knowledge; the effort made in acquiring this knowledge will be reflected in sales.

PROSPECTING

The difficulty encountered in finding customers varies. The retail store obtains prospects primarily through advertising or some other form of promotion, such as display. Many retail customers just walk into stores as a routine matter. In the case of manufacturers' and wholesalers' salespersons, prospecting is different. The ease or difficulty encountered by these sales representatives is affected by such factors as size of the market, location of customers, cost of the product, and competition.

Sales personnel use a variety of prospecting techniques. Some are dictated by management, others are left to the skill and ingenuity of the salesperson. Among the most frequently employed of these methods are the following.

Cold Canvass

The salesperson using this method merely tries to approach every user of the product in the territory (salespersons are assigned specific geographic areas in which to sell). For example, those carrying a line of household tools (hammers, screwdrivers, and so on) would call upon every store which sells that merchandise. This method is time consuming, in that every prospective customer is approached indiscriminately. For example, some might be credit risks, whereas others might not have a need for the goods. Although some businesses frown upon using the cold-canvass method, other companies have enjoyed enormous success with it. Occasionally, the salesperson who practices other prospecting techniques will cold canvass if extra time is available in a particular workday.

Leads

This technique gives the salesperson some indication that specific purchasers might need the product. Rather than just knocking on any door, the salesperson has names of prospects that have been supplied. Leads come from a variety of sources, for example company advertising, sales managers, and friends. Many companies advertise in trade journals that are religiously read by purchasing agents. Purchasers whose interests have been aroused by a particular advertisement might call the company for more information or for specific contact with a sales representative. This is an excellent type of lead, since the prospective customer has taken the initiative to reach the seller. Sales managers often supply leads from which sales can be consummated. For example, the sales manager of an automobile agency might, as a routine matter, check the agency's service department. By determining important indicators such as frequency and magnitude of repairs and age of the automobile, the manager very often suggests to salespersons the names of customers who might be in need of a new vehicle. In the insurance business, salespersons selling auto and life insurance find an excellent source of leads through friends.

Commercial List Houses

There are numerous organizations whose principal business it is to compile lists and supply them to customers for a fee. These lists are arranged according to the characteristics of prospective customers. Thousands of different kinds of lists are available to salespeople. For example, Rolls-Royce, looking for an affluent clientele, might purchase from a commercial house a list of names of people with achievements earmarking them as good prospects.

Other Methods

Other methods employed by salespersons are the endless-chain approach, in which a salesperson secures the names of prospects through the following channels: from someone to whom a sale has just been made (this is used frequently in door-to-door selling); credit agency directories, such as the one published by Dun & Bradstreet, which lists businesses according to classification and also provides credit ratings; exhibitions, such as the boat show presented annually at the New York City Javits Center which serves as a place to get names of interested customers who can be followed up at other times; and spotters, who cold canvass to gather names of good prospects for the regular salespersons.

Besides selection of the most appropriate methods for prospecting, the characteristics of good prospects must be determined by marketers. Among those deemed essential by most knowledgeable salespersons are the following:

1. Does the prospect have a need for the product or service?
2. Is the company considered a good credit risk? Since most transactions are based on credit (at the wholesaler's and manufacturer's levels), an appropriate line of credit (determined generally through affiliation with credit-rating agencies such as Dun & Bradstreet and Credit Exchange) is necessary.
3. Is the prospect you are about to approach actually the buyer? It is necessary to ascertain whose responsibility it is to purchase for a company before the actual contact is made. It is not unusual for an inexperienced salesperson to show a line to an individual only to find that the prospect does not have the authority to buy. This can be a great waste of time. Most large companies have tables or organization from which can be found the name of the person responsible for purchasing.

After careful consideration of the foregoing points, the salesperson is ready to approach the customer.

APPROACHING THE CUSTOMER

The approach differs depending on whether the customer enters the salesperson's establishment (as is the case in retail selling) or the salesperson contacts the customer (as is generally the case in wholesale sales). Whatever the situation, the salesperson's attitude must be conducive to purchasing. Customers should be greeted with a friendly smile. The grumpy-looking salesperson is certain to put the customer into a poor frame of mind. The greeting used to begin a conversation is most important. One should not begin with a question that might bring a negative response. For example, in the retail store, approaching a customer saying "May I help you?" might bring a reply of "No." Although this is typical of retail store selling, it is a poor way to begin a sales presentation. Preferably, a salesperson should begin by saying, "Good morning, I'm Mr. Smith. I'd like to help you with your purchasing needs." This approach is less likely to receive a negative reaction. Another desirable approach is to strike up a conversation regarding an article of merchandise that a shopper is examining. For example, "That chair is as comfortable as it is good-looking. Why don't you try it?" When a customer approaches a salesperson for help, the greeting is less difficult because assistance is sought. A mere "good afternoon" is sufficient. Even "May I help you?" is acceptable, since the fact that the customer is the one who has made the approach negates the possibility of a "no" response.

At this very early point in the sales demonstration, it is time to determine the shopper's needs. Certainly approaching the customer who is examining an item gives the salesperson an idea of what is desired. If the customer is not studying the merchandise, determination of what is needed is a little more difficult. Some brief questions (which become second nature with experience) pertaining to style, color, size (if applicable), will guide the salesperson in the selection of appropriate merchandise. Keeping in mind what the store has available for sale, the salesperson is now ready to show the merchandise to the customer.

Salespeople working on the wholesale level generally arrange for an appointment in advance. The actual initial approach is then prearranged.

PRESENTING THE MERCHANDISE

The actual presentation is the most important aspect of the salesperson's job. Whether the approach used is memorized (although generally unconvincing, that is done by some major marketers) or planned according to a carefully conceived outline, the salesperson should have all the materials necessary to close the sale. In the retail store the actual merchandise available for sale is shown to the prospective customer. Together with good selling technique, this is all that is necessary to complete the sale successfully. Representatives of manufacturers or wholesalers have a number of aids that can be used to dramatize their products. In many cases salespersons carry lines of actual samples, but the nature of some goods does not permit this. For example, the computer salesperson cannot possibly have available a large piece of data-processing equipment. When actual presentation of the goods is impossible and the prospect cannot come to the salesperson's showroom to see the goods, other selling aids are necessary. Even where the goods are available for buyer examination, the very size of the order often warrants additional sales aids. Some regularly used aids are

1. Models of the actual merchandise.

2. Photographs.
3. Copies of advertisements of other customers.
4. Charts or graphs to show sales growth.
5. Manuals giving all the pertinent information about the product in a logical order.
6. Films, such as those used by advertising agencies to show commercials that they have prepared for other accounts.
7. Testimonials of satisfied customers.

Whatever the product, the salesperson should offer strong selling points in a manner that respects the intelligence of the prospect. Buyers are generally too knowledgeable to be taken in by fast-talking salespeople.

HANDLING OBJECTIONS

Prospects indicate that they are possibly ready to become customers in a number of ways. Such questions as "What is the completion date for delivery?" "Is there a cash discount?" or "Are other colors available?" may conceivably signal to the salesperson that a sale is imminent. These are but a few of the indications that a prospect might become a customer. Even after spending time in the consideration of making a purchase, the buyer might hesitate and raise objections. These objections might be excuses telling the salesperson that the buyer is not going to buy, or they might be sincere objections that need further clarification before they are overcome. Whatever the foundation of the objections, the salesperson must overcome them to close the sale.

Most common are objections about price, poor delivery, unsatisfactory product features, and comparison with a competitor's offerings. The experienced salesperson is prepared to handle these objections and does so in a number of ways. One method frequently used by experienced salespersons is to agree with the customer's objection but to quickly add a new selling point. For example, Mr. Walters expresses interest in Style 4863 but declares, "The price is high." The salesperson handling the objection in the manner described might reply, "Yes, but the high standard of construction will guarantee tremendous sales potential." Instead of saying "yes, but" to handle objections, other words such as the following might be used:

1. "Certainly, but have you considered . . ."
2. "You're right, Mr. Adams, however, have you examined . . ."
3. "One of my other accounts felt exactly as you do, but she finally bought from us because . . ."
4. "It is a little longer than our usual delivery period, but . . ."

The foregoing statements are only suggestions. Experience affords the salesperson a wealth of statements from which to choose.

Another method employed in handling objections is to ask the customer questions. In this way a salesperson can separate excuses for not buying from real objections. Examples of some questions are

1. "What's wrong with the range of colors, Mrs. Foster?"
2. "What is your objection to the typewriter?"
3. "What would you consider an appropriate price for electric coffee makers?"

Still another technique that must be used with caution is to deny the objection. The salesperson must be absolutely certain of the information when employing this method. For example,

Customer's Objection	*Salesperson's Response*
"I don't believe we will have it in time for our sale."	"I will guarantee delivery."
"The Acme Company sells it for $1.25 less than your price."	"Our company always sells that item at a price lower than the Acme Company."
"I don't believe the colors will be appropriate to coordinate with the shoe buyer's purchase."	"The colors have been carefully dyed to ensure perfect coordination."

When employing the third technique, only accurate information should be offered to the customer. Any misinformation can lead to mistrust and possible loss of future business from the buyer.

CLOSING THE SALE

When the salesperson feels that all the prospect's questions have been answered, closing the sale should be attempted. Inexperienced salespersons often ask how you know that it is the exact time to close. This knowledge comes from experience. There are signals that may serve as a guide; from there on, experience takes over. It should be understood that the buyer will rarely say, "You've sold me, I'm ready . . ."

Some of the signals are

"How long will it take for special orders?"

"Can I have an additional thirty days in which to pay the bill?"

"When can I expect the merchandise to be delivered?"
"If these items don't sell, will you change them for other numbers?"
"Is the guarantee for one year?"

When the salesperson recognizes what is believed to be the opportune moment, it is time to proceed to close the sale. Choosing the right words at this time might seem difficult to the student of marketing. Using the question, "Are you ready to buy?" is certainly not the correct approach. The use of questions and statements such as these prove to be effective in trying to close the sale:

"Shall we send it express or air freight?"
"Which would you like, Style 602 or style 605?"
"Will that be delivered to the stores or to your warehouse?"
"When would you like it delivered?"
"After this week these items go back to their original prices."
"This is the last day for immediate delivery. Later orders will take four weeks."

Even the most experienced salesperson sometimes finds that the most appropriate time to close the sale has not been chosen. It might take several attempts before a sale is finalized. Marketing students should keep in mind that not every prospect is really a customer and also that not every buyer can be satisfied with a firm's offerings. The buyer's refusal to purchase should be evaluated in terms of what is said. For example, a definite "no" might indicate that the buyer cannot be satisfied. Reactions such as "I'd like to see other styles" or "No, I'm still uncertain" are signals that perhaps more selling is required. Whatever the degree of negativism, a seasoned salesperson should not give up after the first attempt to close has not been successful. The number of times a salesperson should try to close is questionable. Too few attempts might let the customer slip away. Too many tries might tend to make the buyer feel pressured. The right number of times before giving up will eventually be found by experience.

After making an unsuccessful attempt a salesperson must be able to proceed again to a point that will result in success. In order to do this, some information must be kept in reserve that will perhaps whet the buyer's appetite. For example,

"If you purchase today you will be entitled to a 5 percent discount."
"This is the last day of our special offer; tomorrow the price will go up 10 percent."

In retail selling, if consecutive attempts to close are unsuccessful and it is felt that the customer still might purchase the product, some salespeople resort to something called a T.O., or turnover method. This technique involves turning the customer over to a more prestigious department member, such as the manager or buyer. Customers might respond more affirmatively to these people, and thus the department will benefit.

It is important to remember that even if a buyer does not purchase this time, he or she is still a prospect for future business. Courtesy is extremely important to guarantee that the customer can be approached again in the future. It is at this time that many companies lose their favorable image. A disagreeable or disgruntled salesperson can be disastrous in terms of customer satisfaction.

Promoting Future Business

Upon completion of the sale, the resourceful salesperson takes the opportunity to guarantee the customer's future purchases. Experienced salespersons seek to establish a reputation that will encourage other transactions. Spending a few extra moments with the buyer at this time will promote good will needed for future business.

COMPENSATION OF SALES PERSONNEL

Salespersons are remunerated in a variety of ways. To select the one method that will achieve the greatest motivation while guaranteeing customer satisfaction is no simple task for marketers. Each method has its advantages and disadvantages and should be carefully examined by management.

Straight salary is probably the most widely used method of compensation in retail stores although many are now offering commission to their salespersons. It simplifies the company's bookkeeping, but it does not provide incentive.

Salary plus commission guarantees a regular income plus a commission for incentive. The commission is usually small.

Straight commission is generally restricted to manufacturer's and wholesaler's salespersons. This system does not guarantee anything to the salesperson. Earnings are largely in keeping with the seller's own ability and the desirability of the product. Most companies advance a salesperson a sum each pay period. This is known as a *draw against commission*. It is actually an advanced estimate of commission until the time the salesperson's commissions are tabulated. At that point, the difference between the monies drawn and those earned are compared. The salesperson then either receives the difference or owes it to the company.

The quota bonus plan is an arrangement under which the salesperson receives a commission on everything sold over and above a predetermined amount. Sales managers are often paid on a variation of this method. They receive a bonus for sales (of their entire staff) in excess of an established quota for a period.

Variations and combinations of all these methods are common. It is the job of management to find the one that best serves the particular company.

SALES MANAGEMENT AND THE COMPUTER

The use of the computer as a selling tool and a means of controlling the sales force has been growing at a rapid rate. Important uses to which computers have been put in the area of sales management include

1. Producing leads for sales personnel. By matching typical customers against a Dun & Bradstreet data bank of over 650,000 firms, Honeywell Corp. is able to provide each salesperson with all the pertinent data concerning the prospects in his or her territory; the lead is printed out on a 3″ × 5″ index card.
2. Pillsbury's Electronic Data-Processing Center counts the number of stores a salesperson visits, the frequency of his or her visits to each account, and

FIGURE 17–1   NCR's Tower 1632 computer. (*Courtesy:* NCR.)

actual sales against the goals set up in advance. Using this information, the sales manager can spot weak salespeople, instances in which too much time is spent with one customer at the expense of other customers, and territories that are either too large or too small for the number of salespeople allotted to them.

3. CIBA, a large drug manufacturer, used a computer to realign its four hundred sales territories according to the doctor count in seven medical specialties. Included in the program was the provision that the salesperson's home be included in the territory. As a result of the computer's efforts, no CIBA sales territory has a doctor count that is over 4 percent less than the average.

4. Many companies, particularly supermarket chains, by computerizing their transportation and storage functions, have cut costs by combining many small warehouses into centrally located distribution centers.

Figure 17–1 shows NCR's Tower 1632 business computer, which provides sufficient capability for smaller sales organizations.

Important Points in the Chapter

1. Personal qualities such as proper appearance, enthusiasm, good voice and speech, tact, and self-discipline are essential for an individual to become a good salesperson.

2. To be successful, the salesperson must be well informed concerning the company's background, the product, and the competition.

3. Prospecting (the method used to find new customers) techniques vary. Among the most common methods are cold canvass, leads, use of commercial lists, endless-chain approach, and use of credit agency directories.

4. When approaching a customer, proper opening statements should be used. In a retail store, "May I help you?" should be avoided, since it might bring a negative response.

5. If the merchandise is unavailable for presentation during the sale, substitutes should be used, for example scale models, photographs, advertisements, manuals, charts, and films.

6. Customer objections are handled in a variety of ways. The most common methods are the "yes, but" technique, questioning the customer, or denying the objection.

7. If the salesperson is unsuccessful in closing the sale, numerous additional attempts should be made. The salesperson should hold some important features about the product in reserve to be used if repeated closing attempts are necessary.

8. Salespersons are compensated in a number of ways. Most common are straight salary, salary plus commission, straight commission, and quota bonus plan.

Review Questions

1. To which types of jobs can that of salesperson lead?

2. Being tactful is absolutely necessary for good selling. Why?

3. Does enthusiasm mean that a person must employ theatrical tricks?

4. How can a salesperson's enthusiasm or lack of enthusiasm play an important role in selling?

5. Is proper appearance still important for the salesperson?

6. Discuss the various facts the salesperson should know concerning the product.

7. Aside from product knowledge, what must a wholesaler's salesperson generally impress upon prospective customers in order to make a sale?

8. How important is it to be truthful when discussing your competitors with your customers?

9. Which method of prospecting requires the least amount of investigation? How effective is it?

10. Salespersons find lists to be extremely helpful in prospecting. By whom are lists prepared?

11. Is it the salesperson's job to justify price? Why?

12. Why does the salesperson calling at the customer's place of business usually have an easier job at introduction than does the retail salesperson?

13. Which approach is considered improper in retail selling? Why?

14. What are some of the aids used by salespersons to make their presentations more meaningful?

15. Can the computer salesperson demonstrate the product at the prospect's office? If not, how is this problem overcome?

16. Is it ever appropriate to deny the customer's objections? If so, when?

17. Describe the questioning technique of handling objections.

18. What is the quota bonus method of remuneration?

19. Define *T.O.* When is it used?

20. Drawing against commission is a method used to compensate salesper-

sons. Describe this method and indicate which types of salespersons are often paid this way.

Case Problems

Case Problem 1

Lime-Light, Inc., is a wholesaler specializing in light bulbs, lighting fixtures, and lamps. Its goods are specifically for consumers' use, although occasionally it does sell bulbs for use in offices and showrooms. Lime-Light has been in this business for ten years and carries merchandise produced by several leading manufacturers. The merchandise it sells to retail store buyers can also be purchased from other wholesale sources.

Recently, Stuart Klar was hired as a salesperson to represent Lime-Light in the New York metropolitan area. Although he was inexperienced in wholesale sales (he worked briefly in a retail shoe store), his appearance and enthusiasm convinced the sales manager that he could do the job.

After studying the line, learning the important features, memorizing and practicing closing techniques, and so on, he started to make appointments with prospective buyers. He presented himself in a manner that was well received by the buyers, but he was not able to complete many sales.

Perhaps a self-evaluation of his responses to objections raised by the buyers would shed light on the problem. The most common objections raised were

Buyers' Objections	*Klar's Responses*
1. "Your prices aren't better than those of the competition."	"No. But we aren't higher."
2. "The services offered by your company seem inadequate."	"We offer the same as the other companies."
3. "You probably won't deliver on time."	"We always deliver on time."

Questions

1. Do you believe Klar's responses to be sincere?
2. Would you respond differently? How would you answer each objection?
3. Are there any additional points Klar might make to be more convincing? Discuss.

Case Problem 2

Sally Benito was just hired as a salesperson by the Reputable Life Insurance Company. Her experience prior to this job was in retailing (as a part-time sales-clerk while going to college) and in wholesaling (as a salesperson for a paper-and-twine dealer). In both of these jobs she was able to show the product, highlight its important features, and ultimately make her share of sales.

What perplexes Ms. Benito at this time is that because of the very nature of the present product, she has nothing to really show the prospective customers. In the retail job she could allow customers to try on the merchandise. In the wholesale job, the paper bags could be tested and evaluated.

Questions

1. Is it possible to dramatize an insurance salesperson's presentation?
2. What aids would you use if you were Ms. Benito?

18

CONSUMERISM AND THE LEGAL ENVIRONMENT

Learning Objectives

Upon completion of the chapter, you will be able to:

1. Describe the responsibilities of four government agencies in the area of consumer protection.

2. List six examples of legislation passed by state and local governments to protect consumers.

3. Write a brief paper describing, by use of examples, methods by which individual businesses have improved consumer relations.

4. Explain the role of independent consulting firms in the area of consumer affairs.

5. Define Better Business Bureaus and describe their activities.

6. Explain, with examples, the importance of Ralph Nader and other consumer advocates to the consumer protection movement.

7. Discuss some of the problems that have come about because of the consumer movement.

THE ROAD TO A CLEANER AMERICA

Much to the dismay of the consuming public and of the many retailers of carbonated soft drinks, beer and malt beverages, and mineral and soda water, New York State has enacted legislation known as the Returnable Container Law, commonly called the "Bottle Bill." The law went into effect July 1, 1983, mandating that stores clean their shelves of the previously marketed unlabeled containers by September 12, 1983.

The new law not only forced most merchants to set aside additional space for bottle returns but also increased overhead costs due to the additional personnel needed to handle the returns. The nuisance to the consumer was voiced loud and clear but to no avail.

The problem with such legislation as the Bottle Bill in terms of consumer's annoyance has to do with the lack of immediate benefits. While the Truth-in-Lending Act at once puts the borrower on guard concerning interest rates, thus helping with a rational decision, and the Child Protection and Toy Safety Act protects children from unsafe situations, the returnable container law comes off as nuisance legislation.

Most consumers either don't understand the purpose of the bill or have no desire to take the responsibility for cleaner roadsides and reduced space demands, two of the bill's benefits.

When any product- or service-oriented law is enacted, its very being complicates the marketing of that product or service. New York State's Bottle Bill has, among other things, placed the following burdens on producers as well as users:

New labels had to be designed which in addition to the company's logo, ingredients, and so on must have been the words *New York* or *N.Y.*, plus the deposit charge on them.

Retailers must accept containers from consumers and provide refunds if the store carries the brand regardless of whether or not it was bought there, making it conceivable that more containers could be accepted than were actually sold by the store.

Retailers must supply extra space for empty containers, and counters or automatic machines for redemption, which add cost to the operation.

Consumers must pay a deposit of at least 5 cents for each container, store them until they are returned, and bear the burden of making the return.

Dealers must sort the containers by brand for their distributors.

Distributors must pick up empty containers at their own expense, thus adding to the overall cost.

The critics of any legislation argue against its passage. The major objection to the Bottle Bill dealt with increased cost which ultimately would be the consumer's burden to bear. Many have voiced opinions that cleaner roadsides and sanitary landfills could be accomplished more easily than by making the consumer responsible.

Whatever the opposition, the New York State returnable container law is in effect with other states anxious to evaluate its merits. While the consumer is supposed to be the

Beachscape before passage of New York State's bottle bill. (Photograph courtesy of Ellen Diamond.)

winner, many believe it is legislation which consumers don't want and will have to pay for anyway.

INTRODUCTION

Most marketers will agree that we are living in a time of the "enlightened consumer." Not too many years ago the dissatisfactions and unhappinesses of consumers fell on deaf ears. Industry seemed to be able to circumvent consumer complaints and continue in a way that did not really consider any of the problems. No longer do business managers have the luxury of operating their companies in a self-serving manner. Hardly a day goes by without both the broadcast and print media offering their audiences advice, counsel, information, and stories that relate to the plight of the consumer. Is it that industry has finally decided to become more sensitive to the needs of the people, or has it been the work of strong consumer advocates that has forced both industry and the government to become more consumer-minded?

The consumerism movement began in the 1960s and gains strength each day. Briefly defined, "it is the actions of those people or agencies responding to consumer dissatisfaction and protection." Most consumers are not really concerned with who the initiators of consumerism were or why industry or government presently take active roles. The fact that leaders emerged from every aspect of our society in the consumer enlightenment and protection movement is not the important issue. What is most meaningful to marketers is that today's consumers know their rights, the laws that protect them, and the actions to take in the event that their consumer rights are violated.

This chapter will focus on the actions of the consumer advocates who have waged warfare to alert the consuming public of their rights; the various levels of government, its agencies, and leaders who have helped to foster present consumer protection; key legislation that has been enacted; and the role of business in consumerism.

GOVERNMENT PARTICIPATION

Each level of government has become involved, to varying degrees, in the area of consumer protection and enlightenment. From the federal government down to the most local form of government, some type of action has been taken. Although government involvement in consumerism has been taking place since the early 1960s, the roles of the various levels of government are still being redefined. There is still some overlapping and proliferation of consumer programs among the levels of government and even within the same level.

Although there is still something of an air of confusion in the government's roles and responsibilities, the primary goal is to best serve the needs of the public.

The Federal Government

There are a number of reasons given for the active role undertaken by the federal government in the area of consumer protection. Among those which have motivated politicians to get on the bandwagon are

1. No political problem poses as safe an issue as consumer legislation—it has far-reaching appeal for most voters. Although such issues as busing and community integration are likely to divide the voting public, consumer protection is an area that is extremely popular with most people.
2. In terms of governmental expense, proportionately little money is necessary for many consumer protection projects. With continuous budget trimming, the government is amenable to legislation that will not require vast appropriations.
3. Laxity on the part of state and local governments has prompted the federal level to set the tone and initiate consumer legislation. Perhaps, if municipalities had taken an earlier, more positive stance, the federal government would not have involved itself as extensively.
4. Poor product performance of manufactured goods that are sold nationally seems to fall within the jurisdiction of federal legislation. Because most of

this merchandise is not peculiar to one state or city but passes across state lines, perhaps federal, uniform action is more appropriate than individual legislation from the many states and cities affected.

5. A very popular argument is that self-regulation has not worked. Few businesses have taken the requests of citizens to provide better products, more information, and truthful advertising. With business managers showing their allegiance to stockholders by means of higher corporate profits, little was done to heed the complaints of consumers.

The Federal Trade Commission.   The Federal Trade Commission, along with other regulatory agencies, was organized to prevent unfair business practices. Specifically, the FTC is charged with the responsibility of preventing unfair methods of competition and unfair practices in interstate commerce. The commission has steadily played a significant role in protecting the consumer against unfair practices.

Since its establishment in 1914, the Federal Trade Commission's strength has been broadened by the enactment of major legislation. Some of the most important acts that have come under the FTC's jurisdiction are

1. *The Wool Products Labeling Act of 1939.* This act added to the commission's authority, which had been limited to the advertisement of wool products sold in interstate commerce. The act increased the authority of the commission to include in the label the type of wool as well.
2. *The Fur Products Labeling Act of 1951.* In addition to the prohibition of false advertising, this act required that fur garments carry informative labels.
3. *Flammable Fabrics Act of 1953.* With this piece of legislation, the commission was able to establish standards of flammability of fabric and wearing apparel.
4. *Textile Fiber Products Identification Act of 1958.* In this, the most complete product act ever written, coverage includes the prohibition of false advertising and requirements for informative labeling.

At an American Association of Advertising Agencies' annual meeting, Commissioner Mary Gardiner Jones of the FTC, in a talk entitled "The Commission's Consumer-Protection Role," emphasized the commission's three overall objectives to eliminate unfair and deceptive practices from the marketplace.

> First, the commission must see its role as one which is primarily designed to translate the consumer's expectations about the marketplace into enforceable business obligations. Second, the commission must devise its programs with a view to redressing the imbalances of power which exist between the consumer and his seller. These imbalances reflect themselves in the lack of availability of hard data about the products being offered. They also reflect themselves in the inability of consumers either to protect themselves from frauds or deceptions or

to obtain redress if their interests have been damaged when a violation of law takes place. Third, the commission must use its powers so as to supplement or complement the workings of the competitive system where it fails in fact to bring business practices into line with the needs of consumers or to eliminate practices which are false or unfair to consumers or competitors.

Advertising has been and continues to be a major area of concern for the FTC. Many citizens' groups have been formed to voice specific complaints about advertising. In response to these complaints and in line with its statutory responsibilities, the FTC is involved in the following areas:

1. Advertising monitoring—a program in which storyboards, photos, and scripts of commercials of the major networks are carefully examined.
2. Screening the audio tapes of commercials.
3. Investigating the use of testimonials.

The FTC is also involved in setting remedies for truth in advertising. They have established an advertising documentation or substantiation program and a retail store advertising program. They can issue cease-and-desist orders, ask for an affirmative disclosure, or demand corrective advertising to eliminate the residual effects of inaccurate or misleading information in prior advertising.

The Food and Drug Administration.   The responsibilities of the Food and Drug Administration cover not only food and drugs but also cosmetics and therapeutic devices. The FDA is part of the Department of Health, Education, and Welfare. Compliance with its established regulations is enforced through the administration's regular inspection program.

In addition to the general areas of concern, such as proper labeling of foods containing preservatives and artificial coloring and the warning on the labels of drugs that they are habit forming, the FDA has expanded duties, which include

1. Full review of food additives.
2. The devising of a system for the rapid identification of drugs in time of personal emergency.
3. The establishment of minimum standards for devices such as contact lenses, hearing aids, and artificial valves that are implanted in the body.

The Department of Agriculture.   The consumer receives protection in the selection of agricultural products through inspection work carried out by the Department of Agriculture. The department establishes certain standards for these products and a grading system for canned goods. Inspection of agricultural and of meat and poultry products takes place at regular intervals. In addition to the inspection at canneries and packing plants, the department, at the request of manufacturers, inspects their goods to be marketed and issues certificates for these goods.

The Office of Consumer Affairs.   As an outgrowth of President Kennedy's creation of the position of Special Assistant for Consumer Affairs in the mid-1960s came the establishment of the federal government's Office of Consumer Affairs. Until that time the federal government did little in the field of consumer protection and left the responsibilities to the states and municipalities. As consumer awareness increased with each passing day, the federal government felt that it was necessary to initiate its own participation, on a national level. With many agencies already established at the lower levels of government, it was necessary to delineate lines of authority so that there would be no confusion as to responsibility.

Among the areas of immediate concern to the newly established Office of Consumer Affairs were

1. To advise the president on consumer matters.
2. To alert governmental officials of the implications of decisions on consumer-related interests.
3. To redirect complaints to the appropriate office for a course of action to be taken.
4. To assist in the education of the public in matters of consumer concern.
5. To testify at consumerism-related hearings.
6. To offer and seek out industrial information in consumer matters.
7. To assist in the development, organization, and administration of state and municipal consumer programs.

Consumer Legislation.   Since 1964 a great deal of legislation has been enacted which has played a considerable role in the enlightenment and protection of the consumer. The following are among the major new laws.

> *Truth-in-Securities Act (Securities Act Amendment), August 20, 1964.* Provided greater protection to investors by extending disclosure requirements to over-the-counter securities. Required improved qualification and disciplinary procedures of registered brokers and dealers.
>
> *Drug Abuse Control Amendments, July 15, 1965.* Protected public health and safety by preventing both misuse and illicit traffic of potentially dangerous drugs, especially sedatives and stimulants.
>
> *Fair Packaging and Labeling Act, November 3, 1966.* Protected consumers by preventing unfair and deceptive methods of packaging and labeling. Made value comparisons easier by requiring manufacturers to label each product clearly as to manufacturer's name, ingredients, and weight.
>
> *Traffic Safety Act (Highway Safety Act), September 9, 1966.* Increased public highway safety by creating a federal-state partnership for coordinated and accelerated national highway safety programs.
>
> *Bank Supervisory Act (Financial Institutions Supervisory Act), October 16, 1966.* Protected investors by strengthening the ability of federal supervisory

agencies to safeguard the soundness of the nation's financial system and by increased insurance coverage for depositors and savers.

National Commission on Product Safety Act, November 20, 1967. Protected consumers by establishment of the National Commission on Product Safety to identify dangerous products, determine the effectiveness of regulatory laws, and recommend additional protective measures, if necessary.

Flammable Fabrics Act Amendment, December 14, 1967. Protected consumers from flammable clothing and household products by broadening the federal authority to set safety standards as well as the range of fabrics and articles covered.

Wholesome Meat Act, December 15, 1967. Protected consumers from impure and unwholesome meat by offering states federal assistance in establishing interstate inspection systems, providing that federal inspection would be made if after two years no state inspection system as good as the federal system had been established; gave the federal government the power to inspect state plants; and raised the standards of quality for all imported meats.

Automobile Insurance Study Resolution, May 22, 1968. Safeguarded consumers from inequalities and inadequacies of automobile insurance by authorizing a comprehensive study of the existing compensation system, including recommendations for improvement.

Truth-in-Lending Act (Consumer Credit Protection Act), May 29, 1968. Safeguarded consumers by requiring full disclosure of terms and conditions of finance charges in credit transaction, by restricting garnishment of wages, and by creating the National Commission on Consumer Finance to study and make recommendations on the need for further regulation of the consumer finance industry.

Interstate Land Sales Full Disclosure Act (incorporated as Title 14 of the Housing and Urban Development Act of 1968), August 1, 1968. Protected consumers with greater safeguards against shrewd and unscrupulous practices in interstate land sales by requiring sellers to provide potential buyers, fully, simply, and clearly, with all material facts needed for an informed choice.

Wholesome Poultry Products Act, August 18, 1968. Protected consumers from impure and unwholesome poultry and poultry products, just as the Wholesome Meat Act increased protection from impure meat.

Amend National Commission on Product Safety Act, August 4, 1969. A bill to amend the National Commission on Product Safety Act in order to extend the life of the commission for completion of its assigned tasks.

Child Protection and Toy Safety Act of 1969, November 6, 1969. Protected children from toys and other articles intended for children that are hazardous for electrical, mechanical, or thermal reasons.

Council on Environmental Quality Act, January 1, 1970. Authorized the Secretary of the Interior to conduct investigations, studies, surveys, and research relating to the nation's ecological systems, natural resources, and environmental quality and to establish a Council on Environmental Quality.

Amend Federal Credit Union Act, March 30, 1970. Amended the Federal Credit Union Act to provide for an independent federal agency for the supervision of federally chartered credit unions.

Public Health Smoking Cigarette Act of 1969, April 1, 1970. Extended public health protection with respect to cigarette smoking.

Amend National Traffic and Motor Vehicle Safety Act of 1966, May 22, 1970. Amended the National Traffic and Motor Vehicle Safety Act of 1966 to authorize appropriations for fiscal years 1970 and 1971.

Fair Credit Report Act, 1970. Regulates the reporting on credit information and the use thereof. It sets a limit of $50 for consumer liability on lost or stolen credit cards.

Consumer Product Safety Act, 1972. Established the Consumer Product Safety Commission.

Consumer Product Warranty Act, 1975. Increased consumers' rights and responsibilities of sellers under product warranties.

Consumer Product Safety Commission.   Established by the Consumer Product Safety Act of 1972, this commission is one of the most powerful regulatory agencies of the federal government. The commission has the authority to set safety standards for most consumer products, with the exception of such items as food products, drugs, automobiles, and tobacco products. It has the power to list the names of brands and companies concerned with problem products and can prohibit the sale of such products. So powerful is the commission's authority that it can find executives of the guilty companies to be personally liable.

As a part of its regular operation, the commission publishes a list of dangerous products as reported by hospitals. Included in the group most frequently are bicycles, sports equipment, and furniture products.

State and Local Government

The degree of involvement and enlightenment regarding consumer protection at government levels below the federal varies from state to state and from municipality to municipality. Many states and municipalities have established significant laws equal in magnitude to those of the federal government but restricted by state or city boundaries.

Some of the areas of concern that have prompted legislative action on state and local levels include the following:

1. Tenant security deposits
2. Trading stamp company policies
3. Door-to-door sales
4. Unordered merchandise
5. Unsolicited credit cards
6. Credit card irregularities
7. Bait-and-switch advertising
8. Installment purchases
9. Out-of-date packaged goods

Where the federal government has failed to react in a rapid manner, local governments have taken an active role in the protection of their citizens. Although there is sometimes an overlapping of laws enacted by the various levels of government, more attention is being paid to the consumer than ever before.

BUSINESS PARTICIPATION

For many years the complaints of consumers have fallen on the relatively deaf ears of business. That is not to say that all businesses have elected to ignore consumer complaints, but many have responded in less than satisfactory ways. Since the late 1960s, a complete about-face has been made by industry. It does not matter whether the cause has been a self-awakening and response to consumer needs, government action and legislation, or the crusading efforts of consumer advocates such as Ralph Nader.

Many companies have developed and continue to improve programs that benefit the consuming public. The leaders among businesses have been the industrial giants responsible for the majority of the consumer products and services. Smaller companies are also beginning to become responsive to consumer needs.

Industry response has generally been that fraudulent and deceptive practices were never intentional, but that poor lines of communication with consumers have been the principal cause of unhappiness and dissatisfaction.

In an effort to correct problems and to open lines of communication, many types of programs have been initiated. The General Motors Corporation established a Public Policy Committee for internal advice on matters that affect the general public. General Motors, one of the world's largest corporations, has been a major target of leaders of both the environmental and consumer movements. The committee is composed of five members of the twenty-three–member board of directors of General Motors; four are not officers in the company and one is a former vice-chairman of the corporation. The committee's task is to give advice to the board of directors on how to handle such problems as safety and pollution. Although the establishment of such a committee is considered a step toward self-regulation, the organization and composition of the committee is "genuinely preposterous," according to Ralph Nader. Nader in an interview said, "The fact that they couldn't go outside of the company for the men is an indication of General Motors' insecurity. It's so ridiculous that it will backfire." Although not quite as critical as Nader, Philip Moore, executive secretary of Campaign G.M., an organized group of critics of General Motors, said, "While we wish the committee well and will do everything in our power to assist its efforts, we are dismayed to observe that it suffers from the same parochialism as the board itself." Obviously, General Motors' action concerning consumer protection is looked upon with considerable skepticism.

At a conference in June 1970, sponsored by Advanced Management Research International, Inc., entitled "Consumerism, and Its Dramatic Impact on Corporate Profits," many consumer experts from government, business, and consumer interest groups evaluated the consumer information gap. Representing the Maytag Company, probably best known for its washing machine, was the concern's marketing vice-president, Claire G. Ely. In his speech Mr. Ely emphasized the reason that Maytag has been successful since 1893 while many competitors fell by the wayside over the years. Serving the consumer seems to be Maytag's key to success. The company makes available to dealers, without cost, an information tag to hang on every product. The information covered includes the company's name, address, and telephone number so that when problems arise customers can contact the organization directly. To make certain that the consumer is completely satisfied with servicing and repairs, the company sends out field service supervisors to meet and help train service personnel. In this way it can be certain that the customer is satisfied. Examination of Maytag's warranty showed need for change. The small print was eliminated and the warranty was restated in language that was designed to be easily understood. Mr. Ely concluded by discussing the handling of complaints. It is company policy that all correspondence is answered immediately and individually, without the use of form letters. Complaints are always followed up.

Maytag's Information Center has produced a pamphlet on its consumer programs. It fully covers the areas of consumer concern, such as warranty, service training, parts availability, operating instructions, and safety control. The company presents consumer education programs to many types of consumer groups. Also made available is such free consumer education literature as a stain-removal chart.

Maytag people think of themselves as a customer-oriented company. They do not consider themselves good Samaritans or do-gooders but good businesspeople.

The Maytag Company has instituted a multifaceted program to improve its customer relations. Among the features of the program are the following:

1. A team of field service representatives regularly calls upon service personnel to assist in service and repair training. In this way, customers who require service are more likely to be satisfied.

2. The company makes available, at no cost to the dealers, complete information tags to be included with every product produced by Maytag. The tags include all information needed by a customer who wishes to contact the company.

3. Small print, generally misunderstood or not read, has been eliminated from the company's warranties. Instead, simply and clearly worded information is contained in each warranty.

4. Through its information center, Maytag produces descriptive pamphlets, plans consumer-oriented programs, and distributes free consumer education literature.

The Whirlpool Corporation has initiated what they call a "cool line"; the public is invited to call the Customer Services Director at all times. In this way immediate attention is paid to the customer and complaints can be handled more efficiently.

The Ford Motor Company carries out a number of programs to educate the consumer. A few years ago, in an effort to make the public aware of automobile safety, the company sponsored a promotional campaign in this area. Instead of investing all its advertising dollars in promoting style and design, some money was earmarked for safety promotion. Ultimately, the consumer benefited.

The list of companies and their consumer-oriented programs continues to grow. Similar to Whirlpool, Avis and Chrysler have established cool lines of communication. Most businesses now accept written complaints and react to them through written communication. Examples of businesses that use written communications are Nabisco and Pillsbury.

Many retailers, such as R. H. Macy and Sears, Roebuck, provide consumer protection through their standards and testing bureaus. Before goods are offered for sale, they undergo specific tests that separate the inferior from the desirable products. In this way, the consumer is almost certain to be assured of product satisfaction.

Recent studies of many businesses show a definite trend toward consumerism. Some business firms are not likely to confess their sudden expansion into consumer programs, but it is evident from their actions that, in order to survive, the consumer-is-king (or queen) philosophy must be carefully followed.

Independent Consulting Firms

Probably the first national consulting firm specializing in consumer affairs is Kay Valory Consultants. Kay Valory is a former consumer affairs assistant to Governor Reagan of California. After three and a half years and ten thousand letters of consumer complaints as consumer counsel, Mrs. Valory has organized her own firm for the purpose of what she describes as "preventive consumerism." She charges that the expense of government regulation through the many consumer affairs departments is costing the taxpayer many millions of dollars. "The Dear Abby of Consumerism" as she was known in California, Mrs. Valory feels that much of the cost to taxpayers could be avoided if industry became self-regulatory.

Among her clients are a hearing-aid manufacturer and a chain of supermarkets. With offices in such states as New York, California, and Illinois, businesspeople in those areas can avail themselves of consumer affairs counseling for a minimum fee of $50 per hour. The firm's services include the conducting of surveys to measure consumer reaction to products, the development of practical policy changes, and the creation of complete programs to improve the business-consumer relationship.

The Better Business Bureaus

As part of the Association of Better Business Bureaus, there are Better Business Bureaus located throughout the United States. The objective of the bureaus is the promotion of ethical business practices.

All the bureaus are nonprofit service corporations, maintained by business firms to elevate the standards of business conduct, fight fraud, and assist the public to achieve maximum satisfaction from its relations with business. They do not endorse or recommend any security, product, service, or concern, and no concern is permitted to indicate otherwise in its advertising or selling.

Basically, the local offices handle complaints that have been brought about by unfair practices of local businesses. For example, a complaint involving a company located in upper Manhattan may be brought to the attention of the Better Business Bureau of metropolitan New York. If the customer's dissatisfaction is with a company located more specifically in the Harlem area, the complaint would be handled by the Harlem branch of the bureau. In small cities, one central office handles all the complaints; in larger metropolitan areas, branch bureaus are established, because of the enormous number of complaints. The association has an Office for Consumer Affairs in Washington, D.C., to deal with complaints against national companies and to permit information to filter from the government to the local bureaus.

Aside from the handling of complaints, the bureaus operate in a fashion that will stop the consumer from being cheated. Advertisements are carefully scrutinized by bureau personnel in an attempt to uncover false or misleading contents. When the bureau comes across advertising that appears to be deceptive, it makes an investigation. If the advertisement is not truthful, for example the merchandise at the advertised price does not fulfill the vendor's claims, the bureau approaches the seller. Where a merchant refuses to rectify the situation, the bureau might inform the media in which the questionable advertisement has taken place to prevent further promotion (most newspapers, magazines, TV stations, and so on, will not permit unfair advertising). If a law or regulation has been violated, the bureau will notify the appropriate government department, such as the attorney general's office. The bureau does not have the legal power to prosecute, but, as an investigative agency, it has been responsible for bringing legal suits against offenders.

Most of the bureaus make available to consumers brochures designed for their education with regard to purchases. For example, the Education and Research Foundation of the Better Business Bureaus of Metropolitan New York, Inc., has developed a "Wise-Buying Guide Series." These bulletins deal with various consumer products. An example is "The Careful Way to Buy a Car," which outlines such areas as used cars, ability to afford the price, contracts, guarantees, and sales tricks to be wary of.

Trade Associations

Industries organize associations to upgrade and improve their operations and standards. Although the goal of the trade associations is the overall improvement of their industry, the consumer often is the beneficiary of their efforts. For example, most trade associations—such as the National Retail Merchants' Association—frown upon unfair and unethical advertising practices. Self-regulation of advertising has been the aim of many associations. Cigarette manufacturers, having established an advertising code for their industry, enforce substantial fines for its violation. Besides advertising, trade associations are involved in other areas that help the consumer. Although trade associations cannot force businesses within their industries to heed their recommendations, they continue to make meaningful changes that ultimately benefit the consumer.

CONSUMER ADVOCATES

Ralph Nader, Self-appointed Consumer Guardian

Sometimes called the United States' toughest customer, Ralph Nader has become the self-appointed and unsalaried guardian of the interests of over 200 million consumers. Champion of numerous causes, Nader has stirred up enough trouble to warrant industry to reappraise its responsibilities. In his book, *Unsafe at Any Speed*, Nader condemned General Motors' Corvair. Eventually, and perhaps because of the adverse publicity for the Corvair, General Motors halted production of that automobile.

Nader has influenced the passage of the following federal laws:

1. The National Traffic and Motor Vehicle Safety Act of 1966
2. The Wholesome Meat Act of 1967
3. The Natural Gas Pipeline Act of 1968
4. The Radiation Control for Health and Safety Act of 1968
5. The Wholesome Poultry Products Act of 1968
6. The Federal Coal Mine Health and Safety Act of 1969

Other areas of consumer concern that he brought to the attention of the public were the dangers of monosodium glutamate, cyclamates, and DDT. Color television sets, sometimes dangerous because of leaking radiation, were recalled as a result of one of his investigations.

Besides his attacks on business, Nader has leveled attacks on government agencies. He has probed the Federal Trade Commission, the National Air Pollution Control Administration, and the Federal Railroad Administration, among others. To expand his investigations, Nader employs the services of students. Collectively, the group has become known as "Nader's Raiders."

Perhaps the magnitude of his reputation as the consumer's guardian can best be realized through the thousands of pieces of mail that reach him labeled simply: Ralph Nader, Washington, D.C. Although government (federal, state, municipal) and industry are deeply involved in consumerism, most of those involved confess (either publicly or privately) that Ralph Nader began the entire movement.

Although his role of chief consumer advocate continues, Nader has recently received what many consider a personal setback by the defeat of legislation that would have established a new federal agency. In early 1978, by a 227-to-189 vote, the House of Representatives defeated the bill that Nader's group considered the most important bill of this decade. According to Nader, the legislation would have reduced bureaucracy by moving consumer units out of existing agencies and combining them into one unit. At this time, Nader is involved in a variety of other consumerism actions and, from all indications, expects to continue his fight for better consumer protection.

In addition to Nader, many other noteworthy consumer advocates represent government, private agencies, the news media, and other organizations and agencies. TV's Betty Furness, and radio's Linda Sutter, are among the more prominent ones.

TESTING ORGANIZATIONS

A number of organizations were established to bring to consumers product information that will enable them to make more knowledgeable purchases. The best known is the Consumers Union. Through its monthly publication of *Consumer Reports*, potential customers are able to equip themselves with knowledge of various products. For example, the prospective automobile purchaser need only examine the issue on automobiles (they are evaluated each year) to gain enough product information. At the end of each year, Consumers Union publishes an annual volume that covers all products tested throughout the year.

In their own words, "The purposes of Consumers Union are to provide consumers with information and counsel on consumer goods and services, to give information on all matters relating to the expenditure of the family income, and to initiate and to cooperate with individual and group efforts seeking to create and maintain decent living standards."

Consumers Union, established in 1936, is a nonprofit organization. It derives its income solely from the sale of its publications. Unlike the magazine institutes, such as Good Housekeeping and Parents' Magazine, which test products and assign *seals* to satisfactory products, Consumers Union *rates* goods. For example, goods are rated from excellent to poor. By reading the ratings, consumers are able to compare products and are made aware of those that are poor in quality. Often consumers save money by purchasing a lesser known product that has higher quality and a lower cost than that of a better known brand.

PROGNOSIS FOR CONSUMERS

From every indication, the consumer movement will continue to flourish. Both industry and government are investing enormous sums of money and time in the promotion and protection of consumer rights. If either group shirks its responsibilities, it is quite certain that consumer advocates will come forth. While this seems to be a happy and positive situation in which consumers can live, a question that is beginning to be raised must be answered: Will the actions of government cost consumers money? Another question that must be answered involves the anxiety caused consumers by many of the government's consumer protection postures.

The treatment of children's sleepwear with flame-retardant chemicals caused a 20 percent price increase and ultimately a ban on Tris, a major chemical in the manufacture of such material, because of suspicion that it is a cause of cancer. This is one example in which higher prices and consumer anxiety resulted. Anxiety has also resulted from reports of carcinogenicity in certain products, followed later by announcements that the earlier reports were inconclusive. Certain spray adhesives were banned when it was determined that use by pregnant women could cause birth defects. A few months later the report was deemed inconclusive and the ban on the product was rescinded.

The public seems to be becoming more concerned over the effects of some of government's regulation of products and the problems to the consumer that result. In the future, both government and industry must address themselves to the problems that result from consumer protection and plan more carefully to alter the effects.

Important Points in the Chapter _____

1. Participation of the federal government in consumerism is through such agencies as the Office of Consumer Affairs, the Federal Trade Commission, the Food and Drug Administration, and the Department of Agriculture.

2. The federal government has passed numerous consumer laws since 1964. Those of great significance are the Fair Packaging and Labeling Act, Flam-

mable Fabrics Act Amendment, Consumer Credit Protection Act (Truth-in-Lending), and the Child Protection and Toy Safety Act.

3. Industry is somewhat involved in self-regulation. Maytag, for example, has extensive consumer programs.

4. Kay Valory Consultants, headed by a former consumer affairs assistant to the governor of California, is the first consulting organization for consumer affairs. It was organized for the purpose of "preventive consumerism."

5. The Better Business Bureaus handle customer complaints and try to correct false advertising claims.

6. Ralph Nader, the foremost name in consumerism, is involved in righting the wrongs of both business and government in their relationships with consumers. He is credited by many to be the individual responsible for the entire consumer-protection movement.

Review Questions

1. Define the term *consumerism*.

2. What are the purposes of the federal government's Office of Consumer Affairs?

3. How does the Federal Trade Commission involve itself in protection of the consumer?

4. Describe the program that the Federal Trade Commission has designed to combat advertising complaints.

5. Discuss briefly the role of the Food and Drug Administration in connection with consumerism.

6. Which federal government agency concerns itself with standards and grades of products?

7. Cite the most important provisions of the Fair Packaging and Labeling Act of 1966.

8. Name the first private consulting organization specializing in consumer affairs. Whom does it represent?

9. Why has General Motors' Public Policy Committee been criticized by such people as Ralph Nader?

10. Describe the outstanding features of Maytag's consumer education programs.

11. Discuss the role of the Better Business Bureaus and trade associations in connection with consumerism.

12. Ralph Nader is considered to be the consumers' guardian. Discuss briefly some of the areas of his involvement in consumer protectionism.

Case Problems

Case Problem 1

For the past year much criticism has been levied against the olive industry. Companies that produce and distribute olives bottle their products and assign such descriptive terms as *super, colossal, giant,* and *large* to describe the size of their products. Consumers, unable to determine the actual olive size because of the confusing labels, have been continuously plagued by the problem.

Since the descriptive terms used are not in violation of any law, the olive companies have continued to follow their labeling practice. Moreover, many distributors package their olives in cans, which prevents inspection of size.

With the problem ever increasing, Action, a consumer protection association, served notice on the olive industry. They insisted upon labeling reform, self-imposed by the industry, or formal complaints would be made to the appropriate governmental agencies, such as the Department of Consumer Affairs and the Department of Agriculture.

At a meeting of the major olive companies, the problem was discussed. Although a number of suggestions were made, two positions seemed to be dominant. One was to self-regulate and change the present labeling practice; the second was to continue with the current system, since the practice does not violate any laws.

Questions

1. From a marketer's standpoint, which position should be followed?
2. Why?

Case Problem 2

The city of Oceanview has a population of two million and is located in a large Eastern state. Oceanview's major industries are retailing and light manufacturing, with most of the manufacturers' goods being limited to distribution within the city. Over the years, business in Oceanview has had its share of complaints. Both retailers and manufacturers had to remedy poor situations.

To aid consumers, a Better Business Bureau was established in Oceanview. Besides handling complaints, the bureau sought out businesses that practiced deceptive advertising and other unfair practices. In spite of this, complaints continue to mount and the consuming public has become extremely upset. At the present time there is a citizens' movement under way for the establishment of a consumer affairs department. Some of the arguments that have been made are the following:

1. Creation of such a department would call for higher taxes.
2. The federal government has a consumer affairs department. Why can it not handle our problems?
3. If the Better Business Bureau has been unsuccessful, the new department would not fare much better. What more could it do?
4. It is industry's responsibility to self-regulate; why should the government bother?

Questions

1. With which side do you agree? Defend your position in terms of the arguments posed.
2. Are there any additional arguments for either side? Discuss.

19

INTERNATIONAL MARKETING

Learning Objectives

Upon completion of the chapter, you will be able to:

1. Discuss the economic importance of foreign trade.

2. List and describe five different types of areas with foreign trade possibilities and discuss the advantages and disadvantages of each area.

3. Explain the importance of adapting the product and the message to suit the specific trading area.

4. Describe the product life cycle in foreign trade.

5. List six types of foreign operation and explain the situation best suited to each.

6. Explain the importance of maintaining good will in foreign markets, including methods of attaining this end.

THE NESTLÉ CASE

The August, 1973 issue of the British publication *New Internationalist* contained an article called "The Baby Food Tragedy" which was to have a devastating effect on the infant formula industry, with Nestlé as the prime target. The article and other information that followed, including a TV documentary, claimed that Nestlé's marketing of infant formula products in Third World nations resulted in death and malnutrition. The outcry became so intense that a boycott of Nestlé's products was supported by such groups as the National Council of Lutheran Women, the United Presbyterian Church, various Catholic groups, and major unions.

While the uproar singled out Nestlé as the focus of the protest, it was really directed against the whole infant formula industry, of which Nestlé was considered a typical example rather than the sole culprit. The protest was centered upon Nestlé's aggressive marketing policies which, it was charged, subtly suggested that infant formula was more healthful than mother's milk. Specifically it was claimed that

Advertisements picturing healthy babies were understood by Third World mothers as an indication of infant formula superiority.

Free samples given by medical personnel in or out of hospitals promoted the idea that infant formula was superior to mother's milk.

Gifts, commissions, and bonuses were made to health personnel to promote the sale of infant formulas.

Nestlé employed visiting nurses who, it was claimed, were more interested in promoting formula sales than public health.

Labels and other literature were misleading.

The issue grew to international importance. Finally the World Health Organization, a specialized agency of the United Nations, with responsibility for matters of international health studied the problem. WHO produced the International Code of Marketing of Breast Milk Substitutes. Nestlé complied with the code, even going so far as to

Nestlé advertisement for its infant formula product. (*Courtesy:* The Nestlé Corporation.)

provide an Independent Audit Commission led by former Secretary of State Edmund Muskie. As a result of the findings of the Audit Commission, the worldwide boycott was called off. Nestlé is no longer marketed as a substitute for normal mother's milk, to which it is inferior, but as a substitute for native weaning foods to which it is vastly superior.

While the Nestlé case has been resolved, the ethical question has not. Nestlé's marketing in the Third World conformed with the laws of the land and, in fact, was the same aggressive effort that it uses in the Western world. The question is, "Is marketing morality the responsibility of the country in which the goods are being sold, or is it the responsibility of the company doing the selling?" What do you think?

INTRODUCTION

When the domestic market of a highly industrialized nation, such as the United States, becomes saturated through excessive competition, its producers must turn to foreign markets to ensure their continued survival and growth. Since World War II, the world market has increased enormously in terms of population and gross national product. This has had the effect of greatly increasing the importance of foreign markets as a source of sales volume and profits for domestic producers.

Some years ago, foreign trade was generally limited to supplying needs that could not be produced locally. At present, world trade is truly global in nature. Such nondomestic products as German and Japanese automobiles and Japanese TV sets are extremely successful in the United States in the teeth of a highly technical, industrially advanced local competition. Trends indicate a continued expansion in world trade.

Economic Importance of Exports

The growth and importance of world trade to the United States is quite dramatic. In 1981, over $233 billion in exports were sent to foreign markets, while imports exceeded that amount. In total, our trade with foreign sources equaled a significant percentage of the gross national product of the United States. The Department of Commerce estimates that each $1 billion of exports results in 100,000 jobs in the United States. Based on this estimate, foreign exports in 1981 resulted in the employment of many millions of American workers. It is obvious that foreign trade has an importance to the country far beyond the profits made by an individual producer. Naturally, some industries are more involved with overseas markets than others.

Table 19–1 illustrates domestic exports of manufactured products for the period 1970 to 1987. The major products exported are chemicals, food, machinery, and electrical and transportation equipment.

TABLE 19–1. Domestic exports of manufactured products, 1970–1987

Product	1987 Value (mil. dol.)	Percent distribution	Growth Rate (percent)			Ratio of Exports to Product Shipments (percent)			
			1970–1987	1980–1987	1986–1987	1972	1977	1982	1987
Total Manufacturing	**198,355**	**100.0**	**10.9**	**2.5**	**15.3**	**5.6**	**7.4**	**9.1**	**8.2**
Nondurables	60,148	30.3	11.3	2.5	16.6	3.5	4.5	5.4	5.2
Food and kindred products	12,320	6.1	9.8	.2	9.5	2.9	4.1	4.3	3.9
Tobacco manufactures	2,278	1.1	15.7	11.2	53.9	5.7	9.4	10.3	9.1
Textile mill products	1,891	1.0	8.9	-3.8	14.4	2.9	4.3	4.9	3.9
Apparel and other mill products	1,490	.8	11.8	-1.0	26.5	1.2	2.2	2.4	2.1
Paper and allied products	5,676	2.9	10.1	2.8	26.7	4.1	4.9	5.5	4.7
Printing and publishing	1,525	.8	9.4	4.6	17.5	1.3	1.5	1.7	1.2
Chemicals and allied products	26,090	13.2	11.8	2.7	15.6	7.6	9.7	12.5	11.9
Petroleum and coal products	4,479	2.3	13.3	6.7	5.9	1.9	1.4	3.2	3.6
Rubber and plastics products	3,710	1.9	12.6	4.8	26.1	3.1	4.0	4.8	4.1
Leather and leather products	688	.3	15.0	4.4	32.2	1.8	3.8	5.7	7.3
Durables	138,207	69.7	10.7	2.5	14.8	7.4	10.0	13.0	10.8
Lumber and wood products	3,961	2.0	10.8	1.0	31.2	4.1	5.8	7.2	5.5
Furniture and fixtures	550	.3	15.5	2.8	18.1	.6	1.5	2.5	1.5
Stone, clay, and glass products	2,045	1.0	9.3	.9	18.7	2.4	3.4	4.3	3.2
Primary metal industries	4,772	2.4	4.5	-8.3	32.7	2.8	3.0	5.0	3.6
Fabricated metal products	6,185	3.1	8.1	-1.3	11.6	3.9	5.6	6.6	4.5
Machinery, except electrical	41,054	20.7	10.2	1.1	12.9	14.9	19.5	23.3	20.1
Electrical and electronic equipment	24,359	12.3	13.7	5.8	19.3	6.7	10.6	12.7	10.8
Transportation equipment	42,371	21.4	11.5	5.4	11.6	9.2	11.6	15.6	12.5
Instruments and related products	10,191	5.1	11.7	4.1	10.3	12.6	16.6	17.4	16.5
Miscellaneous manufacturing industries	2,719	1.4	10.4	-.9	30.7	7.6	9.4	9.5	9.3

Source: U.S. Department of Commerce, *Statistical Abstract of the United States, 1989* (Washington, D.C.: U.S. Government Printing Office, 1989).

TABLE 19–2. Imports for consumption of manufactured products, 1970–1987

SIC[1] Code	Product	1987 Value (mil. dol.)	Percent distribution	Growth Rate[2] (percent) 1970–1987	1980–1987	1986–1987	Import Penetration Ratio[3] (percent) 1972	1977	1982	1987
(×)	**Total Manufacturing**	**340,089**	**100.0**	**15.0**	**12.6**	**10.0**	**6.1**	**7.0**	**8.5**	**12.9**
(×)	Nondurables	94,298	27.7	13.0	9.0	11.6	4.7	5.4	5.8	8.0
20	Food and kindred products	13,180	3.9	8.0	3.4	5.3	3.9	3.8	3.6	4.2
21	Tobacco manufactures	90	—	10.5	–.4	10.2	.6	.7	1.8	.5
22	Textile mill products	4,780	1.4	9.3	13.0	13.1	5.6	4.2	5.4	8.4
23	Apparel and other mill products	21,503	6.3	18.0	18.6	18.3	7.0	10.3	14.3	24.5
26	Paper and allied products	9,715	2.9	11.3	8.7	18.0	5.6	6.3	6.1	7.3
27	Printing and publishing	1,329	.4	13.7	14.6	7.5	1.0	.9	.9	1.4
28	Chemicals and allied products	14,318	4.2	15.3	10.8	8.5	3.2	3.9	4.5	6.7
29	Petroleum and coal products	13,123	3.9	13.3	–.3	2.2	7.1	8.5	7.3	9.8
30	Rubber and plastics products	6,331	1.9	14.2	12.7	17.7	4.7	5.4	5.1	6.9
31	Leather and leather products	9,930	2.9	16.9	16.6	14.8	15.9	21.2	33.9	54.8
(×)	Durables	245,791	72.3	16.0	14.3	9.4	7.2	8.3	11.2	16.8
24	Lumber and wood products	5,959	1.8	11.2	7.3	10.9	9.4	9.3	8.2	10.2
25	Furniture and fixtures	4,575	1.3	19.6	22.9	14.5	2.6	3.6	5.3	10.6
32	Stone, clay, and glass products	5,560	1.6	14.7	13.7	13.2	3.7	4.0	5.3	8.3
33	Primary metal industries	19,108	5.6	9.9	2.9	4.2	8.9	10.0	14.7	16.8
34	Fabricated metal products	9,617	2.8	14.4	11.8	12.7	2.5	3.2	4.3	6.0
35	Machinery, except electrical	42,319	12.4	18.7	18.1	18.4	5.4	6.3	8.4	16.9
36	Electrical and electronic equipment	45,782	13.5	18.2	16.7	8.5	7.6	10.4	12.4	18.5
37	Transportation equipment	86,658	25.5	16.6	16.0	5.6	9.8	10.2	15.4	20.9
38	Instruments and related products	11,547	3.4	17.5	13.7	8.5	6.7	9.2	10.1	16.0
39	Miscellaneous manufacturing industries	14,666	4.3	15.9	15.2	14.8	13.3	17.2	24.0	37.5

– Represents zero

× not applicable

[1] Standard Industrial Classification

[2] 1970–87 and 1980–87 rates are compound annual growth rates.

[3] Ratio of imports to new supply (product shipments plus imports).

Source: U.S. Department of Commerce, *Statistical Abstract of the United States, 1989* (Washington, D.C.: U.S. Government Printing Office, 1989).

Imports

Foreign trade is not limited to exports. Domestic producers may be finding profitable markets overseas, but foreign products have become extremely important on the American market as well. Table 19–2 shows their importance on the domestic market and the strength of the competition they give to American industries.

In terms of total volume, the United States is by far the largest trader on the global scene. The importance of foreign trade to a country's economy can be measured in terms of the percentage of the nation's imports and exports to total production. A comparison of Tables 19–1 and 19–2 shows that America is relying more heavily on imports and is exporting less. Figure 19–1 indicates that foreign trade is as important to the total economy of the United States as it is to other countries. Note particularly the enormous cost of our petroleum imports.

One industry which has had significant problems in the United States due to an ever increasing percentage of imports is the garment industry. While much of our attention is focused upon automobile imports, the production of clothing from abroad also continues to hamper our economy. The cost of labor is a major factor. Figure 19–1 details the comparative labor costs of the United States and other major garment-producing countries. Low foreign labor costs are one of the reasons foreign goods are less expensive.

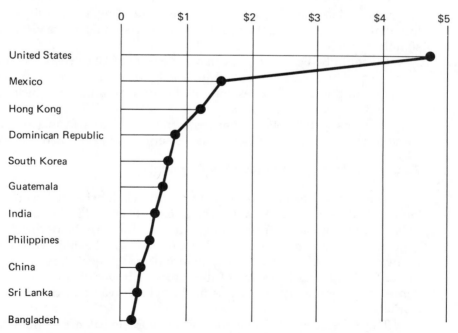

FIGURE 19–1   Comparative labor costs in less developed countries.

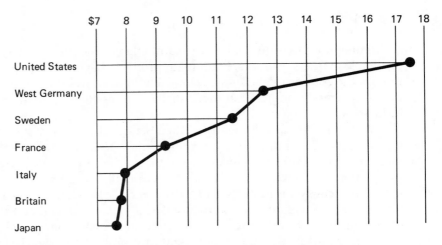

FIGURE 19–2 Comparative labor costs in industrialized countries.

Although a recent report by the University of Missouri-Columbia indicated that 47.3 percent of consumers feel that the imported garments are not as good, consumer reception seems to show that quality is not that important a prerequisite to purchasing.

Bearing this in mind, Van Heusen, a household name in men's shirts, elects to produce their goods in such faraway places as Hong Kong, Taiwan, Singapore, Malaysia, Thailand, and Korea. The company is fully aware of the fact that with proper quality control, the shirts could be made anywhere at significant savings.

It should be borne in mind that the effects of labor costs are not solely in garment production. Figure 19–2 indicates hourly labor costs, fringe benefits included, in the United States and other countries of motor vehicle and equipment industry workers.

It seems to be obvious that aside from any other factors the labor costs alone of other countries will continue to seriously affect our balance of trade.

Balance of Trade and Balance of Payments

The phrase *balance of trade* refers to the relationship between a country's imports and its exports. A nation whose exports exceed its imports is described as having a favorable balance of trade. Through the early 1970s the United States generally maintained a favorable balance of trade. By the mid-1970s this began to change, and for the year 1981 our balance of trade deficit was in the vicinity of $40 billion. This has been one of the causes of a worldwide decrease in confidence in our economy and a loss in the relative value of the dollar in world markets.

There are several reasons for our unfavorable balance of trade:

1. There has been an increase in both the cost and domestic use of oil. Our expenditure for oil imports in 1970 was $3.1 billion. By 1981 it had grown to $61 billion.

2. Our foreign competitors produce more cheaply than we do. This is true despite the fact that in recent years foreign worker salaries have approached and in some cases surpassed the earnings of our domestic workers. Part of the answer lies in the fact that productivity (output per worker-hour) has increased much more sharply abroad than it has in the United States.

3. In the area of technological know-how, our once awesome lead has been narrowed, and in many cases we have been surpassed.

4. The governments of many foreign countries encourage exports by means of special tax breaks for exporters, subsidies, and so forth. In contrast, the government of the United States does very little to encourage exporting.

5. Our once-dominant lead in marketing and customer satisfaction has all but vanished. In many cases, our foreign competitors seem more innovative and better keyed to customer demand than do our native producers.

Balance of payments refers to the excess of receipts of foreign currency over payments of domestic currency. Such receipts and payments include imports, exports, investments, tourism, grants-in-aid, and military spending abroad. As is the case with our balance of trade, our balance of payments at the present time is unfavorable. That means that the amount of money going from the United States to foreign countries exceeds the inflow from foreign countries. This problem is being tackled by our government by such steps as energy conservation (to reduce oil imports) and government negotiation to increase exports (sales of agricultural products to the Soviet Union and China).

CHOOSING AN AREA

There are many factors that must be considered by a company interested in building an export market for its product. The most important of these is the choice of an area that has a satisfactory market demand. This is dependent, in large part, on the stage of economic development of the country in question.

Economic Development

The company that chooses to involve itself in international trade must select the country in which it is to offer its product with great care. The stage of economic development of the various countries of the world can be roughly separated into six groups, each of which has its own unique marketing characteristics. Estimated demand for a company's product is based, in large part, on the economic development of the target market.

The Primitive Nations.   The first stage includes nations in an economic system based on family farming, hunting, and food gathering. There is no marketing system or wealth accumulation that can be used to purchase imports. Countries such as this may be found in parts of Africa and South America. Exports to these countries are generally government sponsored. Such countries are definitely not fertile ground for a marketing program.

The Emerging Nations.   The second stage includes nations that have progressed somewhat beyond the primitive stage. They may be found throughout Africa and the Middle East. Raw materials such as oil and metals are exported, as are surplus agricultural products. This results in surplus wealth available for imports, but the wealth is concentrated in the hands of a few large landholders, a very small middle class, and the government. The majority of the population is still in the primitive farming stage and not available as a market. The government's wealth is used for large projects (dams, roads, and so on), and the remaining wealth is in too few hands to afford a large enough market for any widespread importing.

The Start of Manufacture.   The third stage is characterized by the beginning of the processing of the materials that were previously exported in a raw state. Such products as sugar, rubber, oil, and metals are partially processed before export. These preliminary manufacturing processes employ both native labor and technical personnel from more advanced countries. Although the major part of the population may still be involved in noncurrency agriculture, those that work in manufacturing are paid in currency that is available to buy imported products. This market may be tapped by exporting to native distributors. Typical of the countries in this phase are Indonesia and the Persian Gulf nations.

The Manufacture of Consumer Goods.   The fourth stage is distinguished by the fact that more people are drawn from the farms to jobs in the processing of raw materials, where earnings are paid in currency, so that there is an increasing demand for consumer goods and funds are available for such purchases. Domestic manufacture, particularly in areas requiring small capital, can begin. Textiles, beverages, food, drugs, and other products may be manufactured locally instead of being imported. Frequently, local laws may be passed that encourage such manufacture by restricting competitive imports. Capital goods, such as machinery for local manufacturers, and durable consumer goods, such as automobiles and refrigerators, must still be imported.

The Manufacture of Capital and Durable Goods.   In the fifth stage of economic progress, a country reaches a point at which the money and demand are sufficient to support the manufacture of capital goods and durable consumer goods.

This production may require the importing of raw materials. Although industrialization has begun, the import of foreign products in competition with local industries may be at a very high level. The major economic resources of a country at this stage still rest in the export of raw and semifinished materials.

Exporting Manufactured Products. The final stage of economic development finds the country a full-fledged manufacturing nation involved in international trade. In such countries all consumers have currency and the demand for imports is great. At this point local production competes with foreign imports.

In assessing the probable demand for its product, the company must fit its merchandise offerings to a foreign market whose stage of economic development, as outlined above, is keyed to the company's product. This includes both the type of product and the method of distribution. For example, nations in the primitive, developing, and early manufacturing stages of economic development would offer insignificant markets to an automobile manufacturer. However, there might be some demand from their more affluent citizens. It would be ridiculous to set up a major exporting system, but a simple export system or local agency might be worthwhile.

As a country progresses economically, its wealth and its demand for manufactured products increase. The foreign exporter wishing to tap this market is faced with increasing competition from local manufacturers. That this need not be a deterrent to successful exporting is evidenced by the fact that the major portion of foreign trade is between highly developed countries. Although specialty items, for example Swiss watches, are frequently traded between such countries, many other products are successful despite strong, direct, local competition. Typical are German cars and Japanese cameras competing successfully with highly developed products manufactured in the United States.

Political Development

It would be unwise for any American business to expand its foreign operations into any area that is antagonistic to the United States or so unstable politically as not to be able to guarantee the maintenance of peace and lawfulness that are necessary for commercial success. Companies that make this mistake may find themselves helpless in the face of harassment that the local government either cannot or will not halt. Frequently, emerging nations, desperate for economic investment, are not in a position to attract exporters because they are unable to guarantee peace and stability for any appreciable length of time.

PepsiCo, Inc., recently entered the Mainland China market with its quick-service restaurant, Kentucky Fried Chicken, in Beijing, People's Republic of China as pictured in Figure 19–3. The challenge for an American company was great in this Communist economy but the risk in PepsiCo's move was com-

FIGURE 19–3
Kentucky Fried Chicken operates one of the world's largest quick-service restaurants in Beijing. (*Courtesy:* PepsiCo, Inc.)

pounded by uprisings that took place early in 1989, where student demonstrations for freedom were met with harsh governmental retribution.

Monetary Regulations

Often the monetary restrictions placed on a country by its government are so tight that a foreign company cannot get its investment or profits out of its operation there. Occasionally, a bartering arrangement can be made under which funds can be removed from the country in the form of easily marketable exports. If this is not the case, the company has the choice of waiting for more favorable monetary regulations or investing its profits within its foreign market.

In some cases the monetary standard of a country is so unstable that the value of that country's currency cannot be depended on. For example, Brazil recently devalued the cruzeiro by half. The holder of any contract requiring the payment of a specific number of cruzeiros would have suffered a severe loss. This can be offset by insisting that dealings with a foreign country with an unstable currency be made in dollars, pounds sterling, gold, or any other stable currency.

Habits and Culture

The habits and culture of a country, even those of neighbors, vary considerably. An example of this may be found in the expansion of American-style one-stop supermarket shopping throughout the world. In Buenos Aires, lines begin forming in front of supermarkets at 6 A.M. A Belgian family's evening walk is likely to include a stroll through a nearby supermarket. In Germany, however, the expansion of the one-stop shopping concept was much slower. Germans must shop in many specialized stores to complete their marketing. Unlike American shoppers, they do not consider this a chore but a social event, which they are loathe to give up for supermarket shopping. As a result, the expansion of supermarkets in Germany was less spectacular than expected. Other national differences encountered by supermarkets are in France, higher taxes are imposed on supermarkets than on small shops, and in Italy, there is a political stigma among radicals, holding supermarkets as a prime example of American monopolistic practices. (Despite occasional resistance, supermarkets are spreading rapidly throughout Europe.)

Tariffs and Import Quotas

Many governments attempt to improve the competitive position of domestic manufacturers by imposing tariffs (taxes on imports) and quotas (limitations in the amount of imported goods). Such an act is usually called *protective*, as it serves to protect domestic producers from foreign competition. This practice is most prevalent in developing countries, but it is found among highly industrialized nations as well. For example, the total number of automobiles that Japan may export to the United States is limited.

It is vital that a company, studying a foreign market for its product, take into account not only the present tariff and quota arrangements of the area but possible future changes in such arrangements as well. A seemingly favorable competitive area can suddenly be made unfavorable by a change in a country's tariff or quota system.

Foreign Market Research

Although it is more important to research foreign than domestic markets, in practice such research is rarely done thoroughly. The problem is expense. Information on population, government regulations, family size, and so forth, readily available at small cost on the domestic scene, would be very expensive to gather in many foreign countries. In addition, the foreign market, though large, is split up into many small segments. The cost of researching each area is very high in relation to the total potential volume from that area.

CHOOSING A PRODUCT

One of the most common causes of exporting failure is the inability to adjust the product or the company's message concerning the product properly. This is the result of ineffective market testing or the unwillingness to spend the money required for product adaptation. It is a serious error to assume that a product that is successful in one country will automatically be accepted by a neighbor with a seemingly very similar culture. Successful marketing on the domestic or the foreign scene requires the product to be keyed to customer demand. This may require varying degrees of change in the product or the promotional message.

No Product Adaptation

A few companies are fortunate enough to be able to sell the identical product, with the same promotional scheme, both at home and abroad. PepsiCo, with an outstanding export division, is typical of such companies. PepsiCo's management probably agrees that a changed promotional message might be beneficial, but they feel that the high volume under the present strategy and the cost of the changes rule out the advantages of such adaptation.

Adapting the Product

Perhaps the best way to emphasize the importance of changing the product to meet foreign requirements would be to list several costly foreign failures of locally successful products. Each of the following failures resulted from faulty foreign market research.

Campbell's tomato soup formula was unsuccessful in Britain because the market demand was for a more bitter taste.

General Mills' Betty Crocker division suffered a costly failure in attempting to sell its U.S.-proven fancy frostings and cake mixes in Britain. Another U.S. company researched the market and found that the British take cake at teatime and prefer a dry type of pastry that can be held in the left hand while holding a teacup in the right hand. This company was successful in marketing the type of product demanded by the consumers.

Dry soup mixtures are favored in Europe. CPC International imported the Knorr dry soup line after successful taste tests with canned soups. The product was a U.S. failure, perhaps because dry mixtures need twenty minutes of cooking, whereas canned soups merely have to be heated.

Most companies recognize that product adaptation is a must for successful

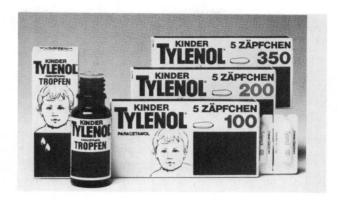

FIGURE 19–4
Tylenol packaging for the German market. (*Courtesy:* McNeil Consumer Products Company.)

foreign marketing. Exxon tailors its gasoline formula to meet changing climatic conditions and Nestlé varies its coffee varieties to meet local preferences. In Germany, the principal soft drink is beer, and it is available in McDonald's. The champ in adaptation is probably P&G which has one hundred different soap formulas to comply with worldwide washing conditions. Figure 19–4 shows Tylenol's package adaptation for children's Tylenol for marketing in Germany.

Occasionally, local conditions make it impossible to penetrate a foreign market. After all, how can you sell washing machine soap in an emerging nation that doesn't have washing machines, or the electricity to run them? Colgate-Palmolive solved the problem by inventing a hand-operated washing machine.

Adapting the Message

Some products can do very well in foreign markets but serve a function different from their requirements on the domestic scene. In such cases, the message requires adaptation, whereas the product can be sold unchanged.

Bicycles and motor scooters are a recreational and leisure item at home but an important means of transportation in many foreign countries. Outboard motors that were designed for and used by hobby boat owners serve admirably as power sources for commercial fishing boats abroad. Small, powered gardening tools, designed for suburban homeowners, are ideally suited to small farms in less developed countries. European dried soups sell well in America, but for making sauces and dips rather than as soup.

Considerable care must be taken in foreign market promotion. Slogans that are highly successful domestically do not always do well in translation. "Let Hertz put you in the driver's seat" was translated for a time as "Let Hertz make you a chauffeur." Similarly, in Germany, "Come alive with Pepsi" became "Come out of the grave with Pepsi." Sometimes, the message translates very well. Kodak and Coca-Cola had no trouble and Esso's "Put a tiger in your tank" was universally successful.

Often, considerations that are ignored domestically become important in foreign cultures. Take colors, for example, black and white, in Japan, and purple in South America are colors of mourning; green is a no-no in Egypt and Malaysia; and yellow liquids remind Africans of animal urine.

Price

Setting prices on products to be sold in foreign markets is somewhat more complicated than domestic pricing. Where cost-plus pricing is used, consideration must be given to transportation, tariffs, special packaging, fluctuating foreign currency rates and the other expenses involved in getting the goods to the foreign markets. Some producers view their foreign sales as "gravy." They reason that overhead and the cost of developing the product are already being carried by domestic sales and therefore they do not attach these costs to their export sales. This permits lower, more competitive pricing for foreign markets.

Dumping occurs when companies charge less for a product on a foreign market than they do on their market. Dumping is illegal in most countries including the United States where several Japanese steel companies were charged an additional 32 percent duty after being found guilty of this practice.

Product Life Cycle in Foreign Trade

The life cycle of a new product follows a pattern either on the domestic or the foreign scene. However, the factors at work on the product are different in international trade. Studies of the life cycle of such products as office machines, motion pictures, synthetic fabrics, electronic goods, and durable consumer goods indicate the following stages in the life of an exported product:

1. Exclusive U.S. export
2. Beginning of foreign production
3. Competition from foreign producers on the world market
4. Competition from foreign producers on the domestic market

By understanding each of these stages, domestic exporters can determine the part of the cycle their product is in and plan their action for the next cycle.

Exclusive U.S. Export.   Since new product research usually has the purpose of satisfying the domestic market, most American new products are designed for a high-income market. Industry in the United States is highly technical in nature and new products require design and other technical changes to fit consumer demand. As a result, new products, although they can usually be produced more cheaply in low-labor-cost foreign factories, are generally manufactured locally so that necessary changes can be quickly and easily made.

As the product becomes perfected and the domestic market broadens, the goods become available for export. At this time export of the product is an exclusive U.S. activity, which is supplied by large-scale American production. As the export trade to any one area grows, the producers of that area become interested in the product.

Beginning of Foreign Production.   Foreign manufacturers, already familiar with the product, begin manufacture as soon as the demand within their area reaches a level that indicates profitability. Blessed with a fully developed product, the foreign producers' developmental costs are minimized. They have the further advantage of being able to study the demand for the product that has been pioneered by the American exporter.

Considering the savings in labor, shipping, duty, and tariffs, foreign producers are usually successful in competing with the American exporter in their local markets. As yet, the foreign producers are still small-scale manufacturers whose production costs, despite a low labor cost, exceed the cost of American producers. Although they can compete very successfully with American exporters at home, their expensive small-scale production costs put them at a disadvantage when faced with shipping costs and tariffs, and their export trade is negligible.

At this stage of a product's life cycle, American manufacturers, although still dominant on the world market, begin to lose out to local producers in specific areas. Since local manufacture begins when local demand is high, the export loss is likely to occur in the highest-volume foreign markets. The result is a decline in the rate of the product's export growth. The decline accelerates as the number of foreign producers increases. American dishwashers are presently in this stage of the export life cycle.

Competition from Foreign Producers Abroad.   When the foreign producers grow in size and experience to a point at which they equal their U.S. competitors, their lower-cost labor market gives them an advantage over American producers on the world market. Shipping and tariff costs are the same. Consequently, when their production problems are solved, lower labor costs give foreign manufacturers a competitive advantage that results in a shrinking of American export volume. The competition faced by American exporters of ranges and refrigerators in South American markets is evidence of this stage. At this point, shipping costs and South American tariffs protect the domestic market from foreign competitors.

Competition from Foreign Producers at Home.   Foreign manufacturers with newer production facilities and lower labor costs, which offset shipping expenses and U.S. tariffs, can frequently penetrate the American domestic market with considerable success. When this occurs, the United States becomes an importer of the product and the export trade dwindles away. Steel and bicycles are typical of products in this stage, as are many other consumer durables.

As more and more foreign countries progress to the point at which their technical productive capacity is such that they can produce for export, the life cycle of export goods will shorten. To offset this trend, many exporters are constructing manufacturing plants in foreign countries to take advantage of the lower labor costs available there.

The length of an export product's life cycle depends on the characteristics of the item. For example, luxury items, expensive products, and products designed to save labor have a longer cycle than inexpensive necessities.

CHOOSING AN OPERATION

There are several ways in which a company may set up a foreign trade operation. Each method has its advantages and disadvantages. The methods run from simple and inexpensive to highly complicated and costly. Many companies begin simply and evolve to the more complicated and expensive operations as their export business grows.

Foreign Agents

Companies whose involvement in foreign trade is on a limited or occasional basis frequently work through foreign agents. Such firms employ export managers who visit the foreign agents from time to time and contact them when a particular item of interest to the agents comes up. The use of foreign agents requires very little effort or expense on the part of an exporter. On the other hand, very little control may be exercised over the foreign operation, and tariffs must be paid by the exporter.

Company-Owned Sales Branches

As the volume of foreign sales from a particular area grows, a company may replace its foreign agent with a company-owned sales branch. This operation results in the complete control of the sales function and permits more aggressive selling and promotion. The use of a company-owned sales branch requires financial investment, risk, and the responsibility for training and managing a sales staff. The sales staff may consist of home company personnel, who must learn about the market, or of foreign nationals, who must learn about the product. The use of company-owned sales branches offers no savings in the way of shipping costs or tariffs.

Licensing

Another method of penetrating a foreign market is by licensing the production and distribution of a product to a local manufacturer. Under this method, the company must find a local manufacturer interested in the production and distribution of the item. The licensee, for a stipulated fee or per unit cost, has complete control over the product for a stated period of time. The use of licenses involves no financial risks and saves tariffs and shipping costs. It has the political advantage of getting a commercial foothold in countries where U.S. ownership is not permitted, tariffs are very high, or import quotas are too restrictive.

Under a licensing arrangement, the exporter has no control over the manufacturing operation. Many exporters oppose licensing, since they feel it is a short-term operation. They hold that once the foreign licensee has the technical know-how to produce and distribute the product, he or she will sever relations with the licenser and retain the business for personal use.

Soft drink companies do very well with licensing agreements. Pepsi-Cola has one with the Soviet Union. It supplies the syrup and know-how, the Soviets provide the equipment and marketing. Pepsi does very well with the deal. Its investment is nil and the licensing agreement is exclusive; that is, no other cola may be sold in the Soviet Union.

Contract Manufacturing

To offset the tendency of licensees to take over the entire business, some companies retain the distribution control but contract out the manufacturing to a local manufacturer. This has the disadvantage of having limited control over the manufacturer. In addition, it is often difficult to find a capable manufacturer, and the management of distribution is often a costly and difficult problem. Sears uses contract manufacturers in many parts of the world, and P&G contracts with local producers for its Italian operation.

Joint Ventures

The total or any part of a foreign operation may be owned by a partnership consisting of the exporter and a foreign firm. Typically under such a deal the American firm would provide the capital and technical know-how, and the foreign firm the management, labor, and political clearances. The investment and consequent risk involved in joint ventures is high. In return for this, the amount of control and share of the profits are correspondingly increased.

One very successful joint venture combines the Mitsubishi Corporation of Japan with Kentucky Fried Chicken. Each contributed 50 percent of the capital and they are equal partners. The Colonel provides the recipes and marketing, Mitsubishi, the locations and chickens. Expansion and profits have been exceptional. On the other hand, Xerox and Rank Limited of England have not done well. Xerox blames Rank's poor marketing and has spent a fortune trying unsuccessfully to buy them out.

A recent entry in fashion retailing via the joint venture route is the one between Barney's, New York, and Isetan Co., Ltd., one of Japan's largest retailers. The venture calls for the two companies to open a series of retail units in the United States, Japan, and other Asian countries under the Barney's name.

Wholly Owned Subsidiaries

In areas in which the marketing program has reached the level at which the rewards are such that large investment is indicated, a company may construct a wholly owned manufacturing facility and distribute through a company-owned organization. This procedure maximizes control, profitability, and risk. Many developing countries offer financial and tax incentives to encourage manufacturing for the resulting job opportunities available to their people. The wholly owned subsidiary is usually a division of the parent exporter and secondary in importance to the domestic operations.

The International Company

The final step in the evolution of a company's foreign trade operation is the international company whose export business is of equal importance to its domestic operations. This requires complete integration of all the company's operations, with manufacturing and distributing facilities throughout the world. The international company's Chicago sales office is not more important than its Bangkok office, and its manufacturing facilities in Dallas take no precedence over its equivalent facility in Milan.

It must be understood that a company may be involved in different export arrangements at its various outposts. Thus, a company with a wholly owned subsidiary in Belgium may work with foreign agents in a less developed African nation.

MARKETING PROFILE

Beecham Group p.l.c.

Beecham Group p.l.c. is an international company involved in the research, development, manufacture, and marketing of a wide range of products, mainly in the health and personal care sectors. The products include prescription and over-the-counter medicines, toiletries, cosmetics, and health-oriented drinks and are sold under three hundred different brand names in more than 130 countries. Beecham generates more than $4 billion in annual worldwide sales and employs approximately thirty-six thousand people.

Headquartered in the United Kingdom, where it employs the major proportion of its work force, Beecham's second largest labor force is in the United States, numbering forty-five hundred people. Major Beecham brands in the United States include Amoxil, Augmentin antibiotics, Tums antacid tablets, Oxy for acne, Sucrets throat lozenges, Aqua-fresh tooth-

FIGURE 19–5
Tums liquid variation
of the tablet. (*Courtesy:*
Beecham Group p.l.c.)

paste, and Massengill feminine hygiene products. The liquid variation of
Tums is shown in Figure 19–5.

In addition to manufacturing and marketing its own products,
Beecham, like other international companies, is involved in alliances or
joint ventures with other companies. In the United States, for example, a
recently signed agreement with The Upjohn Company will enable both
companies to market Eminase, a treatment for heart attacks.

The company's philosophy is to never let old brands die, but to up-
date them and modernize them. A case in point is Brylcreem, a product
launched in 1928 that achieved great success. Its strong brand name ultimately was conceived as old-fashioned, and the company set out to save
the product by updating its packaging, formulation, and advertising. The
new market was young, and it was greeted with a full line of Brylcreem,
which now included shower gels, deodorants, and shaving foam, all relevant to today's young consumer. Since June 1988, the newly launched
Brylcreem has begun to recapture a larger share of the market.

> According to its U.K. managing director, "Beecham has succeeded by going back to the basics of a brand, building on its strengths and assets, and making it relevant today through advertising and new products."

Channels of Distribution

In practice there are five major channels of distribution available to U.S. exporters. They are listed in order of their complexity and cost:

1. Manufacturer—U.S. exporter—foreign importer—foreign wholesaler or retailer—foreign consumer
2. Manufacturer—foreign importer based in the United States—foreign wholesaler or retailer—foreign consumer
3. Manufacturer—foreign importer based in a foreign country—foreign wholesaler or retailer—foreign consumer
4. Manufacturer—foreign wholesaler or retailer—foreign consumer
5. Manufacturer—foreign consumer

The choice of the particular distributive channel depends on the estimated market potential, the amount of capital to be risked, and the amount of control the manufacturer wishes to exert over the distribution system.

MAINTAINING GOODWILL IN FOREIGN MARKETS

Companies that have heavily invested in foreign markets find it important to maintain the goodwill not only of the users of their products but of all citizens of the countries in which they are involved. The following are some of the ways in which this can be done.

Hiring Foreign Nationals

The National Cash Register Company employs twenty-two thousand people abroad, of whom only six are Americans. This indicates to the countries involved that the company sincerely wants to be accepted and that it is helping the country's economy by providing employment to its citizens. The National Cash Register Company believes that it is cheaper to teach its product to foreign nationals than to teach foreign culture to American nationals. Therefore, they employ foreign nationals to sell National Cash Register products to people of their own nationality, and this arrangement works quite effectively.

Investing Profits in Foreign Countries

Another method of improving company goodwill in foreign markets is to build confidence that the operation is permanent rather than just looking for quick profit. This can be done by investing at least part of the profit in the economic development of the country in which the profit was earned. In some countries such investments are forced by currency restrictions. Whatever the reason, increased investment pays off in goodwill and the increases in profits that go with it.

Other Methods

Any company that must depend on foreign goodwill for success must be sure to implant in its American employees a respect for the traditions, customs, and religion of the countries involved. It should support its hosts' economic and cultural development and maintain a high reputation for integrity by honoring all contracts and commitments. There should be no involvement in a country's politics.

Important Points in the Chapter

1. The growth of population and purchasing power of the world has resulted in a market of enormous potential for international trade. The importance of foreign trade to the American economy may be emphasized by pointing out that millions of Americans are dependent on foreign trade for their jobs.

2. Before selecting an area for developing an export trade, careful study must be made of its economic and political development, monetary regulations, habits, culture, and tariff and quota regulations. International market research is important as well as expensive.

3. Although some products can be exported in an unaltered state, many must be adapted to meet the needs of the specific market to which they are sent. Generally, the promotional methods must be adapted too.

4. Products that are exported to foreign markets go through a life cycle consisting of the following stages: exclusive U.S. export, beginning of foreign production, competition from foreign producers on the world market, and competition from foreign producers on the domestic market. High-cost luxury products have the longest life cycle.

5. There are several ways in which a country can set up its foreign trade operation: foreign agents, company-owned sales branches, licensing, contract manufacturing, joint ventures, and wholly owned subsidiaries. The operation chosen depends on the estimated size of the market, the amount of risk involved, and the amount of control required.

6. It is important that a company having business abroad maintain the good will of the country in which it is a guest. This may be done by hiring foreign nationals; investing profits in the country in which they are earned; contributing to worthwhile projects; showing respect for the country's customs, religion, and traditions; and maintaining a high degree of integrity in both commercial and social activities.

Review Questions

1. Explain the importance of foreign exports to the economy of the United States.

2. In selecting an area to which to export, a company must carefully study the economic development of the area. Why?

3. Explain the foreign trade potential of a primitive area. What sort of foreign trade operation is suited to this kind of territory?

4. Discuss the foreign trade possibilities of countries whose economic level has reached the manufacture-of-consumer-goods level.

5. Fully developed manufacturing countries offer the highest foreign trade potential. Why?

6. Explain the success of the Volkswagen in the American market.

7. Why is the state of political development of a country important to a would-be exporter?

8. Discuss the importance of monetary stability in foreign trade.

9. What is the importance of market research in international marketing? What are the difficulties?

10. Why do some products require adaptation to foreign markets?

11. Give examples of products that are successful in foreign markets where they are used for a different purpose than originally intended. Explain the effect of this on foreign advertising.

12. Why do producers who can manufacture new products more cheaply abroad prefer to use local facilities?

13. Discuss the stage in the life cycle of a product in which foreign production begins. Why are American producers able to maintain their foreign markets when foreign production begins?

14. At what point in a product's life cycle do foreign products begin to compete on the American market? Give examples.

15. What characteristics of a product affect the length of its life cycle?

16. Discuss the use of foreign agents in an exporting operation. In what areas would you expect to find agents used?

17. What are the advantages and disadvantages of company-owned sales branches?

18. Define *foreign contract manufacturing*. What are its advantages and disadvantages?

19. Discuss the factors that must be taken into account in making a decision concerning the type of overseas operation to be used.

20. Explain the advantages and disadvantages of staffing an overseas operation with foreign nationals.

Case Problems

Case Problem 1

The Yamata Camera Company of Tokyo is one of the larger Japanese camera companies. Included in the company's offerings is a line of consumer cameras that controls about 8 percent of the domestic market. The line is also produced for the American market by an American company on a contract basis. Judging from the size of the American orders, the cameras seem to be selling very well on the American market under the name of the American importer—a large, highly respected firm that aggressively promotes the line.

The contract with the American company will expire in two years and the Yamata Company is faced with the question of renewing the contract or exporting its proven product to the United States under its own label, as other Japanese camera firms do with considerable success. Cost estimates indicate that the cameras could be profitably offered at a price below the amount the American consumer is presently paying. The Yamata Camera Company is financially capable of carrying the operation.

Questions

1. What are the advantages and disadvantages of renewing the contract? Of direct exporting?
2. If the company decides to export, what channels of distribution should it use?

Case Problem 2

The Garden-Aid Corporation is a highly successful manufacturer of a complete line of gasoline-powered garden tools that are sold to American home gardeners. Since World War II the migration of Americans to individually owned suburban houses has created a tremendous demand for the company's product and Garden-Aid is a large-scale, efficient producer.

The success of the powered garden tool industry has brought many competitors into the field. This has resulted in gradual lessening of sales volume and profits. To retain its place on the industrial scene, Garden-Aid has decided to move into the foreign market.

To date, exports of powered garden tools are very small. Garden-Aid's estimate of foreign demand is so high that competitors are certain to follow Garden-Aid into the international market. To offset future competition in the foreign markets, management has decided to go directly into a large-scale foreign operation at many levels and in many areas. It realizes that each area will require product modification, message modification, and a distribution plan unique to the special problems of the area.

Questions

1. Discuss and give examples of the required product modification, message modification, and channels of distribution for each of the following types of countries.
   a. Primitive nations
   b. Emerging nations
   c. Nations beginning to manufacture
   d. Nations manufacturing consumer goods
   e. Nations manufacturing durable goods

2. Describe the probable life cycle of a powered lawn mower.

20

NONPROFIT MARKETING

Learning Objectives _____

Upon completion of the chapter, you will be able to:

1. Differentiate between profit and nonprofit institutions.
2. List and discuss four characteristics of nonprofit organizations.
3. Indicate the problems involved with developing a marketing program.
4. Explain the marketing mix for nonprofit organizations.
5. Enumerate and explain the four steps involved in the evaluation of a nonprofit organization.
6. Discuss the future of marketing in a nonprofit organization.

OF BASEBALL CARDS AND BALLERINAS

For generations American boys have saved baseball cards. These are wallet-sized cards with autographed pictures of baseball players on the front (the old ones are hand drawn) and the player's vital statistics on the reverse side. The statistics include a brief biography and the player's baseball achievements since turning professional. Some fifty years ago Topps Chewing Gum included a baseball card with its bubble gum and sold the package for a nickel. (Most boys threw away the gum and saved the card—there's a limit to the amount of gum you can chew.) The cards were saved, traded, and even gambled for by matching heads or tails by flipping the cards. The fad is still alive, with many children collecting pictures of their favorite athletes. There is also a lively market for antique baseball cards, with collectors paying thousands of dollars for a particularly rare one.

New York's Feld Ballet kicked off its 1983 season by including cards of six of its dancers along with the subscription forms. The autographed cards were photographs of a member of the troupe taken while dancing, with vital statistics of the dancer on the reverse side. The message read, "Collect the whole set (50 cards), swap 'em with your friends! And while you're at it, subscrib to our Spring season and root, root, root for the home team." (See Figure 20–1.)

The Feld Ballet sold a record 42 percent of its seats from that single mailing. During intermission cards were actively traded. Complete sets were being sold for the astronomical price of $2 a set. The promotion makes sense. The subscribers like to know what the performers look like. Since most seats are too far from the stage to permit this, the cards are welcome. The performers like the cards too since they provide some street recognition. Feld Ballet loves the promotion; it sells tickets and provides a "home team" atmosphere.

The major ballet companies in New York City are the American Ballet Theater and the New York City Ballet. These are staid, old-line organizations, and neither of them showed any interest in the promotion. It's simply not their cup of tea. The Cleveland Ballet, however, is going into baseball cards. Andrew Bales, its president, was quoted as saying, "We're certain that our prima ballerina is worth three Willie Mayses any day."

INTRODUCTION

So far this book has been concerned with marketing for profit-making organizations. This has had the effect of ignoring a very significant portion of our economic life, namely, those organizations whose primary function is something other than the profit motive. It has been estimated that between 25 and 30 percent of our work force and as much as 20 percent of our gross national product are the result of the efforts of nonprofit organizations. Consider the number of people involved in our various levels of government, including the armed

ANTHONY DOWELL
visiting dancer
BORN: London, England
STUDIED:
The Royal Ballet School
PERFORMED:
The Royal Ballet "Alberecht" in *Giselle,*
"Romeo" and the "Prince" in *Swan Lake*
and *The Sleeping Beauty.* Created many
other roles for Sir Frederick Ashton,
and Sir Kenneth MacMillan, and is the
subject of the BBC production entitled
All The Superlatives. 1973 named by
Queen Elizabeth II as Commander of
the British Empire.
BALLET THIS SEASON:
Circa May 10, May 11 & May 12

FIGURE 20–1   "Baseball"-type cards of Feld Company dancers. (*Courtesy:* The Feld Ballet Company.)

The Feld Ballet. (*Courtesy:* The Feld Ballet Company.)

forces, that there are 350,000 religious organizations; add colleges and universities, hospitals, libraries, labor unions, and political parties; and you begin to get some idea of the size of this segment of our economy. Each of these organizations has a message to get across, a marketing path to follow, and a marketing problem to solve. Some, like our religious organizations, need contributions, others need volunteer workers, and the Girl Scouts have to decide which cookies to sell. These are all marketing applications. The problems of course differ. The question of whether the Army should try to attract volunteers by an appeal to patriotism or the promise of learning a technical skill is quite different from a library's decision on how to motivate users to return overdue books. But there are similarities also, and the application of sound, basic marketing principles will help solve both problems.

CHARACTERISTICS

As has been pointed out, although the term *nonprofit organization* includes a wide variety of endeavors, all such organizations have certain things in common that differentiate them from the profit-seeking sector of our economy. These are

1. Service orientation
2. Nonprofit status
3. Visibility
4. Narrow marketing

Service Orientation

By and large, nonprofit organizations are chiefly concerned with services rather than profits. The Salvation Army, for example, offers food and shelter to the homeless and needy; symphony orchestras provide music; and libraries, books. Even in those instances where products are offered, as when a public television station offers a book for contributions in excess of the regular membership charge, or a church has a cake sale, these products are always insignificant to the purpose of the organization.

Many nonprofit organizations do not market either services or products. The political parties, however, market their candidates, vacation areas market their location, and the Sierra Club markets its ideas on conservation of our wilderness areas.

Nonprofit

The principal difference between a profit and a nonprofit organization is its goal. The goal of the International Business Machines Corporation is to make profits for its investors. The goal of a college or university is to educate students and produce scholarly research and writing. Both institutions charge for their efforts and both actively seek out customers, but their basic reason for existence is different. It is true that many major learning institutions own profit-making assets, but this is not the purpose of their existence, and such profits are only used to further their goal.

Visibility

The public demands that nonprofit organizations act in a completely moral, ethical fashion. When these standards are not met, criticism is quick to follow. In recent years, some states have begun to operate state-owned gambling systems. New York State, for example, theorizing that gambling is a fact of life, reasoned that since that is the case, the profits should go to the state treasury rather than the bookies and organized crime. Off Track Betting (OTB) was instituted, and state-run outlets were opened to handle race track betting. While many people opposed this, the majority of the citizenry went along. When OTB began an advertising campaign, the opposition increased. Is it right for the state, a nonprofit institution, to encourage gambling?

Narrow Marketing

Another characteristic of nonprofit organizations is an unequal distribution of their benefits. A city-supported transit system is often subsidized out of general tax revenues, but only used by a limited number of residents. Parents who send their children to private schools help pay for the public school system. How many people actually attend the performances of a publicly supported concert series? This is in contrast to the activities of profit-seeking organizations. General Motors offers its products to everyone, and the use of the product goes only to the individual who pays for it.

These differences tend to make marketing for a nonprofit organization more difficult. Since there are no profits, these organizations are generally short of funds. This requires the seeking out of contributors, who often insist upon some say in the running of the organization. As a result, lines of authority can become unclear. In addition, many nonprofit organizations depend heavily on volunteer workers who may be less dependable and perhaps less competent than a person freely chosen for the job.

Another problem with nonprofit organizations is that they are neither competitive in the services they offer nor accountable to owners for their performance. When Chrysler products lost market share to competitors, a new president was found who changed the marketing mix and dramatically improved the company's profits. In a nonprofit organization this is rarely, if ever, done. In fact, the problem might not even be recognized since there are no stockholders looking over management's shoulders.

While all of these problems tend to make the application of a sound marketing plan difficult, they do not reduce the importance of a sound marketing system to the successful operation of a "not-for-profit" organization.

DEVELOPING A MARKETING PROGRAM

Perhaps the most difficult problem to be faced in developing a marketing program for a nonprofit organization is the fact that the majority of the people involved are not business people. They are, in fact, a totally different breed from those to be found in a "for-profit" institution. They are generally uncomfortable with words like *advertising* and *personal selling*, although they strongly support the posting of notices and other missionary work which is much the same thing. The point is, when there are funds to be raised or a product or service to promote for either a profit or nonprofit organization, the marketing principles are the same, and the degree of success is in direct relation to the proper application of those principles.

In discussing a marketing program for a nonprofit organization it is necessary to understand the diversity of organizations that fall under that heading, and the public's attitude toward them. Some, like religious and charitable groups, are not at all controversial. Everybody loves them. Others, such as those in favor of gun control, those against nuclear power, and those in favor of unilateral disarmament, face large, powerful opposition. Each has its own specific problems that must be treated individually, but again, in each case, the application of sound marketing practices will be beneficial.

A marketing program must begin with a target, that is, a specific group who are likely to become customers. General Motors markets its Cadillacs by seeking out the segment of our society that falls into the socioeconomic level that would be likely to purchase that product.

Charitable organizations have two different types of clientele and are required to aim at two different groups. They must attract both contributors and recipients. Since there is a vast difference between the two, separate marketing schemes must be developed.

Finding a donor market requires segmentation. Research must be developed to determine the type of person likely to donate to this type of organization. Segmentation by age, geography, economic level, and social status must be determined by using the same tools available to the researchers of commercial marketing institutions. In addition, the psychological aspects of giving to this type of organization must be gone into. Why do people give to nonprofit organizations? Some of the reasons are

1. Religious beliefs encourage giving to help the needy and promise future rewards to the charitable.
2. Contributions to properly organized charities are tax deductible.
3. Contributors to charitable organizations believe that the organization does a good job and that their contribution will be used effectively.
4. Within a social group, making a contribution earns admiration and respect. This is particularly true with large, public contributions. Even when the contribution is less than fully public, word gets around and the contributor earns admiration.
5. Peer pressure plays an important part in contributions. As each member of a peer group falls into line, the pressure builds up on the remainder of the group to conform. This is as true in the purchase of an expensive automobile as it is in the making of a large donation. It is standard procedure among charity fund raisers to ask a contributor for leads among his or her friends, because once a peer group has been broken into, other members of the group are a fertile source of solicitation.
6. People feel good about giving. It enhances self-image and imparts a feeling of well-being.

An understanding of the contributor's motives are necessary to the development of an effective appeal for contributions. With this knowledge, the pitch can be tailored to the specific reasons that people have for giving. Motives are not always obvious. For example, there are more people in the United States in favor of gun control than there are opposing such control. Yet, those against control are always able to win when the issue comes to a head. They do this by appealing to a large number of groups, many of whom do not even own guns. Although the majority of the group is interested in hunting, they include in their pitch an appeal to people who feel they need guns for protection against crime, and others, not gun owners, who think that the right to bear arms is basic to the American way of life.

Developing Objectives

The next step in the marketing process is the development of objectives. General objectives are easy, but they are of little help to a marketing scheme. Effective marketing requires specific objectives that can be focused upon. Moreover, they must be limited in number so that a major thrust can be put behind each. For example, the general objective of the U.S. Post Office is to provide us with prompt, efficient mail service. To further these general goals, its specific objectives are

1. To reduce costs and improve efficiency by educating the public on the importance of using Zip codes.
2. To inform the public of the advantages, in terms of cost and efficiency, of using the U.S. Postal Service rather than the host of competing delivery services that are springing up.
3. To raise the status of the Postal Service in the eyes of the public.

The Marketing Mix

Successful marketing for both commercial and nonprofit institutions requires a proper marketing mix. That is, product, place, promotion, and price must be appropriate to each other and blended together.

Product.   In most nonbusiness organizations the product offered is an idea or service. Such concepts are difficult to describe because of the intangibility of their nature. The RCA Corporation can begin with a picture of a television set, describe it in great detail, point out its advantages, and show its decorative nature. Now consider an appeal for Peace Corps volunteers. The advantages for individuals vary with each individual and assignments may vary from the tropics to the Arctic. In addition, RCA guarantees quality control which results in a uniformity of product. Each customer knows exactly what to expect and gets it. This is certainly far from the case with the Peace Corps where some volunteers are thrilled with the experience and others quit long before their enlistment period is over. As in all marketing schemes the product selected must fit the needs of a particular market segment. A church that finds that many of its constituent families include working mothers might decide to provide a day-care center as one of its products. Since successful marketing depends upon the satisfaction of customer needs, the product should not be selected until a need is determined. This will undoubtedly require careful marketing research, an activity as important to nonprofit as it is to commercial organizations.

Some nonprofit products have life cycles. The March of Dimes Foundation was enormously successful in raising millions of dollars annually to combat polio, a terrible disease of children. When the Salk vaccine eliminated polio, the organization altered its goal from the elimination of polio to one of research into birth defects. In effect, they dropped a worn-out product and replaced it with a more salable one. Similarly, Princeton's Educational Testing Service, the non-profit organization that produces the Scholastic Aptitude Test (SAT), has found that college enrollment has been falling in recent years. It has changed its product mix to include a test used by business firms on prospective employees.

Place.   Place, the process of getting the product to the target market, for non-profit organizations requires an understanding of the fact that this sort of organization is comprised of two targets, the contributor and the user.

As far as the contributor is concerned, the place for making the donation is generally at his or her convenience. Most nonprofit organizations are always short of funds and will accept contributions at any time or place the donor chooses. Additionally, any form of donation is readily accepted. This includes cash, checks, credit cards, real estate, businesses, art, stocks and bonds, and even old clothes. The channels used are usually short and direct, that is, from the donor directly to the nonprofit organization. Some nonprofit institutions, to increase their funding, use fund-raising organizations who for a price actively solicit contributions. Charitable organizations try to stay away from professional fund raisers for several reasons. For one, they are very expensive (as much as 70 percent of the donation). Also, fund raisers damage the nonprofit organization's image. Contributors like to think that their total contribution goes to the needy. To learn that a significant portion of their donation goes to a fund raiser might lead them to seek out another charitable organization to be the recipient of their gifts. Where fund raisers are used, it is usually done secretly. Along the same line, some contributors would be upset to learn that a large portion of their donation to some nonprofit organizations is used to pay salaries and other expenses, and this information is rarely published.

Concerning the distribution of the nonprofit organization's service to its users, the place chosen is where it is most needed. Libraries and dramatic groups are placed where they will be accessible to the population centers they service. The Salvation Army locates its food distribution centers in economically depressed areas, and the National Heart Association sends mobile blood pressure units to the locations at which they will be most heavily used. In recent years college enrollment has been decreasing. To offset this trend many colleges and universities have been offering both credit and noncredit courses at satellite campuses or even churches and high schools for the convenience of their clientele.

While channels of distribution for nonprofit organizations are usually direct, middlemen may sometimes be used. The National Safety Council (auto safety) uses schools and local police to give their defensive driving courses as a public service.

Another widely used but little publicized channel involves country clubs. These organizations generally have a pet charity. The members of the individual clubs are usually of the same economic and sociological class with similar interests and attitudes. As a result the selection of the charity is supported by all. Typically, such clubs have annual raffles with the profits being turned over to the charity. At one club, a Cadillac is raffled off each year. Two hundred raffles are sold (the approximate membership) at $200 per raffle for a total take of $40,000. The drawing is held at a big summer party and the winner gets the automobile, which costs $20,000. The remaining $20,000 is turned over to the charity. The raffle buyers get a 1 in 200 chance of winning (good odds for a raffle) at a cost of $200, which the affluent members can easily afford. The winner gets a car; the losers, the satisfaction of giving to a worthy cause.

Promotion.   As is the case with commercial businesses, promotion plays a very important role in the marketing of nonprofit organizations. Although all of the elements of promotion, advertising, publicity, sales promotion, and personal selling are used extensively by these organizations, generally personal selling is the most important element. Although the Armed Forces spent over $100 million on posters, advertising, and other promotion, it was felt that sending twelve thousand recruiters to the various high schools and conducting tours of military bases (another form of personal selling) were most effective. Alcoholics Anonymous uses personal selling most effectively. Recovering alcoholics discuss their problem and eventual improvement with individuals and groups. Their personal experience with the problem is very real to the prospect who is usually desperate for help, and the happy ending thanks to Alcoholics Anonymous frequently clinches the deal.

Although some $2 to $3 billion is spent annually on advertising by nonprofit organizations, much free advertising is available. The Advertising Council is the source of free advertising agency services, and some of the media offer free advertising. An example of one such successful campaign is Smokey the Bear, a forest fire prevention promotion that ran for thirty-five years. Another is the Wall Street Run for Your Heart Fund sponsored by the Timex Corporation, pictured in Figure 20–2.

Advertising is the one marketing area that nonprofit organizations understand. They have been using it for years and some even consider it synonymous with a total marketing program. Colleges and universities frequently use advertising to offset enrollment declines, often with a noneducational appeal. The University of California at Berkeley ads feature "A California Summer," and the University of Arizona advertises summer visits to the Grand Canyon.

Colleges are also heavily engaged in personal selling. College Day in the high schools and Transfer Day at community colleges are annual events at which representatives of the admissions offices of many colleges and universities are present to describe the programs, transferability of course, and life-style at their institutions. This is usually done on a one-to-one basis, the essence of personal selling.

FIGURE 20–2   Nonprofit promotional campaign. (*Courtesy:* The New York Heart Association, Inc.)

Although nonprofit organizations have two distinct sets of clients, the contributors and the users, both can be targeted by the same advertisement. An advertisement by the Lung Association, for example, might include both an appeal for funds and an exhortation to give up smoking. Similarly, the American Heart Association might urge the reader both to watch his or her diet and to make a contribution.

Governments at all levels do a great deal of promoting. At the state and local levels, the promotion is usually aimed at attracting tourists and business enterprises that are either starting new installations or relocating older ones. Attracting businesses is very important to states because companies provide employment for the state residents as well as taxes for the state treasury. In localities that suffer from extensive unemployment, local governments frequently make very attractive offers to potential employers including free land on which to build, the free use of existing buildings, and various tax incentives. Since local need for jobs is great, competition among various localities can be fierce. All types of promotions are used for this. Advertising in trade journals and the business sections of major newspapers to attract prospects is common. Personal selling is then undertaken to convince the prospect of the locality's advantages. Speeches before interested groups and even buttonholing individuals at trade shows are not unusual. Successful businesses that have publicized their intention to expand or relocate are often deluged with direct mail extolling the advantages of various localities. The offers are generally very lucrative. When you consider the desperation of a small Midwest city that has just witnessed the closing of a steel mill, its major employer, you can understand the situation.

Attracting tourists is the other great thrust of state and local government promotion. New York City's "I Love New York" campaign is a good example. Faced with a situation in which companies were leaving and tourism was stagnant, the city employed a major marketing research firm. Extensive interviews and surveys were undertaken to determine the most important tourist interest in the city. It was found that Broadway shows far outranked the other cultural offerings, restaurants, shopping, and other tourist attractions. Having determined the customers' preferences, a large advertising agency was called in to promote Broadway as a unique New York City asset. Casts from Broadway shows were utilized to produce television spots in which they sang "I Love New York." Travel agencies, airlines, hotels, and restaurants cooperated to set up vacation tours, bumper stickers, brochures, and advertisements all proclaiming the theme "I Love New York." The campaign was part of a much larger effort designed to improve business and tourism throughout New York State. As a result of the campaign the exodus of businesses from New York slowed down and the tourist industry improved. A similar campaign some years ago provided Puerto Rico with a solid industrial base. It is interesting to note that one way of attracting business to a locality is to convince executives that the area is a nice place in which to live. The location of the executives' homes seems to be one of the most important factors in business location decisions.

The federal government is, of course, the largest of the nonbusiness promoters. Many of the various departments and agencies maintain large promotional budgets which are used for a large variety of purposes. Advertising is the principal method of governmental promotion, and the combined advertising budget of all agencies places the federal government among the top ten advertisers in the country. Federal advertising has led to considerable controversy since there is always a segment of the population that is offended by the message. When the Environmental Protection Agency opposes the use of "dirty fuel," soft coal operators and their employees whose livelihood depends on soft coal feel that their government is harming them. The very idea of the federal government using tax funds to spread propaganda among its citizens is offensive to many. Consider the way an Amtrak railway rider feels when the trains are late or poorly maintained and he or she reads a newspaper advertisement extolling the excellent service offered by the governmental-operated rail lines. It gets worse when the discomforted rider realizes that he or she is helping to pay for the ad.

Another problem with advertising by the federal government is that it is such a big spender that it becomes an important source of revenue to the media. This fact may be important to the editorial policy of the selected newspaper or magazine. For example, since the government has a wide choice of newspapers to select from, isn't the political party in power likely to choose the one that is supportive of their policies? Much of the print media is so dependent on federal advertising revenues that a truly independent editorial policy may be hard to find.

Price.   A discussion of price in the area of nonprofit organizations must rest on the definition of *price* that includes giving up something of value as a type of price one must pay. Under these conditions, nonmonetary sacrifice may be counted as price. Thus, a volunteer enlisting in the armed services gives up the freedom of civilian life as the price of being in the armed forces, people involved in the Salvation Army give up their time in order to do volunteer work, and the Lung Association requires that we give up smoking as the price we pay for better health.

Some nonprofit organizations such as unions and clubs charge their membership club dues. Where possible, the amounts are set to cover the budgeted expenses with a little left over to meet unexpected expenses. The price set must be in accordance with the services rendered by the organization. There is a considerable amount of competition among these institutions. The college that sets its tuition above that of schools of similar reputation will have difficulty meeting its enrollment goals. Similarly, the amateur theater group must price its admission tickets well below that of competing professional troupes.

Many organizations are financed by a combination of charges for service plus donations and/or governmental subsidies. The U.S. Postal Service charges users for mail delivery and makes up its deficit with a large subsidy from the U.S. Treasury. In this instance competition plays a major role in the setting of price for services. The United Parcel Service, Federal Express, and others compete very successfully with the U.S. Postal Service in terms of both price and service. Any increase in the cost of postage improves the position of these competitors.

Sales Promotion.   Sales promotion for nonprofit organizations takes many forms. These may include exhibitions, shows, and the distribution of books and pamphlets. The U.S. government is the largest distributor of books and pamphlets. Through the Government Printing Office thousands of publications are available at little cost. Other notable promotions aimed at furthering the goals of nonprofit organizations are Jerry Lewis's telethon for the Muscular Dystrophy Foundation and $100- to $1,000-a-plate dinners used by the major political parties.

EVALUATING NONPROFIT MARKETING

Profit-seeking organizations measure their performance by measuring their profits, their gross sales, or their proportionate share of the total market. Nonprofit organizations have a much more difficult problem. Fund-raising campaigns can be evaluated quantitatively, and therefore effectively, but when it comes to quality of service, that is another matter entirely. That is to say, the amount of funds raised by the telethon to combat muscular dystrophy may exceed the goal set, but how do you measure the services provided by those funds? Has the research funded by the foundation put us any closer to the control of the disease? This is a very difficult question to answer, and because this is so, proper measurement of the effectiveness of a nonprofit organization is nearly impossible.

The Performing Arts Foundation of Huntington, New York, is a case in point. This was a local theater group that was funded by a combination of ticket sales and donations. After years of struggle and gradual improvement the foundation was able to move to a large professional auditorium that was built to its specifications. Tickets for the larger theater sold out early, and things looked rosy. Unfortunately, the programs offered during the first season in the expanded showcase were so bad that the group was unable to sell sufficient seats the following season and was forced to shut down. Evaluating the operation in terms of ticket sales would have shown excellent results. An evaluation of the services offered, however, was deadly. Admittedly, this is an extreme case. It illustrates that the evaluation of fund raising is not enough of a yardstick for measurement. The quality of service must be measured as well, and this is difficult. Is the decline in enrollment at a college due to poor public relations or a general shrinkage in the pool of the college-seeking population? Is the increase in attendance at a Salvation Army soup kitchen a sign of better food preparation or bad economic conditions?

Despite the fact that the evaluation of nonprofit organizations is far from a perfect science, it is far from imperfect as well. That is, while it is impossible to get an exact evaluation, the results of a proper marketing audit can be critical to the success of the organization. As in all evaluations of this type, there are four steps involved in the process:

1. Set goals.
2. Check results against the previously set goals.
3. Find out what went wrong.
4. Adjust the operation to correct the shortcoming.

Setting Goals

Goals should be set for each major category in the organization and for each segment within that category. That is, each fund-raising effort should have a budgeted goal, and the sum of these efforts will be used as the total expected income. The American Cancer Society raises money through direct mail, personal selling, advertising, and many other activities. Each should have an individual goal set.

Setting objectives is probably the most crucial part of the evaluation procedure since the whole procedure is based on it. The goals set must be reasonable and well-defined. A fund-raising campaign should have a specific figure set as a goal. "Better than last year" is not a workable goal.

Goals must be set in the performance of the service area as well. The number of tickets to be sold by a symphony orchestra, the admissions expected by a museum, and the number of free meals to be provided are typical objectives.

Standards of client satisfaction are another type of goal that should be set. It is not enough for a performing arts center to sell admissions, it must check customer satisfaction standards as well. How do the letters of complaint compare to those that are complimentary? What were the results of the questionnaire? Did the clients enjoy their meals?

Checking Results

When the campaign or season is over and all the information has been gathered, it is easy to compare the results with the goals set. The problem is in determining whether the goals were illogical or the performance of the organization was at fault. Unreasonably high goals are impossible to meet; those set too low are too easily met. This is a problem for profit-seeking organizations as well. For all organizations goal setting requires considerable care.

Finding the Problem

Pinpointing the problem generally requires marketing research. Museums as well as drama, dance, and musical groups usually provide questionnaires to their members soliciting complaints and advice on future programming. Planned Parenthood uses interviews, as do those organizations concerned with the distribution of food and shelter to the needy.

Researching problems should be an ongoing activity that is not restricted to instances in which the results of a campaign do not meet the goals set for it. Just as the products of profit-seeking organizations must constantly be changed to meet the changing needs of their market, nonprofit organizations must constantly alter their approach to both their donor and user markets.

Adjusting the Operation

When the problem can be pinpointed, corrective action should be taken. A good example is the Girl Scouts of America. From its inception in 1860 the GSA had been a highly successful operation. The organization, comprised of cute little girls in green dresses, selling cookies and being trained to be efficient mothers and homemakers, was targeted to the expectations of its market. By 1969 membership had reached nearly four million girls; however, during the 1970s membership began to decline. It was found that the clientele no longer thought of itself as future homemakers and mothers. Women's liberation was the sign of the times and the stereotype of a woman staying in the home had lost its appeal. The operation adjusted to meet the new demands of the times. Merit badges for cooking and sewing were replaced by computer competency and business. Stress was now placed on gaining self-confidence and achieving career goals. Recruitment was begun in depressed areas with pregnant girls included among those who were asked to join. By 1980, membership rolls had begun to increase again. Nonprofit business, like any other business, must adjust its offerings to the needs of its market.

THE FUTURE OF NONPROFIT MARKETING

At present most of the larger nonprofit organizations employ professional marketers. These may range from a vice-president in charge of marketing to a marketing manager who is responsible to a designated vice-president.

Most of the small- and medium-sized organizations are gradually moving in the direction of professional marketing as well. Smaller organizations that are not involved in a fully integrated marketing plan are turning to marketing specialists for their specific problems. More and more they are turning to advertising agencies for advice. Media ads and spot commercials on radio and TV are becoming more polished because of this. Marketing consulting firms are being hired to conduct surveys, do research, and seek out problems and needs. As more and more nonprofit organizations use appropriate marketing techniques to solve their problems, we shall find a gradual improvement of the fund-raising ability and the quality of service offered by these institutions.

Important Points in the Chapter _____

1. The characteristics that distinguish nonprofit organizations are they deal in services rather than products, they do not seek a profit, their actions are closely monitored by the public, they aim at a very narrow target clientele.

2. While marketing problems are the same for both profit and nonprofit organizations managerial attitudes differ. Nonprofit organizations are often run by unbusinesslike people who are disinterested in or even antagonistic toward marketing ideas.

3. Nonprofit organizations have two distinct markets, donors and users. Since marketing success depends upon satisfying customer needs, each market must be separately surveyed and analyzed.

4. As in "for-profit" marketing, each element of the marketing mix must be analyzed and blended into an effective marketing program.

5. To measure the effectiveness of the marketing effort, the following steps

should be followed: set goals, check the results against the goals, find the problem, take corrective action.

6. Nonprofit organizations are gradually adopting professional marketing. Those organizations that have not yet turned to fully integrated marketing programs frequently use specialists such as advertising agencies and marketing researchers to solve their problems.

Review Questions

1. Discuss the size and importance of the nonprofit market.

2. Differentiate between nonprofit marketing and "for-profit" marketing.

3. What is meant by *visibility* in the nonprofit marketplace?

4. Describe the two targets of the nonprofit market. Why are these markets considered narrow?

5. Discuss the difficulty with management in developing a marketing program for a nonprofit organization.

6. List six reasons that people have for making donations to a nonprofit institution.

7. What is the importance of peer pressure in soliciting donations?

8. Explain the difference between general and specific marketing objectives. Give examples.

9. Discuss and give examples of the life cycle of a nonprofit organization's product.

10. Compare the function of place for both the donor and user markets.

11. What is the role of personal selling in both the donor and the user markets?

12. Explain the arguments used by those who believe that the federal government should not involve itself in advertising.

13. Give three examples of nonmonetary price.

14. Discuss the factors that must be taken into account by the U.S. Postal Service in setting the price for first class delivery.

15. List the four steps that must be involved in evaluating a nonprofit marketing program.

16. Explain the problems involved with setting proper goals.

17. How can a nonprofit concert series check results?

18. How did the Girl Scouts of America adjust their operation to offset declining membership?

19. Discuss the future of marketing for nonprofit organizations.

Case Problems _____

Case Problem 1

Anderson Community College is located in the populous suburb of a large metropolitan area. The school was started in 1960, and from that time until the early 1980s, its growth was constant. By 1980 it was one of the ten largest community colleges in the country. By that time, despite a considerable building program, the school had severe classroom space problems. It had become impossible to arrange course schedules to meet the needs of many of Anderson's students who needed to hold jobs during after-school hours.

The school offers a rich variety of occupationally oriented and transfer programs. Students graduating from the nontransfer programs generally find jobs, and for the others, the great majority of courses are readily transferable to senior colleges. The faculty is generally dedicated and holds more advanced degrees than the faculties of any other community college.

By 1980 the growth rate began to level off. By 1984 many freshmen classes had to be canceled because of a shortage of incoming freshmen. Alarmed by dropping enrollments, the Board of Trustees hired a marketing research firm to survey the following groups: current students, incoming freshmen, high school graduates who did not choose Anderson, graduates, and adults interested in returning to college.

Among their findings were the following:

In Favor

1. Tuition is inexpensive.
2. Student can live at home.
3. Programs are good.
4. Teaching is good.
5. Most courses are transferable.
6. The physical plant is comfortable.

Against

1. Some specific courses are not transferable to some schools.
2. Some of the occupational programs are out of date.
3. Coursework is too easy.
4. Coursework is too hard.
5. There are bad teachers.

6. Many high school students and adults were not aware of the programs.

7. The school's academic reputation is weak.

8. There is no social life.

9. The location is inconvenient for adults seeking college courses.

10. Scheduling is difficult.

Question

1. What corrective action should Anderson Community College take? (All of the elements of the marketing mix should be considered.)

Case Problem 2

The Church of the Apostles is situated in the heart of an economically depressed area of a large urban center. The church is located in what had been an unsuccessful two-story department store that was donated to the congregation some years ago. The church itself occupies the main floor. The furnishings consist of crude benches and a homemade pulpit. The lower floor is used as a dining room and food distribution center. Free lunches are prepared and served by volunteers. The top floor of the building is not used.

During the best of times the church barely gets by financially. The church is not affiliated with any religious denomination and its sole source of funds is donations from its wealthier members and regular Sunday collections. No attempt has ever been made to solicit funds from any other source. Presently, economic conditions are bad, and the parishioners are particularly hard hit. This has caused a twofold problem. First, donations have been sharply reduced due to the economic stress on the local donors. In addition, the demands for food have gone up sharply since unemployment has increased. Another problem is a proposal that has come up to use the upper floor as a child care center. This, it is argued, would permit mothers to find employment, which will ease the financial stress of the area and consequently the church as well. Because of the financial crisis this proposal has been temporarily shelved.

The head of the church is a man of deep religious beliefs. He is a kind and gentle man whose life is devoted to his congregation. Excellent attendance at services and the availability of volunteers is evidence of the devotion of his followers. He has no interest whatever in business.

A committee has been formed to examine the financial problems and propose possible solutions.

Question

1. List and discuss possible solutions to the problem.

APPENDIX:
MARKETING DEFINITIONS

The following is a glossary of marketing terms that has been adapted from a report prepared by the Committee on Definitions of the American Market Association.[1]

ACCESSORIES. See EQUIPMENT.

ADVERTISING. Any paid form of nonpersonal presentation and promotion of ideas, goods, or services by an identified sponsor. It involves the use of such media as the following:

Magazine and newspaper space
Motion pictures
Outdoor (posters, signs, skywriting, etc.)
Direct mail
Novelties (calendars, blotters, etc.)
Radio and television
Cards (car, bus, etc.)
Catalogs
Directories and references
Programs and menus
Circulars

This list is intended to be illustrative, not inclusive.

[1] Ralph S. Alexander, chairman, and Committee on Definitions of the American Marketing Association, "Marketing Definitions," 1960.

Comment. Advertising is generally but not necessarily carried on through mass media. While the postal system is not technically considered a "paid" medium, material distributed by mail is definitely a form of presentation that is paid for by the sponsor. For kindred activities, see PUBLICITY and SALES PROMOTION.

ADVERTISING RESEARCH. See MARKETING RESEARCH.

AGENT. A business unit that negotiates purchases or sales or both but does not take title to the goods in which it deals.

Comment. The agent usually performs fewer marketing functions than does the merchant. Agents commonly receive remuneration in the form of a commission or fee. They usually do not represent both buyer and seller in the same transaction. Examples are broker, commission merchant, manufacturer's agent, selling agent, and resident buyer.

The Committee recommends that the term *functional middleman* no longer be applied to this type of agent. It is hardly logical or consistent in view of the fact that such people perform fewer marketing functions than other middlemen.

ASSEMBLING. The activities involved in concentrating supplies or assortments of goods or services to facilitate sales or purchase.

Comment. The concentration involved here may affect a quantity of like goods or a variety of goods. It includes the gathering of adequate and representative stocks by wholesalers and retailers.

AUTOMATIC SELLING. The retail sale of goods or services through currency operated machines activated by the ultimate consumer.

Comment. Most, if not all, machines now used in automatic selling are coin operated. There are reports, however, of promising experiments with such devices that may be activated by paper currency.

AUXILIARY EQUIPMENT. See EQUIPMENT.

BRANCH HOUSE (MANUFACTURER'S). An establishment maintained by a manufacturer, detached from the headquarters establishment and used primarily for the purpose of stocking, selling, delivering, and servicing the product.

BRANCH OFFICE (MANUFACTURER'S). An establishment maintained by a manufacturer, detached from the headquarters establishment and used for the purpose of selling products or providing service.

Comment. The characteristic of the branch house that distinguishes it from the branch office is the fact that it is used in the physical storage, handling, and delivery of merchandise. Otherwise, the two are identical.

BRANCH STORE. A subsidiary retailing business owned and operated at a separate location by an established store.

BRAND. A name, term, sign, symbol, or design, or a combination of them which is intended to identify the goods or services of one seller or group of sellers and to differentiate them from those of competitors.

Comment. A branch may include a brand name, a trademark, or both. The term *brand* is sufficiently comprehensive to include practically all means of identification except perhaps the package and the shape of the product. All brand names and all trademarks are brands or parts of brands, but not all brands are either brand names or trademarks. Brand is the inclusive general term. The others are more particularized.

See also NATIONAL BRAND and PRIVATE BRANDS.

BRAND MANAGER. See PRODUCT MANAGEMENT.

BRAND NAME. A brand or part of a brand consisting of a word, letter, group of words or letters comprising a name which is intended to identify the goods or services of a seller or a group of sellers and to differentiate them from those of competitors.

Comment. The brand name is that part of the brand which can be vocalized—the utterable.

BROKER. An agent who does not have direct physical control of the goods in which he or she deals but represents either buyer or seller in negotiating purchases or sales for the principal.

Comment. The broker's powers as to prices and terms of sale are usually limited by the principal.

The term is often loosely used in a generic sense to include such specific business units as freelance brokers, manufacturer's agents, selling agents, and purchasing agents.

BUYING POWER. See PURCHASING POWER.

CANVASSER. See HOUSE-TO-HOUSE SALESPERSON.

CASH-AND-CARRY WHOLESALER. See WHOLESALER.

CHAIN STORE. See CHAIN STORE SYSTEM.

CHAIN STORE SYSTEM. A group of retail stores of essentially the same type, centrally owned and with some degree of centralized control of operation. The term *chain store* may also refer to a single store as a unit of such a group.

CHANNEL OF DISTRIBUTION. The structure of intracompany organization units and extracompany agents and dealers, wholesale and retail, through which a commodity, product, or service is marketed.

Comment. This definition was designed to be broad enough to include (a) both a firm's internal marketing organization units and the outside business units it uses in its marketing work and (b) both the channel structure of the individual firm and the entire complex available to all firms.

COMMERCIAL AUCTION. An agent business unit which effects the sale of goods through an auctioneer, who, under specified rules, solicits bids or offers from buyers and has power to accept the highest bids of responsible bidders and thereby consummates the sale.

Comment. The auctioneer usually is a paid employee of an auction company which is in the business of conducting auctions.

COMMISSION HOUSE (SOMETIMES CALLED COMMISSION MERCHANT). An agent who usually exercises physical control over and negotiates the sale of the goods he or she handles. The commission house usually enjoys broader powers as to prices, methods, and terms of sale than does the broker, although it must obey instructions issued by the principal. It generally arranges delivery, extends necessary credit, collects, deducts its fees, and remits the balance to the principal.

Comment. Most of those who have defined the commission house state that it has possession of the goods it handles. In its strict meaning the word *possession* connotes to some extent the idea of ownership; in its legal meaning it involves a degree of control somewhat beyond that usually enjoyed by the commission merchant. Therefore, the phrase *physical control* was used instead.

The fact that many commission houses are not typical in their operations does not subtract from their status as commission houses.

COMMISSARY STORE. See INDUSTRIAL STORE.

COMMODITY EXCHANGE. An organization usually owned by the member-traders, which provides facilities for bringing together buyers and sellers of specified commodities, or their agents, for promoting trades, either spot or futures or both, in these commodities.

Comment. Agricultural products or their intermediately processed derivatives are the commodities most often traded on such exchanges. Some sort of organization for clearing future contracts usually operates as an adjunct to or an arm of a commodity exchange.

COMPANY STORE. See INDUSTRIAL STORE.

CONSUMER RESEARCH. See MARKETING RESEARCH.

CONSUMERS' COOPERATIVE. A retail business owned and operated by ultimate consumers to purchase and distribute goods and services primarily to the membership—sometimes called purchasing cooperatives.

Comment. The consumers' cooperative is a type of cooperative marketing institution. Through federation, retail units frequently acquire wholesaling and manufacturing institutions. The definition confines the use of the term to the cooperative purchasing activities of ultimate consumers and does not embrace collective buying by business establishments or institutions.

CONSUMERS' GOODS. Goods destined for use by ultimate consumers or households and in such form that they can be used without commercial processing.

Comment. Certain articles, for example, typewriters, may be either consumers' goods or industrial goods, depending upon whether they are destined for use by the ultimate consumer or household or by an industrial, business, or institutional user.

CONVENIENCE GOODS. Those consumers' goods which the customer usually purchases frequently, immediately, and with the minimum of effort in comparison and buying. Examples of merchandise customarily bought as convenience goods are tobacco products, soap, newspapers, magazines, chewing gum, small packaged confections, and many food products.

Comment. These articles are usually of small unit value and are bought in small quantities at any one time, although when a number of them are bought together as in a supermarket, the combined purchase may assume sizable proportions in both bulk and value.

The convenience involved may be in terms of nearness to the buyer's home, easy accessibility to some means of transport, or close proximity to places where people go during the day or evening, for example downtown to work.

COOPERATIVE MARKETING. The process by which independent producers, wholesalers, retailers, consumers, or combinations of them act collectively in buying or selling or both.

DEALER. A firm that buys and resells merchandise at either retail or wholesale.

Comment. The term is naturally ambiguous. For clarity, it should be used with a qualifying adjective, such as *retail* or *wholesale.*

DEPARTMENT STORE. A large retailing business unit which handles a wide variety of shopping and specialty goods, including women's ready-to-wear and accessories, men's and boys' wear, piece goods, small wares, and home furnishings, and which is organized into separate departments for purposes of promotion, service, and control. Examples of very large department stores are Macy's of New York, J. L. Hudson Co. of Detroit, Marshall Field & Co. of Chicago, and Famous, Barr of St. Louis. Two well-known smaller ones are Bresee's of Oneonta, New York, and A. B. Wycoff of Stroudsburg, Pennsylvania.

Comment. Many department stores have become units of chains, commonly called *ownership groups* since each store retains its local identity, even though centrally owned.

The definition given stresses three elements: large size, wide variety of clothing and home furnishings, and departmentalization. Size is not spelled out in terms of either sales volume or number of employees, since the concept keeps changing upward. Most department stores in 1960 had sales in excess of $1 million.

DIRECT SELLING. The process whereby the firm responsible for production sells to the user, ultimate consumer, or retailer without intervening middlemen. The Committee recommends that when this term is used, it be so qualified as to indicate clearly the precise meaning intended (direct to retailer, direct to user, direct to ultimate consumer, etc.).

Comment. The phrase *firm responsible for production* is substituted for *producer* in the old definition so as to include the firm that contracts out some or all of the processes of making the goods it sells direct, for example, the drug house that has its vitamin pills tableted by a contractor specializing in such work.

DISCOUNT HOUSE. A retailing business unit, featuring consumer durable items, competing on a basis of price appeal, and operating on a relatively low markup and with a minimum of customer service.

DISCRETIONARY FUND. Discretionary income enlarged by the amount of new credit extensions which also may be deemed spendable as a result of consumer decision, relatively free of prior commitment or pressure of need.

Comment. These are the definitions of the National Industrial Conference Board, which publishes a quarterly Discretionary Income Index Series. Discretionary income is calculated by deducting from disposable personal income (1) a computed historical level of outlays for food and clothing; (2) all outlays for medical services, utilities, and public transportation; (3) payment of fixed commitments, such as rent, net insurance payments, and installment debt; (4) homeowner taxes; and (e) imputed income and income in kind.

DISCRETIONARY INCOME. That portion of personal income in excess of the amount necessary to maintain a defined or historical standard of living, which may be saved with no immediate impairment of living standards or may be spent as a result of consumer decision relatively free of prior commitment or pressure of need.

DISPOSABLE INCOME. Personal income remaining after the deduction of taxes on personal income and compulsory payment, such as social security levies.

Comment. This is substantially the Department of Commerce concept.

DISTRIBUTION. The Committee recommends that the term *distribution* be used as synonymous with marketing.

Comment. The term *distribution* is also sometimes used to refer to the extent of market coverage.

In using this term marketers should clearly distinguish it from the sense in which it is employed in economic theory, that is, the process of dividing the fund of value produced by industry among the several factors engaged in economic production. It is wise to use the term sparingly.

DISTRIBUTION COST ANALYSIS. See MARKETING COST ANALYSIS.

DISTRIBUTOR. In its general usage, this term is synonymous with *wholesaler.*

Comment. In some trades and by many firms it is used to designate an outlet having some sort of preferential relationship with the manufacturer. This meaning is not as widely used or as standardized as to justify inclusion in the definition. The term is sometimes used to designate a manufacturer's agent or a sales representative in the employ of a manufacturer.

DROP SHIPMENT WHOLESALER. See WHOLESALER.

EQUIPMENT. Those industrial goods that do not become part of the physical product and that are exhausted only after repeated use, such as machinery, installed equipment and accessories, or auxiliary equipment. *Installed equipment* includes such items as boilers, linotype machines, power lathes, bank vaults. *Accessories* include such items as gauges, meters, and control devices. *Auxiliary equipment* includes such items as trucks, typewriters, filing cases, and industrial hoists.

EXCLUSIVE OUTLET SELLING. That form of selective selling whereby sales of an article or service or brand of an article to any one type of buyer are confined to one retailer or wholesaler in each area, usually on a contractual basis.
Comment. The definition does not include the practice of designating two or more wholesalers or retailers in an area as selected outlets. While this practice is a form of selective selling, it is not exclusive outlet selling. The term does not apply to the reverse contractual relationship in which a dealer must buy exclusively from a supplier.

FABRICATING MATERIALS. Those industrial goods which become a part of the finished product and which have undergone processing beyond that required for raw materials but not as much as finished parts.
Comment. Examples are plastic molding compounds.

FACILITATING AGENCIES IN MARKETING. Those agencies which perform or assist in the performance of one or a number of the marketing functions but which neither take title to goods nor negotiate purchases or sales. Common types are banks, railroads, storage warehouses, commodity exchanges, stockyards, insurance companies, graders and inspectors, advertising agencies, firms engaged in marketing research, cattle loan companies, furniture marts, and packers and shippers.

FACTOR. (1) A specialized financial institution engaged in factoring accounts receivable and lending on the security of inventory.
(2) A type of commission house which often advances funds to the consigner, identified chiefly with the raw cotton and naval stores trades.
Comment. The type of factor described in (1) operates extensively in the textile field but is expanding into other fields.

FACTORING. A specialized financial function whereby producers, wholesalers, and retailers sell their accounts receivable to financial institutions, including factors and banks, often on a nonrecourse basis.
Comment. Commercial banks as well as factors and finance companies engage in this activity.

FAIR TRADE. Retail resale price maintenance imposed by suppliers of branded goods under authorization of state and federal laws.
Comment. This is a special usage of the term promulgated by the advocates of resale price maintenance and bears no relation to the fair practices concept of the Federal Trade Commission; nor is it the antithesis of unfair trading outlawed by the antitrust laws.

GENERAL STORE. A small retailing business unit, not departmentalized, usually located in a rural community and primarily engaged in selling a general assortment of merchandise of which the most important line is food, and the more important subsidiary lines are notions, apparel, farm supplies, and gasoline. These stores are often known as *country general stores.*
Comment. This is roughly the Bureau of the Census usage.

GRADING. Assigning predetermined standards of quality classification to individual units or lots of commodity.
Comment. This process of assignment may be carried on by sorting. This term is often defined so as to include the work of setting up classes or grades. This work is really a part of standardization.

HOUSE-TO-HOUSE SALESPERSON. A salesperson who is primarily engaged in making sales direct to ultimate consumers in their homes.
Comment. The term *canvasser* is often employed as synonymous with house-to-house salesperson. Because of its extensive use in fields other than marketing, this usage is not recommended.

INDEPENDENT STORE. A retailing business unit which is controlled by its own individual ownership or management rather than from without, except insofar as its management is limited by voluntary group arrangements.
Comment. This definition includes a member of a voluntary group organization. It is recognized that the voluntary group possesses many of the characteristics of and presents many of the same problems as the chain store system. In the final analysis, however, the members of the voluntary groups are independent stores, cooperating, perhaps temporarily, in the accomplishment of certain marketing purposes. Their collective action is entirely voluntary and the retailers engaging in it consider themselves to be independent.

INDUSTRIAL GOODS. Goods that are destined to be sold primarily for use in producing other goods or rendering services, as contrasted with goods destined to be sold primarily to the ultimate consumer.
They include equipment (installed and accessory), component parts, maintenance, repair and operating supplies, raw materials, fabricating materials.
Comment. The distinguishing characteristics of these goods is the purpose for which they are primarily destined to be used—in carrying on business or industrial activities, rather than for resale to or consumption by indi-

vidual ultimate consumers. The category also includes merchandise destined for use in carrying on various types of institutional enterprises.

Relatively few goods are exclusively industrial goods. The same article may, under one set of circumstances, be an industrial good, and under other conditions be a consumer good.

INDUSTRIAL STORE. A retail store owned and operated by a company or governmental unit to sell primarily to its employees.

Nongovernmental establishments of this type are often referred to as *company stores* or *commissary stores*. In certain trades the term *company store* is applied to a store through which a firm sells its own products, often together with those of other manufacturers, to the consumer market.

Comment. Many of these establishments are not operated for profit. The matter of the location of the control over and responsibility for these stores rather than the motive for their operation constitutes their distinguishing characteristic.

INSTALLED EQUIPMENT. See EQUIPMENT.

JOBBER. This term is widely used as a synonym of *wholesaler* or *distributor*.

Comment. The term is sometimes used in certain trades and localities to designate special types of wholesalers. This usage is especially common in the distribution of agricultural products. The characteristics of the wholesalers so designated vary from trade to trade and from locality to locality. Most of the schedules submitted to the Bureau of the Census by the members of the wholesale trades show no clear line of demarcation between those who call themselves *jobbers* and those who prefer to be known as *wholesalers*. Therefore, it does not seem wise to attempt to set up any general basis of distinction between the terms in those few trades or markets in which one exists. There are scattered examples of special distinctive usage of the term *jobber*. The precise nature of such usage must be sought in each trade or area in which it is employed.

LIMITED FUNCTION WHOLESALER. See WHOLESALER.

LOSS LEADER. A product of known or accepted quality priced at a loss or no profit for the purpose of attracting patronage to a store.

Comment. This term is peculiar to the retail trade—elsewhere the same item is called a *leader* or a *special*.

MAIL-ORDER HOUSE (RETAIL). A retailing business that receives its orders primarily by mail or telephone and generally offers its goods and services for sale from a catalog or other printed material.

Comment. Other types of retail stores often conduct a mail-order business, usually through departments set up for that purpose, although this fact does not make them mail-order houses. On the other hand, some firms that originally confined themselves to the mail-order business now also operate chain store systems. For example, Sears, Roebuck and Montgomery Ward are both mail-order houses and chain store systems.

MAIL-ORDER WHOLESALER. See WHOLESALER.

MANUFACTURER'S AGENT. An agent who generally operates on an extended contractual basis, often sells within an exclusive territory, handles noncompeting but related lines of goods, and possesses limited authority with regard to prices and terms of sale. He or she may be authorized to sell a definite portion of the principal's output.

Comment. The manufacturer's agent has often been defined as a species of broker. In the majority of cases this seems to be substantially accurate. It it probably more accurate in seeking to define the entire group not to classify them as a specialized type of broker but to regard them as a special variety of agent since many of them carry stocks.

The term *manufacturer's representative* is sometimes applied to this agent. Since this term is also used to designate a salesperson in the employ of a manufacturer, its use as a synonym for manufacturer's agent is discouraged.

MANUFACTURER'S STORE. A retail store owned and operated by a manufacturer, sometimes as an outlet for the manufacturer's goods, sometimes primarily for experimental or publicity purposes.

MARKET. (1) The aggregate of forces or conditions within which buyers and sellers make decisions that result in the transfer of goods and services.

(2) The aggregate demand of the potential buyers of a commodity or service.

Comment. The business manager often uses the term to mean an opportunity to sell goods. It often has the added connotation of a geographical area, such as the New England market, or of a customer group, such as the college market or the agricultural market.

Retailers often use the term to mean the aggregate group of suppliers from whom a buyer purchases.

MARKET ANALYSIS. A subdivision of marketing research which involves the measurement of the extent of a market and the determination of its characteristics.

Comment. See also MARKETING RESEARCH. The activity just described consists essentially of the process of exploring and evaluating the marketing possibilities of the aggregates described in part (2) of the definition of *market.*

MARKET POTENTIAL (ALSO MARKET OR TOTAL MARKET). A calculation of maximum possible sales opportunities for all sellers of a good or service during a stated period.

MARKET SHARE (OR SALES POTENTIAL). The ratio of a company's sales to the total industry sales on either an actual or potential basis.

Comment. This term is often used to designate that part of total industry sales which a company hopes or expects to get. Since this concept includes a considerable element of "blue sky," this usage is not encouraged.

MARKETING. The performance of business activities that direct the flow of goods and services from producer to consumer or user.

Comment. The task of defining *marketing* may be approached from at least three points of view.

(1) The *legalistic,* of which the following is a good example: "Marketing includes all activities having to do with effecting changes in the ownership and possession of goods and services." It seems obviously of doubtful desirability to adopt a definition which throws so much emphasis upon the legal phases of what is essentially a commercial subject.

(2) The *economic,* examples of which are (a) "That part of economics which deals with the creation of time, place, and possession utilities" and (b) "That phase of business activity through which human wants are satisfied by the exchange of goods and services for some valuable consideration." Such definitions are apt to assume somewhat more understanding of economic concepts than is ordinarily found in the marketplace.

(3) The *factual* or *descriptive,* of which the definition suggested by the Committee is an example. This type of definition merely seeks to describe its subject in terms likely to be understood by both professional economists and business managers without reference to legal or economic implications. This definition seeks to include such facilitating activities as marketing research, transportation, certain aspects of product and package planning, and the use of credit as a means of influencing patronage.

MARKETING BUDGET. A statement of the planned dollar sales and planned marketing costs for a specified future period.

Comment. The use of this term is sometimes confined to an estimate of future sales. This does not conform to the general use of the term *budget,* which includes schedules of both receipts and expenditures. If the marketing budget is to be used as a device to facilitate marketing control and management, it should include the probable cost of getting the estimated volume of sales. The failure to allow proper weight to this item in their calculations is one of the most persistent and fatal mistakes made by American business concerns. It has led to much striving after unprofitable volume, which has been so costly.

A firm may prepare a marketing budget for each brand or product or for a group of brands or products it sells or for each group of customers to whom it markets. See also SALES BUDGET.

MARKETING COOPERATIVE. See PRODUCERS' COOPERATIVE MARKETING.

MARKETING COST ACCOUNTING. The branch of cost accounting that involves the allocation of marketing costs according to customers, marketing units, products, territories, or marketing activities.

MARKETING COST ANALYSIS. The study and evaluation of the relative profitability or costs of different marketing operations in terms of customers, marketing units, commodities, territories, or marketing activities.

Comment. Marketing cost accounting is one of the tools used in marketing cost analysis.

MARKETING FUNCTION. A major specialized activity or group of related activities performed in marketing.

Comment. There is no generally accepted list of marketing functions, nor is there any generally accepted basis on which the lists compiled by various writers are chosen.

The reason for these limitations is fairly apparent. Under this term students of marketing have sought to squeeze a heterogeneous and nonconsistent group of activities. Some of them are broad business functions with special marketing implications; others are peculiar to the marketing process. The function of assembling is performed through buying, selling, and transportation. Assembling, storage, and transporting are general economic functions; selling and buying are more nearly individual in character. Most of the lists sadly fail to embrace all the activities that marketing managers worry about in the course of doing their jobs.

MARKETING MANAGEMENT. The planning, direction, and control of the entire marketing activity of a firm or division of a firm, including the formulation of marketing objectives, policies, programs, and strategy, and commonly embracing product development, organizing and staffing to carry out plans, supervising marketing operations, and controlling marketing performance.

Comment. In most firms the person who performs these functions is a member of top management who plays a part in determining company policy, in making product decisions, and in coordinating marketing operations with other functional activities to achieve the objectives of the company as a whole.

No definition of this position is included in the report because there is no uniformity in the titles applied. Variants include marketing manager, director of marketing, vice-president for marketing, director or vice-president of marketing and sales, general sales manager.

MARKETING PLANNING. The work of setting up objectives for marketing activity and of determining and scheduling the steps necessary to achieve such objectives.

Comment. This term includes not only the work of deciding upon the goals or results to be attained through marketing activity but also the determination in detail of exactly how they are to be accomplished.

MARKETING POLICY. A course of action established to obtain consistency of marketing decisions and operations under recurring and essentially similar circumstances.

MARKETING RESEARCH. The systematic gathering, recording, and analyzing of data about problems relating to the marketing of goods and services. Such research may be undertaken by impartial agencies or by business firms or their agents for the solution of their marketing problems.

Comment. Marketing research is the inclusive term which embraces all research activities carried on in connection with the management of marketing work. It includes various subsidiary types of research, such as (1) *market analysis*, which is a study of the size, location, nature, and characteristics of markets; (2) *sales analysis* (or research), which is largely an analysis of sales data; (3) *consumer research*, of which *motivation research* is a type, which is concerned chiefly with the discovery and analysis of consumer attitudes, reactions, and preferences; and (4) *advertising research*, which is carried on chiefly as an aid to the management of advertising work. The techniques of operations research are often useful in marketing research. The term *market research* is often loosely used as synonymous with marketing research.

MERCHANDISING. The planning and supervision involved in marketing the particular merchandise or service at the places, times, and prices and in the quantities that will best serve to realize the marketing objectives of the business.

Comment. This term has been used with a great variety of meanings. The usage recommended by the Committee adheres closely to the essential meaning of the word. The term is most widely used in this sense in the wholesaling and retailing trades. Many manufacturers designate this activity as *product planning* or *management* and include in it such tasks as selecting the article to be produced or stocked and deciding such matters as the size, appearance, form, packaging, quantities to be bought or made, time of procurement, and price lines to be offered.

MERCHANT. A business unit that buys, takes title to, and resells merchandise.

Comment. The distinctive feature of this middleman lies in the fact that he takes title to the goods he handles. The extent to which marketing functions are performed is incidental to the definition. Wholesalers and retailers are the chief types of merchants.

MIDDLEMAN. A business concern that specializes in performing operations or rendering services directly involved in the purchase and/or sale of goods in the process of their flow from producer to consumer. Middlemen are of two types, *merchants* and *agents*.

Comment. The essence of the middleman's operation lies in the fact that he or she plays an active and prominent part in the negotiations leading up to transactions of purchase and sale. This is what distinguishes the middleman from a *marketing facilitating agent* who, while he or she performs certain marketing functions, participates only incidentally in negotiations of purchase and sale.

This term is very general and also possesses an unfortunate emotional content. Therefore, the Committee recommends that whenever possible more specific terms be used, such as *agent, merchant, retailer, wholesaler*.

MISSIONARY SALESPERSON. A salesperson employed by a manufacturer to call on customers of the firm's distributors, usually to develop goodwill and stimulate demand, to help or induce them to promote the sale of the manufacturer's goods, to help them train their sales personnel to do so, and often to take orders for delivery by such distributors.

MOTIVATION RESEARCH. A group of techniques developed by the behavioral scientists which are used by marketing researchers to discover factors influencing marketing behavior.

Comment. These techniques are widely used outside the marketing sphere, for example, to discover factors influencing the behavior of employees and voters. The Committee has confined its definition to the marketing uses of the tool. Motivation research is only one of several ways to study marketing behavior.

NATIONAL BRAND. A manufacturer's or producer's brand, usually enjoying wide territorial distribution.

Comment. The usage of the terms *national brand* and *private brand* in this report, while generally current and commonly accepted, is highly illogical and nondescriptive. But since it is widespread and persistent, the Committee embodies it in the report.

PERSONAL SELLING. Oral presentation in a conversation with one or more prospective purchasers for the purpose of making sales.

Comment. This definition contemplates that the presentation may be either formal (as a "canned" sales talk), or informal, although it is rather likely to be informal, either in the actual presence of the customer or by telephone, although usually the former, either to an individual or to a small group, although usually the former.

PHYSICAL DISTRIBUTION. The management of the movement and handling of goods from the point of production to the point of consumption or use.

PRICE CUTTING. Offering merchandise or a service for sale at a price below that recognized as usual or appropriate by its buyers and sellers.

Comment. One obvious criticism of this definition is that it is indefinite. But that very indefiniteness also causes it to be more accurately descriptive of a concept which is characterized by a high degree of indefiniteness in the mind of the average person affected by price cutting.

Traders' ideas of what constitutes price cutting are so vague and indefinite that any precise or highly specific definition of the phenomenon is bound to fail to include all its manifestations. If you ask a group of traders in a specific commodity to define price cutting, you will get as many conflicting formulas as there are traders. But if you ask those same traders at any particular time whether selling at a certain price constitutes price cutting, you will probably get a considerable degree of uniformity of opinion. It is precisely this condition which the definition is designed to reflect.

PRICE LEADER. A firm whose pricing behavior is followed by other companies in the same industry.

Comment. The price leadership of a firm may be limited to a certain geographical area, as in the oil business, or to certain products or groups of products, as in the steel business.

PRIVATE BRANDS. Brands sponsored by merchants or agents as distinguished from those sponsored by manufacturers or producers.

Comment. This usage is thoroughly illogical, since no seller wants the brand to be private in the sense of being secret, and all brands are private in the sense that they are special and not common or general in use. But the usage is common in marketing literature and among traders. Therefore, the Committee presents it in this report.

PRODUCERS' COOPERATIVE MARKETING. That type of cooperative marketing which primarily involves the sale of goods or services of the associated producing membership. May perform only an assembly or brokerage function but in some cases, notably milk marketing, extends into processing and distribution of the members' production.

Comment. Many producers' cooperative marketing associations also buy for their members. The fact does not subtract from their status as producers' cooperatives; this is especially true of the farm cooperatives.

The term does not include those activities of trade associations that affect only indirectly the sales of the membership. Such activities are the maintenance of credit rating bureaus, design registration bureaus, and brand protection machinery.

PRODUCT LINE. A group of products that are closely related either because they satisfy a class of need, are used together, are sold to the same customer groups, are marketed through the same types of outlets, or fall within given price ranges, for example, carpenters' tools.

Comment. Sublines of products may be distinguished, such as hammers or saws, within a product line.

PRODUCT MANAGEMENT. The planning, direction, and control of all phases of the life cycle of products, including the creation or discovery of ideas for new products, the screening of such ideas, the coordination of the work of research and physical development of products, their packaging and branding, their introduction on the market, their market development, their modification, the discovery of new uses for them, their repair and servicing, and their deletion.

Comments. It is not safe to think of product management as the work of the executive known as the product manager, because the dimensions of the job vary widely from company to company, sometimes embracing all the activities listed in the definition and sometimes being limited to the sales promotion of the products in the product manager's jurisdiction.

PRODUCT MIX. The composite of products offered for sale by a firm or a business unit.

Comment. Toothpaste is a product. The 90-cent tube of Whosis ammoniated toothpaste is an item. Toothpastes and powders, mouth washes, and allied items compose an oral-hygiene product line. Soaps, cosmetics, dentifrices, drug items, cake mixes, shortenings, and other items may comprise a product mix if marketed by the same company.

PUBLICITY. Nonpersonal stimulation of demand for a product, service, or business unit by planting commercially significant news about it in a published medium or obtaining favorable presentation of it on radio, television, or stage that is not paid for by the sponsor.

Comment. Retailers use the term to denote the sum of the functions of advertising, display, and publicity as defined here.

PURCHASING POWER (BUYING POWER). The capacity to purchase possessed by an individual buyer, a group of buyers, or the aggregate of the buyers in an area or a market.

RACK JOBBER. A wholesaling business unit that markets specialized lines of merchandise to certain types of retail stores and provides the special services of selective brand and item merchandising and arrangement, maintenance, and stocking of display racks.

Comment. Rack jobbers usually put their merchandise in the store of the retailer on consignment. Rack jobbers are most prevalent in the food business.

RESALE PRICE MAINTENANCE. Control by a supplier of the selling prices of his or her branded goods at subsequent stages of distribution by means of contractual agreement under fair trade laws or other devices.

RESIDENT BUYER. An agent who specializes in buying, on a fee or commission basis, chiefly for retailers.

Comment. The term as defined is limited to agents residing in the market cities who charge their retail principals fees for buying assistance rendered, but there are resident buying offices that are owned by out-of-town stores and some that are owned cooperatively by a group of stores. The former are called *private* offices and the latter *associated* offices. Neither of them should be confused with the central buying office of the typical chain, where the buying function is performed by the office directly, not acting as a specialized assistant to store buyers. Resident buyers should also be distinguished from apparel *merchandise brokers,* who represent competing manufacturers in the garment trades and have as customers out-of-town smaller stores in search of fashion merchandise. These brokers are paid by the manufacturers to whom they bring additional business, on a percentage of sales basis.

RETAILER. A merchant, or occasionally an agent, whose main business is selling directly to the ultimate consumer.

Comment. Retailers are to be distinguished by the nature of their sales rather than by the way they procure the goods in which they deal. The size of the units in which they sell is an incidental rather than a primary element in their character. Their essential distinguishing mark is the fact that their typical sale is made to the ultimate consumer.

RETAILER COOPERATIVE. A group of independent retailers organized to buy cooperatively either through a jointly owned warehouse or through a buying club.

Comment. Their cooperative activities may include operating under a group name, joint advertising, and cooperative managerial supervision.

RETAILING. The activities involved in selling directly to the ultimate consumer.

Comment. This definition includes all forms of selling to the ultimate consumer. It embraces the direct-to-consumer sales activities of producers whether through their own stores, by house-to-house canvass, or by mail order. It does not cover the sale by producers of industrial goods, by industrial supply houses, or by retailers to industrial, commercial, or institutional buyers for use in the conduct of their enterprises.

SALES AGENT. See SELLING AGENT.

SALES ANALYSIS. A subdivision of marketing research which involves the systematic study and comparison of sales data.

Comment. The purpose of such analysis is usually to aid in marketing management by providing sales information along the lines of market areas, organizational units, products or product groups, customers or customer groups, or such other units as may be useful.

SALES BUDGET. The part of the marketing budget that is concerned with planned dollar sales and planned costs of personal selling during a specified future period.

SALES FORECAST. An estimate of sales, in dollars or physical units, for a specified future period under a proposed marketing plan or program and under an assumed set of economic and other forces outside the unit for which the forecast is made. The forecast may be for a specified item of merchandise or for an entire line.

Comment. Two sets of factors are involved in making a sales forecast: (1) those forces outside the control of the firm for which the forecast is made that are likely to influence its sales and (2) changes in the marketing methods or practices of the firm that are likely to affect its sales.

In the course of planning future activities, the management of a given firm may make several sales forecasts, each consisting of an estimate of probable sales if a given marketing plan is adopted or a given set of outside forces prevails. The estimated effects that several marketing plans may have on sales and profits may be compared in the process of arriving at that marketing program which will, in the opinion of the officials of the company, be best designed to promote its welfare.

SALES MANAGEMENT. The planning, direction, and control of the personal selling activities of a business unit, including recruiting, selecting, training, equipping, assigning, routing, supervising, paying, and motivating the sales force.

Comment. These activities are sometimes but not generally designated as *sales administration* or *sales force management.*

SALES MANAGER. The executive who plans, directs, and controls the activities of sales personnel.

Comment. This definition distinguishes sharply between the manager who conducts the personal selling activities of a business unit and his or her superior, the executive titled marketing manager, director of marketing, or vice-president for marketing, who has charge of all marketing activities. The use of this form of organization has been growing rapidly during recent years.

SALES PLANNING. That part of the marketing planning work which is concerned with making sales forecasts, devising programs for reaching the sales target, and deriving a sales budget.

SALES POTENTIAL. See MARKET SHARE.

SALES PROMOTION. (1) In a specified sense, those marketing activities, other than personal selling, advertising, and publicity, that stimulate consumer purchasing and dealer effectiveness, such as display, shows and exhibitions, demonstrations, and various nonrecurrent selling efforts not in the ordinary routine.

(2) In retailing, all methods of stimulating customer purchasing, including personal selling, advertising, and publicity.

Comment. This definition includes the two most logical and commonly accepted usages of this much abused term. It is the suggestion of the Committee that insofar as possible, the use of the term be confined to the first definition given.

SALES QUOTA. A projected volume of sales assigned to a marketing unit for use in the management of sales efforts. It applies to a specified period and may be expressed in dollars or in physical units.

Comment. The quota may be used to check efficiency, stimulate efforts, or determine remuneration for individual salespersons or other personnel engaged in sales work.

A quota may be for a salesperson, a territory, a department, a branch house, a wholesaler or retailer, or for the company as a whole. It may be different from the sales figure set up in the sales budget. Since it is a managerial device, it is not an immutable figure inexorably arrived at by the application of exact statistical formulas.

SALES RESEARCH. See MARKETING RESEARCH and SALES ANALYSIS.

SELECTIVE SELLING. The policy of selling to a limited number of customers in a market.

SELF-SELECTION. The method used in retailing by which the customer may choose the desired merchandise without direct assistance of store personnel.

SELF-SERVICE. The method used in retailing whereby customers select their own merchandise, remove it from the shelves or bulk containers, carry it to a checkout stand to complete the transaction, and transport it to the point of use.

SELLING. The personal or impersonal process of assisting and/or persuading a prospective customer to buy a commodity or a service or to act favorably upon an idea that has commercial significance to the seller.
Comment. This definition includes advertising, other forms of publicity, and sales promotion as well as personal selling.

SELLING AGENT. An agent who operates on an extended contractual basis; sells all of a specified line of merchandise or the entire output of the principal; usually has full authority with regard to prices, terms, and other conditions of sale; and occasionally renders financial aid to the principal.
Comment. This functionary is often called a *sales agent.*

SERVICE WHOLESALER. See WHOLESALER.

SERVICES. Activities, benefits, or satisfactions which are offered for sale, or are provided in connection with the sale of goods. Examples are amusements, hotel service, electric service, transportation, the services of barbershops and beauty shops, repair and maintenance service, the work of credit-rating bureaus. This list is merely illustrative, and no attempt has been made to make it complete. The term also applies to the various activities, such as credit extension, advice and help of salespeople, and delivery, by which sellers serve the convenience of their customers.

SHOPPING CENTER. A geographical cluster of retail stores, collectively handling an assortment of goods varied enough to satisfy most of the merchandise wants of consumers within convenient traveling time, and thereby attracting a general shopping trade.
Comment. During recent years, the term has acquired a special usage in its application to the planned or integrated centers developed in suburban or semisuburban areas, usually along main highways and featuring ample parking space.

SHOPPING GOODS. Those consumers' goods which the customer characteristically compares on such bases as suitability, quality, price, and style before selection and purchase. Examples of goods that most consumers buy as shopping goods are furniture, dress goods, women's ready-to-wear and shoes, used automobiles, and major appliances.

Comment. It should be emphasized that a given article may be bought by one customer as a shopping good and by another as a specialty or convenience good. The general classification depends upon the way in which the average or typical buyer purchases.

See comment under SPECIALTY GOODS.

SPECIALTY GOODS. Those consumers' goods with unique characteristics and/or brand identification for which a significant group of buyers are habitually willing to make a special purchasing effort.

Examples of articles that are usually bought as specialty goods are specific brands and types of fancy foods, stereo components, certain types of sporting equipment, photographic equipment, and men's suits.

Comment. Price is not usually the primary factor in consumer choice of specialty goods, although their prices are often higher than those of other articles serving the same basic want but without their special characteristics.

SPECIALTY STORE. A retail store that makes its appeal on the basis of a restricted class of shopping goods.

STANDARDIZATION. The determination of uniform specifications of basic limits or grade ranges to which particular manufactured goods may conform and uniform classes into which the products of agriculture and the extractive industries may or must be sorted or assigned.

Comment. This term does not include grading, which is the process of sorting or assigning units of a commodity to the grades or classes that have been established through the process of standardization. Some systems of standardization and grading for agricultural products are compulsory by law.

STOCK OR INVENTORY CONTROL. The use of a system or mechanism to maintain stocks of goods at desired levels.

Comment. Such control is usually exercised to maintain stocks that are (1) representative in that they include all the items the customer group served expects to be able to buy from the firm involved, (2) adequate in that a sufficient quantity of each item is included to satisfy all reasonably foreseeable demands for it, and (3) economical in that no funds of the firm are held in inventory beyond those needed to serve purposes (1) and (2) and in that it facilitates savings in costs of production.

STORAGE. The marketing function that involves holding goods between the time of their production and their final sale.

Comment. Some processing is often done while goods are in storage. It is probable that this should be regarded as a part of production rather than of marketing.

SUPERETTE. See SUPERMARKET.

SUPERMARKET. A large retailing business unit selling mainly food and grocery items on the basis of the low margin appeal, wide variety and assortments, self-service, and heavy emphasis on merchandise appeal.
Comment. In its bid for patronage the supermarket makes heavy use of the visual appeal of the merchandise itself.

TRADEMARK. A brand or part of a brand that is given legal protection because it is capable of exclusive appropriation; because it is used in a manner sufficiently fanciful, distinctive, and arbitrary; because it is affixed to the product when sold; or because it otherwise satisfies the requirements set up by law.
Comment. Trademark is essentially a legal term and includes only those brands or parts of brands which the law designates as trademarks. In the final analysis in any specific case a trademark is what the court decides to regard as a trademark.

TRADING AREA. A district whose size is usually determined by the boundaries within which it is economical in terms of volume and cost for a marketing unit or group to sell and/or deliver a good or service.
Comment. A single business may have several trading areas; for example, the trading area of Marshall Field for its store business is different from that for its catalog business.

TRAFFIC MANAGEMENT. The planning, selection, and direction of all means and methods of transportation involved in the movement of goods in the marketing process.
Comment. This definition is confined to those activities in connection with transportation that have to do particularly with marketing and that are an inseparable part of any well-organized system of distribution. It includes control of the movement of goods in trucks owned by the marketing concern as well as by public carrier. It does not include the movement of goods within the warehouse of a producer or within the store of a retail concern.

TRUCK WHOLESALER. See WHOLESALER.

ULTIMATE CONSUMER. One who buys and/or uses goods or services to satisfy personal or household wants rather than for resale or for use in business, institutional, or industrial operations.
Comment. The definition distinguishes sharply between industrial users and ultimate consumers. A firm buying and using an office machine, a drum of lubricating oil, or a carload of steel billets is an *industrial user* of those products, not an ultimate consumer of them. A vital difference exists between the purposes motivating the two types of purchases, which in turn results in highly significant differences in buying methods, marketing organization, and selling practices.

VALUE ADDED BY MARKETING. That part of the value of a product or service to the consumer or user which results from marketing activities.

Comment. There is urgent need of a method or formula for computing value added by marketing. Increased attention is being devoted to developing such a formula. At present none of those suggested has gained enough acceptance to justify inclusion in this definition or comment.

VARIETY STORE. A retailing business unit that handles a wide assortment of goods, usually in the low or popular segment of the price range.
Comment. While some foods are generally handled, the major emphasis is on nonfood products.

VOLUNTARY GROUP. A group of retailers each of whom owns and operates his or her own store and is associated with a wholesale organization or manufacturer to carry on joint merchandising activities and who are characterized by some degree of group identity and uniformity of operation. Such joint activities have been largely of two kinds: cooperative advertising and group control of store operation.
Comment. A voluntary group is usually sponsored by a wholesaler. Similar groups sponsored by retailers do not belong in this category. Groups of independent stores sponsored by a chain store system are usually called *agency stores.*

WHOLESALER. A business unit that buys and resells merchandise to retailers and other merchants and/or to industrial, institutional, and commercial users but which does not sell in significant amounts to ultimate consumers. In the basic materials, semifinished goods, and tool and machinery trades, merchants of this type are commonly known as *distributors* or *supply houses.*
Comment. Generally these merchants render a wide variety of services to their customers. Those who render all the services normally expected in the wholesale trade are known as *service wholesalers;* those who render only a few of the wholesale services are known as *limited-function wholesalers.* The latter group is composed mainly of *cash-and-carry wholesalers,* who do not render the credit or delivery service; *drop-shipment wholesalers,* who sell for delivery by the producer direct to the buyer; *truck wholesalers,* who combine selling, delivery, and collection in one operation; and *mail-order wholesalers,* who perform the selling service entirely by mail.
This definition ignores or minimizes two bases upon which the term is often defined: first, the size of the lots in which wholesalers deal, and second, the fact that they habitually sell for resale. The figures show that many wholesalers operate on a very small scale and in small lots. Most of them make a significant portion of their sales to industrial users.

INDEX